CCH®
RETHINKING
STRATEGIC HR

HR's Role in Building
a Performance Culture

DR. JOHN SULLIVAN

Wolters Kluwer
Law & Business

Acting Publisher: Nancy Zukowski

Editors: Joy P. Waltemath, J.D.
    Linda Panszczyk, J.D.
    Elizabeth Pope, J.D.

Production Coordinator: Rebekah J. Grubisic

Cover Design: Erika Dix, Laila Gaidulis

Interior Design: Erika Dix

Layout: Publications Design

This publication is designed to provide accurate and authoritative information in regard to the subject matter covered. It is sold with the understanding that the publisher is not engaged in rendering legal, accounting, or other professional service. If legal advice or other expert assistance is required, the services of a competent professional person should be sought.

ISBN 0-8080-1100-6
©2004 CCH INCORPORATED
4025 W. Peterson Ave.
Chicago, IL 60646-6085
1 800 248 3248
hr.cch.com

ACKNOWLEDGEMENTS

It's impossible to write a book about "rethinking" HR strategy without beginning with the premise that the way most senior HR leaders develop and implement HR strategy is currently lacking. In my 30-plus years of working in HR, I've had the pleasure of meeting literally thousands of senior HR leaders and VPs. Almost without exception, each one was a smart, dedicated, hard-working individual. However, despite their hard work and dedication (with the exception of two individuals), none of these HR leaders ever acted like HR was *the* most important department in a corporation.

Only two HR VPs stand out from all the rest. These two individuals began with the unique understanding that HR has *the* most important role in any corporation–that of building and maintaining a "performance culture" that continually drives every person to perform and then continually to improve. By making fact- based decisions and focusing directly on increasing workforce productivity and company performance (rather than the more traditional HR approach of building relationships, compliance and "getting a seat at the table"), these two visionaries have demonstrated that it is possible for HR to be the most significant contributor to a firm's bottom line.

Just like Columbus, their approach is so different from what others practice that you might be tempted to think that the status quo is the correct way to do HR, but you would be wrong. The business world has changed forever, and the only HR role that guarantees continued superiority is the data-based performance culture approach to HR that these individuals have pioneered. To these "beautiful minds" and landmark individuals, Kirby Dyees and Patty Murray (the former and current VPs of HR at Intel), I dedicate this book.

I would also like to acknowledge the thousands of HR graduates from San Francisco State University who, after "infiltrating" HR departments throughout the West, have refused to "give in" when bluntly told by senior HR turf protectors that, "I don't care what you learned in college, that's not the way we do it here."

Next I would like to acknowledge the endless hard work, intelligent comments and the "find a way" approach that my colleague, Master Burnett, has brought to this book project. He makes the impossible easy and without him, this project would never have been completed.

And finally to my loving wife, partner, chief supporter and best friend, Adeline, thanks for your tolerance and understanding during the writing of this book. If you hadn't sacrificed your own HR career to support my work, none of this would have been possible.
KB & TN

Dr. John Sullivan
January 2004

BIOGRAPHY

BIOGRAPHY

Dr. John Sullivan is a well-known international educator, corporate advisor, professional speaker, author, and visionary in the field of Human Resources. He pulls upon his more than 30 years of experience as a practitioner to identify major weaknesses and propose solutions that raise the bar for performance to the level chief executives expect. As an author, he has published more than 450 articles and five books covering subjects ranging from world-class recruiting tools and strategies to HR metrics. Each year Dr. Sullivan leads a number of workshops and training events at major industry events and leading corporations that focus on "Changing the DNA of HR." Dr. Sullivan is a long-time resident of San Francisco, California, and serves as a Professor of Management at San Francisco State University.

For more information on his background, professional affiliations, publications, or upcoming schedule of events, visit *www.drjohnsullivan.com*.

Also by John Sullivan:
- *HR Metrics the World-Class Way* (Kennedy Information)
- *Improving Productivity the World-Class Way* (Kennedy Information)
- *Recruiting Tools for Line Managers* (Kennedy Information)
- *A Manager's Guide to Innovative Orientation* (Self-Published)
- *The VP-of-HR Newsletter* (Self-Published)

Contents

CHAPTER ONE

Introduction

CHAPTER SIX

HR has an external focus on impacting business objectives

CHAPTER SEVEN

HR uses performance culture tools

CHAPTER ONE

INTRODUCTION

OBJECTIVE

This book focuses on that "missing link" between a good organization and an industry-dominating performance culture—a strategic human resource function that focuses on measuring and increasing workforce productivity.

KEY POINTS

◊ The true definition of strategic HR is a future-focused approach designed to provide a measurable impact on strategic business goals.

◊ It is not possible to become the dominant firm in any industry without becoming a performance culture.

◊ There is a major difference between traditional and strategic HR programs and actions.

WHY READ THIS BOOK?

The rapidly changing world of business is forcing every organization to seek out new ways to increase its performance. Most are applying a patchwork approach, while a very few elite organizations are striving to the highest level of performance—what is known as a "performance culture." Many elite organizations like Intel, Cisco, GE and Wal-Mart have successfully dominated their industry and increased their performance to "world-class levels" by building a culture of performance.

In contrast, many other organizations have attempted to match their efforts by duplicating some of the management tools that these elite organizations have utilized like supply chain, CRM, Six Sigma and lean production. By taking such a narrow approach in order to "catch up," they have sidestepped the most important performance factor in a performance culture—the people and their performance.

This omission is significant because the "human resources" of a corporation are quite often the highest cost factor an organization has, often approaching 50 percent of its variable costs. Any significant increase in the performance of such a high cost factor will have a greater impact on company performance and profit than any other "fad" management solutions.

BECOMING A PERFORMANCE CULTURE

The first premise of this book is that it is not possible to become the dominant firm in any industry without becoming a performance culture, and that the critical element in becoming a performance culture is improving the productivity and effectiveness of the people in the organization. GE calls its version of a performance culture a "meritocracy," while Intel uses the term "paranoia" to send the message that dominating the industry demands continuous improvement in performance as an accepted way of life. Whatever term is used, the intent is the same: every individual and every process must continually improve its results.

The second premise of the book is that the human resource function in most organizations has missed an important opportunity by failing to take the lead in the development of a performance culture. This book provides the aggressive tools and strategies that will allow the HR function to become the newest "corporate hero" by dramatically increasing organizational performance, workforce productivity and profits through the use of performance culture approaches and techniques.

EVIDENCE OF STRATEGIC IMPACT MISSING

Although most people in HR are satisfied with the way they approach HR, the cold reality is that most individuals and HR departments do *not* have evidence that they have a major strategic impact. After 30-plus years of advising managers at over 100 major US and international corporations, teaching HR, writing hundreds of articles and books, and practicing as an HR executive, I have come to two basic conclusions:

- 99 percent of the people in HR feel, believe and think they are strategic.
- 1 percent of the people in HR *know* they are strategic because they have the hard evidence that even a cynical CFO would accept as credible proof of their strategic impact.

The primary goal of the book is to show you new ways to improve the business impact of your HR function by up to 25 percent. Because the goal is so high, the approaches that permeate this book are aggressive ones that are designed to make you rethink everything you do in HR.

As a result of this aggressive goal, few punches are pulled. The book includes numerous critiques and even criticisms of how many HR professionals approach becoming strategic. Yes, it is designed to *provoke your thinking*, and it is also true that the solutions proposed generally are much more aggressive than those proposed by other authors within HR. But if you want dramatic results, you need dramatic solutions.

The book intentionally is not a balanced approach. It doesn't highlight many traditional HR approaches, first, because other authors have effectively covered those approaches, and second, because those approaches are unlikely to increase the business impact of the HR function by 25 percent.

So, if you're ready to be challenged and to see the dramatic difference in the way that top-performing organizations "do strategic HR," you'll find that this book will open your eyes and show you a fresh approach to the "new HR." Incidentally, it doesn't only dwell on strategy, it also includes specific day-to-day steps that you must take in order to become strategic.

This book is intended to provoke and make you think. You will not agree with everything in the book, and some points might even make you mad, but don't despair as long as it makes you re-think the way you approach HR.

ARE YOU STRATEGIC?

If you are currently wondering in your mind whether you or your HR department are really strategic, there is a relatively easy "yes or no test" of whether something that a business does is considered strategic by top management:

METRICS

Whether you are in HR or any other business department, if what you do is truly strategic, it will appear prominently in the annual report.

Take a moment to think about it. It might be a disturbing thought but, like it or not, if your quantified results do not appear in the annual report, you have failed to convince senior management of your strategic impact. The remainder of this book is dedicated to providing you with the tools and strategies that will both increase workforce productivity and get you and your work prominently cited in your organization's annual report.

This book is designed to be easily scanned; do not feel that you need to read it from front to back in order to obtain value. In addition to comprehensive long-term strategies it is also full of standalone tools and approaches that can be instantly applied. Some of the most unique but helpful ones include:

- A clear definition of what is and what is not strategic
- The five distinct levels of contribution that HR can make
- A list of the most-used HR departmental strategies
- Tools for assessing your own strategic level
- How HR routinely "under-costs" its decisions
- A chart on how to make "fact-based" decisions
- How to make a strategic business case to your CFO
- How HR can learn from the success of the supply-chain transformation

- How to use decision filters to improve HR decision-making
- Action steps for becoming more strategic

> *It is a fact that top performers can produce up to 12 times more than the average worker. It is also true that many corporations spend nearly 50 percent of their variable costs on people. If you could find a way to increase the productivity of 50 percent of corporations' expenditures by a factor of 12, is there really any doubt in your mind that you would be declared the "employee of the year?"*

WHY IS IT IMPORTANT TO BECOME STRATEGIC?

"Strategic" is one of the most common terms in business. It is used—and occasionally overused—by every major business function. The word is just as likely to be uttered by senior executives as it is by people that feel that they need to be "more strategic" in order to be recognized or successful. Why all the fuss over this simple word?

DEFINITION

Strategic is so important because "being strategic" means having an impact on the things that are the most important to an organization—the corporate goals and objectives.

Although "strategic" is a commonly used word in HR, there is little agreement about what "being strategic" actually means in practice. That same level of confusion, however, does not exist in other business areas like marketing, product development and supply chain. For example, finance and accounting both deal with numbers and dollars, but finance is considered a strategic function, while accounting generally is not. The primary difference between the two is that accounting focuses on providing reports describing what happened last year, while finance focuses on the future and on increasing profit. As you will see later, there are many characteristics of being strategic, but *being future-focused* and *having an impact on profits* are certainly two examples of those characteristics.

If you are a senior human resource professional it's important to move beyond the use of the word "strategic," because the mere use of the word will not improve your status or recognition within an organization. This is especially true in HR, because it historically has been classified as an "overhead" function. When any function has a history of being administrative or even bureaucratic, it's difficult to overcome that legacy and to become truly strategic.

What is needed to make this transition is a dramatic change in the way you think and act. That dramatic change requires more than increasing HR program efficiency; it requires "out of the box" ideas that have a direct measurable impact on business results.

WHY SHOULD AN INDIVIDUAL BECOME STRATEGIC?

If you want to become a senior manager, becoming strategic is an absolute requirement. You can't survive in the top ranks of management or in any technical field without the ability to think and act strategically. But it's a fair question to ask whether there are any benefits to becoming strategic long before you enter the ranks of senior management. The answer is yes. Some of the reasons an HR practitioner should learn how to think and act strategically early in his or her career include:

- **Job security.** Strategic individuals are looked at by top management as "keepers" and are among the last to be let go during layoffs.
- **Designation as high-potential.** Individuals who "think and act" strategically in the early stages of their career are often "designated" as high-potential individuals. Designation as a high-potential individual will likely provide you with enhanced learning and growth opportunities.
- **Assignments.** Strategic individuals are often selected for assignments on cross-functional teams that can increase exposure and learning.
- **Influence.** Because most managers are strategic, the ideas and perspectives of a strategic thinker are more likely to be sought out and heard.
- **Impact.** If you believe in the value of human resources, acting strategically will increase the impact that you will have on the organization. If you joined human resources to "make a difference," being strategic guarantees that you will make a *big* difference.
- **Resources.** Individuals who think and act strategically generally get more corporate resources and larger budgets because strategic

actions provide a higher return than tactical actions.

- **Promotions.** Strategic individuals are generally promoted faster because strategic skills are needed at the higher levels of the organization.
- **Less stress.** Being future-focused means that you will be prepared for most upcoming "problems," and as a result, you have less stress in your life from organizational "surprises."
- **Bonuses.** If your organization rewards strategic ideas and success, being strategic likely will lead to increased recognition pay, awards and bonuses.
- **Utilize your education.** If you have an advanced degree, especially an MBA, thinking and acting strategically will allow you to utilize the knowledge that you learned in school and apply it to real situations.
- **Exposure to senior management.** Strategic ideas are likely to be presented to and discussed by senior management, and as a result, you are likely to have increased opportunities to meet and present your ideas in front of them.

Remember, you can't become a strategic individual overnight; it's a gradual process. And in a similar vein, the benefits of becoming strategic grow gradually over time; don't expect a promotion to senior vice president overnight.

Want to know if management considers your program to be strategic? Look in the annual report. If you are mentioned, you are—and if you are omitted—you are not!

BE AWARE OF THE RISKS OF BEING STRATEGIC

Becoming more strategic is a legitimate goal for everyone; however, just using the word strategic in your everyday language will not make you more strategic. Being strategic means moving beyond words and instead attempting to do the really hard things. It's important to recognize up front that even though strategic actions have great impacts, they also have high risks and high failure rates. Strategic efforts can get you great rewards, but failing to meet strategic promises can also get you a great deal of unwanted negative exposure.

Unfortunately, becoming strategic is hard to do. It takes time and a great deal of planning and learning. It's also true that many HR departments and individuals that make an attempt to become strategic fail in their attempts. So whether you (or your HR department) have committed to becoming "more strategic," be aware that the risks are high for those who enter the field unprepared. Even senior vice presidents of human resources may not always be acknowledged as strategic contributors.

For example, if you assume that the most strategic executives in a corporation are the highest paid, you might be surprised to know that, according to SEC filings, less than 10 percent of VPs of HR are listed among the top five highest-paid corporate officers in their corporation. On a positive note, those VPs of HR that demonstrate their strategic business impact are well paid. In fact, there are a good number of VPs of HR that bring in over $1 million per year. One VP actually earned over $30 million in one year (with the help of some stock options).

> *Being strategic means doing the really hard things first. If you're trying something new and it isn't hard or risky, it's probably not strategic.*

WHAT IS THE DEFINITION OF STRATEGIC?

It seems these days that almost everyone in both business and HR is striving to become more strategic. While it's a legitimate goal, many practitioners use the word even though they don't know exactly what the word means. It's not enough just to say that you're "strategic," because nearly everyone says that. Rather, it is essential to your credibility that if you assert that you are strategic, you first understand exactly what is and is not strategic.

DEFINITION

A strategic action is a program or initiative designed to directly impact a "business problem." The net result of the strategic action is an increase in measurable business results, where business results are defined as an increase in revenue, profit, market share or a product competitive advantage.

WHAT DOES "STRATEGIC" REALLY MEAN?

There are several different levels of definitions of the word strategic. They run the gamut from the basic dictionary definition to a more focused HR definition. Here are some different definitions:

DEFINITION

A dictionary definition. The technical definition of strategic includes "designed to *strike the enemy at the sources* of its military, economic or political power in order to gain an advantage." For example, a strategic target would be a country's capitol, its source of energy, communications infrastructure, or munitions manufacturing. Strategic criteria are used as a sorting tool to determine which future battles or regions would get the most resources. The meaning of strategic is opposed the term that is on the other end of the "impact" spectrum, which is "tactical." Tactical means designed to impact the enemy at the "local level."

An academic definition. The "textbook" definition of strategic is "the plans made or the actions taken in an effort *to help the organization fulfill its intended purpose."* Purpose in this case is outlined by the organization's mission statement and its corporate goals and objectives.

A business definition. Strategic in business means focused things that affect the entire organization by impacting the corporation's stated goals and objectives (Examples of strategic business objectives include improving customer service, faster product development, and increasing market share, the stock price or employee productivity). Strategic initiatives are positive things that managers do in order to impact the organization's long-term goals and to provide the firm with a competitive advantage. Strategic initiatives vary dramatically from tactical initiatives. Tactical initiatives are those programs, products or functions that have a major impact on reaching *departmental or functional goals* rather than overall corporate goals.

CHECKLIST: FIVE SIMPLE QUALIFYING CRITERIA FOR ANY STRATEGIC PROGRAM

- **Broad impact.** It has an impact across many business units and regions.
- **Focus on future needs.** It has the capability of impacting future needs and problems.
- **Competitive advantage.** It includes the potential to provide a sustainable competitive advantage.
- **Revenue impact.** It potentially can generate at least one percent of revenue or profits.
- **Impact on other corporate goals.** It has a direct impact on long-term corporate goals and objectives in addition to revenue.

Before providing HR's definition of the word strategic, it's important to recognize that top management, not HR, makes the ultimate decision as to what is or is not strategic.

DEFINITION

An HR definition. Strategic in HR means future-focused HR initiatives and programs that affect the entire organization. They impact the corporation's stated goals and objectives and also provide the firm with a competitive advantage in the area of people management or workforce productivity. (Note there are ten essential elements that are necessary to make an HR department strategic; this complete list is provided later in the book in Chapter 4).

Other related HR definitions include:

Definition of an HR strategy. The department's "HR strategy" is the overall approach adopted by the department. The HR department strategy, and the HR plan associated with it, are designed to provide direction as to what the department considers important and to aid in allocating HR resources so that they are concentrated on initiatives that are most likely to increase employee productivity and corporate profits.

Definition of a strategic HR program. In order for a HR program to be considered "strategic," it would normally need to include the following characteristics:

- Be "forward-looking" by forecasting an upcoming problem;

- Be focused on "business problems" rather than HR issues;

- Have a "measurable impact" on workforce productivity; and

- Utilize resources from several HR functions.

Being strategic means being future-focused and concentrating HR resources on solving "business problems" that occur outside of HR.

HOW DO YOU KNOW WHEN YOU ARE BEING TACTICAL?

The first thing that HR professionals should realize is that there is nothing wrong with having a tactical impact. Contributing to departmental or functional goals is an important activity that any HR professional should value. In fact, there are some jobs and initiatives within HR that can have only a tactical impact. For example, it is difficult to have a strategic impact in payroll or benefits administration. The key thing to remember is that, even if your job isn't strategic, by thinking more strategically, you can improve the focus of your programs so that the dollar return is greater and the positive impacts are broader.

Before you can be sure that what you do in HR is strategic, you need to know the difference between strategic and tactical HR actions. Tactical actions have a short-term impact and are generally focused internally.

CHECKLIST: HOW TO TELL IF YOU'RE BEING TACTICAL

There are a variety of things that make an HR action tactical. What you are doing in HR is probably tactical if it has the following attributes:

- **Internally focused.** You are *internally focused* on the day-to-day activities within the HR department. Tactical HR programs "run" without concern for their strategic impact.
- **Focus on cost.** You measure costs (program efficiency) but not your impact on revenue and profits (program impact).
- **Incremental change.** You maintain the status quo within HR by making only subtle refinements in existing programs.

- **Failing to prioritize.** You fail to prioritize programs, individuals or business units so that high-priority business units and programs *do not* receive any special treatment.
- **Failing to coordinate.** You fail to coordinate your functional activities with other HR functions to ensure an increase in the overall business impact of HR.
- **Being reactive.** You or your programs react to events rather than anticipating them in order to prevent them or to minimize their negative impact.

"Being strategic" is a meaningless phrase. Having a measurable impact on specific strategic business goals is the phrase to commit to memory.

LEARNING HOW TO "THINK STRATEGICALLY"

Strategic thinking in HR means that everyone continually compares his or her contributions against the major business objectives of the organization. By constantly thinking like a CEO, individuals can sharpen their focus (time and resources) on the things they do that can impact what the organization has determined to be its strategic objectives. In most cases, you need to learn how to "think strategically" before you can act strategically. In fact, some jobs are so narrow and resource "limited" that most of the time the only choice is to think strategically.

STOP THINKING LIKE AN OVERHEAD FUNCTION

Strategic thinkers continually try to assess the keys to a company's success. Is it the equipment, the buildings or the people that cause a firm to be successful? There are many firms—GE, Microsoft, Cisco and Charles Schwab just to name a few—that clearly succeed not because of their wealth of natural resources or access to sophisticated equipment but because of *their people and their people management practices*. CEOs regularly acknowledge that people are "the" critical success factor in their firms when they use the phrase "people are our most important asset." Why then does HR see itself in such a limited role?

Profit center potential

HR departments have traditionally considered themselves to be an overhead function that added value—but with a limited potential for strategic impact. Unfortunately, that traditional way of looking at HR is a huge step backwards if you want to become strategic. An alternative view is instead to look at the potential that HR has to become a *profit center.*

Learn from others

The first step in thinking strategically is to begin to learn from others within the firm who are known for their strategic impact, especially other so-called "overhead functions" (like operations/supply chain, marketing/branding, IT and even finance) that have clearly moved from the backwater of "overhead" to become critical factors in a company's profitability and success. Even CFOs and CIOs have made the transition from "overhead" to front-line leaders (remember when the predecessor to the CFO was a bookkeeper and the predecessor to the CIO was a typewriter and office machine repair person?).

It's now time for HRM (human resource management) to join the list of top business buzzwords (like TQM, CRM, process re-engineering, branding and supply chain) and overhead functions that have transformed themselves into profit centers and corporate heroes. HR has an opportunity to become even more prominent than other recently popularized business functions because people expenditures can reach as high as 60 percent of all variable costs. As a result, making people management processes more effective can't help but positively impact profits.

It takes more than fancy names like "human capital" and "talent management" to make this impact, however; it takes specific actions on the part of HR leaders. Actions—not words—make you strategic.

EVERYONE MUST THINK STRATEGICALLY

HR executives often boast about being strategic, but all too often that talk fails to translate into action. Separating strategic talkers from truly strategic individuals is admittedly difficult; however, on occasion, it really is easy to see when "being strategic" doesn't permeate an organization. Perhaps an example will illustrate the point.

When you ask most HR professionals to name their department's overall HR strategy, you invariably get a blank look. Most know that there is a strategy but very few actually can put a name to it. If you go the next step and ask line managers from around your company to name the HR strategy, it is unusual to find a single one who can identify their organization's corporate HR strategy. It is not a difficult conclusion to make that when few even know something as simple as the name of your strategy, it is highly unlikely that the strategy is effective.

ALIGNING PRACTICES WITH STRATEGY

The lesson to be learned here is that being strategic requires an approach that permeates everything that's done in the organization. Putting out memos or even issuing a strategic plan doesn't guarantee that anyone will even listen, no less act, strategically. Consequently, begin and end the process of becoming strategic with some degree of skepticism. If you want to know whether thinking and acting strategically is permeating the organization, you need to periodically measure not just knowledge of your strategy's name but also the actions being taken to implement your strategy and the results that are being produced.

DEMONSTRATING THE SHIFT FROM TRADITIONAL TO STRATEGIC

EXAMPLES: BECOMING MORE STRATEGIC

When HR departments move from the "tactical" delivery of traditional HR services towards becoming more strategic, they shift the way they think and act. Their focus changes so that HR time and resources are allocated to totally different programs and actions. Consider the following examples of the transition between traditional HR and strategic HR.

A basic example: A "snap" assessment of the shift in focus

If you are trying to identify whether a department is moving in a strategic direction, here are some of the shifts that you should be able to identify:

Table 1-A.

Tactical	Strategic
HR starts with a focus on . . .	**HR shifts to a focus on . . .**
Treating all programs the same	Programs with the highest impact
Treating all jobs and individuals the same	Jobs/individuals with the highest impact
HR jargon	Business language
HR goals	Business goals and objectives
Process improvement and efficiency	Measurable business results
Internal HR issues	Business unit and corporate issues
Internal company issues only	Both firm and external economic events
Decisions based on experience or intuition	Decisions made with data and facts
Assuming that good people produce results	No assumptions; programs measure results
HR assuming minimal responsibility	Taking responsibility for people productivity

It's important to remember that these shifts in focus are merely indications that an organization is becoming more strategic. The only true way to determine if an organization is strategic is by whether there is a measurable impact on business objectives and results. This brief comparison is designed just to highlight a few of the major differences. A more detailed comparison of strategic and non-strategic actions follows.

A more detailed example: Contrasting traditional HR thinking and strategic HR thinking

The following is a more detailed example that demonstrates the progression from traditional HR thinking toward more strategic thinking, utilizing the way HR measures turnover as an example. As you follow the steps from the traditional to the strategic, you should be able to see the increased business impact. Look in particular for the increased use of benchmark comparisons, more detailed qualitative metrics, and closer examination of "uncounted" costs as the example progresses from HR information points 1 through 8.

Figure 1-1. *The traditional HR approach*
(A turnover reporting metric)

HR information point #1: Our turnover rate is 20 percent.

Comment. *Merely indicating the percentage of people who left provides no business insight.*

↓

HR information point #2: Our turnover rate is 20 percent. However, the industry average is 10 percent and our direct competitor has a 7 percent turnover rate.

Comment. *This new information indicates we're doing relatively poorly compared to others.*

↓

Phase 1 Becoming more strategic:
This begins the strategic thinking phase.

HR information point #3: Our voluntary turnover rate is 20 percent; our involuntary turnover rate is 0 percent. Our direct competitor's involuntary turnover rate is 5 percent.

Comment. *With more information, we now see that we are not terminating a single employee for cause. This could be an indication of weak performance management. Because a direct competitor is terminating 5 percent, they could be dropping their dead wood, thus giving them a competitive advantage.*

↓

HR information point #4: Our voluntary turnover rate is 20 percent, and everyone that left is from a key position or was a top performer. Five percent of the voluntary turnovers are top salespeople.

Comment. *This additional information tells us where the individuals who are quitting are coming from. All positions are not equal, and losing top performers is always a strategic issue.*

↓

Phase 2 The strategic approach:
The final step, advanced strategic thinking.

HR information point #5: Our voluntary turnover rate is 20 percent and we calculated the replacement cost of replacing these key individuals to be $1 million year.

Comment. We've now added the minimal business impact of turnover by calculating the costs of hire replacements.

↓

HR information point #6: We have determined that replacement hires perform at 10 percent below the output level of the individuals that they are replacing. HR has determined that the difference in productivity is because "experienced" individuals know the customer and the product better, and that knowledge increases their ability to sell. The lost productivity of these workers has a business impact of $15 million in sales per year.

Comment. By adding the "uncounted costs" on productivity impact (lost sales) of losing these workers, we finally have begun to act strategically.

↓

HR information point #7: We have determined that of the 20 percent voluntary turnover, 5 percent are top sales people. In half of the cases where we lost a top salesperson we lost at least one key account, valued at over $10 million per year, within three months of the salesperson's leaving. That results in additional lost sales of $50 million a year.

Comment. By moving beyond the reduced productivity and also looking at lost customers, we see that we have been "under-counting" the cost of turnover (under-counting costs is a common HR problem).

↓

HR information point #8: After interviewing top performers and individuals in key positions we found the only reason they left was that they had a poor manager. We also found that, in each case, the manager had been rated as weak in his or her annual management assessment process, but for some reason we failed in even a single case to transfer, correct or terminate the manager. In the past when we terminated poor managers, the increased productivity was two times higher than the costs associated with the termination.

Comment. *We now know the actual business impact of our 20 percent voluntary turnover rate is $66 million per year. But even worse, the primary cause of the turnover was both identifiable and preventable, if HR had been proactive and strategic.*

This more detailed example clearly demonstrates the difference between traditional HR thinking and strategic HR thinking. Using the traditional approach, we gave managers limited information with no benchmarks, and HR certainly did not provide any dollar-impact information.

As HR progresses and becomes more strategic, HR begins to show the cause of the problem, the solution, and the dollar impact of failing to act. If HR provided only the traditional 20 percent turnover rate, management might have assumed that everyone has a 20 percent turnover rate and accordingly would have taken no action. With the strategic approach and identification of $66 million in bottom-line costs, it is clear that HR could have solved the problem by transferring, correcting, or terminating some bad managers.

What is or is not strategic is determined by senior managers outside of HR. They judge strategic actions or programs not by the words that describe them but instead by their actual impact on business results, which incidentally is always measured in dollars!

Figure 1-2. *A final example: The progression from traditional HR actions to strategic actions*

This example follows the work of an individual employee relations specialist and shows the transition from a traditional approach to a strategic approach.

Traditional employee relations approach: The activities of the employee relations specialist included "I put in 10 hard hours every day performing the following activities:"

- **Provide answers:** Answered managers' employee relations questions when they called.
- **Advocate:** Acted as an employee advocate when there were conflicts between managers and employees.
- **Legal issues:** Warned managers to avoid litigation risks.
- **Poor performers:** Urged managers to give "problem" employees a second chance.
- **Grievances:** Processed grievance paperwork.
- **Respond to calls:** Responded to employee relations "situations" when called.

↓

Strategic employee relations approach: The activities of the employee relations specialist included "I put in eight invigorating hours every day because there are fewer "fires" to fight."

- **Provided answers:** Made lists of possible manager questions and answered them on a web site so the information was available 24/7. The net result was that managers could get their own answers anytime they needed them, even when I was not available.
- **Advocate:** Began focusing on employee productivity rather than taking the "little guy's" side. The result was that I began to shift my role to consultant and productivity advocate, instead of "helping" the underdog.

- **Legal issues:** Calculated the real probabilities and risks of lawsuits and educated managers so they could decide when to take a "reasonable risk." The net result was that after calculating the real probabilities, most previous fears of lawsuits dissipated and managers began making fact-based decisions.

- **Poor performers:** When an employee relations event occurred, I calculated the probability and the cost of "fixing" a poor performing employee and compared it to the cost of replacing the employee so that the manager could make an "informed" decision. The result is that we now "release" more poor performers because the data indicated that they never improved, despite all our efforts. It turned out that the ROI of hiring replacement workers was three times higher than for "fixing" poor performers.

- **Grievances:** Began to question whether a grievance could be "predicted and prevented." Began gathering data and looking at a number of incidents in order to identify the root causes. The net result was that I began to alert managers weeks before a minor problem grew into a major one. Grievances were reduced by 25 percent and worker productivity increased by 10 percent.

- **Respond to calls:** Rather than waiting for the manager to call, I sought out "precursors" to employee relations problems. I calculated the potential damage and consulted with the managers on possible approaches to prevent these issues. I also sought out opportunities for "positive employee relations" in order to excite, motivate and challenge workers. The net result was a 15 percent improvement in productivity, 10 percent drop in turnover and a 12 percent drop in absenteeism. Business units that I serve have a 4 percent increase in profit compared to a 1 percent average increase in all other business units.

The difference in both approaches and results is dramatic in this and in the previous example. It should be obvious that strategic actions in HR "look different" and produce dramatically different results than do tactical HR approaches. Numerous other strategic assessment tools can be found later in the book covering both departmental and individual strategic assessment tools. A quick assessment tool for determining the strategic level of individual HR programs follows.

DETERMINING IF A SPECIFIC HR PROGRAM IS STRATEGIC

If you're running a really good best practice HR program, it is common to wonder whether the program is really strategic. Up front it's important to realize that actually adding a strategic impact is quite difficult. In fact, I have found that less than five percent of HR programs actually turn out to have a major strategic impact. That doesn't mean most HR programs aren't important; rather, it just means that the definition of strategic impact for HR is set very high.

Later in the book you will find methods of assessing the quantitative impact of HR programs. However, if you want to do a quick assessment of a specific HR program, here are some non-quantitative "indicators" that show whether your HR program has the potential for making a strategic impact. This checklist is based on the premise that truly strategic programs are well known within the corporation. If you're doing something strategic, the odds are that senior executives will be aware of it and, as a result, they will want continual updates on it.

CHECKLIST: DOES YOUR PROGRAM HAVE STRATEGIC POTENTIAL?

- **Future-focused.** The program is based not on the current but on the future needs of the corporation. At some point, your program team has made a formal forecast of those needs.
- **Program goals.** The program goals are defined in business terms. These goals focus directly on improving business results and improving the overall productivity of the workforce.
- **Responsibility.** The head of the HR program has assumed total accountability for producing results, even though he or she knows up front that HR doesn't have total control over each of the elements and resources that impact the program's success.
- **Breadth of impact.** The results of the program will be felt outside of HR, in more than one single business unit, as well as by customers and stakeholders.
- **Executives are aware.** The CEO is aware of the program by name and/or the COO requests periodic updates on it. The executive committee has discussed the program. If the program utilizes technology, the CIO is aware of it by name.

- **Program exposure.** The program is mentioned in the annual report (assuming the program is operational) or in the CEO's internal annual report of his or her accomplishments.
- **Meetings.** The project or program leader has regularly scheduled meetings on the program with executives outside of HR.
- **Progress reports.** A senior manager outside of HR receives regular progress reports on the project or program. HR receives periodic comments on the report from that senior executive.
- **Revenue impact.** If the program were discontinued, total corporate revenue or profit would go down enough so that the CFO would notice.
- **Bold steps.** Because strategic programs are capable of large results, the program is either bold, contra-cyclical, or the first of its kind in the industry.
- **Worth copying.** Competitors have attempted to benchmark and copy it.
- **Advantage.** The program team has completed a side-by-side assessment that demonstrates that the program provides a competitive advantage.

Not all strategic programs meet all of these criteria, but if you aren't meeting at least 75 percent of them, odds are that you have yet to reach the strategic threshold.

Note: The elements of a strategic HR *department* (as opposed to a *program*) are found later in this book.

Senior executives want to be kept informed about all things strategic. So, if they don't ask for reports on what you are doing or schedule regular meetings with you, then what you are doing is not considered to be strategic.

Before we move on to the specific elements of strategic HR function it is important to take a step back and look at the role of HR in an organization. The next chapter helps clarify the roles and responsibilities of HR by classifying what HR does into five distinct levels of contribution.

CHAPTER TWO

CLARIFYING THE STRATEGIC ROLE OF HR

OBJECTIVES

The last chapter defined what it means to be strategic in HR. It's important to step back and take a broader view, because a common mistake that many in HR make is to focus exclusively on the strategic element of HR. This chapter focuses on more clearly defining the role and the purpose of the HR department.

KEY POINTS

◊ As an alternative to the traditional "four quadrant" model of HR focus, consider instead the five levels where HR can make a significant contribution.

◊ It's important to define "who" HR's customer is—and it is senior management.

◊ HR must take responsibility and accountability for all people management results, even though HR does not have total control over all of the factors that influence those results.

◊ Finally, recognize the problem with "undercounting." It's impossible to measure the strategic impact of HR accurately if you only look at the direct cost savings of cutting programs.

UNDERSTANDING THE ROLE OF HR

Human resources, like all other business functions, must do a range of things well, from basic transactions to the strategic, in order to be successful. Rather than looking just at the "end point" of the spectrum, it is better to understand the *range* of HR activities and contributions.

The "five levels of HR contribution" model

There are few "models" that describe the different approaches or focuses that HR departments should have. Without a doubt, the most famous one is the "four quadrant" or "business partner" model developed by Dave Ulrich at the University of Michigan. Briefly, that model includes as HR's four key roles: administrative services expert, employee champion, change agent, and strategic partner. As effective as that model is, it fails to define clearly what happens in the most important of the quadrants, the strategic one.

As an alternative to the four quadrant model, I offer here the "five levels of HR contribution" model that I believe better describes both the basic and the strategic levels of HR contribution in terms of their strategic business contribution. Although each is important in its own right, the most strategic contributions are in the areas of improving employee productivity, building a competitive advantage, and positively impacting strategic business goals.

ALIGNING PRACTICES WITH STRATEGY

The five levels of HR contribution model

HR "work" can be classified into five distinct levels from the basic to the most strategic. Those levels include:

Figure 1-1. *The five levels of HR contribution model*

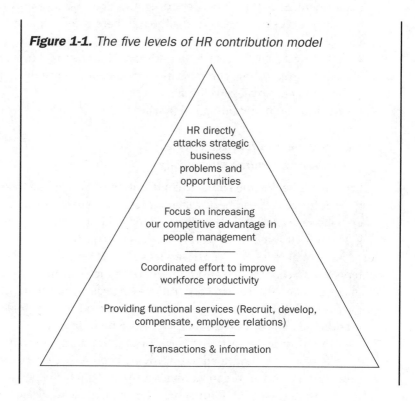

HR directly attacks strategic business problems and opportunities

Focus on increasing our competitive advantage in people management

Coordinated effort to improve workforce productivity

Providing functional services (Recruit, develop, compensate, employee relations)

Transactions & information

Senior HR leaders are constantly seeking ways to become more strategic. However, HR efforts can take on many faces. To make it clearer, here is a model that classifies strategic HR efforts into five distinct levels, from the basic to the most advanced. These levels include:

Level one: Transactions and information

Every HR department must provide basic information, answer employee and manager questions, and complete transactions. These are the oldest but most elementary of HR services:

- Day-to-day HR transactions including new hires, terminations and benefits
- Providing basic information and answering basic HR questions

Level two: Providing functional services

A majority of HR departments provide these essential functions. At this level, each of the services is provided in a separate functional department. Each functional department, *i.e.*, recruiting, compensation, etc., sets its own goals, and although there is some interaction, services are provided relatively independently of each other.

- Providing basic HR services in traditional independent functions including recruiting, compensation and benefits, employee relations and employee development
- Creating and maintaining HR policies

Level three: Coordinated efforts
to improve workforce productivity

Level three begins the strategic contribution of HR. While transactions, information and basic functional services are important, they do not rise to a strategic level because they neither share a common goal nor focus on any key corporate goal or objective.

What makes level three HR services distinctive is that level three represents a coordinated effort, the goal of which is to impact one of the primary goals of every corporation—increasing productivity. In the case of HR, of course, the segment of the productivity goal that is addressed is workforce or employee productivity.

Any effort to impact workforce productivity directly requires specific resources dedicated to improving productivity, metrics for productivity, and an organizational component, which encourages (or forces) the distinct HR functional departments to work as a team for this goal. Improving the overall productivity of the workforce means that HR develops initiatives continuously to increase the dollar value of employee output while maintaining or reducing the average labor cost per unit.

The traditional HR functional work that occurs in level two is too fragmented to have any real impact on workforce productivity. In fact, typically none of the independent functional units in HR even have workforce productivity as a goal. Some of the non-traditional productivity-related HR activities that are "added" to traditional functional offerings include:

- The retention of key employees
- The redeployment of employees from areas of low business impact to high
- Non-monetary motivation and recognition
- Workforce productivity metrics
- Spreading the best people practices within the organization

Level four: Increasing the people-management competitive advantage

Level four provides another strategic contribution. Increasing competitive advantage is an externally focused effort to compare each key HR program and service directly to competitor firms. What makes this level unique is that its focus is outside the organization; prior to this, every HR effort was internally focused. This is another coordinated HR-wide team effort.

Rather than just tracking what competitors do, the goal is to identify and exploit weaknesses and to eventually ensure that our workforce productivity exceeds theirs. Only very elite HR departments fund major efforts in this area.

Typical competitive advantage building efforts include:

- Competitive analysis of your rival's people programs
- Forecasting and workforce planning
- Employment branding
- Competitive intelligence

Level five: HR directly attacks strategic business problems and opportunities

Level five is the highest level of strategic impact in HR. Efforts in this area go well beyond even employee productivity. They attempt to address strategic business problems such as product development, quality, customer service and non-performing business units. Normally only HR departments in performance cultures reach this level of direct business impact. Typical strategic business problem and opportunity efforts include:

- Business unit turnaround teams
- Product problem turnaround teams
- Increasing speed and innovation in product development

- Building a company-wide performance culture
- Identifying M&A targets based on the talent the firms have

As you can see from the five levels of HR contribution model, HR has a range of activities on which to focus. HR responsibilities start with the basic transactions and eventually become strategic at the third level. The fourth and fifth levels focus on goals that few HR departments ever attain, however. The model is similar to the approach used by elite performance cultures in that it includes the most strategic of HR efforts: workforce productivity, competitive advantage and solving business problems. All three of these areas are included in the 10 essential elements of the strategic HR department (which are highlighted in the next chapter).

WHO IS HR'S CUSTOMER?

Management or employees?

It's not unusual for HR departments to debate for endless hours about "who is their customer?" If the goal of your HR department is to become a strategic partner, that debate should end quickly. All strategic business people define their customer as the customer of the firm. Everyone should have as his or her first priority increasing customer value. However, it is also important to define HR's primary "internal customer."

SENIOR MANAGEMENT IS THE INTERNAL CUSTOMER

The goal of most HR executives during the 1990s was earning a seat at the executive table, and most succeeded in becoming a bona fide member of the senior management team. Once you assume that role, it should become abundantly clear that if you wish to be strategic, you must define your "internal customer" as senior management of the corporation. There are a variety of reasons why senior managers must become your primary HR customer. They include:

- The senior managers are by definition strategic. They control strategic resources and business units and, as a result, anyone who expects to have any strategic impact must do it with their cooperation and support. Few if any mid-level managers or employees can ever have a strategic impact, so defining those individuals as your primary internal customers ends any chance of producing strategic results.

- Senior managers control the budget so you must influence them in order to get sufficient resources to do your job.
- Senior managers hold a significant amount of power, and without their support it's unlikely that most of your ideas will get adopted or implemented.
- Senior managers have supervisory responsibility for the line managers under them. As a result, because HR has no direct power over line managers, senior management cooperation is necessary in order to get managers and supervisors to follow HR's advice and to utilize its programs.
- If HR senior executives want eventually to be promoted into other areas of management, they must establish a track record within HR of advocating productivity, profit, and reaching corporate goals, because those are the same things that are advocated in every other business unit outside of HR.

These points highlight the need to establish up front that the senior managers of the corporation (general managers and above) are HR's primary internal customers. HR must identify senior management's business objectives and their expectations when it comes to HR, and then design systems to ensure that HR is contributing directly to meeting those needs and objectives. All HR plans, services and performance metrics must be designed with senior management's goals and objectives in mind.

Identifying senior managers as a primary HR customer has been known to irritate some HR traditionalists. Because they feel so strongly that HR should be an employee advocate, it is appropriate to spend a little time in this chapter demonstrating the negative business consequences of such an approach.

PRODUCTIVITY PROPONENT, NOT EMPLOYEE ADVOCATE

Many traditional HR theorists and practitioners have cast the role of HR as being an "employee advocate," or someone that helps employees when they have conflicts with their managers. In sharp contrast, others (especially those who advocate a performance culture) reject this notion as the antithesis of being strategic. While neither position is totally right or wrong, the "employee advocate" position has some inherent weaknesses. Some of them include:

- HR managers are paid by management and by the business, not by employees. Consequently, HR might not even be credible in convincing employees that HR can be a "fair" representative for employees.
- In most countries, unions are by law advocates for the employee. Whether you have a union or not, advocating for employees could be construed as usurping an employee's right to representation.
- Assuming that employees need an advocate categorizes them as second-class citizens incapable of defending themselves. In addition, advocating for employees might actually make them weaker, which eventually could make them less capable of making decisions, advocating for their own position, and promoting their own ideas within the company.
- Making HR an employee advocate creates an "us-against-them" mentality, when in fact increasing productivity requires both managers and employees to work together as a team. Providing employees with too many third-party options might actually hurt direct employee-management relationships; instead of talking face-to-face, both sides get in the habit of bringing in a third party.

HR professionals are paid by the organization to represent the organization's interests. Because HR's strategic role is defined as increasing workforce productivity, the HR department must assume the role of "asset manager" for the most expensive corporate asset—its employees. A focus on workforce productivity and profitability can get blurred whenever HR takes the employee side because quite frequently, employee self-interest is not consistent with productivity and profit.

Whether we like it or not, HR's job is to help get employees to do things that they wouldn't do naturally. If employees naturally produced at the highest level, we wouldn't need performance pay, firings, rules, training and the other things that HR helps manage.

I admit that on the surface it may sound a little "dehumanizing," but HR's job is to increase the workforce's output using all the motivational and reward and punishment tools available. Some in HR even advocate that their role is to make employees "happy." This also conflicts directly with HR's role in increasing workforce productivity because making employees work harder than they would on their own more than occasionally makes them unhappy, the same way that firing nonproductive employees and layoffs can make employees "unhappy."

If you're going to be a business partner, you need to assume the role and the responsibilities of any businessperson. It is true, of course, that managers can be wrong and that employees can be misunderstood, but, in most cases, employees should advocate their own positions and do it directly to their managers. Only when that process has clearly failed and the company is in legal jeopardy should HR intervene in this important manager-employee relationship.

> HR advises but it does **not** make people decisions. Managers "own" all people problems and are responsible for making all people-related decisions.

CLARIFYING RESPONSIBILITIES IN MANAGING PEOPLE ASSETS

Even when HR professionals accept their role in increasing worker productivity and building a performance culture, they often, not too subtly, complain that it's "unfair" to expect them to manage work-force productivity. Their complaint stems from the indisputable fact that the actions of managers and employees—and so many other factors—impact HR's ability to produce results.

Accepting responsibility without authority is difficult; however, it is not that uncommon in today's complex business world. The remainder of this discussion will highlight the importance of HR accepting responsibility and accountability in spite a lack of control.

TAKING RESPONSIBILITY FOR THINGS YOU DON'T CONTROL

As we have already established, being strategic means producing results that impact business objectives. But in order to take credit for something, you have to take responsibility for it first. What that statement means is that if you want to take credit for some strategic result, you must first assume some degree of "ownership" over that strategic area.

In this case, HR needs to assume responsibility and ownership for employee productivity, so that when employee productivity improves, HR can legitimately take credit for the accomplishment. Unfortunately, all too often HR professionals want to take credit when productivity is high, but they don't want to take the blame and the responsibility when it drops.

Taking responsibility and being strategic go hand in hand.

Many people equate being strategic with having some degree of formal authority or control, but there is really no automatic connection between the two. Strategic individuals seldom have as much power as they would like.

For example, the CFO takes responsibility for all financial actions but, in fact, a CFO has little direct power over how money is spent. In most cases, the CFO doesn't formally own or even possess the funds for which he or she must assume responsibility. Most of the CFO's power comes instead from educating and influencing others, not from any formal authority to fire or even to punish individuals. In short, what CFOs do is take responsibility for the things that they have determined to be important to the success of the organization, even though in most cases they do not have total control or power over the entire situation.

In a similar light, even though HR is classified by some as an overhead function (where overhead functions do not, by definition, have direct line-manager authority), it cannot use this "I'm powerless" excuse if it ever expects to be considered a strategic function. Rather than making excuses, strategic individuals find a way to influence others, so that the net result is that people who "don't have to cooperate" are nonetheless influenced to work together toward a common goal. Taking responsibility for things you don't completely own or control is known as the "captain of the ship" approach.

Did HR sink the Titanic?

Look at an example. If you were examining the sinking of the Titanic, would you say that the captain, the navigator, or the lookout was at fault for the sinking? Before you make a quick judgment, take a step back. Remember on the Titanic there were no equipment failures or acts of nature. The sinking was a series of failures caused by human errors. Who is responsible for failures by humans and the management systems that direct them? If you assume, as most strategic individuals do, that HR is responsible for the performance of the crew, it's not a far stretch to assume that HR was responsible for the sinking of the Titanic.

After all, HR was responsible for hiring, training, setting performance standards, determining staffing levels, and developing performance management systems. And yes, of course, senior management shares some joint responsibility. Still, when you think strategically, you invariably come to the conclusion that when the "people assets" of the organization fail to perform, that failure needs to be "owned" by the only individuals who have the in-depth knowledge in the management of people resources—HR.

Tactical people take responsibility for operating systems. Strategic individuals take responsibility for producing results.

Non-strategic individuals in HR take a narrow perspective and accept responsibility only for the "operation" of people management systems. This narrow perspective guarantees that HR will not be considered strategic; the very definition of strategic moves beyond taking responsibility for the "operation" and instead focuses on taking responsibility for the "results."

If you accept this broader view that HR is responsible for the "output" or results of the people management systems (not just the operation of the systems), then you already are taking a strategic view of HR. If you assume the "captain of the ship" role, you must move beyond accepting responsibility for merely the operation of all people systems. Rather, you must add to that the broader responsibility for the actions and the performance of the employees who were hired, trained, appraised and rewarded by those systems.

When you adopt this view, you accept the fact that you must advise, cajole, educate and somehow influence managers and employees throughout the organization so that they can execute effectively and produce the highest workforce productivity.

ALIGNING PRACTICES WITH STRATEGY

Chief "people" advisor to the CEO

Before leaving the topic of accepting responsibility for all people management, it's important to determine if there are any limits on that people-management responsibility and ownership. This important note is added because many individuals in HR assume that their "people-results" responsibility flows only in a downward direction. In other words, while many vice presidents of human resources accept responsibility for the people and systems "below them," few even consider their people-management responsibility "above them."

When HR takes an upward view, the question that often arises is, "Who is responsible for advising the CEO in the management of his or her executive team?" Unfortunately this is a question most VPs of HR are afraid to address. Yes, it is true that *technically* the CEO is responsible for managing the executive team, but it is equally true that not every CEO gets promoted to that level based on his or her strong people management skills. Accounts of CEOs who lack people management skills are legion and, as a result, those CEOs' executive teams do not operate as an effective unit.

I am not proposing here that the VP of HR actually run the executive team. What I am suggesting is that great VPs of HR must "manage up" and serve as the chief people advisor to the CEO on the management of his or her executive team. Yes, the VP of HR is but one senior executive on the team. Even so, the VP of HR is frequently the one with the most advanced skill in managing people and team performance.

I only know of a handful of VPs of HR who accept this ultimate responsibility for managing up and becoming the chief people advisor to the CEO. That handful of individuals who *have* accepted that role are, without a doubt, the most strategic and have the greatest impact of any VP of HR that I've ever encountered.

"HR is only a tool; it's not the objective."

INCREASING REVENUE IS MORE STRATEGIC THAN A COST-CUTTING FOCUS

When defining the strategic role of HR, one final area that is important to address is HR's historic over-focus on cutting costs. While of course cutting costs is important, it is essential that HR shift its focus away from cost-cutting and focus instead on increasing output and revenues.

Every major corporation strives to increase its profits; however, in striving to meet that goal it is important to realize that there are two distinct parts of any profit-loss equation—revenue and costs. A business can increase profits in two basic ways: first, by reducing costs, and second, by increasing revenue (either by charging more or selling more). In HR, we've traditionally focused on the cutting-costs part of the equation. Maybe that's because it is relatively easy to cut the "people" costs.

UNDERCOUNTING

Unfortunately, cutting people costs can have some disastrous consequences. HR's longstanding practice of "undercounting" costs is one of the prime reasons that HR fails to increase worker productivity. "Undercounting" is the process of omitting the additional costs caused by a bad practice or process because these unintended consequences are not connected directly to the initial action by HR.

Some obvious examples of dubious cost-cutting and "undercounting" might include:

- Hiring workers with fewer skills in critical positions is certainly cheaper than hiring individuals with superior skills, but it may negatively impact product quality and innovation.
- When top-performing workers demand more money, we can release them and replace them with cheaper, albeit less effective, workers, but we might have to hire significantly more workers just to maintain the same level of production.
- We can ignore market compensation rates and underpay in salary and benefits, but that could negatively impact our ability to attract and retain top people.
- We can offer no or poor-quality training, but error and safety rates might also be adversely affected by the poor training.

- We can avoid the risk of firing bad workers and managers but that likely would adversely impact both the quality and the volume of our output.
- We can lay off the "last hired" because it results in less political turmoil, but that might mean we're losing individuals that bring a fresh outside perspective to the way that work is done.
- We could arbitrarily freeze all hiring during lean economic times, but that might force managers to retain bottom performers because they know no replacements are possible.

As you can see, there are some potential negative consequences of arbitrarily cutting costs without simultaneously looking at the impact of cost-cutting on revenues and productivity. In fact, any accountant can blindly cut costs, but it takes a true productivity expert to understand that cutting costs and "undercounting" the impact actually can have a significant negative impact on the firm.

The strategic target for HR is to increase revenues and productivity while simultaneously maintaining or reducing your relative labor costs. If you give any CEO a choice as to whether he or she would prefer increasing revenues or cutting costs, the "increase revenue" option invariably is chosen. Why? Whenever you increase revenue in a competitive marketplace it's obvious that you are improving your products and services, which are long-term competitive advantages. Short-term cost-cutting might actually improve short-term profits, but in the long term, profits may go down. Careless cost-cutting may permanently harm your competitive position and image among your customers.

WHY REVENUES ARE STRATEGICALLY MORE IMPORTANT

HR makes a strategic error when it does not focus on increasing revenue—the other, but more important side of the profit equation. Increasing revenues is a more important HR strategic goal because it demonstrates your organization is meeting customer needs.

When you increase revenue, it means one of two things. You have either increased the volume of the products you're selling or you have been successful at charging a higher price. Both more and higher-priced sales are indications of a superior product and a great branding and marketing effort. When you continually increase revenues you are demonstrating that you are building a competitive advantage in the marketplace.

When you cut costs you are not demonstrating any positive customer impact. Instead you merely are showing your ability to pinch pennies. No one says costs are unimportant, but it is obvious that pleasing customers, increasing sales, and providing a product that can be sold at a premium are more valuable business goals than cutting costs.

Remember that if you fired every employee, your labor costs would reach zero, but your sales, productivity and product development would also reach zero. Books like "Built to Last: Successful Habits of Visionary Companies" by Jim Collins (HarperBusiness, 1994) provide lots of data that demonstrate that increasing customer satisfaction and revenue are long-term survival strategies superior to simple "cost-cutting." Anyone who has ever worked at a consulting firm or in sales knows that the real hero is the one who increases revenues, not the behind-the-scenes person who focuses exclusively on cutting costs.

HR commonly omits the losses from unintended consequences when it brags about cutting costs.

IT'S NOT STRATEGIC TO "UNDERCOUNT" COSTS IN HR

Anyone who understands business realizes that the accounting department tracks only one type of cost. Accounting costs are the actual expenditure of funds for goods and services. For example, if you trained 10 doctors at $1,000 apiece, the accounting ledger will show a $10,000 "cost" entry. These are real dollars, and accounting has done its job by "counting" them.

Following that logic, many in HR think that by cutting the training of those 10 doctors you have "saved" the company $10,000. On the surface, that might appear to be true, but it is actually foolish thinking that any true strategic businessperson would see right through. What you *actually* might have done by eliminating the doctors' training is increase the number of deaths, accidents, lawsuits and accreditation problems.

Doing the wrong thing

If you think like a businessperson and *not* an accountant, it doesn't take very long to realize that there are actually two types of cost-cutting. The first (the one that everyone understands) is reducing actual dollar expenditures, while the second is the dollar costs associated with "doing the wrong thing" (when it comes to spending money).

The costs of doing the wrong thing are well known by strategic managers. These costs can be defined as the costs or losses that result from "doing less than necessary," failing to invest, or failing to account for the unintended consequences of your decisions.

> *Over cost-cutting is best characterized by the phrase "penny-wise and pound-foolish."*

UNDERSTAND THE "UNINTENDED CONSEQUENCES" OF COST-CUTTING

From a strategic business perspective, there are real business costs associated with these three broad areas where cost-cutting goes awry:

1. **Doing less than necessary.** Succumbing to the pressure to reduce costs may have unintended consequences in other business areas. These losses may appear only indirectly in the firm's financial statements.

   For example, cutting the costs of people programs may lead to a dramatic increase in error rates, accidents, missed deadlines and customer unhappiness. And just because there is no accounting "column" for increased customer unhappiness, that doesn't make the costs associated with having unhappy customers any less real. Another possibility is that the costs of losing customers will appear on the accounting ledger, but no one will make a direct connection between the initial cost-cutting and the delayed loss of customers.

   In a similar vein, let's look at HR expenditures on employee safety programs. Even though accounting actually does track both increased accident costs and the reduction in expenditures on employee safety, accounting has no way of connecting the two. This doesn't make any less real the fact that cutting expenditures on safety programs clearly "caused" the increase in accident rates. It just means that the connection will go unnoticed by accounting *unless HR makes the connection* for them.

2. **Failing to invest.** When an organization fails to spend money on a people problem, the problem may go away on its own. More likely, however, it will fester, worsen and possibly even become unsolvable because managers failed to take action early on. In this case, "doing nothing" will cost you "something."

3. **Shifting costs to hide them.** A strategic HR person looks after the interest of the entire corporation, not just his or her own business unit. On occasion, however, HR loses sight of that fact when it undertakes "self-service" initiatives.

   To take another example, HR portals and Intranet information services provide helpful information to managers and employees, but they may also result in a "shifting" of costs from HR to managers and employees. Even though HR may have reduced its own headcount, by requiring manager and employee self-service, HR actually may be increasing overall costs by taking highly paid managers and employees away from their valuable line jobs in order to perform low-level administrative tasks. If HR omits these costs when it calculates its cost of a transaction, it is not being a strategic leader.

Unfortunately, most HR people only understand the limited "accounting ledger perspective" toward cutting expenditures. As demonstrated below, however, there are other types of costs of which strategic HR professionals must be aware. And for each of these "uncounted" cost areas, it's important to realize that, just because accounting may not track them does not make these costs "unreal" to line managers.

FIVE AREAS OF HR COST "UNDERCOUNTING"

At some point, strategic HR professionals must realize that over-cutting or failing to spend have dollar consequences to line managers that reach millions of dollars (even though there is literally no chance that they will ever appear in an accounting ledger). So if you want to be more strategic, you need to look at the unintended consequences of cost cutting.

There are five different "uncounted costs" associated with HR cost cutting. They are:

1. **Over-cutting costs causes "new" problems.** Cutting expenditures may cause "new" problems, which, in the long run, could cost more than the initial cost-cutting saved. For example, if HR cuts out funds in development, recruiting and retention, the resulting problems that will likely result (decreases in retention, learning and the quality of hire) may obscure any savings that resulted from the initial cuts

2. **The costs of doing nothing.** As noted earlier, there are distinct costs related to doing nothing. The cost of doing nothing is similar to over-cutting costs; the difference here is that there is no initial program to cut. There is instead an opportunity to develop a new program when HR initially identifies a new people management problem.

   The "cost of doing nothing" arises when HR allows the problem to fester and worsen over time, either because of indecision or because HR was unwilling to invest money in any new HR program. In either case, however, the costs of the problem to the business are real. These costs could have been minimized or prevented if HR had just done something by investing in a new HR program or solution.

3. **Spending money to save money.** Failing to spend money (or spending insufficient funds) to maintain existing programs may cause problems that cost a great deal of additional money. In this case, funds are not actually cut, but HR refuses to spend additional money to maintain and improve an HR program. Just as failing to do maintenance on a car's brakes can cause expensive accidents, so can failing to invest in people management programs have dollar consequences to the business.

For example, freezing promotions will limit the number of development opportunities that top-performing employees will receive. If, however, you have instead "invested" money in promotions your organization may end up with a net gain. By spending money on promotions you may get increased productivity from the promoted individuals, and you may have "saved" the costs of replacing employees who would have left to take advantage of promotional opportunities at other firms.

4. **Spending money to make money.** Opportunity costs relate to positive revenue-enhancing opportunities rather than fixing or preventing problems that cost money. Opportunity costs in this context occur when HR fails to take advantage of reasonable profit-generating opportunities that, in the long-term, if taken advantage of, would have resulted in increased revenues.

    For example, if you are presented with the opportunity to hire away a top competitor's best salesperson, most line managers would jump at the opportunity because it would both increase your ability to sell while simultaneously hurting your competitor by decreasing its sales revenues. However, if you fail to hire the person because of a hiring freeze, there is a real "opportunity cost" to having such a policy. Failing to spend money when reasonable opportunities arise results in real costs to a business that, unfortunately, do not appear on any accounting spreadsheet.

5. **Cutting costs only to have to replace them.** Frequently HR cuts costs during a downturn by eliminating programs completely. Occasionally, the cost-cutting does not result in any immediate problems. Because business runs in cycles, however, HR may find that if the downturn is short-lived, it will have to rebuild or replace those recently cut programs. It may also find that rebuilding those programs from scratch may be dramatically more expensive than any cost savings accrued during the time that the program was not in existence. In addition, it's worth noting that the slow start-up and weak initial performance of the "rebuild program" may add dramatically to the "uncounted" business costs.

Just because accounting doesn't track them doesn't make the losses associated with "doing nothing" or "doing the wrong thing" unreal losses.

CALCULATING THE "REAL" VALUE ADDED
OF COST-CUTTING ACTIVITIES

The "real" value added to the corporation by any cost-cutting programs that HR might sanction can be calculated in a formula with six elements. The formula looks like this:

> **The actual dollar value of any cost reductions**
> ***minus* the dollars lost in each of these five areas**
> **of "unintended consequences"**
> ***equals* the real cost-cutting value:**

- New problems caused by "over cost-cutting" of existing programs
- Additional costs that result from inaction or "doing nothing" when problems arise
- Additional costs that result from failing to invest in the maintenance of existing programs
- Additional revenues that were lost because the firm did not invest in "new opportunities"
- Additional costs associated with rebuilding or replacing programs that were dismantled during cost-cutting

Although cutting costs seems relatively easy on the surface, there can be significantly higher costs associated with the unintended consequences that can follow excessive or inappropriate cost-cutting.

Once you understand the different roles of HR, the next step that many senior HR leaders take is to select an *overall* HR strategy for their HR function. The next chapter highlights the advantages and disadvantages of the most commonly used HR strategies.

CHAPTER THREE

SELECTING A STRATEGY FOR THE HR DEPARTMENT

OBJECTIVES

The last chapter helped to clarify the role that HR plays in the organization. After understanding their overall role, quite often the next question that arises in the minds of senior HR managers is, "what is the appropriate HR strategy for my organization?"

KEY POINTS

◊ There are many different HR strategies; each is designed for a different need. This chapter presents the top ten overall HR strategies and the advantages and disadvantages of each.

◊ In my experience, building a performance culture is the strategy with the greatest impact. Unfortunately, it is also the most difficult to implement and operate, but if customers and the CEO are demanding increased performance, there is no better way to obtain it.

DEFINITION

An HR strategy is the overall approach that an HR department takes in order to meet its goals. Generally, an overall HR strategy also has a companion strategic plan, and together they provide the direction for both the department's strategic and tactical efforts. An HR strategy shows you what to do "more of" and "less of." Great strategies and their companion plan serve as a directional sign to help employees and managers understand what is important and what is not.

A strategy can also serve as a type of "decision filter" that can help management sort out inappropriate new ideas and programs. A strategy helps HR managers improve or modify programs so that they are more closely "aligned" (in line with or in agreement with) with your organization's strategic goals and objectives.

An example might help illustrate how a strategy provides direction. If your HR department has a strategy that says be "number one" in every HR function, then managers and employees alike know that this is a performance culture where results are the focus. If, however, the HR strategy is "service excellence," then the focus would be on process excellence, even if that did not always maximize results.

There is no single source that identifies distinct HR strategies and which companies use each variation. Consequently, I compiled this list of strategies based on the strategies utilized by companies around the world that I have worked for or advised. Many organizations develop unique strategies by taking some of the key elements from several of the ten core strategies presented here.

The remainder of this chapter highlights the ten different overall HR strategies and provides some insights into the advantages and disadvantages of each.

THE MOST WIDELY USED HR DEPARTMENTAL STRATEGIES

If you study successful organizations around the world, you'll find that there are a finite number of HR strategies in use. Whether you are a senior HR manager in search of a strategy, or you are just a practicing HR professional who is curious about the range of available strategies, the following chapter will provide you with a brief outline of each. Although each strategy is listed separately, many firms use strategies in combination in order to arrive at an approach that best fits their situation.

SELECTING AN OVERALL HR STRATEGY

Organizations select their HR department's overall strategy using a variety of criteria, including:

- The speed of change in the industry;
- The degree of strategic impact required;
- The resources available to the HR department;
- The level of talent in the HR department;
- What HR strategies were adopted by competitors;
- Consultants recommendations; and
- The personal experience or preference of the VP of HR.

Select an appropriate HR strategy using the above criteria.

The strategies themselves are listed below from the easiest to the hardest to implement. Notably, the most difficult strategy to implement is the performance culture, but it also has the potential for the most strategic impact. For example, firms like Intel, General Electric, Cisco, Nucor, and Microsoft have found that a "performance culture" is the best approach to drive their success, while other excellent companies like Hewlett-Packard, Oracle and Dell Computer have adopted an e-HR strategy, where technology permeates everything they do in HR. And finally, numerous other successful companies have achieved good results using the more traditional business partner or personnel strategy.

Each has its advantages, costs, and disadvantages, so compare and contrast them before deciding that any one approach is "the best."

Table 3-A. *Checklist: Ten basic HR strategies*

1. Personnel strategy;
2. Generalist strategy;
3. Business partner strategy;
4. Call center strategy;
5. Outsourcing strategy;
6. Centers of excellence strategy;
7. Self-service strategy;
8. Fact-based decision-making strategy;
9. e-HR strategy; and
10. Performance culture strategy.

Each of these different strategies is discussed in detail below.

TEN BASIC HR STRATEGIES DESCRIBED

1. Personnel strategy

- **Priority and focus**—Low costs, basic transactions and legal compliance.
- **Description**—The personnel strategy embodies the traditional approach to HR and is the most common strategy. HR serves as an employee advocate. A strong emphasis is placed on managing centralized transactions including payroll and benefits. HR is "reactive" with little outreach, change management, or the use of generalists.
- **Likely strategic impact**—This strategy produces a high level of employee interaction and excellence in transactions, but has a minimal impact on profitability and employee productivity.
- **Appropriate for what type of business?**—Small businesses or medium to large firms attempting to minimize costs may find this strategy appropriate. It is often used when a single person runs HR and in a union environment where most "rules" are defined in the union contract.

- **Structure and organization**—HR is centralized and organized by functional units.
- **Functions with large budget and time allocations**—Hourly hiring, payroll, legal compliance and benefits.
- **Functions with low budget and time allocations**—organizational (OD), training, technology, global, call center, workforce planning, generalists in strategic efforts.
- **Degree of management involvement**—All HR work is done by HR, but the lack of outreach by HR allows the managers a great deal of unfettered discretion.
- **Use of technology**—Low; the available technology is focused on centralized payroll and benefits administration.

Table 3-B. Personnel strategy

Advantages/Benefits	Disadvantages/Risks
Transactional excellence	Slow identification and reaction to problems
Low HR operational costs	Difficult to globalize
Simple and easy-to-manage HR structure	Functional silos are common, resulting in a lack of cooperation
Little HR technical knowledge required	Minimal use of metrics makes it difficult to prove economic value during budget reductions
High customer contact	No emphasis on rewarding great people management
	Managers are provided with a great deal of flexibility but little oversight or guidance from HR

2. Generalist strategy

- **Priority and focus**—A generalist strategy involves excellent hands-on "localized" service delivered primarily by generalists.
- **Description**—This decentralized approach attempts to provide different services that fit the unique needs of the business unit or local facility. It relies primarily on the generalist to deliver most HR services. Centralized HR serves primarily as support staff for the generalists.
- **Likely strategic impact**—Medium, because of the slow transfer of solutions between different business units and the lack of co-ordination between independent generalists.

- **Appropriate for what type of business?**—Medium and large firms and firms that are geographically dispersed are good candidates for a generalist strategy.
- **Structure and organization**—HR is decentralized; generalists do most of the HR work. Generalists are physically located in each major business unit or facility. The local HR generalist often reports directly to the general manager of his or her unit.
- **Functions with large budget and time allocations**—Generalists and "business unit" HR staff.
- **Functions with low budget and time allocations**—All centralized HR functions.
- **Degree of management involvement**—High; the service providers are well known and trusted by local management.
- **Use of technology**—Minimal; most transactions are handled at the local level.

Table 3-C. *Generalist strategy*

Advantages/Benefits	Disadvantages/Risks
High customer contact	Generalists can become too loyal to their business unit and less so to centralized HR
Solutions that fit the unique needs of the business unit	Generalists can do too much "hand-holding"
Rapid reaction to local problems	Generalists may have insufficient technical knowledge to solve complex one-of-a-kind problems
High "personal" credibility with local senior managers	Information transfer between generalists in different business units is often limited, and most information is never captured in central HR
Strong relationship-building	Reliance on paper and the lack of technology means answers are slow to get
	Generalist strategy is relatively expensive compared to most other strategies
	Minimal use of metrics makes it difficult to prove economic value during budget reductions
	No emphasis on rewarding great people management

3. Business partner strategy

- **Priority and focus**—Becoming more strategic through building strategic relationships is the approach taken by the business partner strategy.
- **Description**—The model made famous by Dave Ulrich, the business strategy or four-quadrant model divides the basic role of HR into four areas (service delivery, employee commitment, change management and strategic actions). The business partner strategy is the next step in HR evolution after the traditional "personnel" or generalist strategy. The strategy is interpreted by many to emphasize strategic initiatives and to de-emphasize transactions. When it is effective, HR becomes more important and earns a seat at the executive table.
- **Likely strategic impact**—Moderate; strong strategic relationships might not be enough to directly impact employee productivity or profit.
- **Appropriate for what type of business?**—Medium and large businesses that need to move away from the "personnel" strategy and want to become more strategic are good candidates for the business partner approach.
- **Structure and organization**—The strategic elements of HR are centralized, and while there are a moderate number of generalists, their responsibilities are generally non-strategic. This strategy frequently has a top-heavy senior HR management staff that relies heavily on external consultants.
- **Functions with large budget and time allocations**—Strategic consultants, high-level corporate HR staff, outsourcing, legal compliance, vendor management.
- **Functions with minimal budget and time allocations**—Payroll, transactions, workforce planning, metrics.
- **Degree of management involvement**—Medium.
- **Use of technology**—Medium; many have enterprise suites, but relationship-building requires little technology.

Table 3-D. *Business partner strategy*

Advantages/Benefits	Disadvantages/Risks
Strong interpersonal relationships and high visibility with executive management	De-emphasis on transactions minimizes customer interactions
Fast response time to major corporate problems	Many HR professionals evolving from the personnel strategy may not be capable of becoming strategic when placed in strategic roles
Smaller sized HR with lower headcount	Emphasis on outsourcing may mean reduced HR headcount and fewer people to develop for future HR needs
The emphasis on outsourcing means that HR has a narrower but more strategic focus	Emphasis on corporate strategic issues can make the cadre of generalists feel "isolated" from corporate
	Highly centralized corporate unit can become averse to taking risks and may evolve into a "meeting culture"
	Minimal use of metrics makes it difficult to prove economic value during budget reductions
	No emphasis on rewarding great people management

4. Call center strategy

- **Priority and focus**—The idea behind the call center strategy is to "free up" generalists' time (from answering basic HR questions) so that they can be more strategic. HR maintains ownership of transactions but minimizes their costs with a telephone call center.
- **Description**—The call center strategy generally evolves from either the personnel or the business partner strategy. Its primary focus is shifting the answering of basic HR questions to a centralized HR unit. The call center staff is cheaper and is continually available during working hours.
- **Likely strategic impact**—Minimal, unless the generalists actually spend the extra freed-up time being more strategic.
- **Appropriate for what type of business?**—Large corporations are more apt to benefit from a call center approach.
- **Structure and organization**—Call centers generally report directly to HR operations. They often operate relatively independently of both generalists and other HR functional departments. Although

call centers shift some degree of HR work away from generalist and functional HR units, the call center has little direct impact on how the rest of HR is organized.

- **Functions with large budget and time allocations**—Call center staff, call center consultants and generalists.
- **Functions with low budget and time allocations**—Intranet, technology, benefits administration and other HR transactions units, outsourcing.
- **Degree of management involvement**—Minimal, since most HR "answers" are controlled by centralized HR.
- **Use of technology**—Minimal, emphasis on telephone and knowledge-based systems.

Table 3-E. *Call center strategy*

Advantages/Benefits	Disadvantages/Risks
The call center gives more accurate, cheaper and more consistent answers	More difficult and complicated HR problems cannot be solved by call center personnel
Managers and employees do less "answer shopping" and spend less time waiting	Set up time and equipment costs can be significant
Call center staff are relatively low-cost per hour	There can be conflicts between generalists and call center staff
Some call centers also handle HR transactions	Many managers and employees may resist shifting from "their" generalist to a call center
Call centers serve as a central depository for HR answers	A great deal of marketing and education is required to encourage initial use of the call center
Call centers can help in breaking down HR silos because they gather information from so many different sources	

5. Outsourcing strategy

- **Priority and focus**—As is apparent from its name, the outsourcing strategy requires outsourcing HR transactions and, where appropriate, a majority of a firm's existing HR functions, so that the remaining HR team can focus on increasing its strategic impact.
- **Description**—In an effort to free-up senior HR management and generalist time, and to increase HR's strategic impact, HR managers identify the different HR functions that provide the organi-

zation with no competitive advantage. These functions are then outsourced to vendors with superior capabilities. The net result is that HR managers now have increased bandwidth because they have fewer "average" things to worry about. With fewer functions and responsibilities to oversee, HR managers can focus on the relatively narrow areas within HR that have a realistic chance of having a strategic impact.

- **Likely strategic impact**—Moderate to high, if the narrower HR focus actually results in solving the remaining complex people problems.
- **Appropriate for what type of business?**—All businesses can profit from an outsourcing strategy but especially small or large businesses. Outsourcing is especially appropriate in the US where a great deal of outsourcing support is available.
- **Structure and organization**—Outsourcing can reduce or eliminate entire HR functions. The net result is generally a streamlined HR organization. The area of vendor management may become crucial, however, depending on the degree of outsourcing that you undertake.
- **Functions with large budget and time allocations**—The remaining strategic HR functions, outsourcing, vendor management and outsourcing consultants.
- **Functions with low budget and time allocations**—Any HR functions that are partially or totally outsourced (generally benefits, pensions, payroll and sometimes recruiting, compensation and training).
- **Degree of management involvement**—Minimal, because much of the HR work is now done outside the company.
- **Use of technology**—Low within HR; most of the functions that require technology are outsourced, although many vendors utilize web sites to provide their services to managers and employees.

Table 3-F. Outsourcing strategy

Advantages/Benefits	Disadvantages/Risks
A narrower HR focus means more of a strategic impact	HR may select the wrong functions to outsource and, as a result, the firm loses its competitive advantage
Outsourcing allows external experts that specialize in efficient transactions to handle things that internal HR can't do as well	HR must be skilled at vendor management
Takes advantage of "economies of scale" that vendors might have in handling transactions	Outsourcing firms often cannot handle the most complex HR systems (with their customized workarounds), forcing HR to either adopt the "vanilla" approach or drop the outsourcing idea
Reduces the need for HR to invest its limited capital resources in call centers, HR software, and other HR technologies by taking advantage of the investments that already have been made by outsource firms	You can't outsource "broken" systems until they are fixed
	Outsource vendors may be unstable
	Because vendors must make a profit, the overall costs might be higher
	Outsourcing services can seldom be tailored to the unique needs of a company or business unit
	Outsourcing transactions reduces HR's contact with its internal customers
	Without transactions that were once the training ground of future HR managers, HR may weaken its internal talent pipeline

6. Centers of excellence strategy

- **Priority and focus**—Providing internal "consulting quality" help to solve advanced HR problems is the approach taken by the centers of excellence strategy.
- **Description**—Because generalists have the opportunity to solve only "local" problems, they must often bring in outside consultants to help them solve advanced or unique HR problems. Centers of

excellence (sometimes known as centers of expertise) bring expensive outside consulting expertise *inside* in order to solve the most difficult 20 percent of current HR problems directly. By utilizing internal consultants, the knowledge gained after the problem is solved remains within the corporation, which increases the likelihood that solutions are shared. Inside consultants are presumed to be more successful because they understand the culture and how to get things done within the organization.

Some organizations couple the centers of excellence strategy with the call center strategy. By doing so, organizations can expect to obtain better and cheaper answers at the low end, and higher-quality solutions for the more difficult higher-end HR problems.

- **Likely strategic impact**—High, if the centers of excellence maintain the same quality standards as external consulting firms.
- **Appropriate for what type of business?**—Large and global corporations that use a large number of external HR consultants can make successful use of the centers of excellence strategy.
- **Structure and organization**—Centers of excellence generally operate independently of other HR functional units. They often report to a senior HR manager or the VP of HR. In some cases, centers of excellence strategies that also have strong call center components reduce or consolidate other HR functions because most of their high- and low-level work is now handled by others.
- **Functions with large budget and time allocations**—Centers of excellence.
- **Functions with low budget and time allocations**—External consultants, the most experienced staff within existing functional HR departments, outsourcing.
- **Degree of management involvement**—High, because HR is more capable of handling its most difficult "people problems."
- **Use of technology**—Minimal.

Table 3-G. *Centers of excellence strategy*

Advantages/Benefits	Disadvantages/Risks
Major HR problems are identified and solved faster	External consultants may be superior because they may have already experienced similar problems at other firms
External consulting costs are reduced	"Excess HR staff" may be transferred to the centers of excellence, which may degrade the quality of the help they can provide
HR's internal image and exposure are improved because HR is attacking major HR and management problems directly	Budget pressure may, over time, reduce the centers of excellence staffing levels and also staff quality to the point where they are unable to be responsive
	Set-up costs and time can be significant
	Most of the established centers of excellence have not succeeded in practice
	Managers may resist using internal consultants because of their existing relationships with external consulting firms
	If a center of excellence fails, it will send a clear message that HR can't "handle" the most difficult problems. This will negatively impact HR's image and its ability to be strategic in other areas

7. Self-service technology for transactions strategy

- **Priority and focus**—The manager and employee self-service, technology-enabled strategy shifts most HR answers and transactions to the organization's Intranet to "free up" generalist time and to make managers and employees more self-sufficient.
- **Description**—This strategy often is an advanced variation of the call-center strategy, where HR answers and transactions are shifted to the firm's Intranet. Managers and employees are provided access to easy-to-use HR web sites so that they can do their own transactions and find their own simple-to-moderately complex HR answers. Using the web allows answers to be available globally and 24/7.

  The self-service strategy differs from other technology-based strategies (the fact-based and the e-HR strategy) in that it uses technology solely for answering simple questions and completing basic transactions.
- **Likely strategic impact**—Minimal; providing simple answers and transactions (no matter how easy or cheap) is hardly ever strategic.
- **Appropriate for what type of business?**—Global businesses, firms with strong IT staffs and large businesses.
- **Structure and organization**—Although self-service shifts some degree of HR work to managers and employees, it has little direct impact on how the rest of HR is organized.
- **Functions with large budget and time allocations**—Web technology and Web consultants.
- **Functions with low budget and time allocations**—All HR transactional units, benefits administration and call centers.
- **Degree of management involvement**—High, because managers and employees "own" their transactions and accept the responsibility for finding most basic HR answers.
- **Use of technology**—High, but only in the area of HR transactions and simple answers.

Table 3-H. *Self-service technology for transactions strategy*

Advantages/Benefits	Disadvantages/ Risks
Employees and managers may have their own "personal portal," which may also help increase their productivity because of the tailored information it can provide	Shifting "HR work" to managers and employees may decrease their productivity on their regular job. Their time may also be more expensive than HR staff time
Using the web sends a message that HR understands the importance of technology	Line managers may argue that doing transactions "outside of HR" isn't the best use of managers' and employees' time
Answers and transactions can be done anywhere and at anytime	More difficult and complicated HR problems cannot be solved on the Intranet
Web technology can make transactions "foolproof" resulting in fewer errors than the "people dependent" call-center strategy	HR loses a great deal of interaction with its customers
	The set-up costs and time are significant
	HR staff may not have the capability to do the Web site; it may be "less than cooperative" so delays may occur
	Not all managers and employees have easy access to the company's Intranet
	Not all managers and employees are comfortable using computers and the Intranet; a significant amount of training may be required
	Closing down a recently opened call center (and shifting the work to self service) can be expensive and politically difficult
	Generalists may resist the shifting of a portion of their former workload to the web, and they may not use their extra time to produce strategic results
	Many managers and employees may resist shifting from "their" generalist to a web site
	Requires close cooperation between IT and HRIT

8. "Fact-based" decision-making strategy

- **Priority and focus**—Making HR more "scientific" through the use of measures, analytics and metrics is the way the fact-based strategy operates. The goal is to continually improve everything done in HR through the more "intelligent" use of data.
- **Description**—The goal is continuous improvement in every people-management process. The fact-based model follows the supply chain and Six Sigma models in that it shifts the emphasis from "emotional" or "personal experience-based" decision-making to "fact-based" decision-making. Because metrics permeate everything HR does, most HR decisions can be made more accurate by basing them on facts and data.

  In addition, by providing data directly to line managers, the process allows more people decisions to be made "closer to the customer" by the line manager. Some advanced HR departments add forecasting in order to anticipate problems as well as R&D teams to analyze and develop new people management tools. The fact-based strategy uses technology for decision-making but technology does not permeate every area of HR, like it does in the e-HR strategy.
- **Likely strategic impact**—High, because much of the "guesswork" is removed from HR decision-making and decisions are made closer to the customer.
- **Appropriate for what type of business?**—Technology-driven companies, medium and large size firms with enterprise-wide software applications.
- **Structure and organization**—The fact-based decision-making strategy requires no special organizational structure, but metrics and analytics managers must report directly to the senior decision-maker in every HR functional unit.
- **Functions with large budget and time allocations**—Analytics, metrics, reporting and HRIT.
- **Functions with low budget and time allocations**—Functions that fail to improve or that have a low ROI.
- **Degree of management involvement**—High; managers are provided with the data they need to make "intelligent" decisions.
- **Use of technology**—The pervasive use of technology throughout the organization allows HR to gather data cheaply and easily and to distribute reports to managers easily. Analytics software calculates key ratios and identifies important trends. There is also an emphasis on business intelligence-type solutions.

Table 3-1. *"Fact-based" decision-making strategy*

Advantages/Benefits	Disadvantages/Risks
Increases HR business impact by educating managers with data about "what works and what doesn't"	Requires close cooperation with IT and HRIT
Shows that HR is businesslike because it uses the same types of metrics and analytics that the rest of the organization already utilizes	Requires the organization to have existing enterprise resource planning (ERP) software and other data collection and data-mining tools
Allows managers to be more involved and more successful in people decision-making	HR must become experts in metrics and analytics
Allows corporate HR to closely monitor and compare people-management "success rates" between regions and business units and therefore increase the speed of learning and the adoption of solutions that work throughout the business	Providing data and reports about what works doesn't always incite managers to change and improve

9. e-HR (electronic HR) strategy

- **Priority and focus**—The e-HR strategy uses technology to make everything in HR paperless as well as faster, cheaper, better, and globally capable. It provides managers with new computer-based tools in the areas of employee relations, workforce planning, compensation, and recruiting. It also shifts most HR decisions away from HR people and gives them to managers.

- **Description**—Technology and its related software are the mainstay of every HR function and system in the e-HR approach. By eliminating paper within HR, it instantly becomes cheaper, faster and more globally capable. e-HR also takes advantage of new capabilities in e-learning, workforce planning, analytics, online candidate assessment, applicant tracking systems, and Web-based management reports.

  The e-HR strategy follows the supply chain and Six Sigma models to improve decision-making and productivity by using computer-generated data to improve day-to-day decision-making. The e-HR strategy goes far beyond the "self-service" and "fact-based" HR strategies.

  In addition to using technology to handle all transactions and to answer benefits questions, e-HR shifts almost all day-to-day HR decision-making to line managers. Decisions like compensation, candidate assessment, retention and employee relations are no longer made by HR. Managers take "ownership" of their HR problems, and they are able to make better people-related decisions because of the laptop tools and information provided by HR.

■ **Likely strategic impact**—High, because it allows HR to do things that are not possible without technology. Informed (and more accurate) people decisions are made closer to the customer.

■ **Appropriate for what type of business?**—Large and global corporations.

■ **Structure and organization**—HRIT manages the e-HR effort. Eventually every process and HR function must be computerized.

■ **Functions with large budget and time allocations**—HRIT.

■ **Functions with low budget and time allocations**—Call centers.

■ **Degree of management involvement**—High, because most people-management decisions are shifted to managers.

■ **Use of technology**—High; it permeates every program and initiative.

Table 3-J. e-HR (electronic HR) strategy

Advantages/Benefits	Disadvantages/Risks
Globalization is not realistically possible without technology in HR	e-HR set-up time and costs can be significant
Paperless systems are cheaper and faster and line managers can access all HR information, which allows them to make better HR decisions "closer to the customer"	IT can drag its feet or refuse to cooperate
Linked databases can "learn," therefore reducing their future failure rate	Software upgrades can be expensive
Technology can identify potential issues and alert managers of upcoming problems	Technology can quickly become out of date

10. Performance culture strategy

- **Priority and focus**—In this strategy, HR assumes the responsibility for shifting the entire corporate culture so that every aspect of it reinforces performance and results. The net result is that excellent people practices become a sustainable competitive advantage.
- **Description**—HR shifts the responsibility for "owning" people programs and employee productivity to employees and managers. HR ensures that every people-related system focuses on measuring, recognizing and rewarding productivity and results. It makes sure that "performance" rather than "trying" or "effort" permeates the entire culture and everyone's way of thinking.

  The performance culture strategy is the broadest strategy; it has the most impact of all HR strategies because it takes the "captain of the ship" approach to employee performance. As a "captain of the ship," it assumes responsibility, though it doesn't have complete authority or control, over maintaining and increasing the productivity of the company's workforce.
- **Likely strategic impact**—High, if HR can successfully influence the entire organization.
- **Appropriate for what type of business?**—Firms that operate in a highly competitive environment and that wish to be number one in their industry in employee productivity.
- **Structure and organization**—The structure of HR must be changed to become more like a consulting organization. Traditional "do-er" functions like compensation, recruiting and employee relations must be completely reorganized to provide more advice and metrics rather than direct service.
- **Functions with large budget and time allocations**—HR consulting, strategic planning, forecasting, metrics, HRIT and workforce planning.
- **Functions with low budget and time allocations**—All traditional transaction and "do-er" HR functions.
- **Degree of management involvement**—High, because the ownership of people problems is shifted.
- **Use of technology**—High; managers must be provided with easy-to-use, always available "laptop tools" and daily performance information in order to allow them to make better people decisions and continually to improve workforce productivity.

Table 3-K. *Performance culture strategy*

Advantages/Benefits	Disadvantages/Risks
In assuming the role of strategic leader in increasing employee productivity, the performance culture strategy sends the message that HR will do what strategic leaders do—take responsibility for actions across all business units. HR uses its expert knowledge to influence others over which it has no formal control	Many HR professionals may not be able make the transition from HR "do-er" to HR leader
Instead of focusing on HR problems, the performance culture strategy focuses on business problems (and opportunities). It uses its knowledge of people management to find and then implement people management tools that will make a major contribution towards solving these business problems	Managers and employees may not be willing to accept the responsibility for "owning" people issues
By shifting the responsibility and ownership for people problems and worker productivity, it actually increases its strategic impact, because "ownership" forces managers and employees to take people issues more seriously	HR may not have the skills or knowledge required in order to influence the entire organization
HR increases its visibility throughout the organization because it becomes a consultant and productivity improvement expert, rather than just a transaction specialist and information provider	The old corporate culture may resist changing to a performance culture
HR shifts from a function that "does HR" to a function that advises and influences others	Low performers and people who resist change are likely to fight the transition
Instead of focusing on transactions and providing information, HR focuses on identifying and solving business problems through the use of people management tools	Within HR, there will be tremendous pressure to maintain the status quo
	Many traditional HR processes, approaches, programs and tools will need major revision if they are to contribute to a performance culture strategy

Selecting the appropriate strategy

Each of the ten distinct HR strategies that are outlined above has made a significant impact in some organization *because it fits the need at the time*. It is important to emphasize that there are no good and bad strategies, just ones that are appropriate for the organization and the goals that it sets. Before selecting a strategy or transitioning into a new one, it is important to study your organization's business goals and the competitiveness of the industry you are in. Some senior managers will take pieces of each of the strategies and combine them into a "customized strategy" that's ideal for their organization.

It's easy to assume that the best strategy is the one with the most strategic impact. In fact, developing a strategic HR function or a performance culture within a "commodity business," for example, may actually be a mistake. Whatever path you take, it is important to remember that being strategic in HR means having a direct impact on business problems and results. So, in that light, select the strategy that is most likely to have a significant impact on workforce productivity and profits.

COMMON VARIATIONS IN HR STRATEGIES AND APPROACHES

In addition to the basic HR strategies outlined above, there are some significant additions or variations that are often practiced by major firms. These approaches are generally added on top of the primary strategy. Some of those key variations are highlighted below.

- **Employer of choice**—This approach can be added to any of the advanced strategies. The employer of choice strategy emphasizes building the company's external image as an "excellent place to work" by using branding and marketing tools. Those that follow an EOC strategy often try to get on magazine "best place to work" lists and, as a result, they consciously develop people programs with a certain "wow factor" that are designed to make the company stand out. Many that select this strategy also try to make their workplace "fun." The employer of choice approach is generally part of fifth level of HR contribution, and it is frequently utilized in performance cultures.

- **The mature adult approach**—A variation often added by high-tech firms and performance cultures starts with the premise that HR has too many rules and policies that would be unnecessary if everyone in the organization acted like mature adults normally would act. It is probably true that many of HR's rules and regulations are in fact put in place because of the behavior or misbehavior of five percent of the workforce. Immature behavior typically includes theft, abuse of flexible scheduling, and excessive or inappropriate Web usage.

The mature adult approach is managing to the highest common denominator, rather than the lowest. It strives to eliminate many rules and regulations by stating up front to employees that they are at all times expected to act as mature adults would. The consequence of failing to act at the standard is termination. The benefit to the 95 percent of well-behaved employees is that they now have more freedom and significantly fewer rules and controls.

- **Seamless operations and an easy place to do business**—This approach is a customer-focused one that views HR as being primarily a customer service operation that must operate "seamlessly." This means that managers and employees can either call *one* number or talk to just *one* person in order to get most of their issues resolved. A seamless operation requires intense cooperation between the different HR functions so the customer is not "handed off" to many different HR individuals during the process of getting a complete answer to a single event.

- **Brain horsepower**—A strategy variation originally championed by Microsoft, its basic premise is that while most firms focus on hiring and retaining people with certain technical knowledge and experience, it is sometimes better instead to focus on hiring and retaining "brilliant people." The premise here is that the company with the most "brainpower" will win out in a constantly changing business world that requires continuous innovation.

- **Hire attitude to train skills**—A strategy variation made famous by Southwest Airlines, "hire attitude" works on the premise that you cannot have a cohesive team unless every employee shares common attitudes and personalities. The strategy also assumes that it's significantly easier to train skills than it is to change attitudes or personalities.

- **Weed out the bottom 10 percent**—A HR strategy variation championed by GE that has as its basic premise that it's important continually to "weed out" the bottom 5 to 10 percent of your workforce each year in order to continually improve and develop. The threat of being weeded out also serves as a lever to get everyone's attention on productivity. This practice is a key element to a performance culture.

- **Treat employees like volunteers**—The strategy variation focuses on motivation and retention. The basic premise is that if you assume that your employees are *not* being paid, you would have to put an increased emphasis on non-monetary rewards and recognition in order to motivate and retain them. Such a focus forces managers to be less autocratic and to spend more time on the relatively cheap but effective motivational tools of praise and recognition.
- **Follow the leader**—This conservative approach emphasizes adopting new people-management practices only after the top firms in your industry already have adopted them. The strategy allows you to use benchmarking to copy programs that have proven themselves at other firms. It also allows you to avoid the high costs and risks associated with innovation.
- **Prioritization**—While most HR departments strive to treat all employees and managers the same, this approach instead suggests that you focus your resources specifically on the areas with the most impact. This means prioritizing business units, jobs and managers, and treating those with a high priority significantly better than those jobs and business units with a low priority. This practice is common in any performance culture.

Once senior HR management selects the department's HR strategy, the next step is to ensure that that strategy is both understood and implemented. Unfortunately, is not uncommon for a strategy to provide one direction, while past practices or budget allocations send a contradictory message. Not all individuals or departments automatically will accept a new strategy, so it is important to take specific steps to ensure that the strategy is completely implemented throughout HR.

STEPS TO ENSURE THAT YOUR STRATEGY IS IMPLEMENTED

Developing an HR strategy is only the first step in becoming strategic. Normally a strategy is translated into action by developing an HR strategic plan. It's important to realize up front that having a strategy—even a strategic plan—by itself does not automatically change behavior. Many traditional HR plans are long, written reports with a narrow distribution. Many that receive the strategic plan never read it; even more put it "on the shelf" and don't refer to it again until it's time to revise the strategic plan.

If you want your strategy to have a realistic chance of being implemented, you need to realize that:

- Reports by themselves don't change behavior.
- Even though individuals want to be strategic, there are powerful "tactical" forces that drive them to focus on day-to-day activities.
- Many that read the strategy won't see its direct relevance to what they do.

Once you come to the realization that "having a strategy" or even a strategic plan isn't enough to guarantee success, specific steps are necessary to get that strategy adopted by everyone. One of the first steps for assuring department-wide adoption is developing systems that ensure a coordinated effort, where every HR system, measure and reward "reinforces" the plan, and together they drive people to act within the plans limits.

Reinforcing your strategy and your strategic plan

If you want to ensure that HR professionals, employees and managers act in line with your strategy, you need to reinforce your HR strategy. Several ways you can do that include:

- **Staff allocation**—Make sure that HR headcount and time allocations "mirror" the priorities in the strategic plan.
- **Budget allocation**—Allocate the HR budget so that the most dollars are allocated to the program that contributes directly to the highest priority goals. In addition, make sure that individuals on the team share members with the strategic planning team.
- **Metrics and performance management**—Develop metrics systems that directly measure every individual's and department's performance on each of the major strategic goals.
- **Rewards and recognition**—Ensure that recognition and financial rewards both for employees and managers are tied to their contribution to strategic goals.
- **Communications**—Make sure that a significant part of all HR communications highlights the strategic goals, and remind HR employees and managers about your priorities and focus.
- **Hiring, promotion and retention**—Develop criteria to ensure that all new hires in HR have skills and experiences that are in line with strategic goals. Target individuals for retention and promotion

based on their contribution to your strategic goals.

- **A shared goal and reward**—Many HR departments suffer from "functional silos" where different units of HR act independently of each other. Strategic plans seldom succeed when functional units don't work together. One way to solve a problem is to ensure that a portion of each department's funding and bonus is tied to meeting the HR department's overall HR strategic goals. This shared bonus has the impact of forcing disparate units, teams and individuals to work together because their success is now tied to the success of other units

Rather than stand idly by, it's essential for HR leaders to take proactive steps to increase the impact of the HR strategy. That means ensuring that all HR systems and processes are designed to reinforce the strategy so that HR employees, managers, and HR professionals are reminded, every day, of what does and does not have a strategic impact.

STRATEGIC INITIATIVES CAN BE HIGH-RISK UNDERTAKINGS

Being strategic is a high-risk undertaking. The same level of risk applies to implementing an HR strategy. "Being strategic" means having a significant impact on meeting corporate goals and objectives, but, of course, a program with a high likelihood of significant strategic impact often also carries a high risk of failure. Before you jump headfirst into implementing any HR strategy—or the strategic initiatives that accompany that strategy—it's important to calculate the risks.

In my experience, over half of the HR strategic initiatives that I have examined failed to meet their goals. This high failure rate should serve as a warning for those who declare they want to be strategic. Although every initiative is different, the following list highlights some common HR initiatives that are likely to have a high strategic impact as well as a high risk of failure.

Table 3-L.

Examples of high strategic impact, high-risk HR initiatives	Examples of high strategic impact, low-risk HR initiatives
Enterprise resource planning (ERP) software implementation	Employee retention programs
Leadership and executive development programs	Rewarding managers for excellent "people management"
Management alerts and forecasting future people issues	Proactive internal redeployment of employees
Workforce and succession planning	Employee referral programs
Firing or releasing "bad managers"	Recognition programs
Globalizing HR	
Pay for performance	
"What works" sharing	
Forced ranking initiatives	
HR metrics	

In contrast to high strategic impact, high risk initiatives, high strategic impact, low-risk strategic initiatives, these strategic initiatives generally have a high return rate but a correspondingly low failure rate. As a result, they are often good "first choices" to include in initial strategic plan efforts.

The road to becoming strategic is full of potholes, so be sure to begin the process by understanding that it is often best to select "low-hanging fruit" first. And in this case, that means starting with strategic initiatives that have high impact but relatively low failure rates. Consultants and benchmarking can both help you better identify which programs are likely to bring a high success rate, given your resources and organizational constraints.

BENCHMARK FIRMS THAT PRACTICE STRATEGIC HR

Who are the benchmark firms in strategic HR? That is a question I am frequently asked. In response, I always caution against benchmarking because it can lead to copying programs from others. Although it seems a good idea on the surface, it is generally unwise to copy programs wholesale because what makes a program successful at a Cisco or an Intel may not exist at any other firm in the world. Trying to copy programs consistently leads to frustration and failure.

In addition, I've found that the very best firms, in particular Microsoft, Intel and GE, are *ferocious* defenders of their best practices. In fact, a colleague at Cisco once told me that he would share their best practice with me in one small area … but then he would have to "kill me." I *think* he was joking, but when you consider the millions of dollars and thousands of hours Cisco put into the program, it does not make sense that the company would to share it for "free" with anyone who asked casually about it.

These top firms might give you some basic information, but it is unlikely that they will share the really important information as to why a program works or what the results of the program are. Top firms defend their best practices because they *are* worth hundreds of millions of dollars. I have even known senior HR managers purposely to deceive individuals that are attempting to benchmark them.

There is no formal system for identifying strategic HR departments. But because building an external "employment brand" is one of the key identifiers of strategic HR functions, most of the best firms regularly appear on *Fortune* and *Working Mothers* magazines' ranking of best places to work. It is unusual, in fact, for any firm to have a great strategic HR department and not to appear on one of those two lists.

Identifying the firms that top companies benchmark against is another way of identifying strategic HR functions. Through my work with *Fortune* 500 firms, I have found that there is a small set of firms that consistently appear on most top VPs of HR benchmark list. I do not always agree with their selections, but you can certainly learn a lot from these firms. The following list of top firms is derived from the list of firms that senior VPs of HR want most to learn about.

Table 3-M.

1. GE	9. Wal-Mart
2. Intel	10. IBM
3. Southwest Airlines	11. Wachovia Bank
4. Cisco	12. Corning
5. Pepsi	13. SAS
6. Federal Express	14. HP
7. Microsoft	15. Nucor
8. Dell	

CHAPTER FOUR

OVERVIEW OF TEN ESSENTIAL ELEMENTS OF A STRATEGIC HR DEPARTMENT

OBJECTIVES

Once you have selected an HR strategy for your department, the next step is to "operationalize" that definition and plan out what actions must be taken in order to move your department from a tactical one to strategic one. The first step is to identify the factors or elements that must be present in an HR department for it to have a strategic business impact.

KEY POINTS

◊ As an external adviser who is often asked to assess or audit an HR department, I have found that there are common elements, features or characteristics that strategic HR programs all share.

◊ This chapter will give a brief overview of these 10 common characteristics that distinguish strategic HR functions.

◊ Following this chapter, each of the individual elements will be highlighted in detail in its own separate chapter—Chapters 5–14.

TEN ESSENTIAL ELEMENTS OF A STRATEGIC HR DEPARTMENT

When you study successful business functions, you find that the best and the most strategic all share some common characteristics. These are the same characteristics that can serve as a guide in any effort to transform an average HR department into a strategic one. These common essential elements for a strategic HR department are:

1. **HR increases employee productivity.** The primary HR goal is to increase workforce productivity because that is the strategic corporate objective in which HR holds the lead in expertise. HR provides programs and services that result in a measurable increase in employee productivity, revenue and profit. It also builds a strong business case outlining the dollar impact of increased worker productivity.

2. **HR has an external focus on impacting business objectives.** Corporations have other strategic goals and objectives besides increasing productivity. If HR is also to impact the remaining corporate objectives like profit, quality and customer service, it must have an "external focus" on the business problems associated with those objectives. Rather than focusing on "internal" HR objectives, instead the focus is on providing solutions to the business problems faced by the business units. HR must realize that its primary job, after increasing workforce productivity, is to provide solutions that directly impact the remaining corporate goals and objectives.

   In order to ensure that HR impacts corporate goals and objectives, it must continually redistribute its HR budget and time allocations so that the highest percentage of resources is committed to programs that impact the organization's high priority strategic goals.

   HR must also prioritize its customers and its efforts so that they "mirror" corporate priorities. HR is continually adding, cutting back or eliminating HR programs based on their return on investment (ROI) and business impact.

   HR must also have a focus outside the corporation. It must continually track shifts in the external environment, learn quickly and then shift its strategy to adapt to the changing business world.

3. **HR uses performance culture tools to improve a firm's performance.** HR must seize every opportunity it can to improve employee productivity. If an HR department is to qualify as strategic, it does not have to implement a company-wide performance culture; however, it must implement at least some of the tools that are part of a performance culture. This is because these performance culture tools have so great an impact even if they are implemented piecemeal.

   Strategic HR departments develop a performance culture mindset within HR. They also educate managers about the approach and utilize some of the performance culture tools like accountability, differentiation in rewards, penalties for hoarding and prioritizing customers and services.

4. **HR provides a competitive advantage.** HR has an external focus on the competition. HR continually compares what "we do" in HR to what "they do" in HR at both the organization's product and talent competitors. HR provides people programs that exploit competitors' vulnerabilities and whose output or results are superior to the company's direct competitors.

5. **HR makes fact-based decisions using metrics.** HR continually measures the business impact of HR programs. It also uses metrics to proactively identify potential problems and opportunities, and to continually improve. Most people management decisions are made based on facts and data, rather than on opinions.

6. **HR is proactive and future-focused.** HR must forecast and anticipate changes in the business environment so that HR programs can adapt in time. Strategic functions must anticipate and prepare for an entire range of possible occurrences. They must proactively seek out business problems and opportunities, and aggressively provide solutions. HR makes, rather than facilitates, change within the corporation.

7. **HR makes a coordinated effort.** HR must ensure that its programs and staff coordinate their efforts within HR to ensure results, speed, consistency and the highest user satisfaction. In a strategic HR department, there are no functional silos; HR acts as an organization without boundaries.

8. **HR has a global approach.** HR ensures that its programs have a business impact both locally and around the world.

9. **HR builds a brand.** Strategic HR is not satisfied with just running good programs. In addition, HR must build a "great place to work" brand both internally and externally. Building a strong image or brand gives HR stable funding, but it also raises HR's business contribution by increasing retention and providing a steady flow of recruits.

10. **Technology permeates everything.** Technology is the cornerstone of everything a strategic HR department does because without it, the extensive use of metrics, paperless HR, fact-based decision-making, employee and manager self-service, and globalization would not be possible.

Each of these essential elements of a strategic HR department will be covered in detail in the following chapters of this book.

CHAPTER FIVE

HR INCREASES WORKFORCE PRODUCTIVITY

OBJECTIVES

The first and the most crucial element of becoming strategic is to have HR directly impact employee productivity. Although this is just one the many corporate goals and objectives that strategic HR must impact, it is the most important to HR because it is the sole corporate objective where HR is the primary expert.

KEY POINTS

This next part of the book will highlight the important role that increasing workforce productivity (and the resulting profits) plays in being recognized as strategic. It covers:

◊   The importance of increasing productivity;
◊   How to assess and demonstrate whether you are increasing productivity; and
◊   HR programs that are most likely to have a strategic impact on workforce productivity.

Top HR departments, without exception, produce a measurable difference in workforce productivity from their company's competitors. Compared to this element, each of the other nine strategic essential elements pales in comparison, because *here* HR has the primary expertise to increase workforce productivity. HR's attempt to impact other corporate goals is important, but excelling at this is the primary expectation that senior executives have of HR.

Productivity impacts are important because the very definition of "strategic" includes impacting overall business goals and objectives, which invariably include increasing efficiency and productivity. In the HR context, increasing efficiency means increasing employee productivity, where employee productivity is defined as increasing the dollar value of the output of employees/labor while maintaining or reducing the cost of that labor.

If you take a step back and look at all of the things that HR does from recruiting to training to employee relations, it's clear that they are all done to increase the productivity of individuals and the overall workforce. Unfortunately, not everyone in HR understands that fact. Many within HR set HR goals like hiring 45 engineers, retaining a certain percentage of the workforce, or offering a certain number of training classes.

These all might be necessary HR steps. Still, if you're going to become a strategic leader, you need to realize that they are just steps, not the ultimate goal. The end goal of the HR department and every professional in it is to increase the productivity of the workforce.

> *We have an incredible amount of people who work close to the customer—our sales people, our service people. Making them more productive is my number one priority.*
> —Jeff Immelt, CEO, GE

WHAT IS WORKFORCE PRODUCTIVITY?

Productivity is the value of the outputs of a firm, function or business unit compared to the costs of producing those outputs. Measuring a change in productivity is relatively simple. An increase in productivity results when the dollar value of the output increases, without any significant increase in the dollar cost of the inputs. It can also be depicted as a benefit/cost ratio where productivity results when the benefits increase relative to the costs.

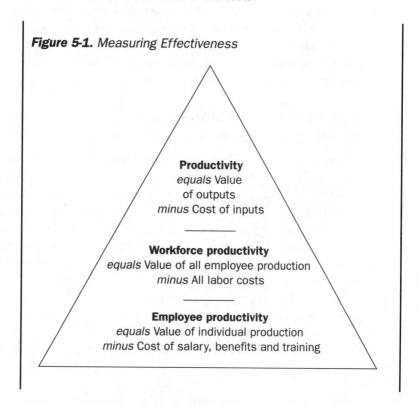

Figure 5-1. *Measuring Effectiveness*

Productivity
equals Value
of outputs
minus Cost of inputs

Workforce productivity
equals Value of all employee production
minus All labor costs

Employee productivity
equals Value of individual production
minus Cost of salary, benefits and training

PRODUCTIVITY IS IMPORTANT IN EVERY BUSINESS FUNCTION

CEOs and CFOs think differently than most VPs of HR. Every senior manager has, as a primary business goal, to increase productivity. The rise of supply chain, customer relationship management, Six Sigma and lean production is a direct result of this desire to improve productivity in essential business units.

Sometimes managers use the term efficiency instead of productivity but both have essentially the same meaning—producing more outputs at the same or lower costs. There are several aspects of productivity that a CEO must address, including the productivity of plant and capital equipment, the productivity of capital and investments and, finally, the productivity of employees.

Productivity develops an important meaning when applied to a particular business unit or function. It becomes the one measure that can be universally applied between business units. Comparing the cost of inputs to the value of outputs makes side-by-side comparisons possible between functions and business units that do totally different things. Even not-for-profit organizations can measure their success by comparing their productivity from one year to the previous year.

LABOR COSTS ARE SIGNIFICANT TO ANY ORGANIZATION

As mentioned earlier, for most organizations, between 40 and 60 percent of all variable costs go to labor or people costs. For many organizations, "labor or people costs" is the highest variable expense in their budget. If nearly half of all expenditures went to supply chain or marketing, everyone would immediately realize the strategic importance of those functions. For some reason, however, most people in HR fail to realize what a large financial impact they have on a corporation.

If you can increase the efficiency of 50 percent of your expenditures by only one percent, you will have made a significant contribution to profits. If at the same time you cut your costs by one percent, you increase the output of that resource by say 5 percent, everyone would take notice.

It's that kind of thinking that is required of strategic HR leaders. They are responsible for making this high-cost asset the most efficient in the industry.

HR's PRIMARY GOAL IS TO INCREASE WORKFORCE PRODUCTIVITY

When senior managers began to recognize the importance of people as a resource to the company, what used to be called the Personnel Department was renamed the Human Resources Department. Like land and capital, managing people effectively became recognized as a key contributor to corporate success.

The VP of HR is the manager of "human resources" just like the CFO is the manager of "financial resources" and the CIO is the manager of "information services." As the department responsible for managing human resources, HR has the same responsibility as any other functional department. It needs to:

- Increase output;
- Increase capabilities or capacity to do more things;
- Provide a competitive advantage; and
- Maintain or reduce costs.

In short, the role of any functional manager is to increase the productivity of the resources that he or she manages. In the specific case of human resources, that means increasing the productivity of employees. Since typically line managers make hiring, firing, pay and other employee-related decisions, the role of HR becomes that of guiding, educating and influencing managers and people processes so that the net result is an increase in employee productivity.

> *The job of HR is to guide, educate and influence managers so that the net result is an increase in employee productivity.*

Unfortunately, not everyone in human resources has made the transition towards becoming the *manager* of human resources within the firm. As a result, HR's strategic impact has been diminished. Do not fall into the trap of believing that HR's role is to make policies, enforce rules, run programs and develop processes, because each of these actions are *inputs*, not results or *outputs*. The final *output* of managing the human resources of the corporation is increasing the productivity or output of the organization's human assets—its employees. The business term for increasing the effectiveness of a company's human resources is workforce productivity.

> *Don't confuse inputs with outputs. Making policy, enforcing rules, running HR programs and developing processes are mere inputs. The output of the human resource function is increased employee productivity.*

FACTORS THAT IMPACT WORKFORCE PRODUCTIVITY

When HR accepts the role of improving workforce productivity, quite often some HR professionals complain that those expectations are unfair because HR doesn't have complete control over each of the factors that impact workforce productivity. While that's certainly true, there are many aspects of business where someone has responsibility for results without total control. In fact, in modern matrix organizations, responsibility without total control is simply the way business is done.

It is certainly important for every manager to understand the factors that impact workforce productivity, so that he or she can make every attempt to influence those factors. The level of workforce and employee productivity is directly impacted by the following factors:

People-related factors that impact productivity

- **Employee skills**—Employees have the right mix of skills, knowledge and experience to fit the work.
- **Employee motivation**—Factors that excite and energize employees including loyalty, rewards, recognition, pride and praise.
- **The manager**—The quality of the supervision and the ability of the manager to develop plans and provide direction and motivation are crucial to success.
- **Team members**—Few workplace tasks can be completed today by an individual working totally alone. Without the support of team members working together, productivity is bound to suffer.
- **Communications**—Employees can't maximize their production without two-way communications, feedback and measures to indicate how well they are doing.

Non-people-related factors that impact productivity

- **Resources**—Sufficient budget to complete the job.
- **Tools and equipment**—The necessary tools, equipment and physical facilities required to do the job.
- **Plans and strategy**—Even the best employees can't produce unless they know what direction the organization is going and what is expected of them.
- **Factors outside the workplace**—On occasion, employee productivity is impacted by things that happen in employees' personal life, or by political and social events.

Obviously, if the HR department wants to improve workforce productivity dramatically, it should spend most of its time and influence on the people-related factors that impact productivity. But HR must also work with other managers to ensure that the non-people-related factors don't somehow negatively impact employee productivity.

A survey of CFOs showed that their top two workforce priorities were increasing workforce productivity and building leadership capabilities.
—Mercer Consulting and CFO research services

HR AS A PRODUCTIVITY CONSULTING CENTER

If HR is to become truly strategic, at some point it must move beyond the "doing things" and "running programs" stage and instead become responsible for ensuring that employee productivity continually increases. HR must serve as a facilitator, catalyst or consultant that provides managers with the appropriate tools to increase productivity. HR should consider itself the "productivity consulting center" where managers can come for answers.

Some of the questions you should be able to answer for managers include:

ALIGNING PRACTICES WITH STRATEGY

What HR practice or tool will increase ...

- Worker motivation in order to increase productivity?

- Employee challenge and commitment so that turnover is reduced?

- The quality of production (reduce the error rate)?

- Customer service scores?

- The volume of output by 10 percent?

- Employee suggestions and innovation?

- The percentage of projects completed on time?

Once HR managers become "experts" in increasing employee productivity, managers and employees alike will beat a path to their door.

HR GENERALLY FAILS TO MEASURE WORKFORCE PRODUCTIVITY

While CEOs and CFOs are continually concerned about increasing productivity in every business, HR departments, almost without exception, fail even to measure their bottom-line impact on workforce or employee productivity. Although it is obvious that HR managers don't have total control over all of the factors that influence workforce productivity, this is no excuse.

If HR wants to be strategic, HR must assume "ownership" of people productivity, just as finance accepts responsibility for investments and IT accepts responsibility for computer operations. Strategic leaders take responsibility for one or more of the critical success factors of the firm. In this case, HR can assume ownership of one of the most costly but influential of the three factors of production (land, labor and capital).

METRICS

How can you measure workforce productivity?

Measuring the productivity of workforce is relatively easy, and it might require little work on the part of HR. Most of the information that is required to calculate workforce productivity is already gathered by the CFO's office. For example, in order to calculate workforce productivity you need only two numbers:

- **The total people costs**—Total people costs are already captured by the finance department on the general ledger (generally, total employee costs includes expenditures for employee salaries, benefits, and training, as well as the cost of operating the HR function).

- **Total value of employee output**—The dollar output produced by employees. Either the dollar value of the employees' output or the economic value they add are both calculated by the finance department on a quarterly basis.

If you subtract (1) the total people costs from (2) the total value of employee output for the year, you get the total value of workforce productivity. If you then compare it directly to last year's number, you'll get the dollar value of any productivity improvement. If you calculate what percentage people costs are of the dollar value of the total employee output, and compare it to last year's percentage, you can identify the percentage that productivity either increased or decreased.

Formula: *People (or workforce) productivity equals Outputs (the value of employee output) minus Inputs (costs of employee salaries and benefits as well as HR departmental costs).*

The HR goal is to produce the highest differential between the value of employee outputs and the cost of the inputs.

REPORTING PRODUCTIVITY GAINS

There are five basic ways to report or express your organization's productivity. They include:

- **The total dollar value**—The dollar value of employee outputs after employee costs are deducted (example–$22 million).
- **Percent of change**—The positive or negative change between this time period and the last (example–a 10 percent increase over last year's).
- **Ratio**—The dollar value of the outputs produced per dollar of inputs (example—2.4 to 1 outputs less costs).
- **Side-by-side comparisons**—You can compare productivity between your own operating divisions (example–department A's productivity exceeded department B's by 12 percent).
- **Benchmark comparisons**—Most managers also would like to compare their firm's productivity to that of their direct competitors or to other benchmark firms. Getting the productivity data of other firms may be difficult because not every firm is willing to share how well they do on these important ratios. Several productivity comparison ratios and their benchmark numbers are available from the Saratoga Institute, which has a long-established reputation for tracking HR metrics. Some industry associations and external financial analysts also frequently calculate some basic productivity ratios.

Note: You can even compare to the productivity between countries. For example, the output for every dollar invested in a U.S. worker is as much as 20 times that of the output per dollar invested in Chinese workers.

VARIOUS HR PRODUCTIVITY MEASURES

If you want to move beyond the basic workforce productivity measure cited above, there are several other productivity measures that you may wish to calculate. Some are simple; others are more advanced. Some of these other productivity measures are listed below.

1. Revenue per employee as a rough measure of productivity

As a base measure, revenue per employee is a good place to start. It is the easiest to understand and to calculate. Revenue per employee is merely the company's revenue divided by the number of employees. Because both revenues and the number of employees are generally listed in the annual report, both calculating your own number and comparing it to other firms are relatively easy to do.

Within your industry, the minimum goal is to have the same revenue per employee as other firms of a similar size. Within your firm, you should expect your revenue per employee to increase each year. The major weakness of this measure is that it doesn't include the cost of the your employees. This is important because, unless you calculate the cost of employees, firms with highly paid employees would have the same ratio of revenue per employee as firms that paid their workers significantly less.

Revenue per employee as a rough measure of productivity		
Purpose	**Weakness**	**Formula**
To get a rough estimate of the value of employee output; easy to calculate using easy-to-find numbers	Leaves out the fact that not all employees cost the same amount	$$\frac{Total\ revenue}{Number\ of\ employees}$$

2. Percentage of labor cost to overall costs

Another simple ratio demonstrates what percentage labor costs are to all total (non-capital) costs. Improving productivity in this case means, at a minimum, keeping the ratio constant.

Percentage of labor cost to overall costs		
Purpose	**Weakness**	**Formula**
To check on whether people costs are being maintained; *e.g.*, does HR hire, motivate and pay so that competitive costs are maintained	Changes in production process (for example, the widespread use of outsourcing or technology) can artificially change the ratio	$$\frac{Total\ labor\ costs}{All\ Costs}$$

3. Profit per employee as a rough measure of productivity

Similar to the revenue per employee calculation, the major difference here is that profit is substituted for revenue. For most, profit it is a more accurate reflection of company success than revenue.

Profit per employee as a rough measure of productivity		
Purpose	**Weakness**	**Formula**
To see the amount of profit generated by each employee	Leaves out the fact that not all employees cost the same amount	$$\frac{Total\ profit}{Number\ of\ employees}$$

4. Revenue per dollars spent on employees

Another measure of productivity is the ratio between revenues and total employee costs. Firms that generate more dollars of revenue per dollar spent on employee costs are the most productive.

Revenue per dollars spent on employees		
Purpose	**Weakness**	**Formula**
The *best* (easy-to-do) demonstration of the relative value (relative to costs) of employee output	Revenue is not equivalent to profit	$$\frac{Total\ revenue}{Total\ employee\ costs}$$ (This ratio can also be reported as the number of cents that must be spent on employee costs to generate a dollar of revenue)

Whatever individual productivity measures you select, it's important to "run them by" the CFO's office to ensure that your calculations are correct.

WHY IT'S IMPORTANT TO MEASURE "PEOPLE PROFIT"

In addition to the productivity measures just presented, there is one additional measure that clearly demonstrates the highest impact that HR can have. It is known as "people profit." If you can only do one calculation in this area, *revenue per employee* or "people profit" would be the appropriate choice.

People profit—Profit per people dollar spent on employees

The ultimate strategic measure is what I call people profit. This ratio answers a key strategic question, "For every dollar I invest in people costs, how much do I get in profit?" It is the ratio between profit and total employee costs. Firms that generate more dollars of profit for every dollar spent on employee costs are the most productive.

This measure is the most strategic because it includes the ultimate bottom-line total profit compared to total employee costs. Managers and HR departments that are effective at managing their human resources will have the highest ratio, and the continual improvement of this ratio gives great credence to the argument that workforce productivity is improving.

For some firms, employee costs are actually quite high (relative to other firms) because they decide to offer higher incentives or hire more qualified people. However, costs are only one side of the picture. If the strategy of investing more in your people in order to get more output *works*, the additional profit generated by hiring these more expensive or more qualified individuals will far exceed their additional costs.

People profit—Profit per people dollar spent on employees		
Purpose	**Weakness**	**Formula**
The best demonstration of the relative value (relative to costs) of having top employees	Profit can be defined several ways	*Total profits* ——————— Total employee costs (This ratio can also be reported as the number of cents that must be spent on employee costs to generate a dollar of profit)

WHAT CAN HR DO TO INCREASE PRODUCTIVITY?

If HR is to be considered strategic by senior management, it must directly impact productivity. Of course, the next logical question is which HR programs are the most likely to produce that impact? Unfortunately for HR professionals, there is no master list available of HR programs that have a high impact on productivity. Although there are many companies and consulting firms that assess the impact of HR programs, most of them wisely choose to keep those results secret in order to maintain their competitive advantage.

Nonetheless, if you are a new director or VP of HR, it's crucial that you invest limited HR resources in such a way that they have immediate productivity impact. In the latter part of this book, I've included many suggested HR actions and approaches that have a strategic impact. But if you are itching to know which HR programs are likely to have the most impact on productivity and profit, here's a quick snapshot of HR programs and initiatives that I have found in practice to have the most impact.

BEST PRACTICE

Programs that typically have a high strategic impact on workforce productivity. Once you do the initial assessment of how productive your human resources are, the next step is to determine how to increase that productivity without at the same time increasing costs proportionally. Here are some high impact tools to increase worker productivity:

Adjusting the HR budget so that resource allocations mirror or align with corporate priorities;

Employee referral programs;

Employee retention programs;

Measuring and rewarding managers for great "people management";

Prioritizing HR resources and services around jobs and business units with the most strategic impact potential;

Measuring and incenting HR functions based on business impact;

Partnering with the CFO on metrics;

Building an external "brand" as a great place to work;

Forecasting and alerting managers about upcoming people issues and opportunities;

Identifying, fixing and removing "bad managers";

Proactive internal redeployment of employees to areas of higher return;

Metrics (to increase accountability) and rewards that are tied to performance and productivity;

Identifying what motivates, challenges and frustrates employees;

Performance management programs that drop poor performing managers and employees;

On-the-job learning and growth opportunities (job rotations and special projects);

Rewards for sharing best practices between managers;

Measures and rewards that cross functional lines in order to increase cooperation;

Better forecasting and workforce planning; and

Increasing pay and reward differentials between top and average performers.

Examples of high-impact but also high-risk HR initiatives

In addition to the above, there are some HR programs that have a potentially high strategic impact but also carry high risks of failure. Before you consider these, be sure you understand the potential downside in costs and likelihood of failure.

- Enterprise software implementation;
- Leadership and executive development programs;
- Management alerts and forecasting future people issues;
- Workforce and succession planning;
- Firing or releasing "bad managers";
- Globalizing HR;
- Pay for performance; and
- "What works" sharing.

TEN MOST COMMONLY USED PRODUCTIVITY IMPROVEMENT "LEVERS"

The ten most commonly used productivity levers are listed in descending order, with the ones that, in my experience, generally have the highest potential ROI listed first. The most commonly used tools that fit each productivity category or lever are listed in the next column.

Productivity lever	The available HR tools
1. Motivate and excite employees	Non-monetary (recognition, praise, feedback); Monetary (compensation, bonuses) and metrics (through competition or avoiding embarrassment)
2. Keep performing employees longer	Retention initiatives, challenge and growth initiatives, improve managers
3. Replace non-performing employees	Hire and fire
4. Improve individual skills and capabilities	On-the-job training, formal training, degree programs, job rotations
5. Improve managers	Develop, replace or redeploy managers
6. Prepare for future problems	Plan, forecast, and alert managers; provide solutions for upcoming problems and opportunities
7. Improve the job "fit"	Redeployment, voluntary internal transfers, promotions
8. Improve people management processes	Increase efficiency and availability through technology, reengineering and Six Sigma
9. Prevent employees from becoming non-performers	Rules, procedures, policies, corporate culture
10. "Fix" non-performing employees	Employee relations, performance management, discipline

LOW-IMPACT HR EFFORTS

There are some HR programs that, no matter how well executed, have proven over time to produce a low strategic impact. Of course there are always exceptions, and I'm not saying that they are not important or that they don't contribute; however, the contribution doesn't normally reach the strategic level where it has a clear impact on workforce productivity.

- Implementing competency programs;
- Improving existing performance appraisal programs;
- Training employees for their "next job";
- Mentor programs;
- Increasing employee benefits and personal portals;
- Outsourcing HR activities;
- Increasing the number of generalists in the field;
- Benefit programs that exceed the industry average in costs;
- Base pay compensation programs without a link to performance;
- Reducing the "cost of hire";
- Reducing the HR-to-employee ratio;
- HR transactions;
- Providing basic information and answering basic HR questions;
- Maintaining HR policies; and
- Employee relations efforts that focus on low performers.

PRODUCTIVITY IS THE MOST IMPORTANT ELEMENT

The most important of the ten elements of strategic HR is increasing productivity and profits. If HR expects to have a continuing strategic impact on a firm's profitability, it must shift the emphasis away from cost-cutting and transactions and toward increasing revenue and workforce productivity. Should HR accept that perspective, HR must focus its resources on programs and initiatives that have the highest likelihood of impacting business results.

The process of increasing workforce productivity begins with setting up the expectation that all HR programs impact productivity. Then HR must develop a set of metrics and measures so it can continually refine and improve workforce productivity efforts. And finally, it must build up its credibility among senior managers as an expert in productivity improvement so that managers will come to HR when they need an increase in productivity or business results.

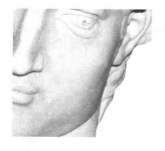

CHAPTER SIX

HR HAS AN EXTERNAL FOCUS ON IMPACTING BUSINESS OBJECTIVES

OBJECTIVE

The second element that differentiates strategic HR departments from non-strategic ones is an external focus on the corporate goals and objectives of the firm. For HR, being externally focused means thinking and acting like businesspeople. Like any other businessperson, HR's goals are the same as the corporation's.

KEY POINTS

◊ An externally focused HR department thinks of itself not just as a business partner but also as a business leader.

◊ As a business leader and problem solver it seeks out corporate problems and aggressively offers itself as a consultant with expertise in solving business problems.

◊ Because HR is a specialist in people management, it uses that expertise as its primary contribution to resolving strategic business issues.

For HR, being externally focused means thinking and acting like businesspeople. Like any other businessperson, HR's goals are the same as the corporation's. In other words, with an external focus, HR adopts the corporate goals and objectives as its own. Its role is simple; make a direct measurable contribution to as many corporate goals as possible:

- Product development
- Customer service
- Market share
- Expansion into new markets
- Increasing the stock price
- Building the brand

Once these goals have been identified, HR's search does not end. The next phase of having an external focus requires HR to seek out business problems that, if resolved, would positively impact corporate goals and objectives.

The third and final phase of an external focus is for HR to monitor the external business and economic environment so that it can be prepared for any upcoming problems or opportunities in the people management area.

DEFINITION

An external focus in HR means:

- Impacting business goals and objectives

- Identifying business problems early and helping to resolve them with people management tools

- Monitoring the external business environment for changes that may impact workforce productivity

Unfortunately, most HR departments tend to be internally focused on their own issues and problems. Only rarely do they have time proactively to identify and focus on external business issues. An internal focus often keeps HR from tracking and responding to changes in the external business environment. These environmental factors (like competitor actions and the unemployment rate) can directly impact the effectiveness of the people management strategies and the tools that HR uses.

Individuals have two choices when they determine their business focus and how they allocate their time. Individual employees can focus on their own job and what is best for them, or they can have an external focus, which means that they spend most of their time doing things that are good for the team. In the same way, a Congressperson can focus on what is good for his or her home district, or he or she can have an external focus—and do what's best for the country as a whole.

These examples demonstrate the difference between an internal and external focus. An internal focus is almost always the first avenue that individuals and organizations take, just because it's just easier to know your own needs and wants. It is this tendency to focus HR time and resources internally on the short-term or tactical issues and opportunities, rather them focusing on external business problems and goals, that differentiates most HR departments from strategic ones.

Let me state up front that there is nothing wrong with spending time on internal HR issues. Resolving internal issues is a necessary and vital contribution to the success of HR. You can't provide either excellent transactional support or consulting services unless you have efficient processes, clear goals and well-trained people. The element that makes an HR department strategic, however, is that in a strategic HR department, the majority of resources are focused on *external* business and environmental issues. This differs from the traditional HR department where, quite often, less than one-third of the resources are focused on external issues.

Strategic HR is a solutions provider. It proactively identifies and solves the problems faced by the business ... using people management tools.

COMPARING INTERNALLY FOCUSED AND EXTERNALLY FOCUSED HR

There are several different areas where an externally focused HR department differs from an internally focused one. Here is an example that demonstrates the differences:

ALIGNING PRACTICES WITH STRATEGY

A side-by-side comparison of the two perspectives

HR internal focus	HR external focus
HR fills all open requisitions	HR ensures that all teams meet their performance goals because their staffing levels were met
HR takes actions like reprimanding a poor performer	HR takes responsibility for improving employees by making poor performers into top performers
HR tracks training attendance	HR focus is on results and demonstrates that increased training correlates with increased output
HR reports that turnover is 5 percent	HR provides end-to-end solutions. It Increases team stability utilizing retention tools, and these efforts lead to a decreased time to market by 12 percent
HR measures success by the number of orientations completed on time	HR focuses on improving productivity, and the time it takes to meet minimum productivity standards for new hires is reduced by 2 months
HR develops metrics and reports	HR warns managers in advance. By providing over-staffing alerts to managers, HR avoids layoffs, thus increasing production efficiency by 12 percent

This table clearly demonstrates the difference between internal and external focus in HR. The internal approach has HR focusing on internal measures, goals and results that, although important, are defined in such a way that they would be only of interest to HR professionals. In contrast, when HR takes an external focus it looks at all problems and solutions in the context of the needs of senior management. In fact, an externally focused HR looks at all problems through the eyes of senior business executives.

Why? Because senior line executives are the ones with line responsibility and accountability for producing business results. HR, in contrast, is a staff function whose job is defined by the line functions it serves. In that staff role, HR must have an external focus to ensure that the services and tools that it provides meet the ever-changing needs of the business and the business environment.

AN EXTERNALLY FOCUSED HR HAS DIFFERENT GOALS

An internally focused HR department defines its quarterly and yearly objectives quite differently than an externally focused one. Here are some examples of internally focused HR goals.

CHECKLIST: INTERNALLY FOCUSED HR GOALS

- Reducing the HR headcount-to-employee ratio
- Cutting the cost of HR services to $1000 per employee (of the firm)
- Reducing the cost of hire
- Implementing new HRIS technology
- Outsourcing more HR services
- Providing an employee self-service portal
- Making HR paperless
- Managing HR vendor relationships
- Generating HR reports
- 100 percent on-time completion of performance appraisal forms

As you can see, internally focused objectives cover topics that are primarily of interest to HR people. In addition, they use words like employee self-service and HRIS technology that again show an internal focus. You might be wondering why a HR goal related to completion of performance appraisal forms is internally focused. That is because although there might be some indirect relationship between performance appraisal forms and improving employee performance, the actual completion of the form itself is the smoke, but not the fire.

The external business goal is the one that focuses on the end result (actually *improving employee performance*). External HR goals focus on the fire, which invariably turns out to be the same as the corporate business objectives and goals that were spelled out at the beginning of the year by the CEO. To help clarify the difference between the two, here is a list of externally focused strategic HR objectives.

CHECKLIST: EXTERNALLY FOCUSED HR GOALS

- Having no project deadlines missed because of talent issues or problems.
- Increasing employee productivity.
- Reducing product development time-to-market as a direct result of HR interventions in the areas of motivation and incentives.
- Turning around the lowest performing business unit so that it becomes profitable within a year as a result of sending in the HR SWAT team.
- Increasing (product) customer satisfaction three percent through performance management interventions in the product call center.
- Increasing product quality eight percent by providing e-training, and reducing the turnover of top performing Six Sigma black belts through targeted retention efforts.
- Increase product sales by one percent by hiring away the top sales people from our competitors.

As you can see, externally focused HR objectives use terms like sales, product quality and customer satisfaction. These terms are likely to be the same ones that are used on a daily basis by the company's executive committee as well as by external financial analysts and shareholders. In direct contrast, the issues and terminology that appear in the list of internally focused HR objectives are likely only to be of passing interest to anyone outside of HR.

> *An external focus means that you define HR successes by the contribution that you make to corporate goals and objectives, such as increased market share, a stronger brand and increased revenues.*

PROBLEMS THAT OCCUR WHEN HR IS INTERNALLY FOCUSED

Theoretically, at least, every HR function should be externally focused because it, like all other staff functions, should focus on the problems and needs of the business units and managers it serves. It's obvious, however, that not everyone in HR buys into this concept. The reality is that most HR departments are primarily internally focused. What are some of the potential problems and negative impacts that come from being too internally focused?

DISCONNECT BETWEEN HR RESOURCE ALLOCATION AND CORPORATE PRIORITIES

In order to have the maximum strategic impact, HR must allocate its budget and time proportionately with the corporation's goals and objectives. HR priorities and expenditures must also mirror corporate priorities and expenditures. Unfortunately, HR seldom makes a formal effort to coordinate its budget and time allocation with either its own or the corporate strategic goals. The following chart illustrates that disconnect.

Table 6-A.

HR budget and time expenditures	Corporate priorities
12 percent—The percentage of HR budget spent on employee relations efforts on poor performers.	0 percent—The percentage of corporate resources spent on fixing or reviving poor performing business units.
10 percent—The percentage of HR time spent in business unit A.	50 percent—The percentage of corporate resources devoted to business unit A.
2 percent—The percentage of HR budget spent on technology.	22 percent—The percentage of the corporate budget spent on technology.
7 percent—The percentage of the HR budget allocated to recruiting.	44 percent—The percentage of projects that are running behind schedule because of an inadequate supply of talent.
47 percent—The percentage of recruiting positions that are funded but remain vacant.	47 percent—Percentage of funded positions that have been unfilled by recruiting efforts.
33 percent—The percentage of the HR budget allocated to classroom training.	88 percent—The percentage of managers that prefer on-the-job training to classroom training.
No priority given to hiring, retaining or developing customer service reps.	#1 priority—The priority given to improving and maintaining customer service.
0 percent—The percentage of the HR budget allocated to a separate retention program for top performers.	#2 priority—The priority given to retaining top performers in key positions.
0 percent—The percentage of the HR budget allocated to a non-monetary motivation and recognition programs.	#3 priority—The priority given to increasing employee motivation.
0 percent—The percentage of the HR budget allocated to improving workforce productivity.	#4 priority—The priority given to increasing productivity.
2 percent—HR budget allocation to diversity programs (0 percent—percentage that the diversity program budget has increased since it became the #1 HR departmental priority).	#1 HR departmental priority is to improve diversity hiring and retention in the firm.

POSSIBLE NEGATIVE IMPACTS OF HAVING AN INTERNAL FOCUS

- **Outsider status.** Internally focused HR departments tend to use a different and less financial language than other business units. By doing this HR runs the risk of being seen as an outsider; someone that doesn't understand the world of business.
- **Budget crises.** Being inward-looking can cause HR departments to allocate their resources according to their own agendas. Spending resources counter to the way the rest of the organization does is highly likely to make HR stand out and perhaps be the first whose budget is cut because HR appears out of touch.
- **Isolated employees.** An internally focused HR department generally also results in isolated employees. This isolation not only can slow the development of the HR staff, but it might mean that their career will be limited to jobs in HR because they are so different that they cannot adapt to any function outside of HR.
- **Information lack.** An internally focused HR may also mean that its information and databases are isolated so that they cannot interact with other business databases. In a fact-based decision world, HR can't survive without access to information that is held by others.
- **Ineffective communication.** Failing to have an external focus can lead to a misunderstanding about what managers need. The result can be a lot of wasted time and energy on programs that aren't appreciated. Poor relationships with managers might also mean a failure to get honest feedback, which also could lead to a high program failure rate.
- **Adversarial relationship.** Too much isolation can lead HR into a *Us vs. Them* mentality that, if left unchecked, can move HR from the misunderstood category into the disliked category,

   Some additional negative consequences that can occur when HR is too internally focused include:
- Because an internally focused HR department is less aware of problems and crises that are occurring outside, HR may be more conservative, slower in decision-making, and less agile than other business units. In fact, HR may develop a meeting culture where getting buy-in and building relationships become more important than providing immediate solutions to business problems.

- HR may have no sense of urgency because the isolation keeps HR people from feeling the heat of bad business results.
- HR may make no attempt to forecast future events, and it eventually becomes backward-looking.
- An insulated HR may not have political credibility and, as a result, it will be the first to have its staff or budget cut.
- HR may fail to conduct periodic self-assessments or audits; this may lead to stagnation and no self-improvement efforts.
- HR might never undertake customer satisfaction surveys because its isolation allows it to be less concerned about what outsiders think.
- HR might sink into a pattern of strongly resisting outside things that were not invented here.
- No environment-scanning can mean that HR will be surprised and unprepared for catastrophic external events.
- HR may resort to the use of soft performance measures, which are not compatible with the rest of the organization's financial measures.

Reducing the cost of hire is an internal HR goal and focus. If HR provides excellent staffing, performance management and reten-tion services so that (product) customer satisfaction increases by 17 percent, then HR is having an external impact.

IDENTIFYING WHICH CORPORATE STRATEGIC GOALS AND OBJECTIVES TO IMPACT

Strategic actions by HR must, by definition, have a strategic impact. Most corporations try to send a message to their managers about what's important by providing them with a list of corporate goals and objectives. The executive committee approves this list; it is often the basis for budget allocations as well as departmental and executive bonuses.

It's obvious that before HR can increase its strategic impact, it must first determine what goals the organization considers strategic. If the HR function has assumed an inwardly focused role, it might not have direct access to these objectives. In those cases, HR must develop a process for proactively identifying these corporate problems and priorities. At some firms, identifying the top corporate objectives is relatively easy, while at others it's substantially more difficult.

BEST PRACTICE

Identifying strategic goals and objectives for an organization:

- **Speeches**—Check the CEO's speeches. Quite often, the CEO outlines the major corporate objectives each year in a speech to all executives or to analysts. These speeches (and the list of objectives) may be available on the corporate intranet.

- **The strategic business plan**—Look in the company's strategic plan. If you have access to the company's strategic plan, the goals are almost always documented there. If the strategic planning department has forecasters, then they are good sources for identifying future problems that the corporation may face.

- **Budget allocations**—Look at the budget. If the corporate budget is distributed, look at which departments and units are getting increased budgets. A large or increased budget is almost always an indication of strategic importance.

- **Bonus criteria**—Ask executive compensation to provide you with a list of the CEO's bonus criteria and compensation factors (these are generally set by the Board of Directors and administered through the executive compensation group). These performance metrics usually provide an accurate representation of what the organization considers strategic.

- **Annual reports**—Read the annual reports for the last few years. Most of them are subtle in how they use words, but if you read carefully between the lines, you can generally identify corporate priorities.

- **Headcount allocations**—Position allocations are often another way to identify corporate priorities. If the business unit is allowed to hire and expand, it's generally a high-priority business unit, as are its products. In a similar light, during budget freezes, those departments that are allowed to travel and purchase items are also likely to be high-priority business units.

- **Analysts reports**—Quite often a financial or industry analyst highlights the strategic priorities in the reports about the firm. An outsider's perspective is sometimes a good second opinion.

- **Ask**—If all else fails, ask the CFO, directors or general managers or the COO for a list of the corporate priorities and objectives.

Even though every firm has its own set of corporate objectives, typical corporate long-term goals and objectives that HR has a reasonable chance to impact include:

TYPICAL BUSINESS STRATEGIC GOALS

- Increasing revenues or profit
- Increasing employee productivity
- Increasing the productivity or efficiency of business processes
- Reducing the costs of labor
- Improving customer service or satisfaction
- Improving product quality
- Reducing product development time (time-to-market)
- Higher margins on products and services
- Improved product features
- Increasing market share/new customers
- Expansion into new markets/regions
- Increasing our return on investment (ROI)
- Increasing shareholder value (stock price)
- Providing or increasing our competitive advantage over our direct competitors

Verifying strategic goals

After you have identified the key organizational objectives, the next step is to verify them with a senior executive in order to ensure that HR doesn't waste its time on outdated priorities. Once you are sure of the corporate priorities, it's important to rank or sort them based on the likelihood that people management is a major or minor factor in reaching the goal. Once HR has identified the goals that have a major people component, the next step is to allocate HR resources for providing a solution to the opportunity or problem.

STRATEGIC BUSINESS OBJECTIVES FOR HR TO IMPACT

When a HR department is truly strategic, it has a variety of direct measurable impacts on the corporation or a particular business unit. The items listed below are all business impacts rather than traditional HR goals and objectives. Because they are the primary measures of strategic business success, they should also be the factors that HR tries to impact. Incidentally, they are also likely to be the things that most line managers are measured and rewarded on, so anyone helping them to meet these goals is likely to be regarded as a corporate hero.

Factors that are relatively easy to impact

- **Employee productivity**—Increasing the output of the workforce while simultaneously maintaining or reducing relative labor costs
- **Costs**—Lower operating costs
- **Volume**—Higher volume of output
- **Quality**—Higher quality of output
- **Errors**—Fewer errors, less waste and fewer rejects
- **Customer satisfaction**—Increased customer satisfaction and fewer complaints

Factors that are significantly more difficult to impact (and more difficult to prove your impact)

- **Innovation**—Innovative ideas that provide a competitive advantage in the areas of product and customer service
- **Time to market**—Reducing the time it takes to develop products and get them to the marketplace
- **Higher prices**—The ability to charge higher prices in the marketplace as a result of improved product features
- **Brand**—Activities that improve our external image and brand
- **Competitive advantage**—Improvement in processes, products or systems that helps obtain or maintain a competitive advantage
- **Expansion**—Any improvement in organizational capabilities that allow the organization to expand into new markets or new geographic regions
- **Funding**—Activities that impact the ability to secure funding and financial resources
- **Market share**—Any improvement in products, customer service or business processes that increase our market share and that help retain current customers or bring in new customers
- **Mergers**—Any activity or improvement that improves the possibility of a successful merger or acquisition (where mergers

and acquisitions increase shareholder value or increase your competitive position)

- **Revenue and profit**—Any activity that increases the firm's top-line revenue or net profit
- **Stock price**—Any activity that positively impacts the firm's stock price

Additional factors that make managers happy

Although most of these factors would not automatically provide a strategic impact, many managers do include them in their strategic goals.

- **Supply chain**—Anything that improves the effectiveness and the retention of your suppliers
- **PR**—Activities that provide us with positive PR exposure and press coverage
- **Continuous improvement**—Anything that spurs individuals and business processes to reduce cycle time and continually to improve their process's output
- **Project completion**—The percentage of projects completed under budget and on time
- **Personal goals**—Anything or anyone that aids them in meeting or exceeding their personal and position goals and the rewards that go with them

Developing supporting HR tactical goals

After identifying the potential business impact areas, HR now has a list of the things that senior managers care the most about. The next step is to develop HR tactical goals and objectives that relate directly to each business objective. Then the VP of HR must redesign HR programs and focus HR resources in order to maximize the HR department's impact on these important business factors. The final step is to then prove to cynical managers that the business improvements are a direct result of your HR efforts and programs.

The results of all strategic programs can be found in the balance sheet or income statement.

STRATEGIC BUSINESS PROBLEMS THAT HR CAN HELP SOLVE

Once you understand the corporation's business goals and objectives, you now know the results that the organization expects. But there is one more thing that you need to know: What problems does the company have that will prevent it from reaching its strategic goal and objectives?

Senior managers are constantly looking for approaches that can help them reach the strategic business objectives of improving profit, raising the stock price and growing the company.

Below is a list of common strategic business problems that are faced by senior managers. The list can be valuable to HR professionals because many of the problems on the list are strategic and are excellent targets for HR. When HR sees that an executive is about to undertake solving one of the strategic business problems, it's a signal that this is an opportunity to participate.

HR managers who think strategically see this as opportunity to develop people-management strategies and tools that directly impact the success of each solution or initiative undertaken. By developing companion strategies to each of these strategic problems, HR can insure itself a major role in the change effort. It's important to note that even though most of these problems are not related directly to HR, there are few approaches that can succeed without effective people-management strategies and tools.

Although no company has all of these problems all at once, it's not unusual for a dozen or so to exist at the same time within the same corporation. The key HR role here is to identify which strategic problems that management has decided to address and to demonstrate that both HR and its people-management tools can play a significant role in making the solution a successful one.

COMMON BUSINESS PROBLEMS FOR HR TO TARGET

Each of the major strategic problems that a firm may have is listed below and is categorized by the area that it impacts.

Product-related (increasing market share)
- Integrate the product line (vertically or horizontally)
- Differentiate the product from the competitors

- Increase advertising or change the adverti
- Increase market research to identify consu
- Improve product design
- Shorten product time to market
- Cut, raise or institute variable pricing
- Improve the brand image
- Introduce or redesign new products
- Improve customer service
- Expand or change the sales force

Expand the size of a company
- Create a joint venture with another firm
- Merge with another firm
- Acquire or buy out another firm in order to complement or diversify your product line
- Acquire or buy out a competitor in order to raise prices and increase market share
- Expand to other regions or globally

Decrease the size of the firm
- Sell off products or business units to focus on core products
- File for bankruptcy
- Sell the firm to competitors
- Go out of business
- Close plants or pull out of regions

Stock-related
- Stock repurchase
- IPO or additional stock sale
- Stock split
- Go private

Work with other firms
- Develop strategic alliances
- Improve the supply-chain
- Sell licenses
- Offer franchises

Management-related
- Fire top management
- Reorganize the management structure (de-layer)
- Downsize/lay off
- Improve retention
- Change the skill mix of the workforce
- Move work to low-cost regions
- Develop a contingent workforce
- Workforce planning problems
- Improve team cooperation
- Improve promotions
- Improve employee recognition
- Spread best practices internally
- Improve the culture

Improve process efficiency
- Decrease cycle time
- Improve quality and service/Six Sigma
- Increase/decrease funding for R&D
- Develop or buy new technology
- Improve outsourcing
- Improve customer relationship management
- Improve lean or just-in-time manufacturing
- Reengineer processes

Financial problems
- Buy or lease property
- Sell or lease current assets
- Change the investment mix
- Implement strategic cost-cutting
- Cut overhead
- Sell bonds

Information gathering
- Identify competitive intelligence
- Provide forecasts and alerts
- Benchmark best practices
- Conduct root cause analysis of internal problems
- Improve reporting

Legal problems
- Acquire copyright, trademark and patent protections
- Sue or threaten to sue our enemies

Miscellaneous
- Change production mix or increase/decrease capacity
- Go into e-commerce

To really make an impact, HR must go proactively to senior managers and propose solutions to one or more of these business problems.

It is this ability to propose pure business solutions to core problems that truly differentiates the good from the great in HR.

STRATEGIC BUSINESS SOLUTIONS THAT HR SHOULD PROVIDE

Even though the goal of HR is to focus on *strategic* problems, the reality is that most HR functions spend their time on solving *HR* issues and problems. And, although these issues and problems are important to HR, they only have an indirect impact on the organization's strategic goals. Most of these HR issues are defined using HR terminology, not business terminology.

EXAMPLES OF TACTICAL HR SOLUTIONS

- Conducting salary surveys
- Doing job analysis
- Providing HR reports
- Conducting exit interviews
- Programs to reduce the turnover rate
- Filling all requisitions on time
- Reducing the cost per hire
- Improving worker satisfaction
- Getting all performance appraisals completed on time
- Processing and resolving grievances
- Answering employees' questions about benefits and compensation

All of these issues are tactical issues. They are important but they still only have an indirect connection to business problems and strategic business goals and objectives. Strategic HR efforts must circumvent this indirect approach and get right to the heart of the matter … making a direct contribution to strategic business goals and objectives. Every corporation has different strategic problems and objectives. The following list will give you some idea of the types of strategic business problems that HR must seek out and make a direct contribution toward solving.

ALIGNING PRACTICES WITH STRATEGY

Strategic business solutions

Reducing labor costs

- Provide management with best practices for decreasing the cost of labor required to produce each unit of product or service

- Develop processes for moving jobs to less expensive labor regions

- Develop new hire and training systems that allow managers to hire less expensive and less experienced workers for their positions

- Provide advice and tools for reducing employee absenteeism, sick leave usage and tardiness

- Provide advice and tools for reducing unnecessary overtime

Increasing output

- Increase the output of the employees in a business unit by identifying the causes of increased productivity (what competencies, knowledge and skills that top performers have versus average performers)

- Provide advice and tools for putting the right person in the right job

- Identify the causes of delays in time-sensitive processes (product development, production and product service) and providing advice and tools for resolving the people-related causes

- Provide tools and advice to help managers improve team cohesion and productivity

- Provide a sufficient pool of qualified contingency workers to handle overload periods

- Provide advice and tools for improving the efficiency of employee scheduling

- Provide managers with post-mortem assessment tools for identifying the root causes of people management problems

- Provide managers with effective performance management systems that rapidly identify, fix or remove poor performing employees

- Provide fast and effective sourcing and hiring

- Provide effective tools for managers to decrease the time it takes for new hires to reach minimum productivity levels

- Provide consulting services to speed up assimilation and reduce the time to productivity after a merger

- Provide specialized services and tools for increasing the productivity of specialized business units like the executive team, R&D and sales

- Develop systems for the rapid sharing of internal best practices, solutions and problem identification between business units

Increasing quality

- Reduce error rates and increase product quality at a production facility through improved training and the refinement of Six Sigma-type processes

- Improve product design by providing advice and tools for improving innovation, idea generation and idea implementation

Improving customer service

- Identify the causes of poor customer service delivery, and provide advice and tools for resolving the people-related causes

- Improve the service delivery and efficiency of call centers and other customer support groups through effective hiring, performance management and training

Employee development

- Provide managers with tools for assessing the development needs of their employees

- Provide advice and educate managers on the most effective tools for improving employee-learning and learning speed

- Provide managers with advice on the most effective on-the-job training and learning tools

Increasing motivation

- Provide advice and non-monetary and motivational tools for improving individual employee productivity

- Monetary incentives—provide effective compensation, bonus and incentives tools for increasing individual employee productivity

- Provide advice and tools for identifying and defusing worker issues and where appropriate, maintaining the union-free environment

Measures and forecasts

- Provide managers with performance measurement tools and dashboards that allow them to identify employee performance problems before they become severe

- Alert managers about upcoming productivity, retention and recruitment issues in their business unit

- Provide forecasts to managers about the future availability of labor and the demographics of the future workforce

Benchmarking and competitive intelligence

- Benchmark other firms' best practices and adapt them to a particular situation

- Track competitors' strengths and weaknesses in recruiting and retention in order to prevent their raiding and to increase the chances of the company poaching their top talent

- Develop exit and post-exit survey programs to identify the factors that cause top performers and key individuals to leave

Other strategic HR programs and tools

- HR turnaround teams that can assess the people-related problems in under-performing business units and provide solutions that will transform them into performing business units

- HR SWAT teams that can be rapidly deployed to assist in people-management emergencies

- Develop and then continually improve company-wide HR recruiting, retention, compensation, benefits, performance management, branding and development programs that ensure a stable workforce and a steady supply of qualified candidates

- Develop strategies for large-scale hiring in order to make corporate expansion a viable business option

- Identify and assess potential firms for merger and acquisition, based on their complementary talent and compatible culture

- Build a talent pipeline to ensure that the firm has sufficient leadership bench strength for future needs

STRATEGIC ACTIONS TO INCREASE HR'S IMPACT ON CORPORATE GOALS

Once HR leaders are convinced of the need to have an external focus, how do they shift HR resources so that they align with or match business objectives? Resource allocation is significant because when an HR department is externally focused, it allocates resources much differently than does an internally focused one. It also undertakes different types of initiatives, it measures different things, and it may also reward different results.

DEVELOPING AN EXTERNAL FOCUS AND A SOLUTIONS-PROVIDER APPROACH

In fact, because every HR department wants to believe that it is already externally focused, assessing time and budget allocations is one of the most accurate ways of assessing whether HR actually has an external focus. Some of the activities that differentiate an externally-focused HR department from an internally focused one include:

- **Making managers accountable**—Generally, once an HR department begins the transition to an external focus, senior HR leaders realize that they can't increase employee productivity on their own. In order to be successful, they need the support and help of every supervisor and line manager. The best way to get that support is to demonstrate to these managers the economic impact of great people management and how, by improving their people management skills, managers will simultaneously improve their business and bonus goals.

  If you haven't had time to make that strong business case, the normal plan B is to use your influence over compensation and performance management to begin measuring and rewarding individual managers based on the quality of their people management. Measuring and rewarding people management results is the fastest way to get managers to pay attention to workforce productivity issues.

- **Measuring the impact on business results**—HR shifts its measurement away from HR efficiency measures and towards measuring the impact of HR programs and efforts on business results. A strong emphasis is placed on measuring workforce productivity and comparing company ratios to the best in the industry.

- **Reacting to negative business results**—When business results are down, HR investigates and undertakes a post-mortem with a team of specialists in order to see if the root cause of the problem is related to weak people-management processes or systems.

- **Acting as a turnaround specialist**—When a business unit has under-performed for a significant period of time, rather than waiting to be called, HR sends a turnaround team to fix the people-management aspects of the problem. HR analyzes the talent needs and re-deploys the right people into the troubled business unit.

- **Forecasting problems**—HR develops analytic tools to study past trends and patterns within the company in order to identify possible precursors to people-management problems. HR monitors what competitors are doing in HR that could impact the organization's hiring and retention. HR alerts managers in order to give them sufficient time to prevent a minor people management problem from cascading into a major one.

- **Monitoring the external business environment**—HR continually tracks external business factors with people-management implications such as the unemployment rate, layoffs and increased hiring at competitors, new tax laws that impact labor costs, the availability of lower-cost employees at sites around the globe, and people-management best practices that might be applicable to the firm.

- **Preparing for a range of solutions**—Once HR begins monitoring the external environment it will invariably learn that the world of business is changing at an increasingly rapid rate. As a result, it is no longer feasible for HR or any businessperson to come up with a single narrow solution. Instead, managers must earn to prepare for a range of options in almost every case. HR managers eventually will be expected to practice "what if" scenarios continually so that there will be no surprises and HR will be prepared for any high-probability changes and problems.

- **Identifying business and manager needs**—HR spends considerable resources identifying the business problems and the people-related issues of senior managers. HR conducts satisfaction and frustration surveys to identify what's working and what isn't.

- **Prioritizing customers**—Because an externally focused HR department is more aware that senior leadership has prioritized certain business units, products and regions, HR must shift its approach from the traditional first-come, first-served or equal treatment for all basis to a prioritized approach that allocates budget and time to mirror the priorities set by senior management.

- **Increasing consulting services**—An external focus means that more budget and headcount are allocated to the problems that occur in the business units. As a result, HR must increase spending in the areas of HR that have the highest external focus and impact. Generally, in the past, those areas of increased spending include consulting services, centers of excellence, SWAT and turnaround teams, and generalist positions (located in the business units).

- **Speed and risk-taking**—As an HR department becomes less isolated, it learns to think and act more like the business units do. And because business units almost always exist in a highly competitive environment, the natural consequence of working more closely with business units is that HR increases its focus on speed in order to match the speed of changes in the marketplace. In a similar light, risk-taking generally also increases because line managers live in an environment that requires them to constantly take risks. If HR is going to solve their problems, it will also need to be able to take reasonable risks.

- **Increasing transfers**—Externally focused HR departments realize that they must not be seen as an outsider. In addition, the HR department must take significant steps to better understand the problems and the people in the various business units. The net result of this realization is generally an increase in the number of transfers and temporary job rotations between HR and other business units. In fact, an excellent indicator of an external focus is when a significant number of HR staff rotates permanently into jobs within the business units.
- **HR rewards and promotions**—HR shifts its approach to rewards within HR. Salary increases, promotions and bonuses are given to those who have demonstrated their ability to impact business objectives, productivity and profits.
- **Increasing focus on brand**—Because HR has an external focus, it is more concerned with the organization's external image as a great place to work. Significant resources are allocated toward getting placed on good-place-to-work lists and on employee referral programs because both result in a long-term supply of qualified candidates.

In addition to revising the way HR spends its budget, an externally focused HR department also tracks and measures the time allocations of its HR professional staff. In order to be strategic, HR staff must spend up to half of its time focused on these external activities. Where appropriate, job descriptions and staffing levels must be adjusted to ensure that the appropriate time and effort is being put into activities that have a strategic business impact.

CAN HR BECOME A PROFIT CENTER?

If you are serious about making a strategic impact, you need to increase revenues or profits. Unfortunately, HR has a history of not focusing on increasing revenues or profits, partially because many people in HR long ago accepted as fact that HR is merely overhead. This negative thinking can create a self-fulfilling prophecy. As a result, many HR departments have decided up front that it is not possible to demonstrate any measurable impact on profit.

Staying in the backwater of overhead functions might have been OK in the past, but times have changed. Now many CFOs and CEOs recognize the value of human capital management. This realization, coupled with technology and new HR tools, now provides HR with an opportunity to become the number one profit center in a corporation. For those that disbelieve that this transformation is possible, here is a roadmap to show you how it's done.

SUPPLY CHAIN, CRM AND SIX SIGMA HAVE DEMONSTRATED HOW OVERHEAD FUNCTIONS CAN BECOME PROFIT CENTERS

Prior to the last decade, overhead functions like purchasing, shipping and warehousing found themselves even lower on the budget totem pole than HR. However, during the early 90s, a radical transformation occurred in the overhead functions of purchasing, shipping and warehousing. These lowly functions transformed themselves into what is now known as supply chain management.

Almost immediately, supply chain began generating a demonstrable profit, primarily through the use of technology, measures and metrics. The bottom line impact was dramatic, measurable and immediate. One firm, Wal-Mart, became the poster child of supply chain excellence, as it turned this lowly overhead function into a significant competitive advantage. The transformation of the supply chain alone was a major contributor toward making Wal-Mart an undisputed market leader (and billions of dollars). The same strategic impact is even more likely in HR because supply chain costs are generally less than 10 percent of corporate expenditures, while people costs generally exceed 40 percent.

Supply chain wasn't alone in making the transformation. Surprisingly, the list of overhead functions that have become profit centers is actually pretty long.

- Finance (even in non-financial firms) has generated profit and stock price increases through investments of surplus capital, recommending stock buybacks and hedging for currency fluctuations.
- Customer service, long in the backwater of top management's attention, has demonstrated how it can generate increased sales and profits through customer relationship management (CRM) tools and strategies.
- Quality control has also made significant progress through Six Sigma programs.

What were the keys to this transformation? How can HR follow the same path and take advantage of the opportunity to become the next corporate hero?

FOUR STEPS IN BECOMING A PROFIT CENTER

Step 1—Understand the CEO's expectations

The first step in becoming a profit center is to understand *who* makes a final determination as to whether you are a profit center or a cost center. In almost all organizations, that right rests with the CEO and the CFO.

Let's start with the CEO's perspective. CEOs are laser-focused on results. A direct consequence of that laser focus is that CEOs themselves focus their interest, time and energy on the short list of things for which their boss, the board of directors and shareholders, holds them accountable.

Understanding those accountability factors becomes the first step in the transformation into a profit center. By identifying exactly what the CEO is measured and rewarded for, HR can then concentrate its resources, time and effort towards having an impact on those factors. For example:

- Customer service—If your CEO is measured and rewarded for customer satisfaction, HR must demonstrate how great hiring, training and the retention of customer service personnel causes customer service ratings to improve. HR must then demonstrate the economic value of each percentage point increase in customer service ratings. Several research studies and numerous companies have found a direct connection between employee satisfaction and customer service scores.

- Sales revenue—If your CEO is rewarded for increasing sales revenue, then HR must demonstrate how, for example, great performance management in the sales area dramatically increases overall sales. The impact can be demonstrated by using a control group of sales people to show how your HR program(s) makes an economic difference (compared to a control group of sales people). If HR can demonstrate that by improving or removing the bottom 5 percent of the sales team it can increase sales by 10 percent, it will have demonstrated that HR programs can directly increase revenues.

The same connections can be shown for improvements in product development, product quality and improved branding efforts. More information is available in later chapters on how to prove that the HR programs are responsible for these changes in corporate performance.

The key lesson here is that the HR department must concentrate its time, budget and energy on those profit-related factors that the CEO cares most about, because improving performance in areas that are off the radar screen provides little economic lift to the firm or to the image of HR.

Step 2—Build a human capital management partnership with the CFO

In most organizations, impressing the CEO isn't sufficient (especially in tight economic times). You must also impress the CFO. You can dramatically improve your chances of being recognized as a profit center if you get early buy-in from the CFO, so the next step in the process is to build an alliance with the people who are responsible for measuring profit … the CFO's office.

Professionals in the finance department are frequently criticized for being one-dimensional. The only language they seem to understand involves the use of numbers and dollars. HR often finds itself in trouble because it has developed the bad habit of using its own language to demonstrate its results, and that language often includes non-quantifiable terms like satisfaction, employee well being and values.

It's no surprise that CFOs quite often don't understand or appreciate the value of such vague terms. Rather than spending an inordinate amount of time trying to get finance professionals to change their perspective, begin to use *their* language. This means that HR leaders must begin to report HR results using the same terminology (*i.e.*, numbers, dollars and ratios) as other important business functions do. For example, customer relationship management isn't satisfied just to report that customer satisfaction has increased; instead it reports the dollar impact of increased satisfaction on repeat sales, customer referrals and product return costs.

Once you adopt this way of thinking and the language of finance, the next step for HR is to make the CFO an equal partner in improving and measuring human capital management. Building the CFO's interest in human capital related issues might be easier than you think; chances are, your CFO has already read in CFO-focused publications about the importance of managing human capital in impacting financial results. CFOs' interest in spreading their influence can be used to your advantage in forming a partnership focusing on the accurate measurement of human resource efforts.

Early in the process, ask for the CFO's office help. If possible, show them how other organizations like Microsoft, Intel, Oracle and HP have developed close working relationships between HR and finance. Offer them a major role in designing your HR metrics and the profit-generation measurement system for HR programs. Be eager to learn about metrics and how to measure and report things the way finance professionals do.

Be equally willing to educate the CFO about the impact that motivation, training, recruiting and retention can have on increasing employee productivity and company profit. If you find that they are especially cynical, let them actually collect the data and calculate the ratios. HR should also consider borrowing a senior finance professional for a short-term job rotation in HR (and vice versa). This "swapping" of professionals helps both departments' understanding of the needs and problems of the other and can go a long way politically in eliminating any past suspicions.

Step 3—Focus HR resources on increasing revenues rather than cutting costs

HR traditionally focuses on cutting costs rather than increasing revenue. Freezing hiring and cutting headcount and training are common HR cost-reduction approaches. Unfortunately, relying solely on cost-cutting measures can be a huge mistake because CEOs prefer increasing revenues (top line growth) to cutting costs. Books that CEOs frequently admire, like "Built to Last," clearly demonstrate that increasing customer satisfaction, building a performance culture and increasing long-term revenue streams are superior long-term success strategies to simple short-term cost-cutting.

The lesson to be learned by HR is that instead of showing an ability to pinch pennies, focus HR efforts on increasing revenues. Work with the CFO, directors and general managers to identify which processes, jobs, products and business units have the most impact on corporate revenues. Then prioritize your HR time and resource allocation in those business areas.

In a similar light, it's important to understand that cutting HR function costs to the bone has a relatively small impact on business success—and it may even have a negative impact on revenues. This minimal cost impact is because total HR department costs are generally less than one percent of all corporate expenditures.

The key here is that the best way to increase revenues is to focus your efforts on the business units, business processes and the jobs that have the most impact on increasing revenues. This might mean, for example, that HR would prioritize its recruiting so that key jobs receive the most resources and the best recruiters. It might also mean that bonus programs and reward systems that increase motivation and performance would be implemented in certain key business units—but not in others. It might even mean that HR would reverse the current practice of spending a great deal of time on problem employees and instead spend more time and resources on top performers.

Step 4—Shift to "fact-based decision-making" and use metrics to demonstrate the productivity, revenue and profit impact of HR

In the first three steps, the focus was on building partnerships; adopting the language of finance and understanding what key business elements have the most impact on revenue and profit. The final step in becoming a profit center is to focus internally on HR. It requires taking the data-based mindset that was used so successfully in finance, supply chain, CRM and Six Sigma, and beginning to use it as the foundation for an HR profit center. Using data-based decision-making means that it's no longer enough to believe that HR programs actually work. Instead, you must now learn to rely on hard metrics to demonstrate to the CEO and CFO's satisfaction that HR programs have a high ROI and positively impact employee productivity and revenue.

VPs of HR must begin the profit-center transformation process by implementing the critical success factors that were essential in the transformation of supply chain, CRM and quality assessment. If you put each of the five success factors in an HR context, it means that HR leadership must:

- Set the unflinching expectation of continuous improvement in productivity, revenue and profit for the entire corporation.
- Require every HR program and function to develop precise measurement systems to assess and continually improve performance.
- Develop reporting processes that distribute people performance metrics (results) to all, in order to spur others to improve.
- Add significant rewards and recognition for HR program success and resource reductions for failure.
- Develop processes for the retraining or elimination of individuals and programs that fail to produce up to these new stretch goals.

The VPs of HR must then begin making all resource allocation and program decisions based on quantifiable metrics and results. In practice, this means that every major HR program and function must begin to demonstrate that:

- It makes decisions based on facts and data.
- It uses technology and metrics to measure program performance and to continually improve.
- It has a positive return on investment.
- It prioritizes and focuses its efforts on business elements that have the most impact on revenues and profits.

After the VP of HR has ensured that each HR program and function is in compliance with the supply-chain inspired, data-based decision-making/metric model, the final step is to develop a business case or reporting mechanism to ensure that the quantified business impacts of HR programs are understood and accepted by senior management.

Most HR professionals go about proving quantifiable impact in the wrong way, so in the following section I will demonstrate in several examples how other HR departments have effectively demonstrated that they are a profit center.

> *Because corporate objectives are the primary corporate measures of strategic business success ... they should also be the factors that HR tries to impact.*

HR DEMONSTRATES ITS IMPACT ON PROFITS

If you ask any senior executive or business analyst how you measure the effectiveness of the corporation, he or she invariably will say either *corporate profit* or *stock price*. Whether HR likes it or not, stock price and profit are what matters. Since it's relatively difficult for HR to impact a company stock price, let's look at the remaining factor that can have the most impact on productivity and revenue. If HR wants to make the transition into a profit center, it must be able to demonstrate the impact of programs and efforts on a company's *profit*.

DEFINITION

Profit is the difference between a corporation's costs and its revenues.

HR can increase profit either by reducing the costs of labor or increasing its output. The following example demonstrates how to measure that a new HR program both decreased costs and increased output so that the net impact on corporate profits was over $2 million.

BEST PRACTICES: HOW HR CAN INCREASE REVENUE AND PROFITS

HR professionals constantly struggle with proving the business impact of what they do. Yet this example illustrates how a single

HR program can achieve nearly 30 different business impacts. It's a simple example: customer service representatives now receive e-learning rather than the traditional classroom training. These aren't highly paid or sophisticated positions, but that doesn't prohibit a business impact exceeding millions of dollars. Although this particular example focuses on training, similar business impacts occur after the implementation of other effective HR programs.

This example assumes that 100 newly hired customer service reps were trained using a new e-learning program. Initial program costs are $250,000. The CFO expects at least a 300 percent return on investment ($1 million in revenue enhancements or cost savings) over the existing fly-in customer service training program.

Initial program metrics were determined jointly between the training department and the CFO's office. The results illustrated here occurred in the one-year period after the e-learning training occurred. A small control group of customer service reps were trained in the traditional manner in order to contrast their performance with that of the e-learning trained group.

Business, productivity and profit impacts of an e-learning program

(NTE = newly trained employees)

- **Output**—Newly trained employees (NTEs) produce 12 percent more output (number and quality of calls) than workers trained in the previous program. This means that these NTEs can handle 12 percent more customer service calls per hour (at acceptable rate of quality). (Since the average customer service rep produces $100,000 in output per year, then a 12-percent increase for each of the 100 new trainees would equal $1.2 million in increased productivity.)
- **Error rate**—Newly trained employees have a 15-percent lower error rate than other Customer Service (CS) employees. Fewer mistakes mean that less work must be redone and that fewer customers are unhappy as a result of these errors. In fields such as medicine and scientific products where the dollar cost of each error can be in the millions, improving error rates is even more essential for business success. (Estimated sales that were not lost due to the lower error rate equal $231,000.)
- **Customer satisfaction**—NTEs have 35 percent higher customer satisfaction scores than the control group. The CRM director

has determined that every percentage point change in customer satisfaction means a 1/10 of a percent increase in sales by return customers. Satisfied customers are also likely to spread the positive word about the firm, and dissatisfied customers are likely to spread their negative experiences. Both are likely to impact future and return sales. (Estimated sales increase equals $2 million.)

- **Reaching minimum productivity levels**—Once starting their job, NTEs reach their minimum output faster. It normally takes customer service reps four weeks to reach the minimum acceptable level of productivity (20 calls per day), while the NTEs reach their minimum productivity in just two weeks, resulting in a 50 percent improvement in ramp-up time. Paying individuals their full salary when they produce below the acceptable standard is expensive. In addition, if the employee has direct customer contact, it is likely that slow time to productivity will also result in inferior service to customers. (Estimated productivity increase as a result of the two-week savings $20,000.)

- **Using lower-cost employees**—The e-learning system is so effective that it works for less skilled and less educated workers. We can now hire high school grads for customer service positions instead of college grads. As a result, we can pay 10 percent less, while getting the same or better results. (Estimated salary savings equals $600,000 per year.)

- **Retention**—NTEs stay 12 percent longer on the job (11 months vs. 10 months). This increased retention rate means not only do we need to hire fewer replacements but that we can also take advantage of the increased knowledge and productivity that come with extended on-the-job experience. (Estimated productivity increase is $20,000.)

- **New positions eliminated**—The NTEs' output increases as a result of the training means that 5 percent of the proposed new positions can be eliminated (at $60k each). This reduces both recruiting costs and salary costs. (Estimated savings of $300,000.)

- **Supervisor's time**—NTEs are more independent and competent as a result of the training. As a result, they require 5 percent less of their supervisor's time. This frees up managers to do more strategic things. (Estimated savings $5,000.)

- **Training time**—The e-learning system trains employees three days faster (training is completed in two days vs. five under the old system). This means that where in the past, replacement workers had to be hired to fill in for five days, now replacements are only needed for two days. (Estimated savings for the cost of temps, $10,000.)

- **Longer periods before retraining**—Because the new e-learning system is more effective, NTEs retain the information they were taught significantly longer. In addition "refresher" courses are available online. As result, employees need to be re-trained only once a year (vs. twice a year previously). (Estimated savings of eliminating an entire training module $100,000.)

- **Sick leave usage**—NTEs have 10 percent lower sick usage and, as a result, fill-in temps were not needed for those days. If employees are more productive and competent as a result of the training, they are more likely to come to work. (Estimated savings for temporary employees $15,000.)

- **Decreased absenteeism**—NTEs have a 5-percent lower absenteeism rate (unrelated to sick leave usage). If employees are more productive and competent, as a result of the training, they are less likely to skip work. (Estimated savings in fill-in temps ($6,000.)

- **Decreased tardiness**—NTEs have 5 percent lower rate of tardiness. Increased knowledge leads to improved results, which excites workers and makes it more likely that they will come to work on time. (Estimated savings for reduced service levels $9,000.)

- **Increased capability**—NTEs offers new competencies and skills in the important area of complaint handling. These increased skills means that the company has 34 percent fewer product returns. Each product return costs $1000. (Estimated savings $33,000.)

- **Customer retention**—The NTEs develop a loyal customer following. As a result, they have a customer retention/repeat sales rate that is 10 percent higher than customer service reps with the traditional training. (Estimated increase in sales $1.2 million).

- **Global capability**—Because the new *e-learning* system includes a language translator, customer service training can occur in any language, anywhere, and at any time. This means the company can eliminate the three different international training programs it used to have to offer in Europe, Asia and South America. (Estimated savings $200,000.)

- **Reduced travel**—The *e*-learning system trains anywhere, so no travel costs or travel time are incurred (formerly 30 percent of the trainees had to fly in for the training). (Estimated travel costs and time savings $125,000.)

- **Lower program costs**—Because the NTEs' training system is electronic and remote, out of pocket training costs for each session are reduced by $5,000.

- **Increase skills**—NTEs have new skills as a result of the new e-training. This means that these "level one" customer service reps can do 20 percent of the tasks formerly done by the more expensive "level two" senior customer service reps. Having the work done by cheaper employees means that we can reduce senior customer service rep headcount by one and replace that position with a level one rep. (Estimated cost savings $20,000.)

- **The need for immediate retraining**—The NTEs failure rate *during* training is 50 percent lower than under the old training program. As a result, fewer customer service reps need immediate re-training. (Estimated cost savings $4000.)

- **The need for later retraining**—The NTE's *on the job* failure rate after training is completed is 25 percent lower than the traditionally trained reps. As a result, fewer employees need to take a refresher course. (Estimated savings $17,000.)

- **A lower percentage are fired**—Traditionally, 10 percent of all newly hired customer service reps were fired before the end of their first year. NTEs are fired at a 50 percent lower rate (5 percent vs. 10 percent), so the net result is that we get increased performance and five fewer new hires need to be brought on board. Potential legal costs savings related to the firings were not estimated. (Estimated savings $75,000.)

- **Expanded service offerings**—Because of our new training, we have increased customer service capabilities that in the past were limiting the expansion of our firm's product offerings by 3 percent. The revenues generated by those services increases our profit by 6 percent. (Estimated profit increase $300,000.)

- **e-learning improves diversity**—The e-learning system works better (than the previous system) for diverse employees. The dropout rate of diverse employees from training used to be 25 percent; now it's down to 10 percent. The net result is 22 percent more diverse customer service reps on the job. Because data indicates that diverse employees (because they mirror the characteristics of our customers) are more adept at handling questions and returns from diverse customers, customer returns from diverse customers are down 23 percent, and customer satisfaction among diverse customers is up 37 percent. (Estimated savings and increased sales $225,000).

- **Continuous learning component**—The new e-learning system has a self-improvement or auto redesign feature that ensures that the program learns from its errors and improves at a rate of at least 10 percent per year. (Estimated impact $500,000.)
- **Ease in recruiting**—The *e*-learning system is so exciting that our employees brag about it and their jobs to their colleagues and friends. This improved image allows us to attract better qualified candidates and reduce recruiting costs. (Estimated savings $15,000 per year.)
- **Ethics and deceit**—The new learning program reinforces the economic value of strong ethical and legal behavior and as a result, there are 1 percent fewer ethical violations and complaints. (No economic value was put on this factor.)
- **Reduced generalist time**—HR generalists in each business unit had to spend an average of five hours per week on retraining the reps. However, as a result of the e-learning system, they can now spend that time spent on other HR issues. (No economic value was placed on this factor.)
- **Branding**—Because of its strong results and innovative program features, the e-learning program was written up in a customer service magazine. This public exposure helps to build our external image, while simultaneously increasing employee referrals. (No economic value was placed on this factor.)

The preceding example demonstrates numerous ways in which a relatively simple program costing $250,000 can have a positive impact on sales, productivity and profits in the millions. HR can decrease the possibility that the credibility of these calculations will be questioned by working with the CFO's office prior to the initiation of the training program. Once finance professionals agree on the way that the data is collected and that the ratios are calculated, it is relatively smooth sailing for HR.

The previous example demonstrated how a single HR program could have a multimillion-dollar impact on productivity and profits. The next section provides a series of examples of how relatively common programs in each of the HR functions can increase productivity and generate profit.

Recruiting impact

Demonstrate that newly hired workers produce more than the average worker (*i.e.,* one already on staff) by directly comparing their productivity in jobs where output is easily measurable.

- For example, demonstrate that the sales people you hire under your recruiting system produce average sales significantly higher than your current employees.
- Next, calculate the dollar differential in output between the new hires and the average existing employee.
- Next multiply that dollar differential amount by the number of new hires, to show the overall revenue impact that new hires have.
- Run a pilot employee referral program in one isolated division and demonstrate the decreased costs and increased quality of hires that result from the pilot program.

Compensation impact

Show that giving a worker a 10 percent raise increases his or her productivity by more than 10 percent.

- Provide evidence that, as the percentage of your employees' pay that is tied to performance increases, so does their output and productivity.
- Demonstrate a correlation between high pay and high productivity. Show that highly paid workers produce more than the dollar value of their wage differential (between them and the average paid worker).
- Calculate the ratio of the dollar value of employee output per dollar spent in compensation and benefits; compare the difference between this year and last year. Show that you are continually getting more for your compensation dollar and also demonstrate that your output per comp dollar is significantly higher than your competitors.

Employee relations impact

Demonstrate that problem employees and bottom performers increase their performance and become average or better performers within a year after Employee Relations works with them.

- Prove the correlation between highly rated (by employees) managers and productivity by showing the percentage increase in productivity that occurs when a highly rated manager replaces an average rated manager in a business unit (and vice versa).

- Next, show that your employee relations and training efforts significantly increase the rating of previously poorly rated managers.
- Demonstrate that your "bad manager identification program" identifies, fixes or removes bad managers months faster than the industry average.

Work-life balance impact

Demonstrate that as the percentage of workers who take advantage of work-life balance programs increases, so does the productivity in their department or division.

- Show that the retention rates of employees increase as work-life balance usage increases. Calculate the dollar impact of keeping key employees months longer.
- Ask new hires why they took the job and demonstrate that the top hires took the job primarily because of your work-life balance offerings.
- Ask top performers (three months after termination) why they left to demonstrate that a lack of work-life balance programs wasn't a significant factor in their decision to leave.

HRIS systems impact

Demonstrate a positive correlation between the increased availability of online HR answers and a decrease in the amount of wasted hours that employees and managers report that they spend *looking* for HR answers.

- Calculate the economic value of reducing those wasted hours.
- Demonstrate HRIS's effectiveness by showing the increased accuracy of HR answers that are provided on the firm's Internet site, as compared to the answers received from (the significantly more expensive) HR generalists.

Training impact

Contrast the difference in sales between those with increased training and the sales people without the additional training. Demonstrate that there is a high correlation or connection between the number of hours a worker receives in training and their productivity.

- Split the sales team and provide one half of the sales team with increased sales training. Do nothing different with the other half.
- Show that lower training hours correlate with increased error rates, accidents and lower product quality. Calculate the costs of errors and accidents to prove the business impact.
- Assess worker performance before training and then show that worker productivity increases immediately after they receive training.

Other HR success stories

"HR provided proven sales competency training. It had a positive ROI impact with an increase in sales by 11 percent, compared to last year."

"Our instant job analysis system found 67 work redundancies that were eliminated through job re-design. Now it costs 27 cents less to produce each product at the same level of quality."

"Our 'It's OK to be a Follower' in certain situations training program increased team decision-making quality by 15 percent and the speed of decision-making by 26 percent. Product time-to-market has been reduced by 5 percent in those teams that went through the training program, resulting in a 7 percent increase in our gross margin rate (every 1 percent change equals a 7 million dollar increase in profit)."

"Our new job simulation selection device is resulting in a 57 percent increase in the day of hire competency and a 38 percent increase in productivity for this year's new C++ programmer hires compared to last year's new hires (where productivity is measured by the total dollar value increase in outputs divided by the dollars spent on people costs)."

"HR analyzed overtime usage patterns and recommended a solution that allowed us to hire temps for peak periods. Total compensation costs were reduced by 4 percent with a surprise 6 percent increase in customer satisfaction as a result of having less fatigued agents."

Demonstrating the business impact of the generalist

Almost every HR department has generalists spread throughout its business divisions. They work hard and are generally well liked, but they seldom can demonstrate the degree of their business impact. The following example, however, outlines how a generalist can impact profit and business results directly.

> The initial goal of the generalist for the first year was to build a relationship with the General Manager of the production division in order to identify the prime business issues and opportunities he faced. One of the HR generalists has been performing a SWOT analysis of their strengths, weaknesses, threats and opportunities for the last month (averaging 23.7 customer contact hours a week). During that time period, the generalist learned that the General Manager has, as one of his primary goals, maintaining the absolute highest product quality in order to give the firm a competitive advantage in production over its closest competitors.

> The next objectives of the generalist were to establish trust and credibility with the managers in the production department and to demonstrate how HR could impact product quality. Although the production GM rated HR the most trusted and most competent of all staff functions in an all-staff function "contribution to productivity" 360-degree survey, the ranking merely provides a good indication of trust; it still doesn't provide evidence of business impact.

> **Identifying the real problem.** As a result of this high level of confidence and trust in the generalist, the GM and the generalist have been able to talk openly and work with the production team to identify their real production quality problems. The generalist has been poring over production charts and Six Sigma results.

> Her conclusion is that the surface symptom of the department problem is the 13 percent "reject rate" of products on the assembly line. Each error cost the firm $3,457 in labor costs and wasted materials. The GM was aware of the high

reject rate but had assumed the problem was related to the quality of the raw material being used in the product.

Effective generalists don't just find problems; they go further and identify the root causes of them. In this case, the generalist went beyond the output data. She looked further and found that the company-wide reject rate was 13 percent, but when she examined the problem more closely, she found that the reject rate for one shift was 21 percent while it was only 4 percent on the other shift. While the *average* reject rate was 13 percent, it was clear the problem was occurring only during the night shift. She further concluded that it couldn't be faulty materials causing the problem because both shifts used the same materials.

After further research, she found the root cause of the high reject rate was actually low skill levels during the night shift at the engineer level 1 and 2 positions on the subassembly table. She further found that four engineers (Boxer, Tanaka, Burnett and Ng) worked on all but 6 percent of the rejected items and were responsible for the high reject rate.

The generalist also completed an analysis in order to identify any possible unintended consequences (additional problems and costs) that might be occurring as a result of the high failure rate. The generalist discovered that the total economic losses are actually triple the production department's $3457 estimate. Production delays (as a result of the 26 percent reject rate) were causing significantly increased costs in the shipping department. Because products were not coming off the assembly line on time, the shipping department had to utilize very expensive overnight shipping services to get the product to the customer. The result was tripling of shipping expenses ($33,000 extra costs).

Even with the use of overnight air freight, the generalist discovered that the product on-time delivery rate was falling from 99 percent to 89 percent as a result of the production problems. By looking through customer correspondence the generalist found that the company was losing 3 percent of its customers as a result of this delayed delivery. The generalist estimated that the dollar cost of unnecessarily losing 3 percent of its customers was $961,000.

The total cost of this problem as calculated by the GM was $3457; however, the generalist's more accurate estimate revealed the *real* cost of the problems caused by these four employees was nearly $1 million.

Implementing a solution. The generalist reviewed her analysis with the General Manager and both agreed that the poor workers were the problem. The GM's initial reaction was to "fire their butts," but the generalist convinced him to let her do some additional analysis. After looking over performance records, interviewing the employees—and their supervisor—the generalist concluded that the four employees were all hired after the yearly quality control training session was held. Their failure was a result of lack of quality control training.

The generalist also noted that the production manager (Short) had been on leave during the last training class and that he was unaware that the four individuals didn't participate. Consequently, the generalist recommended that the reporting procedure be changed so that no more engineers were allowed to miss training. Rather than firing the four employees and incurring the expense of replacing them, the generalist determined—and the GM concurred—that training just might solve the problem.

HR recently had developed an on-line *e*-training course relating to quality control. In fact, course participants had a 94.5 percent improvement in their quality control error rate over the last 18 months. Another division used the new e-training program on production engineers (level 1 and 2) positions, and the result was amazing. Since the course was already developed, the only expense was replacement workers during the time that the four engineers took the e-training class

($1,637). The generalist estimated a 6-week payback period, a 98 percent likelihood of success and a $3,897-to-1 ROI.

It was further recommended by the generalist that production monitor the error-rate problem for two additional months until it could be sure the training worked. The targets were an error rate of 4 percent, the elimination of the extra shipping costs, and late product deliveries had to fall from 10 percent to 1 percent. The production department also included its learnings about the value of the training in the company-wide electronic newsletter "Things that work," so that others could profit as well.

The total estimated increase in revenue by the production department over the next year was $989,000 and, with the company's 10 percent profit rate, that is almost $99,000 of additional profit. Not bad for a month's work by the HR generalist.

Other production managers at five additional plants are likely to take advantage the production department's learning by also reviewing their training participation. This additional training (and the subsequent reduction in lost customers) should result in additional corporate revenue of $3.25 million. The CEO sent an e-mail to the HR VP thanking HR for once again being ... a business leader!

EXTERNALLY FOCUSED HR MONITORS THE BUSINESS ENVIRONMENT

It's hard to miss the fact that the business world is a fast changing place. And with the advent of new technologies and globalization, it is no longer reasonable to assume that the world of business will remain unchanged for any measurable period of time. Successful executives understand the cycle and as a result, they vary their management approach and strategy as the business environment changes.

For example, when the economy is growing rapidly, CEOs shift their management approach to emphasize innovation, growth, speed and time to market. During tough times executives resort to cost-cutting, layoffs and retrenchment. In direct contrast, HR all too often has but a single approach and strategy that it sticks to regardless of the state of the economy and the business environment. As part of its external focus, HR needs to monitor changes in the external environment and then shift its strategy accordingly as the external environment dictates.

Perhaps an example will illustrate the point. During times of high unemployment, most turnover rates drop to near zero. No matter how poorly you treat workers they tend to stay due to their insecurities. As the unemployment rate falls over time employees become more and more willing to leave a job when they are frustrated.

An HR department could ignore the unemployment rate and operate the same retention programs and policies both in good and bad times. However, if HR wanted to be more efficient it would shift that approach. During times when jobs are tough to get HR would spend less time and money on retention because those programs just aren't as necessary during tough times. The same might be true for recruiting: during tough times the same ads that work so well during good times might get you an avalanche of applications that would be impossible to handle during an economic downturn. The key lesson to be learned is that HR must shift its strategy based on environmental conditions.

PROVIDE DIFFERENT HR SERVICES DURING DIFFERENT BUSINESS PHASES

The same may be true for business units within the corporation that are in different phases of business maturity (emerging, growing, mature or declining). For example, a start-up concept business might have few rules and lots of out-of-the-box thinkers, while a mature commodity business might require more accountant types and fewer dreamers in order to be successful. Shifting HR's approach to the business may also be required when other factors change, such as the size of the business, the style of leadership, the product, and the region where the business operates.

The key for HR leaders is that one size can't fit all in a fast-changing world, so HR must shift its strategy as environmental factors change. Instead of a single solution, HR must be prepared to provide a range of solutions just as a company must do when its customers face changing business conditions.

WHAT ARE THE ENVIRONMENTAL CHANGES THAT STRATEGIC HR MUST TRACK?

There are numerous business and environmental factors that, when they change, require HR to shift its approach to solving people problems. When some of these factors change, they impact the effectiveness of HR tools; when others change, they change the demand or need for some HR tools or services.

Some of the factors that HR should track include:

- External business and economic factors
  - The unemployment rate
  - The availability of work visas
  - Conflict and terrorism
  - Hiring growth and layoffs among competitors
  - A change in the demographics and diversity of the workforce
  - Union organizing successes in the industry
  - New technologies
  - Customer demands
  - New product development
  - Turnover rates at competitors
- Factors within the company
  - Profit margins
  - Changes in the company culture
  - Changes in sales
  - Customer satisfaction
  - Resignations and retirements of senior leaders and individuals in key positions
  - New product development
  - Areas with poor productivity and high error rates

HR should coordinate its external environmental monitoring with other business functions—like strategic planning and sales forecasting—in order to triangulate or double-check the information that it receives.

The next section highlights the third essential element in strategic HR—utilizing the tools of a performance culture. A performance culture is a way of doing business throughout the organization that emphasizes results over effort. A performance culture utilizes HR tools like differentiation in rewards, metrics, and competition to encourage performance.

CHAPTER SEVEN

HR USES PERFORMANCE CULTURE TOOLS

OBJECTIVE

The third essential element in a strategic HR department is to utilize performance culture tools in order to improve company performance. To have a broader strategic impact, whenever it can, HR should integrate performance culture tools into traditional HR processes.

KEY POINTS

◊ This chapter outlines what a performance culture is and how HR can implement some or all of a performance culture in order to increase the performance of the firm.

◊ Although this is a difficult strategic element to define and administer, it has one of the greatest impacts of all the strategic HR elements.

◊ Even though the entire performance culture strategy will be outlined in this chapter, HR executives need only select and implement the performance culture (PC) tools that best fit the organization's situation.

WHAT EXACTLY IS A PERFORMANCE CULTURE?

A unique element of the performance culture approach (also known as a performance-driven organization) is that it relies almost exclusively on people-management tools to produce its results. Because it focuses on tools that change behavior, it puts very little emphasis on technology, capital or even strategy, and instead places a significant emphasis on human resource management processes.

> *If your goal is to become more strategic in HR, there is little that you can do that will have a broader impact on your organization's bottom-line performance than utilizing the performance culture approach.*

Although an HR department need not implement an entire performance culture in order to be strategic, it is helpful to understand the philosophy behind a performance culture, even if you are only using some of its tools. Because performance culture tools are so effective, they can have a significant impact on corporate performance even if they are used piecemeal. Utilizing some performance culture tools is a less traumatic solution than implementing an entire performance culture, but it still provides many of the positive impacts on workforce performance.

Every organization has a corporate culture that evolves over the years, but a performance culture differs significantly from most corporate cultures. A performance culture is not so much a "culture" in the same sense as most cultures. Rather than being a series of values or vaguely worded statements, a performance culture is an integrated set of management processes focused on extraordinary performance. It's important to note that it is the *systems, processes and tools* that produce the extraordinary results, not any set of hard-to-define cultural values and beliefs.

The very best firms achieve extraordinary results by organizing and managing their people using this "performance culture" strategy. A performance culture utilizes metrics, incentives, performance management, "paranoia," and a meritocracy, first to increase employee productivity, but also to increase human innovation and risk-taking in the workplace.

Most firms are constantly looking for the "Holy Grail" of how to become and maintain the number one position in their industry. CEOs favor the performance culture approach because it is the most aggressive approach to increasing organizational performance. If you want to become number one in your industry and maintain that status, the most effective approach is to have an integrated management system that ensures that every person, process and organization has a single laser focus of extraordinary performance. And that's what a performance culture is, a coordinated strategic effort to focus everything and everyone on results. If you want to dominate your industry, this is the approach to take.

DEFINITION

A performance culture is unlike most corporate cultures in that it is a consciously planned culture that requires all to have a shared vision (with a focus on performance). Rather than evolving over time like most corporate cultures, it is a deliberate effort by senior management and HR to ensure that every process, system and individual in the organization focuses on results and that anything that runs counter to performance (effort, seniority, time spent, good intentions, etc.) must be redesigned or eliminated. It's not a single "program" but instead a total culture that *overemphasizes* performance in every aspect.

The goals of a performance culture are simple and straightforward. They include:

- **Dominance**—More than just becoming the number one performing firm, the goal is to become the "category killer" firm in the industry (for example, Wal-Mart or Microsoft)
- **Extraordinary results**—Producing results that don't just beat the number two firm but that are so clearly superior as to be labeled "extraordinary"
- **Continuous improvement**—Continually improving at such a rate that competitors can't keep up

As you can see, these are extraordinary goals that are not easily obtained. It takes more than effort and good intentions to dominate the competitors. A performance culture operates much in the same way that the free-market system operates in a capitalist environment. It's highly competitive; results, rather than status or effort, garner the rewards.

A SHARED VISION

The first element of a performance culture is a shared vision that is held by the managers and the employees of the organization. That shared vision has as its central theme the high expectation of being first or second in every major category in their industry. Some firms are happy to do well while others, like GE, demand "championships" as the only expectation.

Most organizations "talk" about performance, but a true performance culture converts that talk into a series of integrated processes and systems where producing exceptional results is the norm and maintaining the status quo is unacceptable. When a performance culture is in place, employees and potential applicants can easily see that performance and continuous improvement are the primary goals. *Everyone* knows that those that meet their goals get significant rewards and recognition and those that do not get little or no rewards.

HOW DO PERFORMANCE CULTURES DIFFER FROM STANDARD BUSINESS CULTURES?

A performance culture differs from other traditional business cultures in that everything in a performance culture is focused on results and performance. In contrast, most traditional company cultures focus on softer things like values, loyalty, equity, and trying your best.

While no company says in public that it doesn't care about performance, the fact remains that most organizations reward loyalty and years of service as much as they do performance. Many companies allow bureaucracies and favoritism to fester. The net result is that individuals often play politics and build fiefdoms.

A performance culture strives to develop processes that fight bureaucratic tendencies and favoritism by building a meritocracy, which is an organization where merit (output and results) is the primary driver of all recognition and rewards. GE, for example, is a company that has one of its primary values to be a meritocracy.

In a performance culture, people, processes, and products are not allowed to remain static. They continually improve because the constant emphasis on metrics and rewards puts pressure on everyone and everything to continually perform and improve. In fact, many consider performance cultures to be "high pressure" in every aspect.

COMMON CHARACTERISTICS OF A PERFORMANCE CULTURE

Most performance cultures share common features. They can be categorized into four basic areas:

- **Rewards**—large differentiated rewards for performance
- **Metrics**—the extensive use of metrics for accountability
- **High expectations**—Industry domination and continuous improvement expectations
- **Rapid learning**—Continuous learning and information sharing

PRINCIPLES OF A PERFORMANCE CULTURE

Not every performance culture is exactly the same; still, most share similar principles or rules by which they live. The following is a list of performance culture guidelines that may be useful even to those not trying to build one within their organization. The basics of a performance culture include:

- **Not everyone can "fit"**—You must be very careful whom you recruit because not everyone can or wants to work in an organization that improves by double digits each year. Those that don't share the performance vision or otherwise don't "fit" must be dropped very rapidly. A fast-moving train is only as fast as its slowest car. There is no assumption that a large percentage of those that work in a performance culture will retire there.
- **Shared vision**—Mixed messages about performance are not acceptable. *All* communications must be clear and precise and carry the message that "average" performance is never the goal and a "show up" culture will never be tolerated. Top performance is the norm, and any conflicting communications or programs must be changed.
- **Outrageous expectations**—The goal of a performance culture is to win *every* time in *every* area where it competes. The goal is often stated as "we should be number one or number two, or get out of the business." In order to reach that goal, every manager must raise expectations continually because the setting and meeting of outrageous goals and stretch assignments is the norm. Performance cultures expect most processes to improve at a rate of between 10 and 20 percent each year.
- **An emphasis on rewards**—Performance must be the primary factor that drives job assignments, promotions, monetary rewards,

praise, and recognition. There can be no rewards for "showing up," trying, or putting in time. Significant rewards and recognition are available for producing current results only. Not only are the rewards available for performance large in relative dollar terms, but there is a major emphasis on differentiating the reward amounts between top and average performers.

- **Individual accountability**—Because the rewards are so large and the penalties are so high, performance cultures make a concerted effort to designate individual responsibility and accountability. Even though performance cultures utilize teams, individual responsibilities and accountabilities are always designated.

- **Confronting problems**—In most organizations "problems" are hidden because it is common to "place blame" on individuals associated with problems (even if it's not their fault). In a performance culture, problem-hiding must be eliminated because the longer that the problem remains hidden, the greater the negative impact and the longer it is before a solution can be found. A performance culture "constructively confronts" all problems rapidly and in a non-personal manner. It is every individual's responsibility to identify, confront and solve problems.

- **Paranoia and sense of urgency**—An assumption of "paranoia" that the competitors might be catching up permeates a performance culture, even though there is no evidence to demonstrate that they actually are. Paranoia means that every process, product, and individual must be improving continually at a rate that allows the organization to maintain a significant lead over its competitors. By assuming that there are "hidden enemies," everyone is forced to maintain competitive intensity and a high sense of urgency. Continuous improvement and becoming the best (or maintaining the lead) in the industry and every functional and process area is the goal for *every individual, process and product*.

- **Differentiation**—Resources are allocated unequally based on corporate priorities. All business units, jobs, managers and employees receive different treatment based on their contribution to the corporation. Equal treatment is *not* a goal and the gap in the amount of rewards, resources, and time allocated between high priority and low priority items is significant. Forced ranking is a common tool, because it forces managers to differentiate.

- **Releasing bottom performers rapidly**—The strong emphasis on performance requires the quick release of those that fail to meet the accepted performance standards. It is not unusual for a performance culture to release 5 to 10 percent of its workforce every year.
- **Competitive "market forces"**—Internal competition is used to develop individuals and to assess their capabilities. Results are openly distributed to spur competition.
- **Talent**—Developing talent is expected and rewarded; hoarding of talent is punished.
- **A hatred for bureaucracy**—There is an inherent dislike for unnecessary rules and approvals. Individuals are treated as mature adults and allowed to make decisions.
- **Change initiatives**—Because everyone is responsible for change, instead of coming from the top, change initiatives are continuous, and they can be initiated from any direction (top down, bottom up and horizontal).
- **Accepting criticism**—Performance cultures know that they are different and, as a result, they expect criticism. However in contrast, excuses like "we're different" and "that will not fit our culture" are not acceptable because the organization still must learn from the very best in the world.
- **A focus on top performers**—In a performance culture all employees are not treated the same. All employees cannot or do not make an equal contribution to the corporation success. As a result, top performers, individuals with key skills, or those that are in key jobs, get first priority with corporate resources. Investing more in individuals with a high ROI just makes good business sense.
- **A meritocracy**—Rewards, promotions, and resource allocations are based on quantifiable results rather than influence, rank or seniority. It's critical that decisions that are made about people are based on objective information and hard performance results. The goal in a performance culture is to become a meritocracy. In a meritocracy everything is focused on results, and it is this focus on results that (1) attracts the very best, and (2) takes away all doubt about what is important and what is not within a company. This combination of the laser focus and a workforce full of top performers all but guarantees success for any company!

Whether your HR department is trying to lead a performance culture initiative or is just trying to learn some lessons from a performance culture, this list of principles can help in improving the focus of your organization toward performance and results.

A PERFORMANCE CULTURE USES COMPETITION TO CONTINUALLY IMPROVE

Market-driven forces and competition generate pressure. External market forces use this pressure to drive out overpriced products and bad ideas. Market forces and competition lead to improved efficiency in external markets, and they have the same impact internally. In fact, in a performance culture, it is that very pressure that drives continuous improvement and competitive advantage. A performance culture uses competition and these market-driven forces to generate pressure that will not allow people, processes and products to remain static. Significant rewards for success and intolerance for failure are major pressure-building forces within a performance culture.

Many consider the "high pressure" aspect of a performance culture as a weakness, and it is certainly true that competition can cause anxiety. In order to avoid excess pressure, HR must develop processes that assess the pressure to ensure it remains within reasonable boundaries. It should also provide development and training activities that improve the "carrying capacity" of the employees in the organization so that they can better handle more pressure. And finally, HR needs to develop "release valves" or tools that can rapidly relieve pressure before it can get out of hand.

It's always important to remember that in business, as in sports, you can change and develop an individual's ability to manage the level of pressure. In fact, in sports, some individuals actually perform better under pressure. The key in a performance culture is to continually utilize competitive forces to put pressure on individuals and teams to perform.

There are two basic reasons behind generating this pressure on employees. The first is that the pressure produces great results, and the second is that if we provide employees with the appropriate training, metrics, rewards and tools, the employees will learn how to cope with the extra pressure.

BEST PRACTICE

Perhaps an example will illustrate the aggressiveness of a performance culture. Costco is a retail chain famous for delivering quality at a cutthroat price. At my local branch, the manager has demonstrated his or her high expectations of employees by prominently posting on the wall, for both customers and employees to see, the top three as well as the bottom three performers, by name, in each key customer service category. Competition, accountability and recognition are key elements in a performance culture, and by publicly acknowledging both the top and bottom performers, Costco sends a clear message that is impossible to "hide" if you are a bad performer.

HR'S ROLE IN BUILDING A PERFORMANCE CULTURE

If HR decides to implement the entire PC (performance culture) strategy, it must utilize PC tools throughout the organization, but the performance culture "mind-set" needs to be "owned" by the organization. There are no performance cultures where the executive team doesn't take ownership of the building and maintaining of a performance culture. The reason that they are so involved is because a PC requires a company-wide mindset.

However, just because building a performance culture is owned by senior management doesn't mean that HR doesn't have an important and strategic role in developing a performance culture or that the firms that don't want a complete PC can't adopt some of its tools. If you look at the characteristics of a performance culture it's easy to see the majority of them relate to people management, which is of course HR's area of expertise. A great deal of building a performance culture revolves around these people management areas.

If your organization has already begun the process of becoming a performance culture, a senior HR manager needs to get involved and take a leadership role in redesigning all of the HR processes that impact a performance culture, especially those that relate to rewards and performance measurement. If your organization has yet to undertake a performance management effort, HR leadership should seize the opportunity to propose it to senior management. But in either case and whether you are invited or not, it's important to recognize that HR has a significant role in developing and maintaining a performance culture because so many of the characteristics of the culture relate to people management.

> *A performance culture is a great recruiting and retention tool for top performers because top performers demand that you keep score. Only bottom performers think that keeping score "spoils the fun" of the game.*

ASSESSING IF YOU HAVE A PERFORMANCE CULTURE

The first step in determining whether your company currently has a performance culture is to compare it to well-known performance cultures. Although there is no natural ranking of performance cultures, most experts would agree that the following organizations put an extraordinary emphasis on producing results:

- General Electric
- Intel
- Nucor
- The Navy Seals
- The New York Yankees
- Dell
- Wal-Mart
- Microsoft
- Oracle

CHECKLIST: ASSESSING WHETHER HR UTILIZES A PERFORMANCE CULTURE APPROACH

An organization does not need to be a "complete" performance culture in order to be successful. Clearly, firms like GE and Intel are recognized by most experts as having more of the characteristics that make up a performance culture than your local Department of Motor Vehicles (DMV)! If you don't currently have elements of a performance culture within your HR department, this quick assessment will show you how you compare.

The previous section outlined some of the basic PC guidelines for the entire firm, while these are focused on the philosophy and workings of the HR department. A list of PC tools for HR to consider using, is found at the end of this section even if it is not considering a comprehensive performance culture implementation.

- **A coordinated effort**—A purposely aggressive and coordinated HR-wide effort to build and maintain a performance culture. Everything from the top to bottom in HR supports and reinforces the laser focus on results. Functional silos and empire building are punished.

- **Focus on results**—A lopsided focus on performance and producing results. Every individual, HR process and system reinforces the importance of producing results.

- **Metrics and accountability**—The extensive use of metrics by HR for the continuous measurement of performance. HR emphasizes the quantitative measurement of results and holds individuals responsible for producing them. Individual responsibility and accountability is the norm. These results are available to all in order to encourage internal competition and "embarrassment" for those that fail to perform.

- **Prioritization**—Equity and spreading resources evenly isn't the goal in HR. Instead, people, jobs, business units, and programs are prioritized depending on their contribution to results.

- **Speed**—Speed is "the" competitive advantage, so excessive rules, approvals, and bureaucracy must be eliminated. HR uses speed because being first results in HR meeting its goals.

- **A magnet**—Top talent is attracted to other top performers like a bear is to honey. The goal of HR is to attract a few of the very best and use them as a magnet to attract other top performers from inside the firm—and from other leading HR departments. Once you get a few, attracting the others is not particularly difficult.

- **Rapid learning**—An emphasis on continuous but rapid learning, sharing of problems, and solutions. Staff are expected to be HR experts and to write and speak in their field.

- **Over-communication**—Open book management and extensive two-way communication is an everyday way of life in HR because a lack of information results in bad decisions that eventually reduce performance.

- **Image**—It is quite common for performance cultures to gain an incorrect external image as a "churn and burn" place where employees are overworked and, even though the rewards are great, there is a heavy burnout rate. As a result HR must manage its image and supplement any negative image within the firm with the fact that it offers extraordinary challenge, growth, and rewards—as well as hard work.

- **Fact-based decision-making**—There is a conscious effort in HR to ensure that decisions are made based on data and not based on emotion and position. HR provides data to managers so that they can also make fact-based decisions.

- **Competition everywhere**—There is a heavy reliance on competition between HR functions to spur extra effort. There is an internal competition for resources, ideas and talent. Because it's possible on occasion to overdo competition, HR also tracks and rewards cooperation and sharing.

- **Innovation is expected**—Because risk-taking is encouraged and even celebrated, a performance culture can expect every individual in HR continually to try new things and innovate. Innovation is *essential*; it is nearly impossible to dominate an industry without a steady flow of workable ideas.

- **Risk taking**—HR makes a conscious effort to encourage and even reward "intelligent" risk-taking. Individuals and teams are encouraged to take "calculated risks." There is also an emphasis on having a high failure rate because failure is an excellent "teacher" in most areas of HR. There is, however, an expectation of rapid learning after every failure.

- **Future focused**—Every HR system anticipates and forecasts so that we are not surprised by the future.

- **Punishment**—There is a conscious effort in HR to punish bad behavior. Individuals are treated as mature adults until they fail to act appropriately.

- **Fight bureaucracy**—HR has a constant theme to "hate" bureaucracy. There is also a conscious effort to eliminate non-performance reward factors such as seniority, loyalty, rank, and effort.

- **Compensation**—The compensation department ties pay to performance and differentiates top pay from the average.

- **Recruiting**—Measuring the quality of its hires helps the recruiting function improve overall workforce productivity.

- **Obvious**—Because it's not possible to keep a performance culture a secret, employees and managers quickly acknowledge that HR leads the firm in becoming a performance culture.

As I mentioned in the introduction, if HR doesn't adopt an entire performance culture, it still should implement as many PC tools and approaches as possible if it wants to become a strategic function.

INDICATIONS THAT A FIRM DOES NOT HAVE A PERFORMANCE CULTURE

Not every organization can be-or even wants to be-a performance culture. Most government organizations, no matter how hard they try, will never be performance cultures. Universities make no attempt to be performance cultures, and any organization that is heavily regulated or has a strong union will have great difficulty in developing a performance culture.

Moreover, some things that are common in standard business cultures would never occur in a true performance culture. Some of the activities and approaches that are inconsistent with a performance culture include:

- Building relationships first is essential for getting things done.
- Seniority or experience is a major part of all compensation or promotion decisions.
- A "meeting culture" exists where discussion is extended to avoid risks and accountability.
- Consensus decision-making occurs where everyone's "buy-in" ensures slow and risk-free decision-making. Votes replace decisions based on criteria and data.
- Everyone in the job gets the same pay (the differential in pay between a top and average performer might be zero, which is not uncommon in a union or government environment).
- 100 percent of an employee's pay is guaranteed; there is no incentive or at-risk compensation.
- Values are as important as whether you produce results.
- Internal employees are given the first choice in hiring.
- Performance bonuses are spread relatively evenly (like peanut butter) among all employees.
- You have a low involuntary turnover rate.
- You have a strong traditional culture that hasn't changed in years.
- Seniority is a criteria for assignments or promotions.
- You have a program that pays for competencies and knowledge over performance.
- You have a strong hierarchical structure.

- You are heavily unionized.
- You use performance appraisal systems that measure skills, behaviors and opinions but not actual output.

Performance culture tools that any HR department can implement

The previous sections highlighted the rules and characteristics of a performance culture. Now it's time to move to the implementation level and to highlight some PC tools.

The following is a list of common tools used by performance cultures. If you want to develop a comprehensive performance culture, the following is a toolkit that can be used to get you started. However, if you only wish to move in the direction of a performance culture, this list can also be helpful.

30 performance culture tools to consider

1. Forced rank employees. Managers seldom relish giving bad news and as a result, most year-end performance appraisals tend to be overwhelmingly positive. One solution to the problem is to require managers to "force rank" their employees. Forced ranking is a process used in almost every performance culture because it does exactly what a performance culture needs—it forces managers to differentiate between top performers and bottom performers.

It's often a difficult program to implement in nonperformance cultures because there is no shared mindset among employees and managers about the importance of differentiation. Much of the resistance to forced ranking, as well as most of the problems associated with it, can be reduced if managers are required to use objective criteria including actual production, sales or output figures.

2. Fire the bottom 5 percent. Another key characteristic of a performance culture is the periodic releasing or firing of bottom performers. Although it takes courage, any organization can take advantage of this strategy. The basic premise is that the truly bottom performers, the bottom 5 to 10 percent, are difficult and expensive to "fix."

Performance cultures track the percentage of bottom performers that later become top performers, but any organization can do the same. If the organization finds that the bottom performers seldom improve in a reasonable period of time, then management moves to the next step of releasing those employees.

The process generally starts with a forced ranking of employees from top to bottom, but standard performance appraisal scores can also be used. Bottom performers are generally given a time period in order to improve but if they fail to improve, the next step is termination. Many organizations pay the released workers an amount of money to leave in order to eliminate any potential legal conflicts, while others release them outright, after checking the performance documentation to ensure that it is sufficient to support their termination decision. Although many individuals—and HR—are reluctant to make hard firing decisions, many companies have found that releasing the bottom performers sends a message to all that performance really does matter.

3. Keep pay at risk. One of the key features of a performance culture is "pay for performance." While in the true performance culture everyone's pay might be at risk, basing pay on performance also can be effective in any culture. Consider offering pay for performance just for key jobs. Be sure to tie the increased pay to quantifiable outputs as opposed to subjective evaluations. Also consider involving the employees affected in determining the best way to measure performance.

4. Constructive confrontation. One of the strong points of a performance culture is that, rather than hiding or avoiding problems, it directly confronts them. Although Intel made the term "constructive confrontation" famous, any firm can benefit from such a process. Constructive confrontation is a process where "intellectual honesty" allows anyone to ask any question and to tell each other what they think without having to worry about the consequences. Constructive confrontation elements include:

- Individuals are given access to almost all information so they can ask "educated" questions
- Anyone can ask anybody any question
- Everyone looks for problems/opportunities
- Knowledge drives individuals to take control/responsibility
- No delay in action is tolerated
- Decisions are "fact-based," not emotional
- Confrontation is based on ideas and data, not personality
- The process dictates that there be no prolonged debate: Decide and then move on

5. Distribute metrics in order to change behavior. Many organizations "collect" metrics, but just collecting them minimizes the potential impact that metrics might have. Whether or not you work at a firm that has a performance culture, you are likely to find that keeping metrics a secret reduces their impact. If your goal is to really change behavior, you need to do more than send out a report on occasion.

One approach that is typical of most performance cultures but that can be used at any firm is to distribute summary metrics that are ranked from best to worst to all managers on a regular basis. By spreading the word with names and in a ranked fashion, you are making performance an open discussion item among your managers. Some of the advantages of distributing metrics include:

- Embarrassing the poor performers, or at least bringing it to their attention that they are lagging behind
- Recognizing the top performers by letting everyone know who they are and how well they've done
- Taking away "ignorance" as an excuse ("I thought everyone was in the same boat as me")
- Identifying the good performers, so that others can learn directly from them
- Showing all what the benchmark top performance level is, in order to raise expectations
- If the tools that the best (and worst performers) utilize are listed in the report alongside their results, you get as an added benefit that others can also know which tools "work" (and don't work) in your culture

In order to get the maximum impact, performance results should be listed by name and they should be ranked so all know at a glance where they stand. Also, list last year's and the best-in-the-industry data for comparison purposes.

6. Share "what works." In a performance culture, rapid learning and sharing is a key to success. Others can learn from cumulative experiences by adopting a "what works" process.

Managers are constantly striving for answers to their people problems. They read, hire consultants, benchmark and, through trial and error, they attempt to identify which tools are the most effective. Unfortunately, the volume of advice and reading material is so overwhelming that they have difficulty sorting through it. And when they do find an answer that seems to make sense they have no way of knowing whether it has a chance of working within the culture and the limitations of their firm. They often find, in fact, that all outside advice is of marginal use because it's hardly ever designed to fit their organization.

An effective way to identify which tools have the most chance of working is to identify the top performing people managers and find out "what works" and "what doesn't work" *for them* within the context of *this organization*. The process is a relatively simple one. It starts by regularly surveying managers about what people problems they face. After compiling a list of the most common problems the survey is given to top performing managers. These managers then list next to each problem the specific tools they have found to be effective and ineffective within the context of their firm. A comprehensive profile is then put together that lists the major problems and the most effective tools based on usage by the best managers.

This "what works" list is distributed to all managers along with a companion list that identifies, by name, which managers have effectively solved which problems, and which managers are currently facing each problem. The second list provides your managers with the names and e-mail addresses of the most effective problem-solvers so that they can contact the manager directly for advice.

By sharing "what works," "who's got the problem," and "who's got a solution," you give managers useful information about what works as well as direct contacts to understand solutions within the context of your firm. The effectiveness of this tool is further increased if managers are rewarded for sharing their best practices and giving advice to others.

7. Cultivate great managers. Managers play an important role in building a performance culture. Because most performance is measured and assessed by managers, they become a crucial element in ensuring that everyone has a laser focus on producing results. A performance culture requires managers to make tough decisions, including rewards and terminations. If managers fail to quantify performance or to use performance data to make people decisions, performance culture cannot succeed.

Unfortunately, many organizations do allow subjective performance appraisals to substitute for actual performance measuring or "counting." HR must ensure that managers are measured and rewarded for great people management. HR should also be willing to take the significant responsibility in ensuring that managers who fail to follow performance culture guidelines are immediately removed.

8. Prioritize the positions that have the most impact on "winning." In a performance culture, positions are prioritized based on the potential impact on a firm's success. Just like in sports, not all positions have an equal impact on team success. That is why a quarterback might average $5 million a year, while a kicker might average $200,000. HR has a long history of treating all positions the same, but that must change in a performance culture. HR needs to work with managers in order to identify the "key" positions that, when staffed with quality talent, have the most positive impact on revenue and profit. HR must redesign its processes and inform staff that these high-impact jobs receive priority in hiring, retention and incentives.

9. Measure and report performance results. Continuous measurements are essential in a performance culture because employees and managers tend to focus their efforts and energies on what to measure and reward. HR must develop a system of metrics for measuring the productivity of individual workers, teams and projects. HR should work with the CFO's office to develop these performance metrics. Once the metrics are determined, the results need to be ranked from best to worst and then distributed to all managers.

10. Recruit the very best in key positions. Recruiting top performers is important whether you have a performance culture or not. However, because a performance culture has such high expectations, it's important that the recruitment system has the capability of recruiting individuals that will thrive in a performance driven environment. Recruiters must focus their efforts on key jobs and business units where top talent will have the highest economic impact. Because this is a performance culture, it is also important to measure and reward recruiters and managers for their quality of hire.

11. Retain the very best in key positions. Retaining top performers, people with critical skills, and anyone in key positions is also essential if you want to meet the highest performance expectations. These key employees must be identified and an individualized plan must be developed to ensure that they are challenged and continually growing. Because almost every organization benchmarks against a performance culture, retaining top people when you're in the spotlight is even more difficult. And, as this is a performance culture, managers need to be measured and rewarded for retaining top talent.

12. Offers significant rewards and pay differentials. One of the key characteristics of performance culture is significant rewards and a differentiation in pay. It's important for compensation to overcome its tendency to allocate pay increases or bonuses relatively equally throughout the organization and instead learn to differentiate pay. To make a significant differentiation, it's important that top performers receive at least 25 percent more pay than average performers, for example. It's also important to tie *everyone's* pay to performance. In a true performance culture, at least 10 percent of the average employee's pay should be at risk, based on his or her performance and results.

13. Focus on top performers. Most HR departments indulge their natural tendency to spend time with the "squeaky wheel." In a performance culture, the exact opposite occurs: HR allocates resources and time *in advance* to ensure that top performers and individuals in key positions get a significant amount of HR consulting and coaching help. HR also must identify any barriers that restrict the performance of these top performers.

14. Release poor performers quickly. Because a performance culture fosters a competitive environment, there are significant consequences if an individual fails. In a performance culture, keeping non-performers can be a disaster as it sends a clear message that performance and results are not really that important. Even in a performance culture, however, most individuals who fail are given a second chance but everyone understands that those who fail a second time are likely to be terminated. It's just not fair to the other workers whose bonuses are based on departmental and firm performance to carry bottom performers for very long. Incidentally, in a performance culture, bottom performers are often "paid to leave" in order to expedite their departure.

15. Move right person to right job. In a rapidly changing marketplace, the needs of the corporation also change rapidly. In order to meet these rapid changes, resources must move quickly from low-return areas to high-return areas. In a performance culture this means proactively identifying individuals and moving them into jobs and business units where they can have the most impact. At most organizations, HR waits until the individual employee decides to move; however, in a performance culture these individuals are identified and moved based on the recommendation of HR. In a performance culture, it's a "crime" to hoard talent, so managers are measured and rewarded on how well they develop and "move" talented employees to other areas of the organization where they can provide higher economic impact.

16. Build and maintain a competitive advantage. One of the tenets of a performance culture is the maintenance of a significant competitive advantage. In HR's case, that means completing side-by-side analysis of the competitors and its own HR practices in order to determine both its deficiencies and strengths. Since performance culture relies heavily on measurements, rewards and punishments, its essential that the firm's be clearly superior to its competitors.

17. Create paranoia and sense of urgency. An assumption of "paranoia" that the competitors might be catching us even though there is no evidence to demonstrate that they actually are is a hallmark of a performance culture. Paranoia means that every process, product and individual must be continually improving at a rate that allows the firm to maintain a significant lead over its competitors. By assuming that there are "hidden enemies," everyone is forced to maintain competitive intensity and a high sense of urgency. Continuous improvement and becoming (or maintaining our lead) as the best in the industry and in every functional and process area is the goal for every individual, process and product.

18. Set high expectations. A performance culture almost by definition has high expectations of its employees. HR's role is to ensure that every manager sets high performance goals. In a performance culture, it is assumed that setting stretch goals and demanding individual accountability are two ways to draw the best performance out of top performers.

19. Demand everyone stay on the leading edge. In a fast-changing world, information and knowledge has a relatively short shelf life. In a performance culture, individuals must maintain the highest skill levels. The performance culture solution is to set the expectation that every employee stay on the leading edge of knowledge. HR's role is to ensure that everyone understands that the latest knowledge, information and skills are essential to performance. HR can also make an important contribution by developing systems that encourage managers to share problems and best practices. The movement of solutions between business units is one of the key success factors in a performance culture.

20. Every system and person must continually improve. Becoming number one in the industry would be sufficient for most companies, but it's not enough if you operate in a performance culture. The goal is not just to become number one; instead, it's to continually improve in order to stretch the lead. HR needs to set an example by adding a continuous improvement element to each of its programs and initiatives. It also needs to measure and reward managers during the performance appraisal process for their success and continually improve every process and output.

21. Change initiatives are continuous from the top down and bottom up. All information and decisions cannot come from the top down; it just takes too long. In a performance culture, initiatives come from the individual with the most information relevant to the problem. HR must develop processes enabling the free flow of information to ensure that ideas, innovations and criticisms come from every layer in the organization. Learning occurs in every level of the organization and, in order to be successful, that information has to be passed quickly without having to go through a tedious hierarchy.

22. Speed is "the" competitive advantage. Regardless of whether or not you have a performance culture, it is becoming obvious that business is changing at a faster rate than it ever has. In order to succeed you must be fast at *everything*. Speed itself becomes a competitive advantage; the margins are so much higher if you get to the marketplace first. HR must ensure that every measurement and reward process has a component for speed. Internally, HR must also speed its own processes so that people-management decisions and transactions are the fastest and most accurate in the industry.

23. Everyone is treated as a mature adult. In most organizations, rules, approvals and policies are implemented to address the "lowest common denominator" of employees. Having restrictive rules and too many approvals unfortunately impacts performance and speed, so HR must take responsibility for eliminating most "broad-brush" rules and restrictions. Then, in the future, whenever an individual does something that's clearly unacceptable, in a performance culture that individual should be punished directly. Generally people are so focused on results and the rewards that go with them that they tend to participate less in disruptive behavior. HR must develop appropriate punishments for those that put personal gain ahead of the team or firm interests.

24. Share forecasts and alerts. An organization where performance is everything can't afford too many surprises. In a performance culture it's HR's role to educate and alert managers well in advance so that they can actually prevent people-management problems from occurring. This requires HR to make periodic forecasts in the areas of recruitment, retention, development and succession planning.

25. Make fact-based decisions. The cornerstone of performance culture is the measurement and reward of results. Individuals receive rewards and recognition for producing measurable output. All decisions should be based, where possible, on objective data and information rather than opinions and emotions. In order for managers to make decisions based on facts, *they must have a steady supply of data and metrics from HR*. In a performance culture, HR must spend its resources on gathering data and distributing it to managers. In addition to this role, HR must also set an example for others by eliminating as much subjectivity as it can in its own decision-making processes.

26. Limit loyalty. Performance is fleeting, so "loyalty" to individuals and processes is dependent on their continued performance. There should be no reward or even consideration given for historical performance. In a fast-changing business world, only present performance matters.

27. Dislike the average. Any organization that strives to be number one in its industry must compare itself to the very best firms. Therefore, there can be no tolerance for mediocrity and what is "average." If the goal is to be the very best, the company must be the benchmark for "best in class," "best in industry," and "best in the world" in all key critical success factors.

28. Practice "open book" management. Open access to information is provided so that employees can have the information that they need to make good decisions.

29. Encourage calculated risk-taking. Individuals and teams are expected to take a large number of calculated risks with rapid learning after a success or failure.

30. Develop talent. Developing talent is expected and rewarded. The hoarding of talent is punished.

Other PC practices

Other common practices in a performance culture that HR can help institute include:

- **Innovation.** Innovation is a competitive advantage so everyone should expect "disruptive" management solutions as well as product innovations.
- **Mass experimentation.** Every employee needs to play a role in trying new things. Rather than just having a scripted approach to new ideas, the firm must encourage everyone first to experiment, and then to choose the ideas that work.
- **Listen to employees.** Continuous, honest, two-way communication channels must be developed between employees and managers.
- **"No boundaries."** HR must implement penalties for creating "silos," fiefdoms or boundaries.
- **Cooperation.** HR must develop systems to encourage, measure and reward cooperation.

If HR decides against implementing a complete performance culture but still wants to be strategic, it should use the preceding list as a starting point for selecting which PC tools to integrate into its traditional HR processes and systems.

WHY TOP PERFORMERS ARE SO IMPORTANT

One of the key elements of a performance culture is that you *don't* treat employees equally. Treating employees equally comes naturally to many HR professionals but it runs counter to most business principles. Companies don't treat all customers the same because some bring in more revenue than others. In a similar light, business units are not treated the same; some get bigger budgets than others because they have more of an impact on business revenues. Why should we treat all employees the same?

A performance culture emphasizes creating a differential between how top and bottom performers are treated. Why? Top performers produce more economic value than average employees do. In business terms, top performers have a higher *return on investment*.

TOP PERFORMERS COST SLIGHTLY MORE

Before you can determine if top performers are worth more than average performers, you first need to determine the cost difference between a top-performing employee and an average one. Of course the amount varies between companies, but in most cases the extra compensation that is paid to top performers averages about 25 percent. It rarely exceeds 40 percent over average workers' pay. There are some cases, however, where top performers actually can get paid less than average performers. For example, in universities, in governmental or in unionized organizations, an individual that outperforms other workers actually may be paid less because of lack of seniority.

TOP PERFORMERS REQUIRE NO MORE MAINTENANCE

After you calculate the additional costs of the salary of top performers, you must also determine if top performers require additional resources in order to maintain their high performance level. Top performers generally are no more expensive to recruit. They actually require less management and training time, and the same approximate amount of equipment and travel expenses.

HOW MUCH MORE DOES
A TOP PERFORMER PRODUCE?

A reasonable businessperson would want to know the differential in performance between top performers and average performers. Several organizations have calculated this, and the results have consistently shown that a top performer can produce three to ten times (12 times for superstars) the output of an average performer in the same job.

TOP PERFORMERS HAVE A HUGE ROI

Now comes the key return-on-investment calculation. If it costs 25 percent more in pay for top performers, do they generate more than 25 percent more in value? The answer is that for 25 percent more in costs, top performers generate up to 1200 percent more in value. It doesn't take a rocket scientist to realize that if you pay an asset (whether it is an employee or any investment) 25 percent more but it produces 1200 percent more in output or revenue . . . you have an outstanding investment.

METRICS

Steps in calculating the dollar difference in output of top performers

If you need to calculate the added economic value of top performers over all others, here are the steps you must take:

- **Identify jobs with measurable outputs**—Start by identifying several jobs with measurable results like sales positions, software engineering, and quality assurance or customer service roles. Because the quantity and quality of their outputs is relatively easy to measure, utilizing them also makes it easier to compare and quantify the differences in output.

- **Calculating output**—Start with the output of the average performer. This is called the *average output per employee.* Then look at the output of the very top performer (or the average of the top 1 percent). This is called the *top performer output.*

- **Top performer increase factor**—Start with the *top performer output* per employee as the base. Then divide the output of the average performer into that number. That is the *top performer increase factor.*

- **Revenue per employee**—Calculate the *average revenue per employee* for these jobs (total divisional revenue for a year divided by the number of divisional employees. If divisional revenue is not available, take the total revenue of the firm for a year and divide it by the number of employees).

- **Revenue increase for top performers**—Take the average revenue per employee and multiply it by the top performer increase factor. That number is the *revenue generated by the top performer.*

- **Value difference between top and average performer**—Subtract the average revenue per employee from the revenue of top performer. The difference is the value added each year by hiring or retaining a top performer.

- **Add additional jobs**—Next, do it for other measurable output jobs. If the ratio (the percent difference) is similar for most jobs (it usually is), use the same ratio for all jobs in the firm. If there is some variance, average the ratios together to come up with the firm's average.

Example

1. Sales for an average salesperson are $150,000. Top employee sales are $400,000.
2. $400,000 divided by $150,000 = 2.6, where 2.6 is the top performer increase factor.
3. Total employees (400) is divided into total revenue ($100,000,000), resulting in $250,000 average revenue per employee.
4. $250,000 times 2.6 (performance increase factor) = $650,000 (revenue generated by top performers).
5. $650,000 (revenue of top performers) minus $150,000 (average revenue per employee) equals $500,000. This means top performers generate over $500,000 per year in revenue more than do average employees. If you hire or retain ten of these top performers, you increase the revenue of the firm by $5M per year.

ACTION STEPS

It's obvious that top performers produce more economic value—that's why it's important to focus on them. However, that doesn't mean you can ignore the rest of your employees. It takes a team to succeed, so you need to treat everyone well, but the key to a performance culture is focusing investment and management time and resources on above-average and top-performing employees.

Once you realize that top performers are a bargain, the next step is to demand that recruiters and HR professionals begin to focus on hiring, increasing the productivity of, and retaining top performers.

Incidentally, a similar logic works when you're considering how to treat your retirees. In some organizations, retirees are treated at least as well if not better than current employees. This is in part because HR often takes into account all of the past contributions made by these former employees. In a performance culture, in contrast, retirees and all others that are no longer in a position to make an economic contribution must be considered second-tier. Of course it's important to treat them well, but never forget to put most of your resources into individuals who have the capability of returning a high ROI.

HOW TO IDENTIFY TOP PERFORMERS IN A PERFORMANCE CULTURE

Because superstar performers can produce up to 12 times more than average performers identifying them becomes a critical element in strategic HR. Once identified, these top performers need to be given adequate resources and attention as well as individual rewards for producing outstanding results. There are a variety of approaches you can use to identify top performers, including:

- **Current performance**—Using current performance as an indicator of future performance.
- **Surveys and interviews**—Asking people "Who might be a future leader?" or "Who would like to be a future leader?"
- **Competency assessment**—Identifying the competencies or skills of leaders and who has them through assessment programs.
- **Leadership behaviors**—Some managers look at "on the job" leadership behaviors or actions as an identifier of leaders.

IDENTIFYING TOP PERFORMERS AND FUTURE LEADERS USING CURRENT PERFORMANCE DATA

In all my years of experience in industry, I have found that identifying an individual's "potential" to be nearly impossible. To avoid the high-potential pitfall I recommend that you instead use *performance* (rather than the *"potential"* of performance) as your primary assessment criteria. Below are some approaches for identifying top performers and future leaders based on their current performance:

- **Top performers**—Identify top performers in all job categories. This can be done by merely comparing their job output, by forced ranking or by utilizing the more traditional performance appraisal scores. Whatever you do, it is important to cover your bases by utilizing multiple measures.
- **Problem solvers**—Great baseball players don't always turn out to be great managers, but those players who demonstrate that they can solve a variety of complex problems are the ones with the highest probability of success in management. You can identify individuals who can solve complex problems by reviewing how they handle themselves in their current job and/or by providing them with opportunities to solve "new" problems that have no clear process or solution. In addition, identify whom other em-

ployees, team leaders and managers go to or request when they face a complex problem.

- **Fast learners**—Because those in senior management positions must deal constantly with uncertainty and the unknown, it's important to identify individuals who learn rapidly in their current job. Typically these individuals read more and different things in order to learn. They frequently scan leading-edge business, functional and industry publications and web sites. Use their current performance appraisal to identify those who learn rapidly. Other options include assigning them problems that require fast learning, or just asking around to identify who is a "fast learner?"

- **Stretch assignments**—By assigning individuals to task forces, teams and "stretch" short-term assignments, you can gather hard evidence about their performance and leadership capabilities. Give a wide variety of employees these opportunities in order to identify "sleepers" (leaders that have not yet come forward). This approach is widely utilized at GE, where stretch goals and stretch assignments are a primary method for identifying, developing and assessing leaders.

IDENTIFYING TOP PERFORMERS THROUGH SURVEYS AND "ASKING"

Many times success and performance are a result of a team effort. A team effort makes it much more difficult to identify individuals who are top performers. One way around that problem is to survey or ask many individuals in order to get multiple opinions about "who" is a leader. Some of the possible approaches include:

- **Use 360-degree assessments**—Use a 360-degree assessment tool to anonymously ask a wide variety of individuals "Who has potential? Who is a leader? Who is a top performer?" By asking a broad range of employees and many levels of management, you increase the odds of identifying any "sleeper" leaders and/or "true leaders." Receiving positive feedback about one's leadership skills from both managers and non-managers can be enlightening, and it is certainly a "win" for both the employee and the organization.

- **Ask other top performers**—Ask other top performers "Who else is good?"

- **Ask mentors**—Identify the mentees of senior leaders, based on the premise that they wouldn't be aiding or mentoring someone unless they saw a great deal of potential in them.

- **Ask employees**—Interview employees directly and ask them who they see as top performers and future leaders. Don't be fooled because of someone's pay or title. Some managers focus on seniority and relationships rather than performance. Someone at the firm always knows who the top performers are, but those in the "know" might *not* include top management!

IDENTIFYING FUTURE LEADERS USING COMPETENCIES

In addition to identifying top performers, a performance culture must also identify individuals that are future leaders or individuals that have the potential to become top performers. Some organizations have used competencies or competency modeling to identify the skills or traits of potential leaders and then "labeled" individuals with those skills and competencies as leaders. I'm skeptical of that approach, as is author Robert Kelley, who after years of intensive productivity research at Bell Labs and 3M reveals in his book, "How to Be a Star at Work," that he could find no common traits among star workers.

Identifying common competencies among top performers and potential leaders is a very complex, time-consuming and expensive approach (for a variety reasons). The most difficult problem to overcome is the definition and measurement of competencies. Most companies identify similar competencies like business acumen, innovation and leadership, but precisely defining what these competencies are and accurately measuring them can become a nightmare. Although I don't recommend the competency approach, some of the commonly used methods to identify competencies include:

- **Assessment centers**—A combination of tests, simulations or "role-plays" designed to identify what skills and behaviors an individual uses to solve complex problems.
- **Competency modeling**—A process of comparing and contrasting the skills, knowledge and competencies of successful leaders (vs. unsuccessful leaders) in an organization. Some firms have successfully come up with a list of leadership competencies, but one of the difficulties is that the skills and behavior required to succeed within the company in the past might not be the same ones necessary to succeed in either the present or the future environment.

IDENTIFYING TOP PERFORMERS USING BEHAVIOR OR ACTIONS

Some firms look at more measurable "behaviors" or actions that are used in their current job instead of looking at individuals' competencies or skills. Here the premise is that you can identify top performers and potential leaders through their work behaviors. Some of the behaviors that managers have used to identify top performers and potential leaders include:

- They have mentored others.
- They are requested by other managers and employees to work on teams or to help solve problems.
- They have spoken at conferences and internal company events.
- They are early adopters of new tools, technology and ideas.
- "A" players are curious and therefore frequently ask questions during presentations.
- They have written articles or are cited by others in their articles.
- They often use technology to do everything faster, cheaper and better.
- They have developed new or innovative processes, systems and approaches.
- They benchmark and directly compare their company's work to that of the competitors.
- They utilize advanced tools and methods to accomplish their major tasks.
- They use metrics to quantify the success of processes, products and services they helped to develop.
- They know the top problems and opportunities facing the industry and firm as well as the steps to take to solve at least one of these critical problems.

Some common "non-leader" behaviors include:

Individuals that are unlikely to be top performers or become leaders also exhibit certain behaviors. They often include:

- They demand job security and guaranteed pay.
- They express a strong need for clear "rules," defined expectations and job responsibilities.
- "C" players put an over-emphasis on process, the chain of command and policies.

- They give indications that they are uncomfortable with ambiguity and rapid change.
- They are strong advocates of seniority and are opposed to pay for performance.

When you develop your selection criteria for top performers, focus on current performance and behaviors rather than "potential." Because few processes are precise, use multiple criteria and methods to identify top performers. Don't forget the final step after you identify your top performers: recognize and reward them for producing outstanding results. It's the ultimate mistake to have any top performer not be aware that you consider him or her a top performer.

A PERFORMANCE CULTURE CAN INFLUENCE THE ATTRACTION AND RETENTION OF TOP TALENT

The goal of becoming a performance culture can never realistically be achieved without attracting and retaining a cadre of top performers. This initial central core of talent acts as a referral agent and a magnet to eventually attract other top performers. In order to build up your initial cadre of top performers, it is essential that you understand what it takes initially to attract and retain your first top performers. Just like an athlete, top performers in business love to win and to work with other winners. They enjoy "putting it all on the line" because they have confidence in their ability to produce. A culture that demands performance and continuous improvement excites top talent for several reasons.

- The focus on performance makes it more likely that the business (and its products) will also be a top performer. Not only is winning fun but the profitability that goes with it increases the total amount of rewards available to all. Focusing on performance means that top performers will get a bigger share of the rewards if the team succeeds. Having a significant reward and recognition differential means that top performers get a much bigger piece of the pie than they would in a normal bureaucracy. The growth that goes with profitability also means more promotions and new project opportunities.
- Top performers love to work around and with other top performers. So, by attracting the initial cadre of top performers, you make

it easy to attract additional top performers. Being around other top performers is exciting, and the synergy forces everyone to get better.

- Excuses are not tolerated and therefore there is less bureaucracy, fewer rules and less whining (all of which top performers appreciate).
- A focus on numbers and metrics attracts top performers—who traditionally produce great numbers and therefore love metrics and measurement.
- Top performers love challenge, growth and great managers. All three are more likely to occur in a performance culture.

To put it another way, the difference between a performance culture and most business cultures is very similar to the difference between capitalism and socialism. A performance culture is a "capitalist-like" culture where the competition is fierce but the rewards are high for those that produce. In contrast, many corporate cultures are more socialistic in that they focus more on equity, effort and helping the little guy than they do on results.

BUILDING A SENSE OF URGENCY AT YOUR FIRM

Hi-tech and start-up firms have it. But many seem to lose it as they get larger and more geographically dispersed. What they lose is their sense of urgency.

DEFINITION

Urgency is roughly defined as a lack of satisfaction with the status quo. The four components of urgency are *speed, focus, discipline* and *commitment*.

Companies and people with a sense of urgency have a passion for continuous improvement. They are often called "paranoid" because their goal is to obsolete their own products and processes before a competitor forces them. Firms with a sense of urgency don't rely on traditional "benchmarking" because that process causes them to improve at a rate similar to the benchmark firms. A sense of urgency demands that the firm set its own pace of improvement. Often the phrase that is used is that the organization "assumes someone is catching up with it, even though it can't see them."

HOW TO INCREASE THE SENSE OF URGENCY

A sense of urgency exists when all employees feel the need to increase their effort, speed and contribution. Urgency causes employees to behave differently because of the negative consequences associated with delay and waiting. It's desirable for a firm to develop a sense of urgency among its employees because it can increase individual, team and business unit output. A sense of urgency can come from a variety of areas, including:

- Personal pride and motivation
- Rewards and punishments
- Metrics and information about project progress
- Pressure from competitors
- Paranoia
- Pressure from technology changes, government or economic conditions

A performance culture is designed to increase everyone's sense of urgency, but there are things that you can do to increase the sense of urgency without implementing a performance culture completely. Tools that can increase the individual or collective sense of urgency include:

- Hire and retain people with a passion for their job and for project completion.
- Periodically measure employee's sense of urgency and reward managers for a high urgency score.
- Offer large "on time" project completion bonuses.
- Tie a large portion of every employee's individual pay and bonus to team performance.
- Offer a significant bonus for every day that the project is completed ahead of schedule.
- Do periodic output measurements for every employee in order to let them know how well they are performing against expectations.
- Provide information to employees about the progress made by direct competitors.
- Provide information to employees about significant changes occurring in technology, the economy or the competitive marketplace.
- Provide periodic updates to employees and managers showing the "time left" to completion.

- Break large projects into smaller parts so that employees can more easily track the percentage of completion.
- Fire the bottom 10 percent of the workers that fail to meet performance standards in order to send a message that there is no tolerance for those that don't perform.
- Post performance charts for all to see their performance.
- Hire people who ask "why?"—those who challenge status quo and who will not accept a no answer when they ask "why not?"
- Set continuous improvement goals to demonstrate that the bar is constantly being raised for the next project.
- Hire winners who win no matter what problems they encounter.
- Develop assessment tools for applicants and employees that measure passion, speed, intolerance for the average, and sense of urgency.
- Incent contractors, suppliers, consultants, temps and other "non-employees."

WHAT CAN REDUCE A SENSE OF URGENCY?

No matter how good a job you might have done in developing a sense of urgency, it's important to recognize that there are still numerous things that can frustrate employees and reduce that sense. It's HR's job to minimize the impact of anything that reduces the organization's sense of urgency.

- Excessive approvals
- Bureaucratic restrictions and rules
- Being kept in the dark about goals and objectives and progress
- Excessive penalties for failing and risk-taking
- Consensus decision-making

The next section highlights the fourth element of the strategic HR department: Building and maintaining a competitive advantage.

CHAPTER EIGHT

HR PROVIDES A COMPETITIVE ADVANTAGE

OBJECTIVE

The fourth element that makes an HR department strategic is providing the organization with a competitive advantage in people-management practices. Building a competitive advantage is an external effort that occurs at level four of the HR strategic contribution model.

KEY POINTS

◊ You must think as though HR is in a constant competitive "battle" with its talent competitors. Once you develop that competitive mindset, it's important to follow up with specific plans and actions.

◊ Some of the essential focus areas include obtaining competitive intelligence, anticipating your competitors' actions, and finally, aiming not at where competitors are, but instead aiming ahead to where they will be.

DEFINITION

A competitive advantage in HR means that instead of building and assessing its HR programs in isolation, HR develops a plan to compare its people-management practices to those of its direct competitors and then improve them in such a way that they are clearly superior in performance. A strategic competitive advantage is generally defined as a people-management program or practice that produces *results* that are clearly superior in critical areas over a relatively long time period.

Developing a competitive advantage is a common practice in business. For example, products are not developed in isolation nor are they developed merely because customers want them. Instead, firms develop products to counter the products of other firms. The same is true in sales. Firms don't just develop a sales approach in isolation, instead firms develop a sales approach that purposely takes advantage of the weaknesses of their competitors' sales approach.

Firms also try to develop a competitive advantage in the area of research. If a firm's competitor begins doing research in one area, then in response to that action, the firm also begins doing research in that area to ensure that the competitor doesn't gain a competitive product advantage.

Incidentally, the most strategic of all competitive advantages comes when, instead of reacting to the actions of others in order to catch up, an organization proactively take actions that give it a competitive advantage first, which in turn forces the competitors to play "catch-up."

It's not unusual for companies to list their product and service offering in a side-by-side chart in order to identify the areas where the company is stronger and weaker. That same product and service comparison can be done in HR in order to identify the areas where HR is clearly superior and clearly inferior.

Compensation was the first area in HR to be concerned about developing and maintaining a competitive advantage. Companies that were hiring a good number of hourly unskilled workers found that if they didn't offer competitive hourly rates, they would lose a substantial number of their workers to a higher-paying competitor.

In response, the compensation department fought to maintain parity by conducting salary surveys that compared the firm's pay rates to those of other companies in the relevant labor market. Compensation's early attempt to compare human resource practices in order to maintain a competitive advantage is a foundation for today's competitive analysis in other areas of HR.

WHY HR NEEDS TO PROVIDE A COMPETITIVE ADVANTAGE

Every competitive firm attempts to beat its competitors. This competition to gain a superior advantage is the heart of a market economy. "Beating a competitor" doesn't happen all at once, however; instead it happens on a product-by-product and program-by-program basis. Although most of the competition is in the product area, it's also important to be superior in other management areas, like customer service and people management.

As we have seen earlier, superior people-management practices have a high return on investment. If you were the manager of a sports team, it would be crystal clear that recruiting, retention and the development of your talent would be a critical success factor in winning. The same is true for organizations. If you hire better people, retain great people longer, and develop people so that they continually improve their performance, you are providing your firm with competitive advantage.

In fact, if you produce more for every dollar spent on people than your competitor, you are clearly providing a cost advantage to your firm. Having great people-management practices may also affect the stock price. Over 20 percent of the factors that analysts look at when assessing the value of the company stock are related to people-management.

Unfortunately, most traditional HR practitioners don't see HR practices as something that even should be compared to a competitor's. These individuals see HR as an overhead function with no critical impact and therefore no need to make a superior contribution. This is what I call "old-think" in HR, and it is certainly not strategic thinking. A strategic HR leader instead starts with the premise that, if its people programs produce better results than the competitors, then HR is providing the organization with a distinct competitive advantage in the marketplace.

BUILDING A COMPETITIVE AWARENESS WITHIN HR

Making human resource management practices a competitive advantage is as much a mindset as it is a set of actions. The most important aspect is to have every member of HR begin to think differently about what they do. There are three parts to this new competitive mindset:

- **Competitive mindset**—Instead of thinking in isolation, HR practitioners need to think about what they do in comparison to what the organization's talent competitors do. In that context, they must continually monitor what the competitor is doing and try to take steps to counter those actions. For example, if a talent competitor is continually "poaching" away talent, HR must react to block their actions. A next step might be to recruit away *their* top talent in order to keep them on their toes, as well as to improve your own firm.

- **Competitive metrics**—That same mindset requires HR managers to begin using more metrics so that they can compare what they do to some quantifiable standard. The ideal comparison is to compare your firm's results with your talent competitors. However, just getting in the habit of comparing your results to the industry's best or even the industry average may be a great kick-start and a "win" by itself.

- **Competitive "paranoia"**—The last element of a competitive mindset is "paranoia." "Paranoia" here is a healthy concept made famous by Intel. This "paranoia" requires HR managers and employees to begin assuming that their talent competition is constantly improving, catching them, or even gaining the lead. That way of thinking gives HR people a sense of urgency and the goal of continuous improvement. If HR assumes that it must improve its practices as fast as its company must improve its product, then HR is well on the way to becoming a competitive advantage for the firm!

Gaining a competitive advantage is an aggressive approach to HR that requires you to assess your competitor's "vulnerabilities" and then to take proactive action to take advantage of those weaknesses. If you are going to be strategic, you cannot take a "can't we all just get along" approach to HR.

IN WHAT AREAS MUST HR BE SUPERIOR?

The first rule of building a competitive advantage is that it's important to be superior only in those areas that have *a critical impact* on business success. As a result, the process of building a competitive advantage begins with identifying the critical success factors in your industry or product area.

DEFINITION

Critical success factors are the things that "cause" firms to perform better than others. In other words, firms that have a lot of these critical success factors do well and those that have few of the critical success factors do poorly.

Because building a competitive advantage doesn't require superiority in every area, it is also important to identify those areas where being great doesn't make a significant difference in the company's success and, as a result, excelling there actually might be a waste of money. In those noncritical areas, the organization needs to be just average because being superior in noncritical areas makes little economic difference.

Perhaps an example can illustrate the point. All professional football teams have both a logo and a quarterback. Because all teams have both, just having the logo or quarterback doesn't create an advantage. But what if one team develops a "super logo" that is clearly superior to the other team's logo. Having a better logo does not provide a competitive advantage because a logo is not a critical success factor for a winning football team.

Past experience has provided data that when a logo gets better there is no impact on the team's winning percentage. However, if one team drafted the best quarterback or poached the best quarterback from the competitors, that would be a competitive advantage. Having a superior quarterback has proven to be, over time, a critical success factor that is necessary for a professional football team to win.

You can identify the critical success factors for your firm by doing your own analysis or by looking at the work of others. When I advise firms, one of the first things I urge them to do is to identify the critical people-management programs that are essential to their company's success. Several consulting firms have done a similar analysis with the Human Capital Index created by Watson Wyatt, Inc. (one of the best). Unfortunately, it's difficult to generalize because having great people produces a greater competitive advantage in some industries like sports, while in other industries (like the wine industry for example), the grapes, the land, and the materials have a much larger impact than the workers picking the grapes.

But with that being said, below is a list of factors that generally do and do not have a significant competitive advantage in the people-management area. Note these programs were selected based on the premise that most of your jobs are professional jobs because the significance differs for hourly and production workers.

Effective competitive advantage factors

Generally these provide a competitive advantage (for professional jobs) if you provide superior results:

- Recruiting
- Retention
- Having great managers
- Rewarding managers for great people management
- Metrics
- Honest two-way communications
- Growth and development opportunities
- Providing employees with some control over their work
- Leadership development
- The internal movement or redeployment of talent
- Pay for performance
- Incentive programs

Ineffective competitive advantage factors

These often do *not* provide a competitive advantage (for example, if you offer above "average" programs):

- Basic benefits programs
- Personal portals
- Outsourcing HR programs

- Performance appraisal systems
- Mission statements for HR
- Most "next job" training
- 360 degree appraisals
- External executive recruiting

It's important to remember that if the company has a superior offering in an effective competitive advantage area, that means that the superior program will result in improved employee productivity or some other *measurable economic advantage.* Just because a program is on the ineffective competitive advantage list does not mean that workers don't desire it, it just means that having a great program does not provide a measurable economic advantage.

Let's look at benefits as an example. Benefits are a high-cost item; and even though employees are well aware of benefit offerings and they are clearly interested in benefits, proving that your firm offers superior benefits, as compared to a competitor, is actually quite difficult. As a result, if one company provides a clearly better benefit package in economic terms, that does not mean that the benefit package will be perceived as being significantly better by its workers.

Because basic benefit packages are difficult to compare and expensive to provide, the "perception" of the breadth of your benefit program may be more important than the actual difference in what you offer compared to your competitors. I realize that for some this is difficult to swallow, but I've never found a company that, after it did the analysis, could demonstrate that (at least for professional jobs) offering anything above average in "basic" benefits had any impact on recruiting, retention or employee productivity.

There is another area where HR programs frequently do not provide a competitive advantage, and that is in the area of outsourcing or the use of vendors. Using a vendor, no matter how superior the vendor is, often turns out *not* to be a competitive advantage because that same vendor frequently does the same work for your competitor. So, even if service and product is superior, there can be no competitive advantage if your competitor has the same product or service.

The lesson to be learned here is either to make a deal with your vendors that they not provide similar services to your competitors, or develop your own program or service that better meets your specific needs. This last option is quite often possible because most vendor offerings are not tailored to your specific situation. Custom-designed solutions that are done in-house can sometimes have better results than a technically superior vendor product that just doesn't fit your company's unique situation.

ASSESSING WHETHER YOUR PROGRAMS ARE SUPERIOR

Many HR professionals try to prove that they offer a competitive advantage by merely comparing programs. In other words, HR says "we have a program and they don't," or "our program has five features and their program only has two." Neither of these approaches can be 100 percent successful because simply "having a program" doesn't mean much.

In contrast, a competitive advantage exists when the program or process produces better results in the areas that are crucial to the company. Whether or not your recruiting program, for example, has five Internet options does not guarantee that it produces hires that perform better on the job than the antiquated paper-based system run by your competitor. The lesson to be learned here is that you compare *results*, not just programs, when you're attempting to prove a competitive advantage.

COMPETITIVE INTELLIGENCE HELPS BUILD A COMPETITIVE ADVANTAGE

Many professionals in HR are conservative in their approach to business, and as a result, they are frequently shocked when they learn that it is part of their responsibility to do competitive intelligence (CI) about competitor firms. Once they get over their initial trepidation, they realize it's only logical that, in order to "beat" the enemy, they have to know what the enemy is doing now and what it is planning for the future.

DEFINITION

Competitive intelligence in HR is a process of gathering information about strengths and weaknesses, current practices and future plans of competitors so that the organization can "leapfrog" ahead of them.

If you are unaware of how CI is done, work with the competitive intelligence staff within your own business units and piggyback on their processes and sources.

BEST PRACTICE

How competitive analysis helped a firm dramatically improve. A large copy machine company was getting killed by its competitors. Their own copiers were often more expensive, less reliable, and had fewer features than their Japanese counterparts. So, the company bought a model of each of the competitor's copiers and put the competitor's copiers in the lobby of their main building.

Next, they took out all of their own copying machines and required that all copies by their employees be made on the competitor's products. Engineers, sales people and managers were almost universally impressed. As a result, the company stopped "bad-mouthing" the competitor and instead started focusing on how the competitor did it so well.

APPROACHES TO COMPETITIVE INFORMATION-GATHERING

One approach to gathering competitive intelligence is a joint benchmark-sharing approach where the firms agree up-front to share data (the model used in compensation surveys, for example) about what each is doing. Although on the surface it might seem with both companies sharing, there is no competitive advantage, the secret to success is how fast a company acts on the information. Consequently, your success depends on your ability to act more quickly and do more things with the information you capture from benchmark sharing.

The second approach relies on gathering public information about your competitor. Have your Information Specialist and other resources find whatever they can that has been written about your competitors. The process generally includes searches of their web sites, SEC filings, press releases and public and academic articles.

The last is the most aggressive approach, involving classic business approaches to competitive intelligence-gathering. It can be powerful but difficult to do.

- Competitive intelligence generally starts with direct market research where a market research firm interviews (or conducts focus groups with) current and former employees, suppliers, and consultants that work with the firm.
- Also interviewed are your own employees and managers who have been employed or interviewed by your competitors.
- Some professional competitive intelligence firms talk to private detectives to advise them about how to gather information or to find out directly what others are doing.
- In some cases "mystery shoppers" are sent to competitors' job fairs and events to see first-hand what is happening.
- Some firms purposely interview all candidates who apply from the target firm just to ask them about people practices and problems.
- Some companies hire the same consultant or consulting firm as their competitors use because they know what type of advice the competitors are getting.

DEMONSTRATING A COMPETITIVE ADVANTAGE

There are numerous ways that an HR department can assess whether it or its programs have a distinct competitive advantage. Some approaches are widely used but clearly have some obvious flaws, including:

- A side-by-side program-to-program feature comparison
- A side-by-side comparison of dollars spent in each program area
- A benchmark study (by consulting firm or industry group) that uses "expert opinion" to rate or rank the programs
- A comparison of the revenue-per-employee ratio between the two firms

STRATEGIC APPROACHES TO ASSESSING COMPETITIVE ADVANTAGE

- A comparison of your program results or outputs to the "best-in-class" results published by industry associations. The logic here is that if your results are the same as or very close to the best-in-the-industry scores, you must, by definition, be beating the competitors.

- An overall comparison of plant-by-plant employee productivity (output versus cost) between the competing firms.
- A rating of the program offerings by managers who recently came from the competitor (and by former employees who went to the competitor).
- A side-by-side output of results comparison in the areas of recruiting, retention, percentage of pay at risk, etc.

Getting data for results comparisons can be difficult. Quite often consultants that work at both firms, former employees of the competitor that now work for you, and industry associations can provide you with some relatively accurate estimates. If you're really feeling bold, consider "trading" last year's results with the HR professional at your direct competitor. It is difficult, but it can—and does—happen.

THE DIFFERENCE BETWEEN BENCHMARKING AND COMPETITIVE ANALYSIS

Many HR departments participate in benchmarking where they seek out best practices from other firms; this is not the same as the competitive analysis required to build a competitive advantage. Benchmarking finds out what the best firms are doing, but it does not automatically find out what direct competitors are doing.

Competitive analysis is a side-by-side comparison between your firm and your direct talent competitors in each of the critical HR areas. Competitive analysis focuses primarily on comparing people performance "results" rather than identifying the HR department's best practices. Best practices information might indeed help your firm to improve your performance at some point, but first you must identify whether there are any performance differences between your firm and your competitors.

PRODUCT COMPETITORS VS. TALENT COMPETITORS

Before conducting any competitive analysis, it's important to identify which firms are your true competitors. Most firms miss the boat when it comes to identifying their competitors. Most assume that their competitors are the same companies that they compete against in the product or service area. That narrow assumption can be a major mistake because there are two types of competitors: product competitors and talent competitors.

In some cases, you need not compare your firm's HR performance to that of your direct product competitors; you might not draw talent from the same talent pool. For example, two manufacturing firms may both manufacture paper cups that they sell wholesale. Both firms are product competitors because they both sell wholesale products to the same customers. But if your firm is located in Washington and your product competitor is located in Georgia, your *product* competitor might not be your *talent* competitor. This is because paper cup manufacturers recruit their talent only from their local geographic area. Because of the geographic distance between your firm and your product competitor, it is highly unlikely that anyone will leave your firm for the competitor, or vice versa, regardless of the strength of either's HR programs.

The lesson to be learned here is that you must perform your competitive analysis of HR programs against your *talent* competitors, which are the other firms that *people you are recruiting (or trying to retain) consider as desirable employers.*

It is important to identify all of your talent competitors for your competitive analysis because while every organization probably knows its product competitors, in some cases, talent competitors are completely off the radar screen. In fact, many of your talent competitors could be well outside of your industry. Once they are identified, HR must undertake a side-by-side assessment in order to identify where your firm is superior (or inferior) to your "talent competitors."

> *In the war for talent, just like in any other war… if you misidentify the enemy, you will lose a lot of battles.*

IDENTIFYING YOUR TALENT COMPETITORS

Before you start comparing yourself to other firms, it is crucial that you pick the right firms to compare yourself to. A large firm might actually have three different groups of talent competitors depending on which jobs your firm considers crucial to its success. The three different job categories are:

- **Local hire jobs**—A talent competitor for "local hire" jobs where most of the hiring is done within a local commuting area. These tend to be hourly service and retail jobs.

- **Professional and technical jobs**—Professional or technical jobs that are not industry- or product- specific such as programmers, finance and HR. For these jobs you might recruit throughout the region or across the US, but because the talent is not industry- or product-specific, your talent competitors might end up including major firms outside your region and industry.
- **Professional and technical jobs specific to your industry**—Professional or technical jobs that are product- and industry-specific. In these cases, your product competitors and your talent competitors are likely to be one and the same. This is especially true for jobs that require industry-specific experience, contacts or skills. For jobs like dress buyer, the competition may indeed be only other clothes stores or firms. Chip designers, chefs, pilots and musicians are also examples of jobs that tend to be industry-specific

The next step in identifying your talent competitors (and the firms you must maintain a competitive advantage over in people practices) is to identify which factors determine whether your talent competitors are the same or different than product competitors. Before you make your final determination on which firms you must develop a competitive advantage over, consider the following factors.

Factors that can make your talent competitors different from your product competitors:

- **Isolated geography**—In small towns or in remote areas, all firms within commuting distance will be competitors for talent because they are the only major employers to choose from.
- **Dominant employer**—In small- to medium-sized towns or in remote areas where there is one large dominant employer, the dominant employer automatically becomes a talent competitor to all other small- and medium-sized firms. This is because of the scope of job and promotion opportunities, and often pay if it is a unionized plant (for example, Hershey's Chocolate in Hershey, Pennsylvania)
- **Your firm is the only firm in the area from your industry**—If your firm is the only firm in your industry that has a facility in the region, then it is likely that none of your product competitors are also talent competitors (especially for jobs without relocation benefits).
- **Entry-level and customer service jobs**—Companies (especially retail, hospitality and service) with many jobs that require little training (or where firms themselves train new hires) may find that

every local firm would be a talent competitor. If your firm has a large number of more sophisticated jobs with a shared skillset that is not unique to your industry (like customer service reps, programmers, accountants), then all firms in the geographic commuting distance are likely to be talent competitors. Starbucks' branches, for example, compete for talent with all local retail stores, not just coffee shops. Banks may compete directly with manufacturing and hi-tech firms for programmers and accountants.

- **College hires**—Some technical majors like engineering, education and nursing accept jobs primarily in a single industry but other majors like business, humanities, or MIS may consider all employers equally.
- **Remote or "at home" work**—For some jobs, geography is less relevant. Firms with a large number of jobs that are remotely located, work at home or that hire people that work out of a car might compete for talent with all firms with similar jobs (for example, writers, web service people, telephone sales).
- **Senior management positions**—Competition for senior management jobs is almost always the region, the entire US or even the globe because relocation is offered. Some senior management jobs are filled from product competitors while the rest (approximately two-thirds) are filled internally or from other industries.
- **Employers of choice (EOC)**—If you work at a recognized "employer of choice" (EOC) (generally firms that are listed on the *Fortune* or *Working Mother* best places to work lists), your talent competitors for top talent are likely to be only other "employers of choice." Competitor EOCs are as likely to be outside your industry as in it (partially because many industries have only one EOC).
- **Other**—People that have transferred recently to jobs in different industries may still be a talent target because they are experienced and could still return to their former industry.

ACTION STEPS FOR IDENTIFYING TALENT COMPETITORS

Once you realize that you have a broader range of talent competitors, your next step is to determine, by name, which firms you must build a competitive advantage over for each of the three major job categories.

The steps to take include:

- Assume product competitors within your geographic region are also talent competitors.
- Assume all well known "employers of choice" within your geographic region are talent competitors for all jobs that are not product-specific.
- Ask your new hires on their first day where else they applied (or considered).
- Identify the firms that all new hires came from (over the past two years), and assume any firm with a large number of hires is among your talent competitors.
- Look at employees who quit, and then identify where the departed employees went (Benefits often knows this, or ask departing employees in the exit interview.) Assume these firms are talent competitors.
- Survey current employees and ask them what other firms they would consider going to if they were to leave.
- Ask interviewees what other firms they considered, applied to or that have made them offers.
- Ask applicants (ask people on the web site or on the job application form) what other firms they considered.
- Ask your recruiters which firms they "share" candidates with at job and career fairs.
- Ask executive search and other recruiting consultants that work for your firm whom they find to be talent competitors.
- Ask management and HR consultants that work with your firm whom they consider your talent competitors to be.
- Do focus groups or surveys at trade fairs and seminars, and ask participants, "who do you consider to be employers of choice in your functional area, its region and its industry?"
- Do surveys or visit classes at universities and identify who students would consider as potential employers.
- Identify all major employers within commuting distance (the Chamber of Commerce will have a list by employee population), and compare your HR programs and strategies to the largest ones.
- Identify firms that offer remote or distance work opportunities (organizations like "New Ways to Work" keep a list of them) and see how your approach and jobs compare to theirs.

- Consider tracking the "cookie" of visitors to your jobs' web site to see where they *currently work* (from their web domain since many search while on the job), where they were *before* they visited your site, and where they go *after* visiting it

It's important not to forget that many firms lose the competition for attracting and retaining talent because they misidentify the "enemy." The consequences of such an error can be deadly. Misidentification of your talent competitors can result in improperly designed recruiting and retention tools. In the recruiting area, offers that are designed to be superior to your product competitors might not work against talent competitors that are from different industries.

The key is to do your research first, narrow down your list of firms and then focus exclusively on building a competitive advantage against each talent competitor in each of the three major job categories.

ACTION STEPS IN BUILDING AN HR COMPETITIVE ADVANTAGE

After you've developed a competitive mindset, there are some other actions that HR can take to provide its firm a competitive advantage in people management and HR. (Note: a longer list of possible actions can be found in Chapter 20 entitled, "Examples of strategic actions and approaches.")

Some competitive advantage actions include:

- **HR program comparison**—Do a side-by-side HR program comparison just to get a basic idea of what they have compared to what you have. Even though it is best to compare program results, is often hard to produce results when you don't even have a program. Do a program comparision first.
- **Results comparison**—When you can obtain the data, do a side-by-side analysis comparing the results of your HR efforts and those of your direct competitors.
- **Differentiate the tools**—Many companies use the same tools out of habit. However, if you are going to build a competitive advantage, you cannot use the same tools as everyone else. For example, if your direct talent competitor relies exclusively on certain sources in recruiting, it's important for your HR department to use some variation of that tool. If two firms use the same tools, no matter

how effective the tools are, there is no way that your firm can have a competitive advantage.

- **Demand continuous improvement**—HR can't assume that it is aiming at a fixed target. Instead, assume that there will be a steady rate of improvement in your competitors' HR programs, and then set goals for meeting or exceeding that improvement rate in every critical HR program in your firm.

- **"Non-copyable" programs**—A competitive advantage means that your HR programs produce results superior to your competitors. A problem arises in that whatever your competitive advantage, it is highly likely that your competitor will quickly copy what you do. Rapid copying is especially true in the area of outsourcing because it's relatively easy for them to sign on with the same vendor that you use, therefore negating your initial advantage. Smart HR departments instead develop programs that, by design, are hard to copy, so that even though the competitor tries to copy the program, in essence you have lengthened the time where you maintain your initial competitive advantage.

- **Improve fast**—Continually improve all elements of the people-management process at a rate faster than competitors improve theirs, so that all of their tentative "catch-up" actions offer no business advantage. Also, implement programs with such high quality that even when they do copy you, it doesn't work as well as your own programs!

- **Forecast more accurately**—Forecast and monitor the business environment so that you are aware of any possible changes before your competitors. Then act quickly in order to stay ahead. Develop strategic forecasts and an HR plan that allows you to be better prepared for business changes than your competitors.

- **Measure results**—In order to create a competitive environment, you need keep score. That means that HR must continually track the areas and programs where it is ahead, equal to or behind its talent competitors.

- **Aim ahead of the target**—Forecast where you believe competitors will be in six, 12 or even 24 months, so that you constantly aim where competitors are headed and not where they are currently.

- **Anticipate their next move**—Develop and continually run "what-if?" scenarios to ensure that HR has a plan "B" for the entire range of possible occurrences. Train other managers how to do the same.

You don't have to try each of these actions in order to build a competitive advantage. Start with just a few in order to get into the habit of thinking and acting competitively. As you get more comfortable, then try a few of the more advanced approaches.

PRACTICES GUARANTEED NOT TO PROVIDE A COMPETITIVE ADVANTAGE

Generally, these "generic HR" practices guarantee you won't build a competitive advantage.

- Read the same publications so you don't know anything different.
- Adopt every new HR practice at the same time "they" do.
- Outsource any critical HR function so that you get the same services as others.
- Buy off-the-shelf training that all can buy and isn't customized to your needs.
- Buy standard industry tools like behavioral interviewing (that all can buy).
- Buy the "same" software from vendors that will also sell to your direct competitors.
- Hire the same consultants that others do so you won't have superior advice.
- Avoid metrics as long as possible because you are afraid of them (even though they are essential to winning).

CHAPTER NINE

HR MAKES FACT-BASED DECISIONS USING METRICS

OBJECTIVE

This chapter highlights the fifth element that makes an HR department strategic, making fact-based decisions using metrics.

KEY POINTS

◊ An essential element in any HR department's attempt to become more strategic must be to shift to fact-based decision-making and the metrics that support that type of decision.

◊ Although HR has a long tradition of making decisions based on intuition, feelings and experience, that tradition must end if HR is to increase its strategic business impact.

DEFINITION

Fact-based decisions are decisions made with numbers (metrics) and data rather than emotion.

Although fact-based decision-making is relatively new to HR, fact-based decision-making is common in almost every area of business, from finance to marketing to production. It does occur within HR in a few firms like Intel and Microsoft, but most other VPs of HR are just now learning the important role that metrics and fact-based decision-making plays in making a strategic impact.

When people ask how to easily differentiate between world-class and average HR departments, the one factor that dramatically stands out is the extensive use—or lack of use—of metrics (numerical measures) to assess HR success. The very best firms like Intel, Cisco and Microsoft are metrics "fanatics," while the worst use only personal judgment, feelings and instincts to judge their success.

WHAT IS FACT-BASED DECISION-MAKING?

DEFINITION

Most decisions that have been made in business are *executive* or *managerial* decisions. Executive decisions are decisions made by managers based on their feelings. They may be feelings that are "educated" by years of experience, or even a good deal of intelligence, but they are still decisions made without "facts." In contrast, fact-based decisions are decisions made using facts, data or metrics.

In the last decade, business decision-making has changed from its traditional reliance on executives or managers to just decide, to a more reliable and precise fact-based decision-making. Most decisions are now "fact-based." Almost everything in business has been reduced to numbers. For example, product decisions that used to be made by people frequently have been turned into a metrics-driven process at successful firms like Wal-Mart, GM and Best Buy.

Human protectionists in HR don't want to admit that, in some cases, the limited knowledge, time or experience that people have makes their decisions inferior to decisions that can be made with the help of metrics and sophisticated forecasting techniques. HR might wish that it weren't true, but in fact, it is true in more cases than we care to admit.

In order to increase its strategic impact, HR must make fact-based decisions in these areas:

- Allocating HR dollars and headcount
- Technology purchase decisions
- Internal HR promotions and new hires
- Performance and productivity assessments
- How HR customers and services are prioritized
- Retention targets and what tools are used to retain individuals
- Additional spending in benefits
- Whether to outsource and with what vendor(s)

EXAMPLES OF FACT-BASED HR DECISIONS

As mentioned earlier, there are two types of HR decisions. The first and most common are executive or management decisions. Individuals using whatever criteria they might deem appropriate make executive decisions, the most common criteria being their experience, their intuition or their "gut feelings." I'm not proposing that this type of management decision be eliminated entirely, but they should be relegated to non-strategic HR decisions.

Instead, what HR managers need to do is to shift to the more consistent and accurate form of business decision-making known as "fact-based" decision-making. This type of decision-making demands that facts and data be the primary basis for those decisions.

Some examples of fact-based decision-making in HR include:

- Recruiting dollars are allocated only to sources that produce at least a 5 percent diversity hire rate.
- HR programs that fail to improve their results by at least 10 percent each year can receive no headcount or budget increase.
- HR generalists' bonuses are tied to the percentage of employee productivity improvement in their business units.

- No HR professional can be promoted without successfully completing a business finance class.
- No new HR program can be funded if it does not include a customer satisfaction measure.
- HR budget allocations are made based on the program's estimated contribution to increased workforce productivity.
- New additions to benefits will be selected based on the preferences of the organization's top performers (top 25 percent).

HOW TO RECOGNIZE FACT-BASED DECISIONS

If you're having a difficult time understanding the difference between executive/management decisions and fact-based decision-making, here is a simple comparison table that shows how the two styles address the same problem. This side-by-side comparison demonstrates the superiority of fact-based decision-making in HR.

Problem statement—HR needs to cut its budget by 10 percent.

Table 9-A.

Executive/management decisions	Fact-based decisions
Mary quit, so we might as well shut down her program.	Mary quit, but she left a well-trained replacement that has run the program in her absence at a 100 percent percent efficiency rating. The program has the highest ROI and manager satisfaction of any HR program.
Cisco shut down their XYZ program so we might as well shut down ours, too.	Cisco cut their program but their turnover has doubled since it was cut. The XYZ program is rated by managers as having the highest impact on productivity and retention. Also, its benefit/cost ratio of 2.7 to 1 is the second highest in HR.
I never really liked John, so I'll cut his program as a way to get rid of him.	John receives the highest ranking of any HR professional on our annual survey of managers. The program he operates is so important with managers that they voluntarily funded half the program's costs. It has a 31 percent ROI.
If I shut down the HR call center program, I can save five headcount, which will make me look good to the CFO. The managers can still get their answers by reading the manual.	The five call center staff members are among the lowest paid people in HR, so cutting them will save little. The call center itself saves every manager and employees an average of ½ hour per week in HR "answer shopping." These uncounted cost savings (e.g., the reduced management time) is worth five times the costs of the call center each year.
No one in HR really likes running a call center because they don't see this job as strategic. Rather than force someone into the job, I'll shut it down.	The call center gives 50 percent faster answers and 75 percent more accurate answers than our generalists do. Managers have a 98 percent satisfaction rate with the call center.
Leadership training is the most expensive program we have in HR so I will eliminate it in order to look good and to save a lot of money.	Our company is facing a leadership shortage and we have been unable to hire the necessary leadership talent externally. Our leadership program has developed 75 percent of our top-performing managers. In addition, it is rated by the senior executives as having the highest impact on the business of any HR program. The program ROI is 137 percent.

It's apparent that he traditional HR decision process includes some logic, but that logic is not backed up by data. The fact-based decisions contain little emotion or political concerns, but they do demonstrate the value of the HR programs and individuals using dollars and numbers.

More examples. Other routine decisions made by HR include the following:

Table 9-B.

Executive/management decisions	Fact-based decisions
All of our employees have been working hard and putting in a lot of time, so I think I'll reward them by giving them a 5 percent raise.	Our employee productivity is among the lowest in the industry indicating that we are getting little economic benefit, even though we pay 20 percent above the industry average. Studies of previous across-the-board raises of 5 percent have shown no positive impact on productivity, retention or recruiting. Instead, our research has found that a 5 percent increase in the performance bonus for individuals in key jobs results in a 15 percent increase in productivity.
One of our hourly employees stopped me in the hallway crying because her child was sick and she said that our medical benefits didn't cover the entire medical bill. I hate to see our employees cry and suffer, so I am going to increase medical plan coverage by 5 percent.	We never make an HR decision based on a single incident. We investigated the incident and found that the employee had failed to take advantage of the policy clause for extraordinary expenses. Further research found that we currently pay the second-highest medical benefits in the industry and that any further increase in benefits had no positive impact on retention, productivity and recruiting.
I think I'll just transfer John rather than fire him for sexual harassment because I just know if we do fire him we will get sued.	John's performance caused us to lose a $10 million customer. Our attorneys checked the case and found there was a negligible probability of us being sued. Our research data suggests there is a 91 percent chance John will repeat the sexual harassment. As a result, we terminated John—and fired the HR person for weak decision-making.
I want to be more strategic, so I'm going to drop or outsource most of our HR administration and spend more time attending meetings and building relationships with senior executives.	We have data to prove that conducting transactions helps us better understand employee productivity problems. In a pilot study, we found that eliminating administration reduces manager satisfaction with HR by 22 percent. We also found that even though eliminating administration gave generalists an average of 12 more hours per week free time, employee productivity and manager satisfaction with HR decreased during the pilot.

COMMON FACTORS IN FACT-BASED DECISION-MAKING

Making fact-based decisions in HR means deciding on a certain course of action based on one or more of the following factors:

- Improved employee productivity
- A positive benefit/cost ratio
- A high ROI
- A positive increase in revenue or profit
- A positive impact on a business problem faced by senior management (slow time-to-market, high production costs, low product quality, etc.)
- A pilot study that provided relevant data
- Split-sample tests in order to prove whether programs work

EXAMPLES OF EXECUTIVE/MANAGEMENT DECISION-MAKING

The following list provides some examples of HR decisions *not* based on facts.

- The person's loyalty or length of service determines how he or she will be rewarded.
- The fact that it didn't work before, so we're not going to try it again.
- The fact that it didn't work at Company X, so we're not going to try it.
- The fact that Company X has one, so we need one also.
- We really liked the book/article that described the practice, so we're going to try it.
- Professor X and our consultant recommend it, so we're going to try it.
- We really don't feel comfortable with metrics, so we're not going to implement them.
- We don't like doing administrative tasks, so we're going to outsource that process.

The two different listings demonstrate that while the non-fact-based decision-making relies on emotion, relationships, guesses and intuition, the fact-based decision-making instead bases its decisions on facts and data demonstrating increased productivity, retention or other business impacts.

DECISION FILTERS FOR FACT-BASED HR DECISIONS

If HR is to be successful, it must shift from basing decisions on whatever criteria individuals choose towards making fact-based decisions. Excellent fact-based decisions are decisions that meet three basic criteria. They are decisions made using:

- Objective decision criteria
- Facts and data supporting the criteria
- An established minimum quantifiable "passing score"

Decision criteria are a series of screens or filters that help determine if a decision is a good or bad one. If HR is to be strategic, it must develop a set of objective decision criteria for use in evaluating new program ideas. A decision criterion is a filter that screens out ideas and proposals that do not fit the minimum requirements for acceptance. If an idea or program fails to meet each of the filter criteria, the program must be revised until the idea meets each of the filter criteria. These decision filters work together like a "funnel" to eliminate non-conforming ideas.

But just having the decision criteria is not enough; each of the criteria must be quantified so that everyone knows the passing score for each criteria. When facts, data or numbers are added to objective decision criteria, the result is fact-based decision-making.

Some examples of HR strategic decision filters with the minimum "passing score" include the following, where the proposed HR program or idea has:

- A positive ROI of over 10 percent
- An impact on employee productivity of over 1 percent
- A low initial investment of less than $100,000
- A success rate of over 75 percent
- The capability for immediate start up (*e.g.*, within six months)
- A short payback period (*e.g.*, within one year) for the initial investment
- No new headcount
- Evidence that it is demanded by the managers (at least one GM or director specifically requested it)
- Evidence that it provides us a competitive advantage that can be maintained for at least six months
- A set of performance metrics (including response time, customer satisfaction, output, and cost per unit of service)

- A continuous improvement element embedded in the process with an estimated improvement rate of over 10 percent per year
- A set of measurable goals and objectives
- Prioritization by customers, jobs and business units that it will serve, to ensure resources go where they have the most impact
- A global reach that impacts at least 75 percent of our international business units
- A technology component that includes paperless transactions and approvals and, where appropriate, manager access
- A single individual responsible or accountable for the program where the consequences of failure are specified

In order to make fact-based decisions, HR must develop a set of decision filters to ensure that program decisions are made based on objective criteria. Each decision criteria should have a measurable "minimum passing score" to ensure that only the programs and ideas with the most strategic impact receive resources and support. Good fact-based decisions are objective rather than subjective.

WHY USING METRICS IS ESSENTIAL IN STRATEGIC HR

Metrics and fact-based decision-making go hand in hand. Fact-based decision-making means that, rather than using personal judgment to make HR decisions, facts and data are used. Since metrics include facts and data, they are an essential part of fact-based decision-making.

Metrics are quantified measures of performance. Without them, proving results is difficult, and individual and team accountability is almost impossible. Because they provide managers with the type of information they need to improve the quality of their decisions, metrics are an essential management tool.

Metrics use numbers to accurately "describe" some situation (usually output or performance). When done correctly, a metric takes away all doubt about what was and wasn't accomplished. The metrics recommended below also provide a standard against which you can compare your performance. These metrics allow you to more clearly see how you are doing because they include not just your performance number but also a "benchmark standard" number, which allows you to compare your results to a standard.

YOU CAN'T BECOME A CHAMPION UNLESS YOU KEEP SCORE

If this were the Olympics, it would be obvious that you couldn't become a champion without measuring results. In fact, the definition of a champion is "the one with the best results." In the general business world, the use of metrics is part of life. CEOs, CFOs and shareholders all measure results. Within all major firms, all projects, products, and business units are evaluated on the basis of numerical results. In direct contrast, however, many within HR resist using metrics—HR's dread of metrics is almost the equivalent of dreading a root canal.

WHAT DOES A METRIC LOOK LIKE?

Not everyone agrees on what a metric should look like but in my experience, the very best include the following six elements, including these preliminary issues:

- **The goal to be met**—What specifically are you trying to accomplish with the process, tool or program? It is often the output of a process (for example, effective sourcing).
- **A benchmark number**—A benchmark number for comparison purposes. You can compare to last year, the initial goal, an industry average, or many others, etc. (for example, the industry average for referrals is 30 percent).
- **Definition of all key terms**—Every key word, data element or goal must be clearly defined so there is no doubt about what counts or doesn't count. Formulas should also be determined in advance to ensure consistent measurement over time.

  Then the actual measures:

- **The quantity or number**—A number that reports the quantity (volume or amount) of the process output (for example, 80 percent of our hires last year came from referrals).
- **A measure of quality**—A measure of the quality of the output (for example, did it work, error rate, usability).
- **Additional submeasures**—When relevant, include one or more of the following submetrics, such as
  - Time (when completed, response time, time to completion, deadlines met)
  - Money (cost, revenue)
  - Satisfaction (whether "they" liked the process or result)

THE BENEFITS OF USING METRICS IN HR

Metrics help you manage better. They tell managers what to do "more of and less of" and they allow HR managers to focus their limited resources on tools and strategies that have the most business impact. If you need a further push, here is a list of why metrics are beneficial in HR.

- **Metrics eliminate confusion**—Employees and managers receive so many mixed communications and messages that deciphering what is important can be difficult. Without having to give a speech or write a memo, metrics define what is important and they also tell the person precisely what level of performance is expected.
- **Metrics allow you to focus on your high priority issues**—Metrics tell everyone what is a high priority. Metrics help focus everyone's attention on the important issues. If what you measure is also closely tied to your budgeting process and your rewards, you are on your way.
- **They help drive continuous improvement**—Comparing metrics between different time periods tells you whether and how fast you are improving. Metrics help focus recognition and attention on those programs that are continuously improving. It also gives stagnant programs a benchmark to compare themselves against.
- **Metrics allow you to come across as an expert**—Experts are respected because they emphasize evidence and data rather than conjecture. To be credible, it is essential that you differentiate facts from opinions in your arguments. Specifically in technical departments (and anywhere within high tech and financial firms), "numbers and data" are the "language" that everyone uses. If you use "another" language that substitutes feelings for numbers… no one will listen to you because they will interpret the over use of opinions as meaning that you just don't have any facts. The best managers in business shift so that eventually they are making mostly "fact-based" decisions.
- **Distributing metrics can change individual behavior**—Only rewards change behavior faster than distributing ranked metrics to all. By ranking and distributing your results metrics, you provide visible side-by-side comparisons that can be embarrassing to some and rewarding to others. Both spur employees and managers into action.
- **Metrics are superior to culture in changing the behavior of your managers**—Instead of solely relying on your corporate "culture"

to drive actions, you should instead rely on metrics and rewards to send the message about how you expect people to behave in certain situations. You will find that by simply changing the metrics and rewards you can quickly change the behavior of most everyone. In contrast, most find that changing a corporate culture is extremely difficult and slow, which inevitably slows the needed change in behavior.

- **Metrics tell you what to stop doing**—Quantifying and comparing the success of every program points out to HR managers where resources should be cut and who should be punished or fired. Rapidly cutting underperforming assets (and shifting them to high ROI programs) is an effective way of improving your efficiency and strategic performance.

- **Metrics can build coordination/cooperation**—Metrics that cross departmental lines can encourage cooperation. When work is broken up so that two or more functional units independently handle parts of it, there is often conflict and a lack of cooperation. However, cooperation between the groups can be increased by using a metric (and a reward) that measures the final output, after all parties complete their work. Cooperation increases because both units eventually realize that neither unit can succeed unless the other unit also does its part. This "Superordinate" goal or metric demonstrates to both units their degree of interdependency.

- **Metrics can help to build self-confidence**—Assigning a "passing score" to a task allows you to compare your work to a standard. Individuals can then easily compare their work to that passing score to determine how they are doing. For the best performers, that comparison helps to build their self-confidence. Metrics can also give you legitimate bragging rights if you come out on top.

- **Using metrics sends the message that you are "new school"**— "Old school" HR professionals often carry a reputation of being resistant to metrics and to change. By using metrics (and also technology), you send the positive message that you think differently and have business acumen.

- **Metrics tell you what to reward**—If you work under a pay-for-performance system (we all should) metrics tells managers who and what to reward and punish. Incidentally, rewarding what you measure makes things happen much faster.

■ **Modern ERP and any other HR software systems make it easier**—Because the best new HR software programs include metric elements, it is now much easier to find the data you need and to calculate the metrics. Some software even contain analytics modules which can help you forecast trends and avoid errors.

■ **Metrics help you ensure that you are meeting your goals and customer needs**—It's easy to assume that your internal customers are happy with you but it's better to find out for sure. Customer satisfaction metrics allow managers to know who is happy and who isn't. In addition, if you provide senior management with a year-end report that proves that you have met each of your yearly goals, you send a quick but clear message that you did what you promised.

"Remember . . . without data, it's just an opinion."

WHY SOME PEOPLE RESIST METRICS

Most people enjoy working in HR because they enjoy working with people and helping others with people problems. This is especially true in the "softer side" of HR, including activities like organizational development, coaching, mentoring, training, and leadership development. Concerns for "dehumanizing" people began in the 1950s with fears about the introduction of universal IDs, even Social Security numbers. Historically, many argued that universal IDs, and the application of numbers to individuals in general, created a situation whereby the unique aspects of individuals would be minimized.

In most cases, the reality is the opposite, and those who continue to cling to this excuse are behind the times. The world *has* changed. Credit card companies, insurance companies, political parties, and even your local grocery store have realized that delivering "individualized" service requires that you have data to help you distinguish wants, needs and behaviors unique to each person. In the global fast-changing world, numbers and data have become "king." They represent the key measurement of business success and the determinant of whether you will get future funding.

Although most utilize metrics primarily to build a business case, strong people advocates need them too. As a strong "people advocate," you care about people and improving the quality of their work/life balance. But how can you know what their actual needs are without the use of metrics that identify what is needed? Metrics derived from surveys and focus groups help you understand worker needs and their frustrations.

The value of metrics doesn't stop at determining employee needs. Once you have identified their needs and implemented "people programs" to meet those needs, you aren't finished. It is also essential that you continue to use measurement systems to ensure that the programs actually are meeting the goals you established. And since people-programs are so chronically under-funded, it's also important that you get it right the first time, because there won't be funds to try something else.

Even if you are a die-hard people advocate, consider the value added by using metrics. Metrics don't really dehumanize; rather, they can help you improve your efficiency and responsiveness. Remember, in the end, if you don't agree with the metrics, you are still free to include emotional elements in your decision-making if you so choose. The metrics just give you another option.

THE CONSEQUENCES OF NOT USING METRICS

Failing to utilize metrics can have a number of negative consequences. In addition to the obvious (you will lose a lot of budget battles), there can be other consequences. For example, it's difficult to attract and retain top talent when you don't keep score, because top performers love to keep score. They want to win, and you can't tell them who is winning without metrics.

If you fail to use metrics, there are also some personal consequences. First, your personal pride will suffer because you won't know precisely whether you met your personal, professional or departmental goals. In the highly competitive world of HR it is also true that failing to use metrics will negatively impact your opportunities for pay increases, bonuses, promotion, and yes, even your job security. Merely working hard—in HR as in other areas of business—is no longer sufficient. There are negative consequences if you can't prove you're doing a great job.

FACTORS THAT ARE FORCING HR TO USE METRICS

Technology makes fact-based decisions possible—As the use of technology spreads, capturing and analyzing data in all fields becomes easier. When more HR departments become paperless and more managers and employees have access to computers and the Web, the ability to sort data and distribute reports becomes easier. As it does, the pressure to make metric-based decisions will also increase.

Business process improvement sets the trend—The second driver of metrics use is the success of supply chain management. The supply chain process has transformed a "backwater" operation (warehousing, ordering and shipping) into a widely talked-about profit center. Supply chain succeeded mostly because it shifted to 100 percent metric-based decision-making.

Other overhead functions have also noted this dramatic shift, and they also have started to move toward fact-based decision-making. Managers fell in love with the effectiveness of these data-driven programs, which were successful primarily because they substituted data-based decisions for subjective ones.

Globalization and mergers also force managers to shift to fact-based decisions—The globalization and consolidation of companies through mergers means that firms are now much larger and their workforces are spread over huge geographic areas. Mergers and globalization have made it difficult to get to know geographically dispersed managers, much less to trust them to make informed decisions.

Once the face-to-face contact that is possible in smaller firms has been lost, it becomes obvious that you you can't assess performance "remotely" without metrics and quantifiable goals. Global competition means you must make fast decisions and, in most cases, fast "fact-based" decisions are more consistent than fast "gut" executive decisions. Great fact-based decisions are decisions made by experienced humans using the data provided by measurement and metrics.

"A metric is a way to demonstrate accountability."

Metrics can help improve your relationship with the CFO and CIO—The fourth reason to adopt metrics and fact-based decision-making is that CFOs love fact-based decisions. CFOs live in a world full of facts and devoid of emotions and emotional decision-making.

In a highly competitive world dominated by CFOs who want to cut your budget, business function and program managers no longer have a choice, they must demonstrate their economic value using metrics. CFOs want everyone to be accountable. If you are in a situation where charm has run out as an option, then it's probably time to consider switching to metrics in HR to prove your impact.

Using metrics sends a clear message that you are "business-like." Tracking and quantifying your results can—almost instantly—get the CFO and CIO on your side because it demonstrates that you think and talk like they do (*i.e.,* you both now make fact-based decisions). By measuring results, you are demonstrating to top management that you are results-oriented. Reports that include numbers and metrics make the CFO happy, not just because they are easier to read than most wordy HR reports, but also because they make your results more easily comparable to what others do.

It is unlikely that any of these four trends will slow down in the immediate future, so now is the time to jump on the metrics bandwagon before someone in authority uses your lack of metrics as an excuse to cut your budget ... or to cut you.

> *"What you measure and reward takes away all doubt about what is important."*

CRITERIA FOR SELECTING METRICS

Not all companies are the same. Each has its own culture and focus. Some emphasize performance in every area of the business while other firms narrow in on only one area, like costs or quality. Because using metrics gets almost everyone to focus on what is measured, it is important when selecting departmental metrics that the metrics selected reflect the values and goals of the corporation.

METRICS SELECTION FACTORS

Accordingly, when you select departmental metrics for HR, use the following five factors:

- **Reflect the culture**—Select HR metrics that reflect the culture and values of the firm. If, for example, you work for an engineering firm where quality in precision matters greatly, make sure you also select a set of HR metrics that also focus on quality imprecision.

- **Mirror the business goals**—Before you pick which metrics to use in HR, make sure that they align or directly track to the corporate goals and objectives. Remember the sum of all performance metrics (from the departments) should equal the overall company performance metrics.

- **Mirror your product's critical success factors**—If your organization produces a product or service, it's important to identify factors that must be present in order to ensure the successful development and sale of your product. These are critical success factors (CSFs). In overhead functions like HR, it's important to ensure that even though HR is an indirect function, it can contribute directly to the product success. As a result, the metrics HR selects should relate directly to the products' critical success factors. For example, if product development speed is essential for success, select HR metrics that also focus on speed and time to market.

- **Focus on results, not just process**—Many HR departments only measure process efficiency. Although process efficiency is clearly important, it is far better to focus on the output of your processes. A recruiting process, for example, could measure the cost per hire (which would be a process efficiency factor), but a better overall metric would be measuring the value of the increased output (productivity) that results from hiring more productive people for the next two years. The cost of the transaction is less important than the "output"—the performance of the person you hire (i.e., a superstar employee like Tiger Woods).

- **Select metrics that relate to business goals**—There is no magic here. Your department and your firm have certain measurable objectives that must be met. It is your job as a manager to determine which outputs will lead to the successful completion of each of the major business goals or objectives. If metrics measure performance and output, which output or result area should you select to measure? While there is no simple answer, most process, product or program results can be categorized into several distinct areas. They include the possible business output or result measures below:

Table 9-C.

ROI, ratios and value comparisons—Productivity	
Profitability	Efficiency
Volume/number/dollars—Market value	
Amount	Size
Volume	Yield
Goal attainment percent	Effectiveness
Quality—Consistency	
Accuracy	Reject rate
Reliability	Error rate
Feature-richness	
Usage/usability—Dependability	
Capability	Availability
Defectiveness	Clarity/understandability
Customization	Changability
Utilization percent	Breadth of choices
Usability	Ease of use
Complexity	Durability
Safeness	Convenience
Variability	Accessibility
Compatibility	
Service/satisfaction—Satisfaction rate	
Number of complaints	Return rate
Loyalty—Repeat usage/re-visit rate	
Brand inclination to buy or use	
Visibility—Awareness	
Positive image	PR/press exposure
Costs—Cost per unit	
Percentage of cost overruns	
Time/speed—Timeliness	
Percentage on time	Cycle time
Speed of improvement	Reduced management time
Innovation—New idea generation	
Innovativeness	Patents/copyrights
Agility—Flexibility	
Adaptability/agility	
Other—Ease of administration	
Coordination required between different business units	

WHICH TYPES OF METRICS ARE AVAILABLE TO HR?

Soft and hard HR metrics

When you are selecting your HR metrics, it is important to realize that CFOs break metrics into two different degrees of believability. Those that relate to items not counted in the budget or financial ledger are known as soft metrics, and those that are included in the budget or financial ledger are known as hard metrics. Just in case you didn't already guess, CFOs are biased in favor of hard metrics.

Perhaps some examples will illustrate the difference.

Soft HR metrics

Not really metrics—"I think my program works, "managers like me," "no one complains," "we are all working really hard here," "we've instituted five new programs," etc., cannot be considered program measures or metrics.

HR time savings—shifting HR work so that employees and managers (on paid time) do the work that used to be done by HR is not really considered cost savings. Although these actions might save on the HR budget, there is no net savings to the firm. In a similar light, shifting employee costs to consultants, outsource vendors, contractors or temps may result in headcount savings to HR, but real costs may actually go up.

Time and cost savings from HR process re-engineering—Streamlined HR processes and reduced paperwork, for example, generally are considered soft metrics because HR offers no proof that HR headcount will actually be reduced. If HR asserts that employee or manager time was saved (as a result of fewer calls, reports or approvals required) it is still a soft metric unless HR can first prove that time-saving actually occurs and second that the "saved" time is actually shifted to greater on-the-job productivity.

Employee satisfaction and less stress—Although happy employees may seem on the surface to be a valuable thing, CFOs wonder if the higher satisfaction or the reduced stress are a result of lower standards and less pressure to perform.

Hard metrics

Increased on the job performance—Demonstrating that individual employee performance increases are the result of a new program, for example, that a new recruiting program produces hires with 25 percent higher job performance during their first year (compared to those hired under the old hiring system) and an industry-low 1 percent termination rate in the first year.

Return on investment—Showing that invested dollars bring a high rate of return. A new incentive program spends $1000 more per salesperson per month, for example, but the sales revenue increases by an average of $100,000 for every salesperson under the new incentive program. It returns $100 for every $1 invested (the firm average ROI is 2 to 1, and the next best in the firm is 8 to 1).

Program impact—Where a single program has an immediate demonstrable impact, such as revenue increasing 17 percent within two months of the sales team's completion of the new sales training program. Other sales teams that were not trained had no increase in revenue.

Correlation with performance—When the productivity or performance increases proportionately with program usage increases. For example, productivity increases by 10 percent in departments that increase training expenditures by 1 percent (and vice versa).

Revenue per people cost dollar—Measures the marginal performance of the organization as it relates to spending on people programs; for example, revenue per dollar spent on employee costs went up 32 percent after the performance management system identified and released the bottom 5 percent of employees in a business unit.

Decreased costs—Where actual labor costs are reduced. For example, a new scheduling system in manufacturing resulted in a 10 percent decrease in people costs per unit of output within a week of implementation. Decreased labor costs, however, are not automatically a positive thing if they result in decreased productivity, reduced quality, or slower time-to-market.

SINGLE PROGRAM METRICS AND INDEX METRICS

There are basically two types of metrics:
- A single metric, which measures the output of just one particular process or program, and

- An index metric, which, in contrast, combines several individual process measures into a single uniform "index."

Example: Single metrics for strategic HR

Using a strategic HR example, here are eight individual metrics that can be used:

- Revenue (or profit) per dollar spent on people (productivity)
- Turnover of the top 10 percent of the workforce
- Turnover of the bottom 10 percent of the workforce
- On-the-job performance of recent hires (average output and tenure)
- Percentage of key employees whose pay is based on performance (pay at risk)
- Percentage of employees who are satisfied with their managers
- Turnover rate of poor managers
- Manager satisfaction with HR
- Time to fill key jobs
- Diversity ratios of the workforce

Example: Single metrics in recruiting

Using a recruiting example, here are eight individual metrics that you could use:

- Quality: On the job performance of the hire
- Source effectiveness (quality and retention rate per dollar of cost)
- New hire failure rates and the retention of new hires
- Recruiter effectiveness
- Manager satisfaction
- Applicant satisfaction
- Speed of hire (percent of target dates met)
- Diversity of hires

Some HR departments utilize an array of single metrics to monitor weekly or monthly HR performance. This array of metrics is generally called an HR dashboard.

WHY YOU SHOULD CHOOSE AN INDEX FOR STRATEGIC HR PERFORMANCE

Although single metrics have great value, when you utilize too many of them they can overwhelm you. Too many single metrics may overwhelm you with details so that you never see the big picture. With a quick glance, however, an index metric allows you to see the performance of particular function or program. An index metric provides you with a single number that makes comparisons between this year and last, as well as between different business units, easy to make. Combining multiple factors into a single index initially takes a little work, the resulting index is an easy-to-use and easy-to-quote indication of performance.

Not everyone uses index metrics in HR, but there are a variety of examples that you can see every day. Some of them include:

- Stock market indexes like the Standard & Poor's and Dow Jones
- Economic indexes like the Consumer Price Index
- Physical indexes like the air pollution index
- The homeland security/terrorist alert index

Using employment as a focus, the following is an example of how an HR index can work. If you need to compare performance between completely different and unique divisions and you need a common comparison metric, an index is the best approach. In this example, an employment index is highlighted.

An employment index is the averaged score of several weighted recruiting measures. It is a simple indication of recruiting "health," and it's easy to track on a single chart. In these indexes, any score below 100 is considered below average and below 90 indicates a more serious problem.

Indexes can be used as a type of alert or great "smoke detector." If you track them over time, you can demonstrate to managers that a dropping score is a warning indicating that management action is needed immediately if you are to avoid a further decline. Two examples of recruitment indexes are provided below.

METRICS

Performance index for recruiting

The normal or expected score = 100

Needs immediate improvement = a score of 90 or below

Excellent performance = a score of 110 or above

Weight	Performance factor	Two-year baseline score
25 percent	Performance of hires	1.0 average new hire performance appraisal score
25 percent	Percent of hires from referrals	40 percent of all hires come from referrals
20 percent	Time to fill	60 days from data requisition
15 percent	Manager satisfaction	90 percent very satisfied on year-end survey
15 percent	Diversity hiring ratios	10 percent diverse hires

HOW IS AN INDEX ELEMENT CALCULATED?

Calculating an element within the index

This example features one of the five elements of the employment index, the performance of hires, in order to demonstrate how it would be calculated.

The performance of each new hire is measured at the end of the first year. The standard performance appraisal score is used. Start with performance appraisal scores of all hires over the last two years. Add all of the performance ratings altogether and divide by the number of all hires in order to get the average new hire performance score over the last two years. That number, 1.0, for example, becomes a baseline against which all changes are measured. A 1.0 score on a new hire performance appraisal becomes equal to the normal or expected score (most indices generally use 100 as a standard "norm" number).

$$1.0 = 100$$

Accordingly, if you hired one hundred new people last year and their average performance appraisal score was 1.0, then the performance of hire *base* score would be 100, indicating it is average. Anytime actual performance appraisal scores varied from that 1.0 average by a certain percentage, the element score of 100 would then be changed by the same percentage variation.

In order to weight the factor you would then multiply that index number by the factor weight (in this case, 25 percent) and you would get the final factor score of 25. Since 25 is the average or normal score on that particular index factor, the number 25 indicates that the performance of your hires is merely average, neither bad nor good. A score of 20, for example, would indicate a poor performance rating of new hires, while a score of 30 would indicate that you are hiring top performers.

Calculating an index element when a "negative" score is good

For most index elements, as performance improves, the number increases (*e.g.*, as applicant satisfaction improves, the score goes up). For some index elements, the reverse is true, however. When the score of the element decreases, it is an indication of good performance.

For example, when time-to-fill for positions decreases, it generally means that a recruiting process is working better because the number of days it takes to hire someone has decreased. On the surface, this reverse trend appears to be a problem because when the overall index increases, it means that good things are happening. With this individual factor (time to fill) the opposite is true. There is however, a procedure for "reversing" the direction of the score, which solves the problem.

For example, if the time to fill decreased 10 percent (54 days compared to the last two years' norm of 60 days) instead of lowering the standard score in the index by 10 percent, you would instead "reverse" the percentage change (improvement) and increase the element by 10 percent. An improvement on the index must be reflected by an increase in the element score. As a result, a 10 percent decrease in time to fill would, in fact, *increase* the base element score of 100 by 10 percent to 110. Therefore, the final score is 110, which reflects a 10 percent increase in the performance of the time to hire factor.

How to determine the appropriate "weight" of an index factor

All indexes "weight" each of the items in the index. That weight reflects the relative importance of the item to HR managers. The higher the weight assigned to a particular factor, the greater impact—either positive or negative—performance will have on the overall index. For example if you assigned a 50 percent weight to a particular factor, if that factor drops by even 10 percent, the overall index will drop significantly (a minimum of 5 percent). In contrast, if that factor is weighted only 5 percent weight, then even a dramatic change would have only a minimal (less than 5 percent) impact on the overall index.

Assigning weights to factors is not magical. You just assign a high weight to factors that your boss or your company really care about and low weights to less important items. Over time you adjust the weights so that eventually when the index reads 100, you are comfortable, and when it reads 110, you have no doubt that you are clearly exceeding expectations.

DEVELOPING METRICS FOR MEASURING HR RESULTS

Whether you are setting up a new HR program or metrics for an entire HR department, there are certain steps you need to take in order to be successful. The following section outlines the key steps in setting up a program success measurement system.

STEPS TO TAKE DURING THE PROGRAM DESIGN PHASE

Long before you begin the start up phase of any new program, there are certain steps regarding program goals and accountability that must be completed. They include:

Accountability for program success—Identify the specific individuals that are "accountable" for the program's success. These are generally program managers; they are the ones that generally are rewarded if the program meets its goals and punished if the program fails.

Goals and outputs—Identify each of the different program goals and outputs. Program goals are generally derived from either potential program outputs (i.e., service 24 customers a day, double the number of training program offerings) or the problems that the program was set up to alleviate (i.e., reduce turnover from 10 to 5 percent, eliminate sexual harassment lawsuits).

Remember that whatever goals you select for the program automatically become program metrics. Whenever you list a specific program goal, be sure to define it, not just in the volume or dollar amount of output you expect, but also include a quality of the output element (i.e., service 24 customers a day with a 95 percent or above satisfaction rate) Time, money and satisfaction measures should be added to each goal as appropriate.

Be aware that goals can never be defined exclusively using words. Goals must also include at the minimum two different numbers:
- the minimum passing score required to satisfy the goal, and
- the score or performance level that is necessary to be considered excellent (see the next two items in this listing, below)

Passing score—For each separate goal you must define, using numbers, a minimum acceptable score (a.k.a. "passing" score). If your program produces a number below this level, it is assumed that the program has failed to meet the goal. In academic terms, the passing score would be the minimum score required to avoid an "F" grade.

Excellent score—For each separate goal you must define, using numbers, what score it takes to be rated as excellent in performance. In academic terms, this would be the minimum score for an "A" grade.

Weight the goal—In most cases, every program goal is not of equal importance. Being on time, for example, might be more or less important than being under budget. Prioritize or weight each different program goal and output, depending on the relative importance to the organization. Generally, program goals are assigned weights so that the total for all goals equals 100.

STEPS TO TAKE DURING PROGRAM START-UP

Assuming that you obtained funding and you are ready to begin the process of starting up the program, there are several other important steps you must take to ensure an accurate and effective metrics program. They include:

Elements of a program measurement system

Responsibility for overall program metrics—Designate someone to be responsible for designing and maintaining program metrics. Where appropriate, give them the authority and resources they need to implement metrics when the program becomes operational. Offer them rewards for accurate and efficient measurement.

Benchmark other measurement systems—Benchmark other similar internal and external program measurement systems in order to identify the factors essential for accurate and efficient metric systems. Also, identify any potential measurement problems and their potential solutions.

Three types of program performance measures

Determine program output measures—Determine your primary program performance measures. Most of these primary measures will be related directly to each of the program's goals that are set during the program design phase.

Include financial measures—Determine if, in addition to standard program performance measures, you also want to include financial measures (ROI, payback period, cash flow, profit etc.) in your program assessment.

Include efficiency measures—Determine what program efficiency measures you want to monitor (efficiency measures are internal process measures) for program improvement. These are minor measures which may not have to be reported outside of the program's staff.

Other metric system steps

Determine the formulas and definitions—Assign someone responsibility for determining the "formula" for calculating each of the individual program performance measures. In addition, define all key terms clearly and precisely so that everyone is on the same page when they use or measure the item connected to the word.

Who will calculate each performance measure—Every individual program goal and performance measure must be calculated. The process begins by assigning an individual the task of calculating all of the elements that appear in each formula. Someone must be assigned the responsibility for requesting the data needed for each formula and then for performing the final calculations. Individuals typically assigned the role of calculating a performance measure might include the CFO, vendors, program managers, and program analysts.

How to measure "new" data—After someone is assigned the role of calculating the formula for each performance measure, that person must determine what is the best way to measure each element (that is not already collected) that appears in the formula for which they have responsibility. Prior to making a decision, the responsible individual should examine what measurement systems have worked in the past, both internally and externally. Be sure to include cost, compatibility with other systems, accuracy, privacy and "degree of intrusiveness" in the decision criteria.

When to measure "new" data—The individual responsible for collecting new data must determine the best time to accurately measure each item (weekly, monthly or quarterly). Develop a measurement timeline with dates for each new measure.

Data sources for existing data—Some of the data needed to calculate each formula are already available either inside or outside the corporation. The individual responsible for calculating the formula must determine where, when and how they will obtain this existing data for their calculations.

Data accuracy—The individual responsible for requesting existing data must measure and assess the data's accuracy. Individuals responsible for collecting new data must develop a system for anticipating potential data accuracy problems prior to program start-up. Data accuracy and integrity must be assessed directly once the data collection program becomes operational.

CIO check—Because the CIO is responsible for most corporate data, it's wise to run your measurement system plans by the CIO's office to ensure that your approach for collecting new data is sound and that the existing data you need is accurate and available.

CFO check—Because the CFO's office is the one that makes a final determination as to whether your metrics are credible and acceptable, it's also wise to run your entire measurement system plan by the CFO's office for revision and approval. Involving the CFO in the plan and providing some degree of CFO "ownership" can help head off potential problems.

Reporting results—Determine the best way to deliver and report program results metrics. Determine who should receive the report, in what format, and when. Consider providing users with several different media choices. When appropriate, get the CFO's opinion on your reporting plan.

Pre-test the entire measurement system—Pre-test the entire measurement system (if possible) before the HR program becomes operational, and revise if you identify problems. If pre-testing is not possible, consider getting outside measurement consultants to assess your plan.

Operationalize—After the HR program begins operation, begin collecting data and assess the effectiveness of the entire metric program. Revise, if necessary, after your first measures are taken.

Weight the results—At the end of the first quarter of program operation, collect the information, insert into the formula, and calculate the results for each program goal. Take that final performance number and weight it in the same proportion as the goal/output was weighted when you prioritized your goals initially. Do this for each separate goal, and then combine them to determine the proportion of the program's goal that you have met and whether your HR program has been a success or failure. Repeat the calculations each quarter; do a summary after the first year of operation.

Report learning—Identify any "lessons learned" from the first and subsequent quarters' measurement process. Revise and improve your measurement system and share your successes and failures in the measurement area with other program managers.

Implementing a metric system to assess HR program effectiveness requires a great deal of time and energy. Avoid the temptation of skipping a step because, if you do, you leave yourself vulnerable to the many potential criticisms that can come from financial, metric and data experts. Unfortunately, if you fail to be precise in your program measurement system, you are likely to pay the price in program credibility and future funding opportunities.

The next section will highlight another critical element in becoming strategic, which is being proactive and future-focused.

CHAPTER TEN

HR IS PROACTIVE AND FUTURE-FOCUSED

OBJECTIVE

The sixth element that makes an HR department strategic is being proactive and future-focused. This is an extremely desirable goal, but in practice it is seldom obtained. Instead, most HR practitioners are reactive and present-day focused.

KEY POINTS

◊ Being proactive and seeking out potential problems in order to minimize them is critical for strategic HR. This is being future-focused.

◊ Workforce planning and forecasting tools allow HR to identify future issues before they are an unwelcome surprise.

◊ The combined approaches of being proactive and future-focused give HR an opportunity to act like a true strategic leader by aggressively identifying future problems and opportunities. By being prepared, HR provides itself with a chance to both build its image and to increase its impact.

DEFINITION

What do proactive and future-focused mean?

In this case, being proactive means seeking out strategic business problems and opportunities, while being future-focused means utilizing forecasting and workforce planning to prepare for the future.

HR is not alone in its focus on present-day issues. The speed of change in the business world makes it difficult for anyone to forecast the future, and an increased emphasis on producing quarterly results has caused almost everyone to take a reactive, short-term perspective. Becoming strategic requires you to do the hard things, however, so it's probably time to accept that, in order to be strategic in HR, you must be simultaneously short- *and* long-term focused.

In the strategic sense, seeking out business problems differs from the traditional HR approach where functional managers seek out day-to-day operational problems that are unlikely to have a major strategic impact. Instead, HR needs to seek out "future strategic problems"—problems that may exist currently but are likely to grow into major problems that could seriously impact the business in the next year.

The key is for HR to identify them early and to propose solutions to line managers that address the part of the problem that is caused by weak people-management. By proactively seeking out problems HR is aggressively, rather than passively, attempting to impact corporate results.

BEYOND THE BUSINESS PARTNER APPROACH

This position varies from the traditional business partner approach, where you build relationships with managers and then you respond rapidly whenever the managers call with a problem. The basic difficulty with this reactive approach is that managers are not always adept at early problem identification. In fact, they are often great pro-crastinators and frequently don't recognize how serious a problem is until it is too late. Then, by the time the call comes, the problem may have become so severe that there is little that anybody can do.

To avoid this problem, stop relying solely on managers to identify problems at an early enough stage to make a difference. Instead, develop "sensing mechanisms" in HR to identify both potential and real problems at the early stages. In both these cases, HR can be truly strategic by minimizing and even preventing problems.

When HR seeks out strategic opportunities, it is looking not for problems but for areas where new ideas, initiatives or programs might provide an opportunity to increase product development speed, improve product quality or improve customer service, etc.

WHY BE FUTURE-FOCUSED?

Being future-focused is a common characteristic of everything strategic. Why? Strategic problems are generally solved with strategic resources, and there's almost always a delay in gathering and applying strategic resources. As a result, the problem must be a "future problem." In other words, in order to apply strategic resources to a problem, you must look far enough ahead so that there is time for the strategic resources to arrive and to have their desired impact.

Individuals who are future-focused spend approximately 25 percent of their time on planning and anticipating what is likely to happen in the next 6 to 24 months. In some industries where there's a long lead-time, like in nuclear power, managers must look as many as 10 years in advance, because that's how long it takes to design and build a nuclear power plant.

HOW TO BE PROACTIVE AND PREVENT STRATEGIC PROBLEMS

Everyone spends a good percentage of their time reacting to problems; it is only natural to focus on the squeaky wheel. HR is constantly reacting to problems in retention, compensation, recruiting, etc., and of course there is nothing wrong with that unless you spend all of your time *reacting* and none of your time *preventing* people-management problems. A strategic approach requires HR to act like a fire fighter.

BEST PRACTICE

Act like you are preventing fires

Yes, fire departments react to phone calls and then dispatch a truck to fight the actual fire. But there also are actions that fire fighters take to prevent fires. Note that these underlying actions also should be taken by the human resource department:

Prevention—The fire department studies past fires and tries to determine their causes. It also looks for any patterns so that this information can be utilized to prevent future fires. Utilizing this information, fire codes are developed so that there is a reduced likelihood that a fire will occur. Fire departments also make *periodic visits* to ensure that fire codes are being met.

Early warning—Systems are developed to warn that a fire is in its early stages. Heat sensors, *smoke alarms* and fire alarms are early warning devices designed to alert help early enough that the fire doesn't get out of control.

Mitigating actions—Once a fire begins, it's important to reduce or mitigate the damage. *Sprinklers* and automatic fire doors are mechanisms developed not to prevent fires but to minimize damage once they start.

Fast response—Once notified that there is a fire, the fire department reacts quickly because it assumes in advance that fires will occur. As a result, the fire department develops a *rapid response team* to attack the fire before it gets out of control. The rapid response team is assigned to get there first and is trained to use *"what—if"* *scenarios.* This team has *special tools* so that the moment it arrives it can assess the situation, take immediate action, or call for additional help when necessary.

Rapid learning for future prevention—Once a fire is put out, another group of specialists performs a *post mortem or failure analysis* and identifies the fire's causes. That information is *disseminated widely* so that others can learn from this fire. This *feedback* is used by others to revise fire codes and develop processes so that similar fires can be prevented in the future.

As you can see in this fire department example, there are five basic elements in strategic firefighting. Perhaps it's not a surprise that the best HR departments use a similar five-step approach in attacking and preventing strategic people-management problems.

FIVE STEPS OF PROACTIVE HR

Strategic HR leaders do more than react to problems; they reach out to try to prevent problems. They also try to identify problems in their early stages. If you would like to follow a similar strategic problem prevention strategy, here are the steps to take.

1) Proactive prevention

Proactive HR leaders study people-management problems in order to identify patterns and symptoms. They realize up-front that people-management fires can be prevented if their causes are identified. Some of the steps that HR should take in proactive prevention include:

- **Identify causes**—Study past people-management problems and identify their root causes. Be sure and separate the obvious "symptoms" of people problems from the root causes.
- **Identify patterns**—Study multiple people-management events, even though they seem unrelated, to see if there are identifiable patterns or if they have similar causes.
- **Early warning indicators**—Determine if there are visible early warning symptoms or signs that can be utilized as early warning indicators. For example, long before people quit a job, they frequently check on the separation benefits, stop putting in extra hours, or begin sprucing up their resume. Educate HR staff and

managers about these early warning signs. Look especially at statistical indicators like employee turnover or absenteeism that can be used by HR to identify any "soon-to-become" problems.

- **Periodic visits**—HR leaders must periodically visit both top- and bottom-performing business units in order to get a sense about what's really happening. HR professionals need to be trained to look for the symptoms of problems. They must also train managers to do the same.

2) Early warnings

HR must develop systems to warn managers and HR about the early stages of people-management problems. Some of the things that HR can do to be proactive include:

- **Decision trees**—Frequently people-management problems occur when no HR person is available. Managers that work in remote locations or during off hours or shifts need help as well. HR can develop a "decision tree" to walk managers through the early steps of a people-management problem.

DEFINITION

A decision tree is a series of questions and answers. It can be on the Internet or a printed document. It works by asking managers a series of questions about an incident and, depending on the answer, it takes them through additional questions until eventually at the end of each "branch" there is a recommended course of action. Solutions can range from "ignore it" to the more severe "call police." Most modern software includes a decision tree in its troubleshooting programs. Although decision trees take some time to put together, once compiled they work well without any additional need for outside assistance. Advanced decision tree systems known as "expert systems" can be put on the company's web site. These electronic systems can actually improve themselves over time as they learn from experience.

- **FAQs**—This approach is less sophisticated than the decision tree but it can have some value for isolated managers. It's merely a series of "frequently asked questions" and answers that were developed as a result of analyzing similar people-management problems that occurred in the past. It includes a listing of the questions that a manager would be expected to raise when encountering a particular people-management problem. Answers should be tested with HR experts and managers to see if they are complete and understandable.

- **"Smoke detectors" or "heat sensors"**—Long before departmental productivity reaches its bottom, there are often warning signs of tension, anxiety or anger. The concept of smoke detectors is pretty simple. Certain events in HR, even if they can't be predicted, can at least be stopped at the "smoke stage" before they turn into full-blown catastrophes. Runaway employee turnover and strikes almost always have "precursors" (predictors) that, if tracked, can give advance warning of likely events. Unfortunately, most HR departments are reactive at best. They are so busy day to day they forget to spend the necessary time preventing people-management problems. Even large HR departments don't forecast external events (like unemployment rates, changes in market share, competitor actions, etc.) that directly impact their operations.

- A planned strategy that includes data and information gathering can provide HR and line managers with sufficient lead-time so that they can successfully minimize any damage. HR needs to identify these precursors or indicators of festering people-management problems. Some potential precursors or early warning signs that indicate that there are hidden people-management problems include:

  Early warnings for specific departments or business units:
  - A popular manager or supervisor quits or leaves "unhappy"
  - An increase in the number of complaints and grievances
  - Increased turnover of high performers
  - Decrease in 360-degree or employee satisfaction survey ratings
  - Decrease in productivity or production
  - Increased error rates
  - Increased accidents
  - Increased rumor volume

- Exit interview comments
- Increased open-door visits or call center/hot line calls
- Decreases in applications and offer-acceptance rates
- "Coffee talks," focus groups, and employee conversations reveal they are unhappy.
- Authorization card/union activity
- A sudden increase in absenteeism/ tardiness in a department
- Increased refusal of overtime
- An increased percentage of internal transfers or applications for transfers
- Poor departmental performance results
- A high number of project failures

3) Mitigating actions

Once it is clear that a manager or business unit has a people-management problem, it's important to try to reduce or mitigate the damage. I call these tools that mitigate or minimize the damage once the people-management problem occurs "sprinklers."

- **People problems' sprinklers**—Once a people-management problem occurs, these semi-automatic tools can swing into action to help minimize the damage. Some HR sprinklers include having HR generalists interview the parties, or having employee coffee talks, gripe sessions and "open door" practices.
- **Decision trees & FAQ's**—These items described in the last section can also be utilized as mitigation tools.

4) Fast response

Once the HR department has been notified that there is a people-management problem, it's important for HR to react quickly with the right people and tools. A strategic HR department studies past problems and which responses and tools had the most impact. HR uses that information to develop effective responses. Some that you might consider include:

- **Rapid response/SWAT team**—Most HR departments rely on generalists or individual employee relations specialists to handle people-management problems. While many of these individuals are good at a wide variety of things, they may not have the skills to handle a particular type of problem. Consequently, another approach is to develop a SWAT team. A SWAT team is a small but well-trained rapid response group that is dispatched when there is a major or unique people-management problem. SWAT team members are trained by using "what—if" and "if—then" scenarios that were developed from previous high-difficulty people-management problems. Although SWAT team members might have other duties, they have backup so that in an emergency situation, they can be released to attack the problem. Some organizations that have "centers of excellence" in HR have attempted to use them to resolve people-management issues. Unfortunately, in many cases they are unable to respond appropriately because they are not trained for fast response situations.

- **Peer managers**—Although employees cause many people-management problems, many of the root causes of these problems are the managers themselves. While most managers work well with HR, sometimes it takes another manager to intervene in order to get them to really listen. A peer manager is another working manager who is proficient at solving people-management problems. Peer managers are also selected because they have had a good working relationship with the manager in the past, and would be assigned to the problem area to work directly with HR and the individual manager to identify and resolve the issue.

- **Outside consultants**—Because HR departments are frequently understaffed, they sometimes cannot react quickly, no matter how talented they are. In these cases, it is sometimes possible for HR departments to find competent fast-reaction help by using outside consultants who already work with the firm. Generally they are selected and prepared in advance for the role, and frequently they are former or retired employees.

- **ER specialists or generalists**—Some organizations have well-trained employee relations specialists or occasionally even generalists who know the culture and the background of the business unit better than any outsider could. In these cases these individuals can be sent alone or as a complement to another rapid response solution.

5) Rapid learning for future prevention

Once the people-management problem is resolved, it's crucial that HR learn rapidly so it can identify other similar people-management problems currently occurring, as well as prevent similar problems in the future. The key is to identify the root causes of the problem and which tools proved to be most effective in resolving it.

- **Postmortem team**—A postmortem team is comprised of individuals who are skilled in identifying the root causes of people-management problems. This analysis of disasters is often called "failure analysis." Team members are often scientists, people with law enforcement backgrounds, or psychologists. They are good at interviewing as well as sorting through data to identify symptoms and problems. After reviewing their results with senior HR managers, the team then disseminates the results of their investigation widely to other managers. Specific areas to be covered include any early warning signs, which tools were most effective, and the root causes. They might also recommend changes to HR processes or policy.

- **Cross functional team**—When resources are limited, another option is to use an already existing cross functional team to study the problem and recommend solutions to prevent further occurrences.

Summary of the five proactive steps

Many organizations excel at preventing disasters and responding rapidly to problems. The military has a rapid deployment force, police departments have SWAT teams, the Centers for Disease Control has quarantine teams, and the Forest Service has "jump teams." All use similar strategies and all have an excellent records in finding and preventing catastrophes. The key lesson here is to learn by "parallel benchmarking" so that people-management problems with a large impact on employee productivity can be prevented or reduced.

> *"Telling managers about "yesterday" is like rehashing bad news. It has no value. Nothing will wow managers more than putting a stake in the sand and predicting a future event. If you accurately forecast what will happen, your status as an expert in people-management will forever be etched in their mind."*

WHY YOU MUST DO WORKFORCE PLANNING

It's no secret that the economy goes up and down in cycles. Looking ahead, whether the current economy takes another downturn or rebound is imminent, it is important to learn how to anticipate and smooth out the negative impact of the "talent cycle." It's time to review the errors of past years and to begin to put resources and time into workforce planning.

ECONOMIC AND BUSINESS REASONS

- **Be ready for the economic upturn**—Accurate economic forecasts are even more necessary during a downturn because senior managers want to explode out-of-the-box with the right talent as soon as the economic recovery begins.
- **Anticipate and deal with rapid change**—The ever-increasing rate of change in the business cycle (instant bankruptcies and industry consolidation) requires more accurate forecasting of both the economy and what competitors are doing. Companies must develop alerts or "smoke detectors" that give managers advance warnings before minor workforce issues become major ones.
- **Redeploying resources**—As internal business priorities change in response to rapid external change, it is essential that businesses be able to rapidly redeploy or redistribute skills and people to business units and jobs with a higher ROI. Even if you forecast well, there will still be cases when you will need to quickly react and adjust by shifting resources within the firm.
- **Globalization**—As business is becoming increasingly global and physically distant, it is no longer possible by simply "walking around" to know the labor needs in dispersed business units and in distant geographic regions.
- **Company size**—As companies increase in size relatively quickly (often due to mergers), identifying future leaders and workforce needs becomes almost impossible because you can't know everyone and see them in action. Instead, a formalized workforce planning process that uses technology to bridge the gaps and metrics to assess performance is required.

- **Integration after mergers**—As industry consolidation increases as a result of mergers the need to have plans to rapidly integrate two workforces and cultures will continue.
- **Flat organizations**—Tight economic times force organizations to cut costs and organizational charts get flatter as mid-level management positions are eliminated. Fewer management positions generally also mean fewer promotions; consequently the need increases for plans and strategies to motivate, challenge and develop workers in other ways.
- **Immigration restrictions**—Increased homeland security issues now make it more difficult to bring in international workers in order to fill short-term needs. As a result, better local recruitment plans and remote work options are needed.

HEADCOUNT AND RETENTION REASONS

- **Smooth out the fluctuations in the hire/ layoff cycle**—Managers and employees alike seek to smooth out the sudden "peaks and valleys" in employee headcount. The boom and bust cycle (the recent round of layoffs after a period of unprecedented hiring) needs to end because it is expensive, it dampens morale, and it hurts a company's external image as an employer of choice. Effective plans can identify workforce "fat buildup" long before it gets out of control (and thus requires a layoff).
- **The retirement bubble**—The coming "bubble" of baby boom retirements (predicted to be as high as 40 percent of managers at some firms) will mean a dramatic shortage of senior experienced leadership in most companies. Workforce plans are needed to fill the "gap" through alternative development and staffing strategies.
- **Predicting retirement accurately**—Longer life spans coupled with instability in the economy and the stock market means predicting when workers will choose to retire becomes much more difficult. At the same time, more accurate projections are necessary in order to avoid surpluses or shortages of senior talent.
- **The war for talent**—As competition increases for valuable "top talent," firms must develop plans that are more sophisticated and tools to fight off "talent poaching." Firms must also simultaneously develop recruiting plans to identify and poach away the very best from other firms.

- **Increased turnover and impact on succession**—There is a decrease in employee loyalty to any one company due to:
  - changing worker values,
  - recent layoffs, and
  - the availability of the Internet (which makes job searches so much easier)
- These factors mean higher overall turnover rates and more difficulty in predicting employee tenure. Shorter and less predictable employee tenures means:
  - an increased need for succession planning (targeted employees may be gone before they can be promoted) and
  - effective "just-in-time" recruiting to respond to sudden vacancies
- **Shifting worker expectations**—Changing worker needs and interests (with increased demand for work-life balance) must be forecast in order to provide sufficient lead time to respond to them.

SKILL-RELATED REASONS

- **Candidates' skill levels**—The decrease in the number of technically trained candidates graduating from college (especially in engineering) means recruiting will be more difficult. In many cases the quality and skill level of candidates entering the workforce is also on a steady decline.
- **Employee skill obsolescence and learning speed**—In a rapidly changing world, worker skills quickly become outdated. As a result, it's important to track employees' current skills through automated skills inventories, which should improve the utilization of these skills. Rapid learning plans and strategies are also needed to increase the firm's overall learning speed and "what-works" sharing.
- **Predicting succession**—As the skills needed to do most jobs change more rapidly (or become obsolete), it becomes more difficult to plan worker succession because the current skills may be irrelevant for future jobs.

OTHER REASONS

- **Diversity**—More workforce diversity means it's essential that both companies and managers prepare for different and unique needs of these diverse workers. Also as the economic value of a diverse workforce becomes more apparent, the desire to attract and retain diverse workers will also increase.

- **Weak managers**—As endless scandals about senior managers get more publicity and "Dilbertization" (making fun of managers) drives quality people away from management positions, the overall quality of management will decrease. Lower-skilled managers will need more advanced (but simpler and easier to use) workforce plans. Firms must also develop processes and plans to identify bad managers rapidly.

We have just highlighted 19 different reasons why workforce planning is essential for any business. Strategic HR professionals realize the value of utilizing workforce planning to ensure continued long-term workforce productivity. An essential element of workforce planning is forecasting future events. Forecasting can be done independently or in conjunction with workforce planning efforts.

"Being prepared is better than being surprised. And you avoid surprises by looking ahead."

WHAT IS WORKFORCE PLANNING?

HR suffers through business cycles because it has no strategy to react differently during the different phases of a company's business cycle. Even though HR managers have been through business cycles many times, they seem routinely surprised when the next phase hits them.

Other functions are puzzled over HR's inability to prepare accordingly. This image of being unprepared for the changing business cycle certainly does nothing to help HR's image and brand. The process of preparing HR for these inevitable ups and downs in the business cycle is called workforce planning.

The primary reason for being future-focused (*i.e.,* doing workforce planning) is economics. If done well, having a future focus will increase productivity over the long run, cut labor costs, and dramatically cut time to market, because you'll have the right number of people, with the right skills, in the right places, at the right time. The reason having a future focus works is because it forces everyone to begin looking toward the future. A well thought-out future-focused strategy encourages both HR and managers to plan ahead and to consider all eventualities. Effective workforce planning also prevents surprises.

Traditionally much of HR has been backward-focused. HR distributes reports telling managers what happened "last year." HR responds to hiring needs not a single minute before a requisition is formally issued. HR probably doesn't even receive, much less read, the company's business plan or the sales forecast. As a result, it is unlikely that HR will become "forward-looking" without a dramatic shift in the way it works and thinks.

> *There is great value in becoming forward-thinking. For example, everyone knows that people who accurately forecast who will win the Super Bowl are significantly richer than historians who can only describe last year's game.*

WORKFORCE PLANNING DEFINED

To many individuals in HR, workforce planning is synonymous with being future-focused. Workforce planning is a formal process designed to ensure long-term workforce productivity by making sure that the firm has the right number of people in the right jobs with the right skills.

Workforce planning is a systematic, fully integrated, organizational process that involves proactively planning ahead to avoid talent surpluses or shortages. It is based on the premise that if a company forecasts its talent needs, and the actual supply of talent that is or will be available to meet those needs, then it can be more efficiently staffed. If a company is more efficient, it can appropriately avoid the need for layoffs or panic hiring.

By planning ahead, HR can provide managers with the right number of people, with the right skills, in the right place and at the right time. Workforce planning might be more accurately called talent planning because it integrates the forecasting elements of each of the HR functions that relate to talent, including recruiting, retention, and redeployment, as well as leadership and employee development.

MAJOR COMPONENTS OF WORKFORCE PLANNING

There is no standard format or formula for a workforce plan. Some workforce plans contain many components while others contain just a succession plan for senior managers. There is no one-size-fits-all model. While there are some basic components that all plans should include, there are some supplemental components that can and will work better for some companies than others. The following is a list of the most common components of a workforce plan:

- **Forecasting and assessment**—Estimating the internal/external supply and demand, labor cost, company growth rates, revenue and output
- **Succession planning**—Designating leader replacement, leader and/or key employee position progression plan, fast track
- **Leadership development**—Designating high potential, coaching, mentoring, position and project rotations
- **Recruiting**—Estimating needs for headcount, positions, location and timing, sourcing plan
- **Retention**—Forecasting turnover rates, who is at risk, retention strategies
- **Redeployment**—Redeployment process, eligibility, designated move to/from areas
- **Contingency workforce**—Designating percentages, designating jobs
- **Potential retirements**—Designating who is eligible, when, replacements, alternative work arrangements for retirees
- **Performance management**—Forced ranking, identifying who should be managed out
- **Career path**—Designating qualified individuals, position progression path, career counseling
- **Backfills**—Designating key position backups
- **Job rotations and intra-placement**—Designing intra-placement, job posting systems
- **Environmental forecast**—Forecasting industry and environmental trends, competitor assessment
- **Identifying job and competency needs**—Skills and interests inventories
- **Metrics**—Planning and forecasting effectiveness metrics

FORECASTING IS AN ESSENTIAL ELEMENT IN BEING STRATEGIC

Most HR people assert that they are strategic yet they are repeatedly surprised by events that occur around them. Being strategic by definition equates to looking and planning ahead so that you can be prepared to act quickly when either a positive or negative business or economic event occurs.

WHAT KIND OF EVENTS SHOULD BE FORECASTED?

It doesn't take a rocket scientist to realize that the world of business is changing and that anticipating what types of events may occur is essential. Some of the events that HR needs to prepare for also appear almost daily in newspaper headlines. They include:

- Physical disasters
- Stock market downturns
- Accounting irregularities
- A significant decrease or increase in product demand
- Mergers and acquisitions
- Bankruptcy of a major competitor
- Terrorism, wars and civil disruptions
- Labor shortages and surpluses
- Failed government approvals (*e.g.*, pharmaceuticals)
- Class action lawsuits

Although individual events are, by themselves, difficult to forecast, few would argue about the inevitability of the above types of events increasing in frequency as the eyes of the global economy closely scrutinize the efforts of American corporations to rebuild their positions.

> *"Think of forecasting as the elimination of surprises. It doesn't have to be full of statistics. In order to be successful it need only educate and inform managers about the range of possibilities they are likely to encounter in the near future."*

IT'S ONLY FORECASTING

Because most HR people are so busy every day, they don't have time to take a step back and look at the future. Because they don't do it very often, HR people often look at forecasting as something beyond their skill level. Nothing can be further from the truth. Great workforce forecasts are not (I repeat, not) statistical documents. If they confuse you or put you to sleep, no one will read them, much less use them.

Most people subconsciously forecast on a regular basis. Rather than being rare, forecasting is common in your everyday life. For example:

- People who set the odds for winning the Super Bowl are forecasting (which team has the highest and lowest likelihood of winning)
- Weather people forecast every day
- Every time you take a umbrella with you when you go to work in the morning you are forecasting (rain during the day)
- People who prepare budgets are forecasting (they estimate the amount of money it will take to produce the targeted production levels)
- When you maintain a savings account for your son or daughter's college education, you are forecasting (that your children will attend college and how much it may cost)

Even when you buy donuts in the morning for the office you are forecasting how many people will be there and how many donuts each will eat. Even though forecasting is part of our everyday lives, some HR professionals still get nervous when asked to forecast next year's need for new employees. Take a step back and realize that forecasting is just using information to draw logical conclusions. Forecasting then becomes "demystified."

THE IMPORTANCE OF FORECASTING

In my experience, the most crucial element of workforce planning is the forecast, because accurate forecasts provide sufficient time to prepare for problems and take advantage of opportunities. If the forecast is wrong, it's like constructing a building with a weak foundation. Only bad things can happen when you don't understand the future, including production lags, slow product development and unhappy customers because of delays due to talent shortages.

The two primary purposes of workforce forecasting are:

- To predict the gap between future needs and the availability of talent in order to develop plans to close that "gap," and
- To give HR and management a "heads-up" about future workforce problems and opportunities so that these decision-makers have sufficient time to develop a plan of action to handle the forecasted issues.

FORECAST A RANGE, NOT A SPOT

Most workforce forecasts fail to hit their target. Part of reason for this is because most forecasts are too narrow. In order to avoid misleading managers, it's important for each individual forecast to provide a specific projected "target" number, but also to provide a high and low forecast number. This has the effect of converting the forecast from a single number to a broader range. Include in this range the high number (that reflects the best-case scenario) and the low number (that reflects the worst-case scenario). Now that you have a broader target, you are more likely to hit it.

The next step is to then prepare contingency plans for the entire range of eventualities, not just a single forecasted number. Preparing for the range requires several variations in your plan but those variations also better prepare you for any unexpected events.

It is very difficult, for example, to predict the exact score of the Super Bowl. It's much easier to predict a likely range that the final score will fall within. Similarly, guessing an individual's exact weight is nearly impossible, but guessing weight within a range of 10 pounds is significantly easier. Another advantage of providing a range is that when you do so, you in effect notify users of the forecast that some variation is highly likely. This warning both educates and effectively forces managers to develop plans and solutions for all eventualities within that range.

FOUR ELEMENTS OF WORKFORCE FORECASTS

Workforce forecasts provide managers with "heads-up" projections. Those projections come in four separate parts.

The first part of the forecast projects the growth rate of the business. If you don't accurately know how much a business will grow or contract, you are liable to either "under-hire" or end up with a surplus of employees. Both are expensive propositions.

The second part of a workforce forecasts outlines the organization's needs (sometimes known as demand), which covers the number and type of employees needed in the future.

Third, the forecast provides recruiters and managers with information about vacancies, and estimates how many current employees will need to be replaced.

Finally, the fourth element of forecasting estimates the availability or supply of talent. It educates and informs managers about how much talent the company realistically can get through external recruiting and what talent must be developed internally.

Each is described below:

- **Growth forecast**—The first and most important step is for the workforce planning team (working in conjunction with other forecasting teams within the firm) to forecast the growth rate of the industry and the firm. After the growth rate is projected, future revenue and the number of units of production also must be estimated. The projected number of output units and revenue will be used to project the number and types of people that will be required to meet the increased or decreased output. Accurate growth rates prevent "overhiring" or undertaking unnecessary layoffs. Growth forecasts generally include the expected growth rate but also include estimates of the best and worst-case scenarios.

- **Talent needs forecasts**—The "needs" element is designed to provide managers and HR professionals with a view of the number and type of employees needed in the future. It gives managers and recruiters a "heads-up" warning so that recruiting can provide the right number and quality of new hires to meet the organization's growth needs. Development and training professionals use the estimate to calculate the number of employees that need to be retrained or developed. Advanced "needs" forecasts also include projections on the increased costs of employees (compensation) and new competencies and skills that will be required.

- **Forecasts of vacancies**—Even if the recruiting function brings on the needed number of new employees to meet growth projections, that number must be adjusted upward to allow for internal turnover. Vacancy forecasts project the number and type of employees that must be replaced due to normal turnover and retirements. More detailed forecasts also project when, in what jobs, and where (in a general sense) these vacancies will occur.

■ **The availability of talent**—Once managers and recruiters know the organization's "needs," they will also need to know about the availability of talent. Most "availability" forecasts first look *internally* to see what talent currently is available and what portion of existing employees and managers can be "developed" to meet future needs. Next, availability forecasts project the *external* supply or availability of talent. This is especially important in job areas that require advanced training or advanced degrees (where there is projected shortfall). Availability forecasts also warn managers of talent shortages that cannot be filled due to recruiting. This provides managers with time to try other approaches, like substituting technology for labor, and people-development programs like re-training, apprentice and leadership development.

"Being strategic demands that you look at the big picture. That means you must forecast and prepare for the future. Without forecasting and workforce planning, HR will continue to get blindsided by "surprise" internal and external events."

ALERTING MANAGERS ABOUT UPCOMING PROBLEMS

Part of the definition of being strategic includes focusing on "future problems" in order to either prevent them or have a plan ready to handle them effectively if they actually occur. The question that often arises, however, is "what do I look for?" The answer is that you look for *early warning signs*.

There are two types of warning signs or precursors that indicate that you may have an upcoming people-management problem. Precursors are events or data points that occur immediately before a serious problem materializes, and consequently they can be helpful in predicting future events. First, you need to look internally for precursors in financial and operational ratios. Later you look at external factors.

Note that the numbers used as examples are representative of a large high-tech firm.

I) Internal early warning signs to monitor

Internal financial and performance ratios that might indicate potential people-management problems:

- **Profit-related precursors**—Profit projections change by more than 10 percent
- **Revenue related**—Revenue projections change by more than 10 percent
- **Revenue per employee**—The ratio changes by more than 5 percent
- **Market share**—Competitive market share changes by more than 5 percent
- **Customer orders**—Sales/orders have changed by more than 10 percent when comparing this year to last
- **Percentage of profit from new products**—The percentage of our total profit that comes from recently introduced products (introduced in the last two years) changes by more than 10 percent
- More than 25 percent of the product divisions are unprofitable

Internal "people" indicators of potential people-management problems:

- Employee head count growth exceeds 5 percent
- The ratio of "overhead employee" headcount as compared to regular employee head count changes by more than 5 percent
- The ratio of employees to managers changes by more than 10 percent
- Employee turnover changes by more than 5 percent
- HR spending per employee exceeds 1 percent of all costs or it changes by more than 5 percent
- Recent (within the last three months) freezes on salary changes, requisitions, promotions or hiring
- The level of approval required for new requisitions changes

Internal product, plant and inventory indicators of potential people-management problems:

- The backlog of unfilled orders changes by more than 10 percent
- Percent of plant capacity utilized changes by more than 10 percent
- Warehouse inventories are changing by more than 15 percent or inventory turnover is increasing by more than 10 percent
- The number of products in beta testing or the product pipeline changes by more than 10 percent

- Product development time (time to market) changes by more than 5 percent
- The percent of overhead costs (relative to all costs) changes by more than 5 percent

Corporate culture-related indicators of potential people-management problems:
- The results of 360-degree or employee surveys decline by more than 10 percent
- Employee grievances or complaints increase by more than 5 percent
- There has been a recent freeze (within the last six months) on internal purchasing (computers, travel, free food, etc.) and/or the CEO/CFO has written a memo requesting managers to cut costs

II) External early warning signs to monitor

Potential changes in economic conditions could cause people-management problems; actions by competitors also could impact an organization's people-management planning.

Economic factors. When the economy is growing, sales increase and, generally, so does hiring and the need for retention efforts. In contrast, when the economy begins to shrink it's essential to reexamine hiring and consider reducing headcount in anticipation of a decrease in sales and profits. There are many economic factors that serve as early warning signs, including:

- Consumer spending changes (for retail/consumer goods and service firms), corporate spending changes (for industrial goods and service firms), and government spending changes (for military and government goods and service firms) by more than 5 percent
- GNP growth changes by more than 10 percent in the U.S. (and in countries in which the organization has a significant number of employees)
- The unemployment rate changes by more than 25 percent
- Currency Valuation/International Exchange Rates shift (in either direction) by more than 10 percent (which can have an impact on the cost of products and materials and also affect the purchasing power of the consumer)
- Analysts' recommendations to sell or hold stock of the organization or its direct competitors change

- Stock price indexes (NASDAQ/ Dow Jones) decrease by more than 10 percent over a six-month period (which can impact future investments and thus growth potential)

Competitive and industry factors. Actions by the firm's competitors could also be warning signs to monitor:
- Profit growth changes by over 10 percent at competitors (or for the industry)
- Revenue growth changes by over 10 percent at competitors (or for the industry)
- Large scale layoffs by other firms in the industry
- Hiring freezes are announced at competitors (or for the industry)
- Competitors, both weak and strong, are already announcing lower earnings forecasts or decreased sales
- Employee turnover at competitors changes by over 25 percent (or for the industry)
- Plant productivity/output at competitors changes by over 25 percent (or for the industry)
- Other firms open or close plants, or go bankrupt
- Suppliers are already announcing layoffs, lower earnings forecasts, or decreased sales
- Precursor or lead firms (identified by past patterns of early layoff announcements that preceded but predicted our own upcoming need for layoffs) are now scaling back hiring by more than 10 percent, or announcing lower earnings forecasts or decreased sales
- Spending on R&D at competitors changes by over 25 percent (or for the industry)
- The number of available jobs listed on competitors web sites changes by over 20 percent

Previous industry patterns reoccur.
- In industries where products often become commodities, margins are dropping and the product is in danger of becoming a commodity (indicating the need to become a low-cost producer)
- In industries that undergo boom and bust cycles, previously occurring economic patterns that have led to a decline in sales and the need for layoffs are recurring
- In companies undergoing rapid growth, company growth rates are slowing. This indicates the repeat of an industry pattern where

rapid growth inevitably leads to intense competition and then a fallout to a few players

- In industries undergoing rapid technological growth, technology growth rates are slowing. This indicates the repeat of an industry pattern where rapid technology growth inevitably leads to periods of technology stagnation

- The number and the size of layoffs reported in industry layoff reports changes by 10 percent

- The merger rate in the industry changes by over 10 percent (indicating that the organization may also acquire firms, which may lead to headcount surplus)

Because not every organization has the resources or the time to forecast or engage in workforce planning, it's important to explore alternatives to the traditional approaches.

ALTERNATIVES TO WORKFORCE PLANNING OR FORECASTING

The most important element of a strategic HR department is to forecast the future. Forecasting allows you to give managers a "heads-up" warning about the company's future. If HR can provide managers with sufficient time to plan ahead and to act differently, many significant workforce planning problems can be avoided.

If, despite all your good intentions, you don't have the time or resources to prepare a forecast, there are some alternative action steps you can take. Under "plan B," even though you can't forecast, there are still some positive steps to take that have almost the same impact as forecasting.

ALTERNATIVES IF YOU CAN'T FORECAST

You can survive without forecasting if you develop "just-in-time" processes and a wide range of contingency plans.

- **Utilize other company forecasts**—Companies traditionally do several types of forecasting, including strategic business planning, financial/budgetary forecasting, and production and sales forecasts. Because sales and budget forecasts are the easiest to obtain, they are frequently used by HR in lieu of its own forecasting. Strategic business planning forecasts are generally the most comprehensive but they're also difficult to come by because they contain business secrets. Production forecasts can also have some value but they are generally short-term in nature.

- **Use vendor forecasts**—If you have the resources, consider paying outside consultants, information specialists and vendors to supply you with alternative forecasts (or information). You can then either use their raw data or use their forecasts exclusively.

ALTERNATIVES IF YOU CAN'T DO WORKFORCE PLANNING

- **Develop effective redeployment plans**—If you don't have a process for forecasting business downturns and maintaining the appropriate sized workforce, you can mitigate this potential over- or under-supply weakness by having a strong redeployment process.

DEFINITION

Redeployment is the movement of a significant number of workers from an area of lower importance to a business unit or job that has been designated as a higher priority. Redeployment processes allow you to move surplus workers internally to shortage areas, thus avoiding the need for a layoff in one area and rapid hiring in another. Redeployment plans can also help smooth over the problems caused by over-hiring.

- **Develop just-in-time processes**—A just-in-time (JIT) process is one that is designed to react instantly to an event. If managers don't have a forecast or an advance warning system, the next best thing is ensuring that people-management processes each have just-in-time/instant ramp-up or ramp-down capabilities. Including a JIT element in every management system allows you to respond instantly to an event at the same level of quality as if you were warned well in advance (as a result of an accurate forecast). Fifteen-minute oil changers and most fast food restaurants operate with just-in-time systems. While they might also have a forecast, their real key to success is a series of instant response processes.

- **Have a larger-than-normal contingency workforce set aside**—Most of the problems with workforce forecasts occur because HR consistently overestimates growth and, as a result, over-hires. That problem is compounded because if growth estimates are too high, excessive headcount also results. In most corporations, there is no easy way to reduce labor costs rapidly because managers are afraid to fire any permanent employees. Some organizations attempt to use performance management to resolve that "surplus" employee issue but a superior option is to require managers to maintain a significant percentage of their workers as contingent workers. Managers are less reluctant to release part-timers and contractors; consequently, having a fixed percentage of the workforce designated as contingent makes it easier to cut costs and employees within a relatively short time period.
- **Identify and track precursor patterns**—Instead of looking at reams of financial data to come up with a statistical forecast, instead try to identify precursors (something that precedes an event) that warn you about what is to occur. For example, if a police officer pulls you over and asks for your driver's license, you are soon going to get a traffic ticket. That's a precursor: it's not a 100 percent certainty, but once it happens, the odds are that the predicted next event will soon follow. By looking at historical patterns, it is often easy enough to identify precursors to growth. If the precursors are obvious you can reliably use them in lieu of a formal forecast.
- **Require backfills for all key positions**—If you don't accurately predict turnover, you might end up with some sudden vacancies and no one to fill the positions. However, there is another alternative to forecasting turnover: that is to require the manager of each key position to designate someone in advance to take that position if it becomes vacant. The designated person would be required to be cross-trained and prepared to fill in. Designating a "backfill" is a form of succession planning without the complicated processes. This alternative helps to limit the trauma often caused by sudden turnover.
- **Practice "if-then" scenarios**—If you don't have the time or resources to forecast, a viable alternative is preparing for best- and worst-case scenarios. Requiring each manager to train continually on "if-then" or "what if?" scenarios will ensure that they are prepared for the same range of possible events that, if feasible,

you would have forecasted. If you train for all eventualities, you minimize the likelihood of any surprises, which is precisely the goal of forecasting.

The only way to get good at forecasting is to practice and continually refine your estimates. The goal isn't to get a perfect forecast; it is only to provide managers with a "heads-up" warning about the range of people-management problems they are likely to encounter. Once you realize that forecasting isn't about statistics but is instead an educational process designed to inform managers about likely problems, the stress level will decrease immediately.

In a more positive light, remember that everyone loves the forecaster who identified the winning lottery number or picked the winning Super Bowl team. So get started; here's your chance to become a hero.

The next section of the book demonstrates the importance of coordinating and integrating the different HR functions and programs, so that all work in unison.

CHAPTER ELEVEN

HR'S EFFORTS ARE COORDINATED

OBJECTIVE

The seventh element required in a strategic HR department is to ensure that the HR department's efforts are closely coordinated. HR faces many challenges on the road to becoming strategic, but the most common one is the selfish and territorial silo behavior within too many HR departments.

KEY POINTS

◊ The first step toward making a coordinated effort is to understand the impact of poor integration. In order to identify the consequences of poor integration within HR, robust metrics are needed.

◊ The second major step involves offering rewards for cooperation and "boundaryless" behavior.

◊ The final step is to communicate clearly with all HR employees about the interrelated nature of their jobs.

Having a coordinated effort in HR is a critical success factor for having a strategic business impact. At first glance this might seem like a minor item, but in reality most HR departments have fragmented efforts. These fragmented efforts often mean that managers and employees have to search for answers and, more often than not, have to suffer through numerous handoffs between functions within HR.

Because HR is an organization that provides information services, it must act like any other service organization: HR must build a reputation as an easy place do business. It must provide its customers with one-stop shopping and a minimum number of handoffs between individuals. The fact that the HR department operates as a series of functional silos is no secret to managers or even to most HR professionals. If you want a high-performing HR department, you need a high degree of cooperation between each of the department's functional units.

DEFINITION

The management terms for a well-coordinated department are "boundaryless" or seamless. In brief, this phrase means that instead of every HR function and program acting independently, they operate smoothly as a unit, so that the customer never realizes that administratively they are dealing with numerous different functional units.

Having these different organizational cylinders or silos work together is very much like the workings of an auto engine. When different cylinders are firing out of sequence you get a rough engine. Within the HR department, when the different functional units don't work together, you get the same low performance. It's important to recognize that even though HR departments can operate without this coordination, it is unlikely that they can produce a strategic result.

WHY HR MUST COORDINATE ITS EFFORTS

Individual HR professionals are widely known for their cooperation and willingness to be team players. As individuals, HR professionals are courteous, responsive and knowledgeable. Unfortunately, individual spirit and effort cannot result in satisfied customers if the customer is constantly being shifted between numerous functions and individuals. And that is the paradox. Individuals in HR are cooperative and team players, while the view that HR customers have is of a fragmented collection of independent HR functions.

Functional silos and efforts that are not coordinated cause nothing but frustration for customers of HR services. When a manager or employee has a problem, he or she sees it as a single problem. When they visit HR, however, they are told instead that they have a fragmented problem that requires them to visit multiple Web sites and/or talk to numerous different HR functions. HR seems almost to see most problems through the "eyes of a fly," which split simple problems into a complex, multifaceted array of different problems. Perhaps some examples will illustrate the point.

When an employee is fired, the only things the employee is concerned about are being paid and finding out about benefit coverage. However, when HR terminates an employee, they see multiple problems including:

- A payroll problem;
- A benefits problem;
- A COBRA problem;
- An ID badge problem;
- A security (walk out) problem;
- An equipment, key and uniform turn-in problem;
- An exit interview problem; and
- An legal documentation problem.

When you think about most of the events in HR (for example, recruiting, promotions, retirements and performance management), they cannot be successfully completed without cooperation of multiple independent HR functions.

Here's another example to illustrate the point. When a new hire is made, many HR functions and programs are involved:

- **Recruiting**—Sourcing, interviewing and selecting;
- **Compensation**—Job analysis, writing the job description, setting the salary range and approving the final salary offer;
- **Benefits**—Benefits information and the initial sign up for benefits;
- **Payroll**—Initial sign up for payroll;
- **Relocation**—Relocation services;
- **Orientation**—"On-boarding;"

- **Training**—Initial training and training required of all new hires;
- **Legal**—Designing the offer letter and providing an overview of the screening process; and
- **Generalists**—Polishing the job description, on-site orientation and interviewing.

It's obvious that if these nine different HR functions don't work together, the overall hiring process will not produce excellent results. A lack of cooperation between these different units will delay the process to the point where we might lose most quality candidates due to the delays.

The lesson to be learned is that any employee, faced with many different problems, is likely to feel overwhelmed and frustrated. That frustration is likely to be exacerbated once the employee realizes that he or she must visit at least eight different functions and as many as 20 different individuals in order to accomplish the simple exit task. The stress and daunting task of filling out forms and talking to 20 different individuals makes an already difficult termination even worse. If HR could define the problem as "getting an employee out quickly without increasing the likelihood of litigation" and make every individual responsible for that, there might be a renewed interest in working together as a unit.

PROBLEMS WITH A FRAGMENTED HR EFFORT

The many different HR strategies that an HR department can operate under were outlined earlier in this book. Unfortunately, when most of them are implemented, the resulting HR departments all share a common flaw. That universal flaw is the existence of functional silos within HR that all too frequently operate as if they were independent units. Managers and employees both frequently complain about these independent fiefdoms and wonder why there isn't more integration and coordination between these units. The net result of this confusing maze of functions is often a lack of accountability where *no one* in the HR department accepts responsibility for minimizing the number of pass-offs and ensuring that functions work in unison.

A functional silo arises when each HR function such as recruiting, retention or compensation acts as though it were an independent entity rather than as an integrated component of a much larger system.

In many cases, one HR function seems to have little concern or even interest with respect to what the other HR functions are doing.

Among the many problems caused by this silo approach:

- Frustration and a waste of time on the part of managers and employees;
- Answer-shopping, where employees and managers call numerous HR individuals (wasting their time) in order to find the answer that they want;
- Managers and employees doing nothing because of their distaste for dealing with HR;
- The different HR functions developing their own software and databases that cannot communicate with other HR or other business functions;
- Reduced cooperation meaning less sharing of solutions and information between functions;
- Independent HR functions that tend to develop their own jargon, acronyms and language that neither employees nor other HR functions can understand;
- Submitting data to multiple functions and working with each independently;
- Poor interfunction communications meaning more confusion and errors;
- Higher HR costs due to wrong information and the high number of hand-offs; and
- A weaker HR image and brand among senior executives because they see HR as a bureaucracy.

A chain provides strength only when each individual link is strong and working in unison with the other links of the chain. If one link were to fail, the entire chain fails. An HR department is no different. All of the functions that make up HR must be charged, in unison, with providing the services and support that enable managers to achieve their business objectives. No HR department can achieve excellence in accomplishing that unless each link (HR function) in the chain is strong and working in concert with the others.

If you manage an HR function and you strive for greatness, you must first understand the factors that cause this lack of coordination.

WHY IS HR SO UNCOORDINATED?

There are a variety of reasons why HR functions all too frequently act as independent silos. The most common three reasons for silo-like behavior within HR are:

- **Narrow measures and metrics**—When HR departments measure performance, they often do it narrowly, within their own functional units. Unfortunately, these silo metrics tell only a small portion of the total story. When you measure the effectiveness of a single HR function or program, you see only a narrow picture.

  It's similar to measuring the effectiveness of a football team based only on defense, which wouldn't be an accurate indication of the team's success. If the overall team is to be successful, you must have all units working together. That means that you must also measure the success of the offense and the defense working together—that is, you must measure winning.

  Within HR it is quite uncommon to find a unifying metric that measures overall HR effectiveness and the contribution that each function makes to the overall effectiveness. Without a unifying metric, a measure of seamless transactions and a measure of how each HR functional unit cooperates with others, it's almost impossible for HR to build cooperative behavior and to meet a common goal.

- **No rewards for cooperation**—Most HR departments have no overall HR performance reward that makes one HR function's success dependent on the success of other HR functions. Rewards are important, because teamwork and cooperation occur much faster when they are rewarded. When you fail to tie HR pay to HR departmental performance, you miss an opportunity to remind HR professionals about the key role that they play in overall HR departmental performance.

- **Vertical training and promotion**—In many HR organizations individuals are promoted vertically within their function. The number of transfers between the different HR functions is extremely low at the bottom and the middle of the HR organization. Most companies have no cross training or job rotation programs, which provide different HR functions with the opportunity to learn about the needs and the problems of the other HR functions. A lack of cross training and interaction also means a lack of understanding and an us-versus-them mindset.

THE GOALS OF A COORDINATED HR EFFORT

If your goal is to have a strategic HR department, then you must ensure that the department works together in unison in order to provide a coordinated effort. Some of the goals you should set in order to ensure a coordinated effort include:

- **One-stop shopping**—Wherever possible, whether it be a Web site, a phone call or a personal visit, the person should be able to get the answers to simple problems in one location.

- **Limit handoffs**—In those cases where someone must be passed off to other HR units, that handoff should be done by the original HR person. In addition, the total number of handoffs should never exceed three. Wherever possible, the customer should never know that they are now working with a separate entity when they are passed off because it is a seamless transition.

- **No jargon**—The person with the problem shouldn't need to be an expert in HR in order to find the right person with an answer. In other words, without knowing more than the basic generic name of the problem, the employee should be able to find the right person or place with the solution.

- **Tie related problems together**—Related problems or the steps within a single problem should be treated not as separate problems, but instead as a single event.

- **Same-site answers and transactions**—Individuals should be able to get the answer to their questions as well as the transaction completed without having to go to different individuals or places.

- **Boundaryless**—Individuals within HR that do build empires or hoard information should be punished.

- **Free information flow**—Systems must be developed to ensure the smooth flow of information and data (in a consistent format) between the different HR functions.

- **Customer service**—High-quality accurate answers, short response times, satisfied customers and 24/7 service are the expectation.

STEPS TO INCREASE INTERFUNCTIONAL COOPERATION

Some firms have helped to solve the coordination problem by formally uniting diverse HR functions under a talent management umbrella, while others have instituted policies, metrics and rewards. If you decide to undertake the task of building a "silo-less" HR department, there are a variety of things that you can do to help bring that about. Here are some steps to begin the process.

- **All HR functions must share a common goal**—Set one or two superordinate goals for the whole HR department. (A superordinate goal is one that is powerful enough that all want to achieve it but that can't be met by individual functional effort alone.) Design these goals so that each function has a marked impact on whether the goal is met. This goal should be so compelling that HR employees will subordinate their own personal goals and the goals of their function in order to meet them. Examples of superordinate goals might include getting the firm listed on "great places to work" lists, winning an HR Optima award, getting the department written up in *HR Executive* magazine, or increasing the firm's revenue per employee by $25,000. If you involve each function in setting the superordinate goal, you'll also increase the chances of it being understood by everyone and that they will accept it.

- **A unifying HR index metric encourages working together**—A metric or measure that everyone can impact helps build cooperation. Develop a single comprehensive HR index that reflects the overall performance of the HR department.

DEFINITION

An index is a single number that reflects the performance of the unit (the Dow Jones or the S&P are examples of business indexes). This single number is derived by combining a group of individual metrics into a single number.

- Make sure that most HR functional units and individual con- tributors can impact a majority of the sub-items in the index. An example of what key performance metrics might be included in the single combined HR index follows.
  - **Revenue per employee**—Dollars generated per employee can be used as a measure of overall people productivity for the firm;
  - **Overall HR success rate**—The percent of the overall corporate HR goals that are met;
  - **Responsiveness**—Average response time to requests for infor- mation;
  - **Errors**—Average accuracy of answers provided to users of HR services (obtained by using "mystery shoppers" to request information);
  - **Recruiting**—Average time to fill for key jobs. (Average number of vacancies is not an HR performance measure—it's a measure of corporate growth—but the time to fill such positions is an HR metric);
  - **Retention**—Retention rates of the top 20 and the bottom 10 percent of employees;
  - **Bad manager turnover**—Turnover rate among managers who rate poorly on management satisfaction surveys;
  - **Performance of new hires**—The average performance appraisal scores for new hires (compared to last year's average);
  - **Diversity**—As measured by diversity ratios in hiring, promotion and employee retention;
  - **Manager satisfaction with HR**—As measured by a survey of managers asking them to rate HR's contribution to meeting their performance goals; and
  - **Overall employee satisfaction**—As measured by periodic em- ployee surveys.

Remember that setting HR-wide cooperation metrics helps focus people because it sends a message to HR employees about what is important and what is less important.

- **Rewards that encourage cooperation**—Make at least five percent of each HR employee's pay based on meeting the target numbers for the overall HR index. Also, be sure that any individual rewards that a team member gets are automatically increased by a fixed percentage when the overall HR team meets its goal (spurring both individual effort and cooperation among team members).

- **Make sure that functional metrics overlap**—Make sure that the functional performance metrics that are used by each individual HR function include some common metrics—that is, that the same metrics appear in every different HR function's list of performance metrics. Common metrics should include response time, user satisfaction, accuracy in answers, and manager satisfaction with the individual HR function. Track silo-busting success and report your successes to all in order to encourage continued silo-busting activities and team cooperation. If your firm has a Six Sigma program, use it to set consistent standards for quality across every HR function to provide a common ground for comparisons and a shared experience for all.

- **Cross-departmental rotations**—Require that HR functions periodically rotate employees (start with key employees) between each of the functional HR units. Familiarity breaks down barriers and helps individuals understand the unique problems faced by other HR functions. Rotations can be permanent, for a short project duration, half time each day, or one day a week.

- **Cross-functional promotions**—Change the HR internal promotion process so that the promotion plan requires individuals to go through other HR functions in order to become an HR manager.

- **Into-the-field rotations**—Require HR employees to spend at least one week a year working in a "line" department to help them understand their customer needs. Field experience also helps HR employees to understand why employees and managers sometimes dislike HR as a result of having to deal with disjointed HR functions. In contrast, employees and managers can learn that HR professionals do understand the business and don't mind getting their hands dirty.

- **Learn from managers of supply-chain related functions**—Invite managers from your company's supply chain process to offer suggestions on how to improve the coordination and the problem handoff between the different HR functions. Supply chain professionals are the undisputed coordination-of-services experts.

- **Isolated databases**—Most HR databases and software are designed for a specific function. There is often no clear integration between the databases of the different HR functions and, as a result, no individual can access and use all of the different data required to solve a complete problem. HR must work with IT to ensure that every HR database is integrated with each of the others and that each HR function has access to every other function's information and database. Information hoarding must be eliminated.

- **Language and acronyms**—A time-tested way of avoiding outside criticism (and to remain an independent silo) is to utilize your own functional language and acronyms that outsiders cannot understand. If HR is to be integrated, it must minimize the use of acronyms. Outlaw "HR-babble" and provide online glossaries and dictionaries so that others outside the department can easily learn and understand what is going on.

- **Set department maximums on "transferring problems"**—Customers tend to prefer one-stop shopping; managers and employees are no different. Provide cross training and set procedures so that no customer of HR can be transferred between more than two functions and three individuals in order to get an answer or to solve a problem. Where possible, provide a single unified telephone number or Web site so that managers don't have to guess about whom to call.

- **Communications and info-sharing**—Provide open access and shared information sources so all of your HR employees know what is happening. Openly sharing information also helps team members feel like they are part of the action and the decision-making process. Develop communications and information-sharing systems to ensure that a best practice or learning from one HR function is rapidly transferred to all other HR functions. It's equally important that failure or bad news is also shared rapidly so that other functions can avoid the same problems.

- **Outlaw territorial behavior**—I've seen HR managers sabotage or delay the programs of other HR professionals until they got their "buy-in." VPs of HR must punish boundary-building or boundary-protecting behaviors and also model positive boundaryless behavior. Talk to people at GE (the leaders in this area) about how this can be accomplished.

- **Make those people who cooperate into heroes**—Seek out individuals in HR that exemplify cooperation and integration. Provide individual recognition and rewards for those that serve as role models. Make sure every individual in HR is rated or ranked on boundaryless behavior. Distribute the ranked individual results to all so that peer pressure will build on the non-cooperators.

- **Hire people who will cooperate**—When recruiting team members into HR, make sure that recruits have a shared vision, similar values and have exhibited boundaryless behaviors at previous jobs. Recruit and select individual team members that share the practice of helping others first—that is, *hire the unselfish*. Have a planned program to drop high maintenance, territorial team members. Talk to people at Southwest Airlines for approaches to hiring "cooperators."

- **Develop a sense of community**—Develop HR departmental mission and vision statements that highlight integration and cooperation. Make sure that every function's yearly goals overlap with those of interrelated functions to help develop HR departmental cohesion. Provide opportunities to work on cross-functional teams and hold events that help members from different functions to get to know and form a bond with their counterparts in other related HR functions. Provide chances for shared fun in order to give team members something to talk about and to build relationships between teams.

- **Integration management**—Provide the HR team with a strong manager that anticipates and rapidly resolves team conflicts. Develop systems and rules to ensure that integration issues are rapidly identified and confronted in a non-personal manner. Make someone accountable for integration.

   Other tips on building team cohesion and cooperation. Listed below are additional tips on building cooperation.

- Identify and make it clear that your team faces a common external enemy or threat to pull all together (like in wartime).

- Ensure that there is a significant shared punishment when the team fails.

- Demonstrate your winning team record and a positive external image to all in order to foster a feeling of being part of an "in" group. Develop a shared history for your group and company and use it to build a sense of identity.

- Allow for joint goal-setting so that all feel they had some say in where you are going as a team.

- Involve the employees in creating a compelling vision for the team. Hold meetings to develop a common shared vision that is so compelling that people will not leave for a lesser vision outside the company.

- Communicate to your employees the interrelatedness of their jobs, the intensity of the competition, and the need for maximum effort. Develop a feeling of interdependence on your team.
- Make your team one that is hard to join, making membership more desirable and elite.
- Have a significant initiation process that all go through. This gives members a common bond and set of experiences (like boot camp).

The next section will cover the eighth element of strategic HR, being globally capable.

CHAPTER TWELVE

HR HAS A GLOBAL APPROACH

OBJECTIVE

The eighth element of a strategic HR department is a global focus. A global focus does not mean just having a few international services like relocation and expatriate services. It means moving beyond traditional HR thinking, where low labor costs and having a local distribution source and sales force were the primary reasons for placing talent globally.

KEY POINTS

◊ HR is critical to the success of the global company. A successful globalization effort will require HR not just to change the way it thinks but also the way it acts.

◊ The critical success factor of a globalized HR department is the capability to handle a variety of diverse situations from a distance. Globalized HR is very similar in concept to situational management and managing remote workers.

◊ A globalized HR will require new technology, new processes and new programs. In addition, it will probably require that HR hire some new people with different global competencies than its current staff.

Few would argue against the point that the world is becoming more global. Business leaders have known for some time that, if you want to succeed in the global business world, then it is essential that your firm expand its production and sales efforts around the world. Only recently have business leaders begun to realize that you can also successfully expand customer service and even research and design work outside of your home country.

Globalization is invariably in the top three on any CEO's priority list. Unfortunately, it rarely has the same strategic priority within HR. This is not say that HR departments don't have global efforts because most do. However, most of these HR efforts result in the development of an independent global HR program rather than a new way of thinking that permeates every person and every unit of HR.

DEFINITION

A global focus means that each and every HR department looks for opportunities to expand the productivity of its workforce—both in the home country and outside of it. This global perspective means that you move operations globally because of the wealth of talent and ideas that can be found around the globe, not just to cut costs.

The critical success factor of a globalized HR department is the capability to handle a variety of diverse people management problems from a distance. In that sense, globalized HR is very similar in concept to situational management and managing remote workers.

- For example, in recruiting, it means a new perspective where "best in your home country" is replaced by a talent pool that includes "the best in the world."
- In retention and compensation, it means developing localized tools and strategies that are completely different from those that HR is accustomed to using.

In a capsule, it means that every service and program in HR must be capable of working anywhere in the world without an HR person there to directly oversee it.

Effective globalization is as much part of the mindset as it is a set of HR programs. Thinking globally forces you to consider other perspectives and ways of thinking. Globalization requires you to accept and work closely with people who are significantly different than those with whom you have been accustomed to working. When you work in a global HR department, you learn to think in different time zones and to see things from the cultural perspectives of others.

WHY HR MUST BECOME GLOBAL

There are a variety of benefits that accrue to a business with an effective global HR approach. In addition, as other firms move to a global people-management approach, what is now a competitive advantage will turn eventually into a necessity as everyone moves in that direction. Some of benefits of going global include:

- **More candidates**—A broader recruiting pool of candidates from around the world allows you to minimize the impact of local labor shortages by recruiting from labor surplus areas.
- **Better candidates**—Expanding your recruiting capability allows you to get the very best candidates from around the world. You hire top talent who would be unwilling to move to your home country.
- **Reduced costs**—You can lower the costs of labor by moving the work to low labor cost areas.
- **Leadership development**—An increased number of diverse development opportunities for building talent through short- and long-term international assignments will become available. Having a strong global HR function will also help you attract the best HR people because of the learning and development opportunities it provides.
- **Diverse ideas**—Global employees with different backgrounds and experiences provide different perspectives and ideas.
- **Increased sales**—Having staff in a particular area allows you to better understand that area. And because your global workforce more closely represents the profile of your global customers, your product sales will likely improve.
- **Leadership gap**—As baby boomers retire in the United States and companies face a shortage of leadership, they can attract leaders from countries that have a surplus of leadership because they didn't have the same postwar baby boom.
- **Process improvement**—Having business units in many diverse business climates allows a company to pretest business processes,

equipment and ideas in several diverse business situations before eventually rolling them out to the entire company.

- **The "why question"**—Working in a global company forces you to re-examine everything you do because of the increased number of "why" questions that you get from international workers (a "why" question is when international workers repeatedly ask you, "Why do you do it that way?").

GLOBAL-THINKING DECISION FILTERS

The most difficult transition in an effective globalization effort involves a massive change in attitude and behavior inside of HR. Globalization cannot just be the name of a department or a part of someone's job title. Globalization instead must become an essential element of everyone's job. Unfortunately, what commonly happens is that people in HR begin to talk globally relatively quickly but they fail to change the way they act.

The best practice is to develop a global-thinking filter. A global-thinking filter is merely a set of criteria or filters through which every new idea and program must pass. This decision filter forces you to include global elements and global impacts in every idea or program that is proposed. These filters help screen out any new programs, new hires, and ideas that fail to meet the globalization test.

Essential global "filters" that every HR program and initiative should meet:

- **International experience**—For new hires or transfers, does the candidate have international experience, education or travel so that they understand the unique needs of different geographic regions?
- **Language**—Does the individual, software, web site, program, training manual, etc., have multilingual capabilities so that it can be used by people all around the world?
- **24/7 capability**—Because everyone in a global corporation is located in a different time zone, it is essential that new programs in HR have at least partial 24/7 capability.
- **Diversity of thinking**—Does the individual candidate, consultant or vendor have an understanding and tolerance for different ways of approaching a problem? Are they tolerant of different cultures, races, religions and beliefs?

- **Technology for information-sharing**—Because of the physical distance and the expense of bringing international workers together, it is important that any new program or process utilize technology and be paperless. By utilizing technology, workers around the world can rapidly but inexpensively communicate and share information.

- **Global capability**—Make it a minimum requirement for program approval that all new HR programs, technology and processes have a global capability. If they do have a global capability, managers and employees around the world have equal access to excellent HR programs.

- **Global staff**—Make it a minimum requirement for all major functional and cross-functional teams to include members from international offices. Even if they must attend remotely it's important to require that everyone get their perspective. Incidentally, it is equally important to make global staff members team leaders and managers of major HR projects in order to send a message that both they and headquarters staff are equally capable of managing projects.

- **Testing and rollouts**—Periodically initiate new HR programs in international offices to make those offices feel like they can come first when it comes to acquiring new programs. In a similar light, periodically pilot new HR programs in global locations. Develop metrics to ensure that a significant percentage of all HR initiatives come from, or are rolled out in, remote locations. Prohibit any program from starting in the home country that does not have an international rollout component that will be activated within a specified time period (6 to 12 months).

- **Budgeting**—In any new HR program, it is essential that sufficient funds be allocated in the budget for global operations. No program can be approved with U.S.-only funding.

- **Purchasing**—Globalization also means a shift in HR buying habits. A portion of all HR outsourcing, vendor services, technology, software and consulting purchases should come from countries other than the home base, in order to further expand interactions with individuals from different countries and cultures.

- **Field rotations**—Globalization requires the frequent interaction between local country and global workers. The best interaction is face-to-face and on the job. In order to expedite that kind of learning, every major function should be required to set aside a certain percentage of its short-term projects, transfers and promotions for global workers. A functional metric needs to be developed to ensure that a significant number of home staff are going to global offices and vice versa.

- **Opinion gathering**—All too frequently the majority of the new ideas that are adopted by HR leadership come from the home country. On occasion, international ideas don't get a fair hearing because remotely located workers lack the political clout and contacts that headquarters workers have. HR must develop processes to ensure that the business proactively seeks out ideas and opinions from remotely located employees. Safeguards should also be put into effect to ensure that a reasonable number of global ideas actually reach the VP of HR's desk for consideration.
- **Metrics and rewards**—The final, but perhaps the most important filter, is that HR leadership must implement metrics and rewards for acting globally. Programs and managers must be measured on their global actions and behaviors. Some portion of every HR leader's bonus must be based on acting globally. Individual HR professionals must also be recognized and rewarded for designing programs with global impact and for accepting global assignments.

THE CHANGING BUSINESS WORLD REQUIRES THAT "ONE SIZE FITS ONE"

Everyone would like the world to be a simple place where simple solutions can be applied uniformly. Unfortunately, though, the world is becoming increasingly complex. Political unrest, oil shortages and natural disasters make doing business around the world an ever-changing challenge. You can no longer treat every country the same. For example, when one country is going through rapid growth, another country has a shrinking economy. The diversity that we have learned to value in the United States is certainly a given if a company does business in multiple countries around the world. As a result, most global situations require a range of solutions to fit the unique set of circumstances in that place and at that time.

Some HR departments have recognized this need for localized service by allowing business units in each country to operate independently. While this might sound like a good idea on the surface, examine what this means in practice. Allowing each country to operate relatively autonomously directly inhibits the corporation's ability to move and react rapidly as a unit.

And here lies the dilemma that faces most HR managers: How do you get consistency in operations and information flow across the world while simultaneously allowing for some degree of local autonomy and control? The answer of course is that all HR solutions (and their related processes) need to share a common base that is consistent (for example, technologies and metrics). However, there needs to be some portion of the approach that can be customized to fit local needs.

While many HR solutions are developed in a "one size fits all" model, what is actually needed is a mass customized approach where "one size fits one." For example, several HR globalization efforts have focused on developing standardized processes and policies around the world. In fact, this is the exact opposite of what is needed. What managers really need is some degree of flexibility in policies and procedures that allows each manager to apply a personalized solution that fits their unique needs.

There is no "magic mix" formula to tell you exactly how much customization versus centralization that you need, unfortunately. The ideal solution is much like an avocado—one part is hard and unbending (the seed) while another portion is pliable (the fruit). There are a variety of factors that should be considered when choosing what parts of HR will be flexible, including the performance of the unit, the availability of metrics and technology, and the uniqueness of the local business economy.

PROBLEMS WITH MOST HR GLOBALIZATION EFFORTS

Poor program design can doom international programs to mediocrity. The first lesson to be learned: Do not view all problems through the eyes of the United States. Instead, try to view a problem from both the corporate and the international manager's perspective. Because it is important for HR professionals to be aware of the array of problems that can occur during globalization efforts, below is a list of some of the common problems that have occurred in major corporations.

A focus on transactions—A major part of any effort to understand global management practices includes knowing how to attract and retain talent and develop and increase productivity at numerous sites around the world. Unfortunately, what HR actually does when it globalizes is frequently relatively simple and transactional in nature.

For example, the most common HR programs that directly relate to globalization are relocation and expatriate programs. All too often when HR ventures into other broader global services, vendors, consultants, or lawyers do most of the actual work. Few people would argue that relocation is a strategic HR function.

Manager satisfaction—It's not unusual for international line managers to expect little direct help from corporate HR. For example, at one large high-tech firm, international managers were polled about what they thought about corporate HR. The responses were uniformly negative (no translating difficulties here). They ranged from "they never listen to us" to "we are the last to get new HR programs and, when we do, they are barely modified versions of the U.S. program." A strategic HR manager cannot be U.S.-centric. He or she must instead strive to provide an equal level of services to all managers, regardless of where a manager is physically located.

It is also not surprising to find that few HR programs measure management's satisfaction with HR's contribution to productivity. Few HR departments make the effort to poll their international managers to measure their satisfaction levels, and even fewer take the time to compare workforce productivity between different regions and countries. You can't improve productivity at remotely located businesses if you don't know which ones are performing at the highest levels.

A "follower" mentality—Businesses are seeking leadership in the process of globalization. In order to be strategic, HR must proactively take the lead in seeking out opportunities to assess new countries and new global opportunities. Unfortunately, HR all too often waits for management to tell it what country the firm is moving into, and after that business decision has already been made, then HR begins to build programs to fit those expansion plans. As a result of this follower's approach, when it comes to globalizing, most HR professionals and functions are not major players. The programs they offer and the skills that they have are limited in scope and U.S.-centric at best.

Information collection—Not all HR professionals have traveled internationally and even fewer read publications not written in English. As a result, many HR professionals are not able to do competitive intelligence and market research into the local people practices of each region.

If a firm's remote business units are to beat their competition, they can be no different than corporate business units. They need to know the benchmark people-management practices in the country, as well as the best people practices that are employed by the competitors. Providing information about the people practices of the region and the direct competitors is beyond the capability of most global HR functions because they do not do competitive intelligence, benchmarking, or market research on worker expectations outside of their home country.

Metrics—It's difficult to observe or assess the work of the people who work at remote locations. However, corporate management still needs to assess their productivity. Few HR departments have developed consistent performance appraisal and productivity metrics that can be assessed from a distance. Performance metrics allow managers to compare the performance of remote business units and to react long before any problems get out of hand.

Knowledge and learning—A significant percentage of HR professionals have a minimal knowledge of international business, remote management, and the HR practices of other countries. HR managers all too frequently make the assumption that U.S. business practices can be easily implemented "as is" in any country. This U.S.-centric approach causes HR professionals to skimp on their learning about international people-management practices. This lack of knowledge can limit opportunities for HR. For example, everyone knows that mergers and acquisitions are a major tool for corporate growth, but what HR team has the capability of identifying and assessing international firms that would be great takeover targets because of their similar culture and their depth of talent?

Treating all countries in a region the same—It's relatively easy to stereotype countries. It's not uncommon for managers to overgeneralize and assume that all countries in a region (for example, South America, Asia or Europe) are the same. Assuming that all countries on a continent have similar human resource practices and laws is a *huge* mistake that can harm not just talent management but also product sales.

Focus—HR frequently fails to integrate all HR functions into the global effort. Most global efforts just include compensation and relocation, but globalization efforts should be broadened to include well-developed programs in recruiting, training, performance management and productivity improvement. The direction of HR program development must also shift. HR has a tendency to develop its programs in its home country first and then later transfer them to international sites. This one-way movement tends to make non-American employees feel like second-class citizens, especially when the programs they develop are summarily rejected at corporate because they were not invented.

Recruiting and retention programs—Few U.S.-based corporations have done the research to determine which unique set of factors increases retention and recruiting success in different regions of the world. Most experienced recruiters know that it requires market research to identify the very best sources and to understand candidate acceptance criteria. Using U.S. concepts and definitions for diversity around the world is also a common practice in HR, even though the definition of, and demand for, diversity varies significantly throughout the world.

Retaining local managers after training them—A large problem in global operations is that once you identify and train local management talent, everyone will try to poach them away. This is especially true in geographic regions where Western-trained managers are scarce. The retention issue occurs because it's difficult to hide well-trained managers in developing regions. Odds are that other major firms have also moved into the region and they see that your organization's already-trained and experienced talent is an optimal target for their recruiting efforts.

Now that we have identified some of the common problems that occur when globalizing HR, it's time to shift our attention toward solving these problems.

BEST PRACTICES IN GLOBALIZING YOUR HR FUNCTION

There is no standard roadmap for successful HR globalization efforts, but the first move is to avoid all of the errors that others have made before you. Take advantage of the best practices that made a significant contribution to the success of the globalization effort. Some excellent globalization practices are listed below.

FOCUS, PROGRAM DESIGN AND PLANNING

- **Agile HR solutions with a range of options**—Both within and outside the United States, managers need people solutions and tools that fit their environment. In a global company there is a wide range of different business environments making it essential that all new HR programs and processes be either broad enough to fit most variations or agile enough to "flex" to meet most of the rapidly changing conditions that will be encountered throughout the global organization.

  Agility and speed must be part of all programs so that they can change to meet the differing social, legal and speed-of-change conditions in different regions around the world. Programs must also anticipate the extremes in unemployment, economic growth, and the availability of technology solutions.

- **"Once you move them a mile"**—Managers at Hewlett-Packard often use a phrase "if you move them a mile, it's the same as moving them 1,000 miles." What this phrase means is that once you move workers physically away from their boss, the same remote management tools apply whether you move them one mile or 1,000 miles. Independent of globalization, more and more workers are physically being located away from their U.S. corporate offices (at remote offices, at home, or continually on the move). This trend toward remotely locating workers allows HR to use any remote workers to develop tools that also can be used for globalized operations.

  No matter how far you move the employee, managers will never be able to maintain employee productivity levels if they continue to rely on the current "face-to-face" approach to management. Because of these shifts, HR needs to develop remote tools and metrics that allow managers to manage employees as effectively as if they came in to headquarters everyday. Because remote management and global management are remarkably similar, HR gets a two-for-one benefit because most of the effective remote management tools can also be applied to the global work force.

- **Utilize the global hand-off**—One of the most effective tools for increasing productivity and decreasing development time is the global hand-off of projects. A global hand-off is where parts of a project are completed during normal working hours in a particular location and at the close of business they are then handed-off to the next time zone to the west. These handoffs continue on to other time zones all around the world. This allows projects to be worked on continuously, 24 hours a day. As firms acclimate to this hand-off method, it can result in a rapid improvement in product development cycles and in time to market. This approach is effective for both HR and non-HR projects.

- **Equity is local**—The equitable treatment of employees is a difficult issue anytime, but it is especially difficult in a global company. It is an impossible task to guarantee equity around the world because of the diversity of the economies of the different countries. Trying to equalize all practices, pay and treatment is a time-consuming task.
- A better approach is to define equity as a local issue throughout the company. Make it known that all you can reasonably expect is for the local managers to provide equity within their regions. While it is a fine goal to attempt to provide equity globally, it is a monumental task, which is almost impossible to reach. However, this local equity provision does require that you provide multiple opportunities for those who wish to move to regions where the compensation or other practices better fit their personal needs.

INFORMATION GATHERING AND METRICS

- **Competitive intelligence and "what works" sharing**—HR must expand its competitive intelligence and best practice gathering capability to include international firms and regions. HR must know about the best people practices everywhere in the world. Of equal importance is the rapid sharing of what works between managers around the world. GE calls the rapid sharing of information around the world "global brains."
- HR must learn to treat information about successes, failures and learning like a "hot potato" and develop processes and systems to rapidly pass it around the organization in order to insure that all managers have an opportunity to learn about and adopt best practices. Without rapid learning and sideways communications, the company faces the risk of repeating the same mistakes around the world.

Just as those who ignore history are bound to repeat it, those who fail to learn from local mistakes are bound to have them repeated in numerous global locations.

- **Two-way communications**—Top-down communications are slow and they can frustrate remotely located managers. Honest two-way communication and feedback are essential for effective globalization and remote management. HR must take an active role in seeking out the opinions and ideas of managers and employees from remote locations. One successful element of a global HR program is that remotely located workers feel like they are listened to and appreciated. A primary goal of HR globalization is to develop a process that allows the firm to identify the unique needs of global or remotely located managers and employees. This can be accomplished in a variety of ways, including e-mail surveys, "pulse surveys," telephone focus groups, net meetings, and with individual telephone interviews.

- **"Repeat back" communications**—It's fairly common for global employees to feel intimidated when they're using English or even just when they're talking to headquarters staff. As a result of this uneasiness, they are unlikely to complain or speak up when they don't understand something. In order to combat this lack of understanding, HR must learn to ask international managers frequently to "repeat back" what was just said and what it meant to them. This "repeat back" feature helps to minimize errors due to cultural and language differences and to ensure that the message came through clearly.

- **Metrics not culture**—Corporate cultures vary significantly in their strength and application around the world. If you want to change behavior rapidly around the world, it's essential to use other tools in addition to the corporate culture. Many organizations have found that metrics and rewards are the most effective drivers of change in a large geographically dispersed organization. In addition, metrics can help rapidly identify which people practices are the most and least effective in the different regions.

QUALITY AND COMPETENCIES OF THE STAFF AND EMPLOYEES

- **Hire globally within HR**—Once HR determines the essential competencies for a global-thinking person, HR needs to begin using those criteria to hire, transfer and promote HR professionals. Utilizing these criteria will eventually lead to the hiring of a significant number of non-U.S. nationals to work in the HR function. This also means that a significant percentage of the department's HR professionals will work full time outside the United States while they remain an integral part of the HR team.

- **Learning rapidly**—Above all, if every HR service and function is to become a global service provider, everyone in HR must begin to broaden his or her learning. This learning must begin by reading international business journals, visiting international business web sites and learning about the business practices of each of the countries in which the firm currently (or may soon) do business. HR professionals must also develop their own global learning sources so that they can understand the very best global HR practices.

- **Internationalizing HR program development**—Learning and program development must be a two-way street. Everything can't start at "corporate" and then generate outward. Globally developed programs and learning from around the world must also flow into, and be adopted by, corporate on a regular basis. HR must make a concerted effort to ensure that non-corporate ideas are recognized, rewarded and promoted just as often as those developed at "corporate." The goal is to ensure that remotely located managers and non-corporate based HR professionals don't feel like second-class citizens.

- **Put the work where the talent is**—In a world where talent can be difficult to acquire and retain, it is essential to learn to put the work where the talent is. Instead of automatically moving work to the United States, the global approach is to gather data on where there are labor surpluses, high education and experience levels, and low labor costs. The next step is for HR to encourage management to move both hourly and professional work to those talent surplus areas.

The next chapter in the book highlights the ninth strategic element in HR, building an HR brand.

CHAPTER THIRTEEN

HR BUILDS A BRAND

OBJECTIVE

The ninth element of a strategic HR department is building an HR "brand."

KEY POINTS

◊ Building an HR brand can have a tremendous impact.
◊ Not only can brand building increase the applicant flow and lower turnover rates but it can also improve HR's internal reputation and improve its chances for increased funding.
◊ Although building a brand is clearly not an easy task, its strategic benefits and business impacts far outweigh its initial costs.

DEFINITION

Branding is the process of creating an image of being a "great place to work" in the minds of the target audience of applicants and employees. It is a concept borrowed from the business side of the enterprise.

Part of any HR branding effort is the goal of becoming a "magnet" organization that almost automatically attracts top performers from all the major organizations within an industry. Organizations like SAS, GE and Cisco, for example, all have built their businesses with a "great place to work" brand as a cornerstone.

There are two schools of thought regarding building a brand and image within HR. The most common approach is the traditional one, which is based on the premise that good work by itself automatically will be recognized and rewarded, so that no marketing is necessary. The second school takes a bolder approach and assumes that HR, like any other overhead function, must market itself proactively and build its image in order to improve its effectiveness.

A majority of HR departments take the more traditional approach, while a few like Cisco, Southwest Airlines, the Container Store, Agilent Technologies, and Edward Jones have taken a more aggressive approach in building their HR brand and image. Cisco and GE, in fact, forever changed the world of HR by developing people programs that everyone talked about. *Fortune* and *Working Mother* magazines have continued that trend by making an organization's people programs the "trigger" for being listed as a great place to work.

HR can no longer refuse to "brag" about its people programs. If it does, it is affirmatively hurting the organization and its ability to attract and retain top talent. Leading edge organizations have taken a proactive approach to HR branding and image-building because of its high ROI and positive impact on recruiting and retention.

HR branding goes by several different names, including employment branding, best place to work branding or employer of choice branding. Traditionalists in HR may believe that departments that build up their brand do it to build their own egos. If that were true, however, the effort would be to build an individual's own personal image as an HR professional rather than the organization or department's image. Instead, the primary reason that an HR department builds its brand is to improve its impact and effectiveness.

Building an HR brand and image is a strategic necessity in a world where branding and image-building are pervasive. Almost every major company invests in building its product brand because of the high economic impact that those efforts produce.

Product branding is designed to develop a lasting image in the minds of the consumer so that consumers automatically associate quality with any product or service offered by the owner of the brand. An HR brand does the same in that it creates an image both internally and externally that makes people want to work for the organization because of its excellent people-management practices. Once the brand or best place to work image is set, it generally results in a steady flow of high-quality applicants and an increased retention rate. Employment branding uses the tools of market research, PR and advertising to mold the image that employees and applicants have of what it is like to work at the organization.

As you build a strong external brand in HR, the side benefit is that your internal image also will improve as executives see the positive recognition that your well-designed people programs have brought to the organization. Such recognition instantly moves HR from being considered merely administrative to being considered a strategic contributor.

WHAT IS AN HR BRAND?

DEFINITION

An employment brand is a long-term recruitment and retention strategy whose goal is to build a company's image as a great place to work. Employment branding is a tool designed to provide a steady flow of applicants for all jobs over a long period of time. Because it also builds the image of the organization among employees, it also has an impact on employee retention.

The four basic elements of HR image building and branding are:
1. Building the HR department's internal image
2. Getting "talked about" in industry and business publications
3. Getting on "best place to work" lists
4. Becoming recognized as an employer of choice

Each of the four HR branding elements makes a direct contribution toward HR's effort to be strategic.

THE GOALS FOR HR BRANDING

A successful HR branding strategy includes the following goals:

- To develop a common theme or brand so that current workers tell friends and contacts a consistent story about what it is like to be an employee of the organization
- To build and reinforce the public's image of the organization's culture, work practices, management style, and growth opportunities
- To coordinate the employment brand with the company image and its different product brands
- To continually monitor the organization's "good place to work" image both inside and outside the organization to ensure the brand remains strong
- To energize the best potential candidates to apply for jobs at the organization
- To increase the number and quality of employee referrals
- To increase retention rates
- To promote good PR and strengthening of the product brand image when the organization is mentioned in articles and books citing the best companies
- To build an effective image so that customers and strategic partners are also attracted by the favorable image
- To increase employees' motivation because of a shared pride in where they work
- To increase the organization's name recognition along with developing a positive image in order to influence stock price

THE FOUR ELEMENTS OF HR BRANDING

1. BUILDING THE HR DEPARTMENT'S INTERNAL IMAGE

Most people would agree that HR professionals are not "braggers." As a group they tend not to have big egos or blow their own horn, while others in sales and marketing are known for aggressively building their image among senior managers. In fact, most HR professionals I meet strongly resist any internal image management efforts. I would certainly agree with that approach *if* other functional departments didn't aggressively build their own internal image. I would also note that the recent efforts of supply chain management, Customer Relationship Management (CRM), and business process reengineering all received major funding for their efforts, at least in part as a result of their internal image-building efforts.

> *If your goal is to make double-digit improvements in HR, you must realize that you will fail to reach that goal without additional financial resources. An effective way to acquire those additional resources is to build your image among senior managers as a "profit center" and a key contributor to corporate success.*

Marketing the HR department internally certainly bothers those who believe that hard work alone is automatically recognized and rewarded by senior management. This passive approach, however, runs counter to a strategic approach, in which you plan ahead and leave little to chance. Just like the organization, HR *could* let its product speak for itself. Or, in addition to providing an excellent product, it could also proactively build and maintain a "brand image." It is the latter, combined approach that strategic HR departments take.

Building the HR department's internal image among senior managers requires a marketing and PR approach. Building your image begins with identifying the key decision-makers or most powerful individuals within the company. HR then identifies their individual preferences (*i.e.*, the criteria that each uses to assess programs and functions). Next, HR develops an "influence" plan to educate these individuals about the work HR does and its impact on their job and area of control. That plan is generally compiled with the help of the organization's internal branding and PR experts.

This education process might include short talks at staff meetings, one-on-one presentations, involving these decision-makers as advisors in HR strategy development, and "business case" reports that demonstrate HR's direct impact on the success of each business unit. The education and influence effort is of course subtle but the intent is clear. The goal is proactively to educate and influence key individuals so they understand both the goals and the business impact produced by HR.

By undertaking such an aggressive effort, HR sends a clear message that it wants to be a "power player" in the corporation, not because of ego, but because of the significant costs of labor to the business and the positive business impact that results from HR's influence.

2. GETTING TALKED ABOUT

Although many organizations strive to become what is known as an "employer of choice," it is a lofty, difficult and probably an unnecessary goal for most organizations. A cheaper and easier alternative is to become a "talked about" place to work. Getting talked about is easier than you think. The strategy focuses on purposely doing extraordinary or innovative things in the workplace that will be picked up by the media. Doing innovative things for your workers will not only get you mentioned in the media but it will also give your employees something positive to "talk about" when friends ask them what it is like to work there.

There are two elements in the "getting talked about" strategy. The first is proactively providing your employees with something to talk about to their friends and professional contacts, and the second is being written up and talked about by industry and business media.

Becoming talked about uses the principles of "viral marketing" to spread the word to potential candidates about the great people-programs at your organization. It is a planned strategy that utilizes market research techniques to improve what employees say about your organization. The underlying premise of this approach is that word-of-mouth is a much more effective way to spread your message than formal advertising. Hearing or reading about your organization from a third-party source is more credible and believable than standard company PR pieces and recruitment advertising.

Getting your employees to talk about you

The first element of "getting talked about" is providing your own employees with information about your great people practices. Something to talk about might be something as simple as special treatment for a sick worker, free soft drinks at work, an innovative contribution to the community, or even a unique approach to flexible work hours. Something to talk about may be a "story" about how you treated an employee—or anything that employees would find significant enough to pass on. The important thing is to continually provide employees with some positive feature in the workplace to talk or brag about to their friends.

Unfortunately, "Dilbert-like" management miscues are often the only thing employees have to talk about when someone asks, "What is it like to work there?" HR needs to utilize market research techniques to determine exactly what employees currently say when outsiders ask them about the organization. This is especially true if you are relying heavily on employee referrals because referral programs increase the frequency of times in which employees have an opportunity to talk about their organization.

The message employees send must be consistent and clear. HR needs to provide them with a great message to pass on, because employees' family and friends ask them frequently about their work. At most organizations, employees do want to respond with a positive story, but they can't if they don't know any.

Providing employees "stories" is primarily for recruiting purposes, but it also has a retention side benefit. Employees who gain positive reinforcement from friends when they tell them about their company's people practices are more likely to be proud of the company. If the stories are clearly superior, this image-building effort will increase an employee's referrals while simultaneously reducing their interests in leaving the company. Having friends and family spread the story of your great people practices further enhances your image *at no extra cost*.

Media exposure

The second element of being "talked about" is being talked about in industry and business media. The goal of being talked about is the same as of any PR effort, to improve your image and to spur action. In this case, the goal is to increase the awareness that top performers at other organizations have about your organization's people practices. The long-term goal is to spur them to apply for a job at the organization sometime in the future.

Becoming "talked about" is a deliberate PR effort that includes:

- Getting the organization profiled in articles
- Authoring articles about major business problems and your organization's solutions
- Having your managers speak at conferences and public events
- Utilizing regularly occurring company PR and product events to spread your "great place to work" image
- Having the organization's great people practices highlighted in benchmark studies
- Getting your managers quoted in leading publications in stories that discuss people programs and great people management

Stories to tell

It's not enough to have the best management practices; you also must publicize them so that employees and potential applicants are aware of them. Some examples of management practices that should be publicized as part of your "talked about" initiative include:

- Demonstrating that your products "make a difference." Show that your products and services change lives and make the world a better place to live
- Outlining the company's economic success as a market leader and as an innovator in products
- Demonstrate the company's steady job growth, job security, and history of few layoffs
- Show that you offer the best technology, equipment and tools to help do a great job
- Highlight your generous approach to flextime and working at home
- Show how performance is recognized and generously rewarded
- Demonstrate that there are numerous promotional opportunities as well as chances to learn and grow
- Highlight diversity programs and successes
- Showcase your best management practices and any unique or outstanding benefit programs

Being "talked about" reinvigorates your employee referral program

There are never enough recruiters to spread the word about a great company. However, if you turn every employee into a recruiter you will find that it is much easier to get the message out. A great referral program has employees, their friends and their families "talking up" the organization during every waking hour. Successful referral programs make sure that employees have enough information about the company's people programs so that they can spread the best message to others.

Effective referral programs have few administrative rules, and they expedite referrals in the hiring process. In addition to a bonus for each referral, they ensure that employees and managers who actively refer are recognized and rewarded as part of the regular performance appraisal and employee recognition processes.

Working at a talked-about company gives you status equivalent to that of a famous celebrity or movie star. The results of a talked-about strategy can be spectacular. Once you get each and every employee talking about what a great place they work, the flow of high-quality applicants will increase dramatically (by as much as double). Then your only problem is how to sort through them.

3. GETTING ON "BEST PLACE TO WORK" LISTS

Almost without exception, companies that win awards for being a great place to work have no difficulty in recruiting and retaining talent. In fact, if your organization is highly placed on best places to work lists, recruiting becomes more of a resume-sorting problem than a candidate-finding problem.

For U.S. organizations, the ultimate recognition is to appear on the *Fortune* "great place to work" list. The importance of being on the *Fortune* list grows every year. The popularity of the list among employers is also growing (*e.g.*, the number of potential applicants is currently close to 1000 and steadily rising). The *Fortune* list is increasing in popularity because more and more HR departments realize that building a brand as a "great place to work" has a long-term impact—and one of the highest ROI's of anything you can do in HR. Getting placed on the *Fortune* list guarantees you additional publicity in your local region as well as throughout your industry.

Of course, getting on the list is hard work. In order to succeed in getting placed on the list, you must have a strong HR brand manager, high scores on employee satisfaction assessments, an "inventory" of great people programs, and a great deal of tenacity. Some of the organizations that appear consistently in the *Fortune* list include Cisco, the Container Store, Edward Jones, Intel, HP, Agilent and Wegman's Markets.

4. BEING RECOGNIZED AS AN EMPLOYER OF CHOICE

The ultimate long-term recruiting and retention strategy is to build a reputation as an "employer of choice" (EOC). An employer of choice is a conscious corporate-wide HR strategy that is designed to re-make a company image as "a great place to work." This employer of choice brand strategy combines the "talked about" and the "list" strategies into a comprehensive HR branding strategy. The ultimate goal is to become a "magnet organization," with a reputation or brand that is so strong and positive that it can, on its own, act like a magnet to draw applicants from all industries and all regions. The principle works for companies in a manner similar to how "magnet" schools attract students from every area.

Where most employment strategies are short-term and "reactive" to available job openings, building an employer of choice brand is a longer-term solution designed to provide a steady flow of applicants. EOC is a term used to designate a company that, because of its status and reputation as a great place to work, is always the first choice (or at least on the short list) of world-class candidates. One obvious advantage to the company is that it can easily attract and retain the top talent it needs to produce a quality product.

In addition, EOCs get name recognition, which helps reinforce the organization's product brand. There is no plaque awarded for EOC status but there are many benefits that can accrue to a organization that reaches it. Organizations widely considered to be an employer of choice include Microsoft, SAS, Hewlett-Packard, Intel and Starbucks. Because there are generally only one or two employers of choice in every industry, becoming an EOC is a high-risk HR strategy.

BENEFITS OF BUILDING AN HR BRAND

There are a variety of benefits that accrue to an HR department with strong brand strategy. Some of those benefits include:

Name recognition and exposure

Nothing will get you noticed faster among potential applicants than getting on the *Fortune* list. In addition to being noticed by those that actually read the magazine, getting on the list also guarantees that your organization will be highlighted in several industry and local publications because reporters and journalists will frequently call your organization to ask how you handle different human resource management problems. All of this publicity adds up to significant name recognition that becomes your "employment brand."

Benchmarking

The distinction from being mentioned in industry publications and being placed on the best place to work lists will open up numerous benchmarking opportunities for you. Companies that, in the past, wouldn't even return your calls for benchmarking information will now respond the next day. In addition, your HR department will get an increasing number of benchmark calls from leading organizations asking you how you operate. This recognition will dramatically build the pride of your HR function, and it might also provide you with ideas on additional HR programs that you might "borrow" from other organizations.

Quality and number of recruits

A strong HR brand guarantees you prominence but, even better, it assures an increased flow of top-quality applicants—in some cases, as much as double the flow of applications prior to the branding effort. The quality of the applicants also will increase because people from other regions and industries will learn about the features that make your company a great place to work. Remember that attracting great applicants is similar to a restaurant's attempt at attracting customers. The publicity of getting a great review will have a much greater impact than any newspaper ad ever could.

Lower costs

The name recognition that you receive by being talked about and for being on the *Fortune* list will last for years. The improved reputation will invariably increase applicant flow and will allow you to decrease your normal advertising costs and recruiting expenditures because your web site alone will provide more than an adequate volume of high-quality candidates.

Retention

Ranking on "best of" lists and being mentioned in industry publications will impact employee retention rates. External recognition builds pride among your current employees and serves to remind them of the many positive benefits of being a part of your organization. Being recognized as the "best" makes it a more difficult decision for employees to leave the organization. Few other organizations offer such quality people programs; in addition, if employees leave a great place to work, their friends and family will wonder out loud, "What were you thinking?"

Referrals

A strong HR brand as a great place to work builds employee referrals, because employees now have much more to talk about when initiating a recruiting conversation.

Sales

Improved brand has an indirect impact on sales and market position due to the increased publicity that occurs following the media spotlight on great places to work. Several studies have produced evidence that being known as a great organization translates into increased sales because customers directly associate being a great place to work with perceived product quality.

A source of pride

In addition to the financial benefits of making the *Fortune* list, most companies seize the opportunity to publicize their ranking. For example, Wegman's Food Markets, a five-year veteran of the *Fortune* list, has provided all employees with brightly-colored T-shirts that recognize this significant accomplishment. Continental Airlines, also a 5-year veteran, has painted the accomplishment on the side of its airplanes. By ensuring that both employees and customers are aware of your employment brand, you increase both customers' and employees' pride in the organization.

LOW COST THINGS YOU CAN DO TO BUILD YOUR HR BRAND

Here are a variety of no-cost things you can do to begin building your employment brand.

- Benchmark and learn all you can internally from successful product and employment brands. Do the same externally (especially look at Cisco, GE, HP and IBM).
- Assess your organization's current management practices, benefits, culture, etc., to identify what you "have to sell" and what you need to improve.
- Do a quick survey or assessment of your current employment "image" among employees, applicants and general public using surveys and focus groups.
- Calculate the potential ROI for branding and sell the idea to management.
- Develop a catchy slogan that highlights your very best "great place to work" feature(s).
- Develop a people-program inventory that lists each of your organization's unique HR or people programs. This list should be used as ammunition to highlight your best practices in marketing pieces and in media articles.
- Identify company products and programs that involve innovation, help save lives or protect the environment. Use these stories and examples in recruiting materials.
- Rename some of your successful people programs with "catchy" names that grab people's attention.
- Do a side-by-side comparison of your benefits and people programs against those of your talent competitors. Identify areas where you are clearly superior.
- Identify and assess your competitors' employment "brand" against which you'll be competing. Develop a branding strategy that highlights the differences between you and your competitor.
- Compose one or two-paragraph profiles of individual employee "success stories" for use in articles and on the web site.

- Work with the CEO's office to get top executives to mention your organization's great people practices both in their internal and external communications. When necessary, write that section of the speech for the CEO.
- Apply for listing in the *Fortune* 100 Best Places to Work list.
- Work with the PR department to identify public events that the company is sponsoring. Send managers and recruiters to talk about the company's great people practices. The recruiting department should also add a few of the marketing staff to its advisory team to offer suggestions and to coach recruiters on the latest marketing tools and strategies.
- Work with the sales department to identify public sales events and trade shows where materials highlighting your great people practices can be displayed.
- Quantify the participation and usage of your work-life balance and other similar high-profile people programs. Quantifying the usage sends a more powerful message than merely saying "we have a program."
- Rank potential media and tools to convey branding efforts (based on what your target audience reads or attends), and then select the initial media and methods to convey the branding message.
- Review articles that mention different companies' people programs. Then develop a list of the criteria used by local publications when they select a company or people program to feature. Utilize these criteria for selecting which program stories you should highlight in your branding effort. In addition, build relationships with local publications and their reporters. Volunteer to act as sources, and encourage them to write stories on your great people and management practices.
- Identify the target market (the type of candidate you are trying to attract) for your branding efforts. Develop a target profile for them (who they are; where to find them; what they read; events they go to; etc.).
- Get key managers to write articles and give talks at industry association meetings. Be sure they include great people practices in their materials.
- Get managers to give talks at community meetings and at the local Chamber of Commerce that highlight your people practices.
- Invite family and friends of employees on site to see "what it is like to work here" and the importance of employees' work so

that they will help spread the word on what a great place your organization is to work.

- Offer benchmarking sessions on your great "people practices" to teach your customers and suppliers how you do great people management in an attempt to get the attendees to spread the word.
- Profile key employee success stories and best management practices on your corporate career web site. Periodically highlight your great people practices in internal publications to remind employees of the great things you do.
- Cosponsor "career workshops" in schools to build your image early.
- Ask the union, if you have one, to help spread the word about what a great place to work you are.
- Encourage local college professors to visit and write "case studies" and articles about the company's people practices.
- Participate in industry-wide benchmarking studies to help build your visibility.
- Have HR leaders speak at public HR seminars and write articles for HR trade publications about your people practices. Have them join the boards of local nonprofit groups and associations to help spread the word.
- Include marketing and branding experience in the criteria you use to hire additional recruiters.
- Create a process to measure and evaluate the program's effectiveness, monitor its progress, and improve it.

Low-cost branding tools

If you have a little money to spend on HR branding, here are some low-cost things to do.

- Re-energize your existing employee referral program and set "targets" for referrals from each department. Include participation as part of the normal performance appraisal process. Provide employees with cards listing the top ten reasons why it's great to work for your company.
- Encourage employees to put decals, license plate holders, etc., on their vehicles to broadcast their loyalty. Sell or distribute employment-branded items (hats, T-shirts, pens, etc.) that depict work at your organization.
- Participate in community clean-up programs; get your organization named on "clean-up" highway signs.

- Develop an alumni club for ex-employees and retirees. Involve these former employees in the process of spreading the word.
- Distribute logo book bags, T-shirts, and other similar items to children; sponsor school events.
- Work with the advertising department to place ads that occasionally highlight your great people and management practices as well as your products.
- Train and reward managers for excellent people-management performance.
- Conduct surveys of college students, business writers, academics, executive recruiters, and influential business leaders as well as your employees to assess your perceived strengths, weaknesses, corporate culture and image.
- Revise recruiting practices to include "wow" elements to make a lasting impression. Continually review your recruitment strategy and team capabilities.
- Have the CEO or HR vice president write a book about the organization's people-management practices.

POSSIBLE DISADVANTAGES OF BEING AN EOC

There is also a downside to being an employer of choice. Some of the possible problems include:

- Executive recruiters often target your organization's management and its employees.
- The strength of the corporate culture makes changing it (as well as many operational changes) difficult.
- Because of their "fame," the organization's employees have a tendency to become overconfident. Performance measurement and willingness to accept criticism often diminish due to this overconfidence.
- The company's image must be defended continually. Minor errors can be blown out of proportion by the press.
- Pay levels (and thus costs of production) can be high due to the high cost of maintaining a world-class workforce.
- New recruits may have unrealistic expectations based on image that can turn into disillusionment if everyday reality does not match.
- EOC helps a organization grow, and this increase in size makes maintaining the culture and EOC status difficult over time.

Becoming an EOC is not for everyone but if you are in an industry where getting the very best employees is the top factor contributing to the organization's success, it may be for you. Even if you do not adopt the total strategy, using parts of it may result in an increased applicant flow.

MEASURING YOUR EMPLOYMENT BRAND

Having a "brand" is not sufficient to achieve success. To be truly successful, most branding efforts must continuously improve and evolve so that your organization's brand is always stronger than that of your talent competitors.

> *Every company already has an "employment brand," be it good or bad, because those connected to the company including its employees, investors, and customers talk about the organization. There is no way to stop the casual conversation that creates most "word of mouth" brands, so the key to success is to manage the current message so that it tells the story you want told.*

The key to any continuous improvement process is:
- Assessing where you are now, and *then*
- Assessing the impact of any improvements that you make.

THE FOUR LEVELS OF EMPLOYMENT BRAND MEASUREMENT

The effectiveness of an employment brand (*a.k.a.* "strength" of the brand) can be measured on four different levels. When you design your measurement system, it's important to ensure that you measure each individual level of your brand. The four levels of measurement include:

1. Media exposure

Counting the number and the "quality" of your media "hits" (a hit is defined as an instance when your company's name is associated with good people-related practices in the media).

> *Example metric: Number of times cited*—Count the number of times each month that your organization's HR and people practices are mentioned positively by name in major

media outlets that service your target audience, including industry and business news publications and television programs. Next compare your appearances in the media to those of your direct talent competitors.

2. Great place to work name recognition

Assessing how many individuals *recognize* your organization as a great place to work. High name recognition means that when a discussion turns to great people practices, individuals mention your organization by name as a positive example.

Example metric: Positive name recognition in your **target** *population*—It is important to measure your organization's great place to work name recognition specifically among your target population (those that are the most qualified for your jobs). When this target population is surveyed, it should identify your organization as one of the great places to work. Track this percentage to gauge the impact of your branding initiatives.

3. Detailed knowledge

Measuring how many individuals know *"why"* your organization is a great place to work goes beyond simple name recognition; individuals must know something about your organization's specific people programs or unique offerings.

Example metric: Your target population is knowledge-able—Ask the general population, your target population and highly qualified individuals what *specifically* they know about your organization's people practices. When asked, they should be able to list the specific reasons they feel that make your organization a great place to work.

4. The brand results in action

Having awareness of your brand is not enough; you must assess if your brand actually causes individuals to *take action* as a result of their knowledge of your organization's people practices (*i.e,.* your brand drives them to apply for a job at your organization).

Example metric: An increased flow of applications—Organizations with a superior brand receive a steady flow of employment applications, even when they are not currently running any job ads or other active recruiting efforts. Track the application rate, the quality of applicants, and the regularity of applicant volume to measure the impact of your branding initiatives.

While many brand managers use words rather than numbers to describe their success, it is very important to remember that brand strength is not a name but rather a *number*. What this phrase means is that it is essential that you convert the descriptions of your "employment brand strength" from words to numbers. Why? Because not only does the use of numbers impress the CFO, but numbers also allow you to rapidly identify any weaknesses in your branding program and to continually improve them over time.

Now it is time to move to the tenth and last element of strategic HR, the extensive use of technology. The next chapter will highlight the impact that technology can have on HR effectiveness.

CHAPTER FOURTEEN

TECHNOLOGY PERMEATES HR

OBJECTIVES

The tenth and last essential element in a strategic HR department is that technology permeates every area of HR.

KEY POINTS

◊ Technology plays a critical part in making an HR department strategic; information and knowledge have become the keys to business success, and HR must respond to that change. Business is demanding "faster, better and cheaper" answers from every business function. HR can't get faster, better and cheaper without the extensive use of technology.

◊ Technology will allow HR to "shift" HR decisions closer to the customer. Line managers will have laptop access to information that will improve the quality of the people management decisions that they make daily.

◊ Technology allows HR to increase its capabilities, so that HR can do things that it never would have even considered before.

HR IS BEHIND THE TECHNOLOGY CURVE

There are two primary reasons why the extensive use of technology is an absolute requirement if an HR department is to become strategic.

1. As HR continues the trend to de-emphasize transactions, the sole remaining functions in HR are those that provide information and advice to managers. As HR moves toward becoming strategic, then, it begins the transition to becoming an information provider and a productivity-consulting center.
2. Each of the individual ten essential elements of a strategic HR department requires the use of technology. For example, the essential elements of forecasting and metrics rely on technology for their very existence. Similarly, globalization and a performance culture both require technology in order to succeed because paper is too expensive and slow to move between offices.

Throughout most of its history, HR has completed most of its tasks relying on people rather than technology. That's probably a natural tendency; because HR is a people function, its first option is always to solve problems utilizing people. Even though most HR departments have adopted some new electronic technologies in the last few years, there are very few HR departments that can say that e-HR and technology permeate everything they do.

In direct contrast, other business functions are light years ahead in the extensive use of technology. For example, supply chain, manufacturing and even finance have learned to increase their capabilities by relying heavily on technology. Medical departments have dramatically improved their effectiveness because they have learned to utilize technology to move beyond the human capabilities (and limitations) of their staff.

Extensive use of technology has not just transformed businesses functions, but entire businesses. For example, with its extensive use of supply chain technology, Wal-Mart has moved from merely a regional retailer to being a "category killer." The US Air Force is another organization that has shifted from relying solely on people judgments to relying on technology to win battles.

What these diverse business units and organizations have found is that technology can improve, not just efficiency, but more importantly can dramatically increase capabilities well beyond anything that was previously possible. In short, technology allows organizations to do things that in the past would have been called "impossible." It is this increased capability that makes technology an essential element in HR.

In a paperless environment, for example, employee files are transmitted around the world in seconds. Analytics software allows HR to not just report results but analyze them electronically in order to determine root causes and trends. Some software programs can even project into the future. Some technologies go one step further and will alert the individual manager electronically about an upcoming high-probability problem in the department. These systems can even offer electronic suggestions on how to resolve or prevent the problem.

People just don't have the same capability as computers to analyze real-time data or to forecast trends. As human beings, most of us are reluctant to admit that technology can surpass human capabilities. Perhaps a better perspective is that technology can help complement human capabilities so together, we can do more.

Another advantage of HR technology is that it can make HR faster and more globally capable. For example, because strategic HR departments are paperless, they can send a file to any manager in the world in seconds, they can provide line managers with daily information on employee productivity, and managers can approve hiring requisitions instantly, no matter where they are in the world.

In contrast, paper-based employee files need to be hand-carried or mailed, paper reports can only updated once per month, and approvals can take weeks if a manager is on the road. In all three cases, a paperless HR allows everything to be faster and more efficient because HR is not burdened with the disadvantages of paper.

PIECEMEAL VS. "TECHNOLOGY DOMINATES"

HR departments take two basic approaches to adopting technology: the piecemeal and "technology dominates" approach.

Piecemeal. Those that take the piecemeal approach look at HR technology as a helpful tool to be used in limited areas when problems arise. For example, when corporate travel gets too difficult or expensive, many firms then adopt an e-learning program. Also, when resume volume becomes excessive, firms buy an ATS system. This approach to technology is reactive; it has no comprehensive plan to guide the introduction of HR technology.

Although most HR departments are looking to technology as a tool to help them reach their goals, many current HR systems are not strategic because they focus solely on the transaction side of HR. Transactions and operations issues are important, obviously, but no one would argue that great transactions are strategic.

HR also takes a piecemeal approach in the management of HR technology. Currently, most of the technology in HR is "owned" and managed by the HRIS department. If technology is ever to be "owned" by the various HR managers, that centralized HRIS ownership must change. Many professionals in HR have been able to avoid learning about technology because they have been able to rely on HRIS to install and manage everything for them. Once the technology ownership shifts to them, HR managers will be forced to learn more about technology and to develop a better understanding of how it can improve their effectiveness.

When an organization undertakes the "piecemeal" approach, areas that have the most potential for increasing HR's strategic business impact include improving employee productivity, metrics, forecasting, and improving line manager decision-making on people issues.

Technology dominates. In direct contrast to the piecemeal approach, firms like Cisco, Microsoft and Hewlett-Packard have set as a foundation of their HR strategy that technology must "dominate" everything they do in HR. Of course, part of the reason they select technology as a foundation is that they are technology companies. Even so, the primary reason for making technology a foundation is that they could never have achieved the strategic HR impact levels that they have without the pervasive use of technology.

When you compare companies that follow the "technology dominates" strategy to companies that have adopted the piecemeal approach, not only do they vary in their use of technology, but they also vary in their strategic results. The difference in strategic results is so dramatic that I have come to the conclusion that it is not possible to become strategic in large or global firms without following the "technology dominates" strategy. On the surface, that might seem like an outrageous statement—if numerous other business functions had not already successfully taken the same route.

STRATEGIC HR IS PRIMARILY
AN INFORMATION PROVIDER

When you examine precisely what HR does, you realize that mostly it provides information. HR provides two types of information. The first is operational information that relates to processes, transactions and coverage. The second but more strategic is information that helps managers make better people decisions. That information includes advice on problems, metrics, alerts, forecasts and productivity improvement.

If you examine these two types of information, you soon realize that the operational information you provide has less of a strategic impact than the decision-making information you provide. And if the current trend where HR outsources or converts most operational and transactional processes to self-service continues, then most of what remains in HR is providing decision-making information.

Take a step back and think about it: when an HR department becomes strategic, it essentially becomes a strategic information-providing function. Once you get out of the transaction business, there is little for HR to do other than provide information and advice. Even when HR provides training, it is providing information to managers and employees. HR provides basic operational information about coverage, policies, rules and process steps, but it also provides a higher level of information for decision-making, such as information on trends, risks, benchmarks, and recommended actions based on past incidents.

HR is not unique in undergoing this transformation to "information provider." Finance underwent that transition several years ago. As an information provider, finance has become more strategic rather than transactional. While finance used to focus on handling money and making investments, it now focuses on providing information to managers that improves their ability to make fast and accurate business decisions. As experts in finance, it provides strategic information, not just for pure financial decisions, but also for business decisions with financial components.

HRI—Human Resources Information

Once HR decides that it is primarily an information provider, it's an easy jump to the next step where all information will be provided in electronic format, similar to how information currently is provided in finance, quality control and supply. Once HR makes the transition from HR into HRI (**H**uman **R**esource **I**nformation) it becomes clear that electronic technology must be the foundation for everything HR does.

HR operational information

After a function makes the transition to strategic information provider, the type of information that it provides to managers changes also. It shifts towards providing "decision-support" information and away from operational information.

Examples of HR operational information include:
- Information relating to rules and policies
- Information relating to procedures and transactions
- Historical information about what happened "last year"

HR decision-support information

In contrast to operational information, decision-support information helps managers solve and prevent people-management problems. Strategic information helps managers make better decisions. This decision-support information tends to be focused on identifying and preventing problems as well as forecasting future issues. Examples of decision-support information include:
- Comparison and benchmark data
- Information on trends and patterns
- Forecasts of future events
- Alerts about imminent problems
- Advice on preventing problems
- Information on "best practices" and "what works" within the firm
- Risk assessments and alerts

PROVIDING INFORMATION REQUIRES TECHNOLOGY

Once an HR department decides to make the shift toward becoming a strategic information provider, the essential role that must be played by technology becomes clear. Computer technology is the ideal platform for providing information. In fact, the computer department at most corporations carries the name "IT" because the department uses technology to manage information. There is a wide variety of technology that HR can use to manage, analyze and provide information, including the company's intranet, the Web, and even e-mail. In addition, HR can use computer technology to do trend analysis, calculate metrics and to prepare customized reports.

There's a tendency for HR departments to stop at that point, but to proceed to the next strategic level, HR must provide managers with "laptop" access to all HR information. This is the ultimate step in HR technology where managers have real-time access to the information they need to make people-management decisions. By providing (on their personal laptops) 90 percent of the information that managers need to make their people management decisions, HR makes the final strategic step—it allows managers to "own" their own people problems.

Performance almost always improves when managers stop blaming "HR" and instead take responsibility for identifying and resolving their own people problems. With appropriate decision-support information right on their laptops, managers can now make most of their people-management decisions independently of HR. This shift in ownership allows HR to concentrate on more strategic issues and on the remaining 10 percent of the people-management problems where HR's advanced expertise is really needed.

> *If your firm is large, if it's in the technology industry, or if it's a global firm, you can never reach your strategic potential in HR if technology does not dominate everything you do.*

HR's NEW SERVICE DELIVERY MODEL

Technology is changing the way that HR provides services. In most organizations, HR services are delivered on a face-to-face basis. When a manager or employee has a problem, there are progressive steps that are taken in order to get an answer to their question. There are two ways to approach this "progression," the traditional and the new HR approach.

The traditional HR progression of service delivery

PERSON

PHONE

DESKTOP

Person—When a manager has an HR problem that requires HR assistance, the first choice is always to go to one HR person and get a face-to-face answer. Almost always that person was the manager's "own" generalist or an on-site specialist.

Phone—If a manager cannot find an HR person to respond "face-to-face," the second choice is to call a HR person. Either a generalist or specialist at headquarters is called in order to get the answer.

Desktop—If the manager cannot find a person, whether face-to-face or on the phone, the final but least desirable option is to look up the question in the desktop HR manual. Managers dislike this option because paper manuals are often incomplete and time-consuming to use.

The "new" HR progression of service delivery

The "new" HR shifts its service delivery emphasis from "face-to-face first" to one that uses technology first. How to get an answer is directly reversed from the traditional approach.

DESKTOP

↓

PHONE

↓

PERSON

Desktop—When managers have an HR problem that requires HR assistance, they first use the computer on their desk (or their laptop/PDA) to access the company intranet. The HR intranet will contain both quick answers plus detailed back-up information. The intranet is superior to the "face-to-face" meeting with an HR person because it contains a panoply of answers a manager needs, and it doesn't require any waiting for HR to "get back to you." The intranet is also available during off-hours when generalists are not. It is also accurate; available in multiple languages, and searchable by key words.

Phone—If the manager doesn't have access to a computer or if by chance he or she has a very complicated question that cannot be answered on the intranet, the next step is to use the phone. Phoning for HR help in the new service delivery progression means calling an HR call center. The call center is superior to calling individuals because it's always available during business hours—as opposed to contacting a specific individual who might not be at their desk. Other superior features of the call center include operators trained to find answers more quickly and accurately since they handle such a high volume of similar calls and the supervisor constantly checks the accuracy and the completeness of the responses.

Person—If the manager requires a very sophisticated answer that can be found neither on the intranet nor via the call center, the manager would then contact an HR person for a face-to-face meeting. Managers often prefer this option; however, face-to-face meetings are expensive and often ineffective because the HR representative doesn't always have the answer immediately available. If the question is a really sophisticated one, the manager could contact someone at the HR "centers of excellence." A center of excellence is a specialized internal consulting group that would have the capability of handling the most sophisticated HR problems.

As you can see, the progression for a manager to go through to get an answer is completely reversed in the "new" HR. This new model uses technology both in the call center and the company's intranet. It provides more accurate answers—at any time of the day—and from the HR department's perspective these services are cheaper to provide.

Managers can be very traditional, however, and they may actually prefer to talk face-to-face. In order to encourage or even force managers to get a majority of their answers from the intranet or the call center, a strategic HR department must guarantee that those tools actually provide easy-to-find, accurate, and complete answers. Face-to-face conversations with an HR person then can be reserved for the most sophisticated people-management problems and issues.

BENEFITS OF USING TECHNOLOGY

There are many advantages to utilizing HR technology.
- Improve your managers' decision-making on people issues by providing them with "real-time" data
- Provide information and HR services 24/7
- Aid in standardizing HR processes and procedures throughout the organization

- Improve measurement accuracy
- Improve recordkeeping accuracy
- Allow HR to compare cases, analyze trends, provide alerts and forecast
- Facilitate rapid learning from mistakes with system feedback loops
- Increase HR's ability to manage a global HR function, including providing HR information in multiple languages around the world
- Provide increased security for employee records
- Help HR gather and share information with other company databases
- Provide instant data and access to reports by anyone at a minimal cost for each report
- Increase speed in transaction processes
- Make it easier to gather, analyze and report standard performance metrics
- Provide instant communications through e-mail, the Internet and the Web

STRATEGIC HR SOFTWARE APPLICATIONS

A variety of software applications are available to HR. Some serve primarily a transactional purpose while others are more likely to have a strategic impact. The most strategic ones include:

- **Expert systems**—These are electronic decision trees that walk a manager through a routine problem by a series of questions or "prompts."
- **Analytics**—Software that analyzes trends and helps managers in identifying problems.
- **Heuristics**—A software program that helps identify similar events and patterns, even though the problems are not directly connected.
- **Smoke detectors**—Software programs that identify precursors or leading indicators that can give managers an indication of a festering or upcoming problem.

TECHNOLOGY IS REQUIRED FOR
THE ESSENTIAL ELEMENTS OF STRATEGIC HR

Let there be no mistake about it: Each of the 10 essential elements of a strategic HR function requires the use of technology. Without it, most of these essential elements would not even get underway, much less succeed. What is the impact of technology on the essential elements of strategic HR?

HR increases employee productivity and corporate profits. To dramatically increase employee productivity, you first must be able to measure it. Technology is essential for both measuring productivity and for identifying and solving the problems that cause productivity to decrease. *e*-HR allows both managers and HR professionals to learn rapidly, which is important in continuous improvement and for increasing productivity.

HR uses performance culture tools to improve a firm's performance. A performance culture relies heavily on speed, performance measurement, and rewards to increase performance. Technology enables speed as well as accurate performance measurement.

HR provides a competitive advantage. One of the prime ways that HR can differentiate itself from its competitors' HR functions is by being an early adopter of HR technology. If HR uses technology to increase employee productivity, it can develop or maintain a lead over the competition.

HR makes fact-based decisions using metrics. Obviously the basis for fact-based decisions is the information provided by the HRIS system. Technology allows HR to widely distribute metrics to managers.

HR is proactive and future-focused. Being future-focused requires planning and forecasting. Information technology is an essential element in accurate planning and forecasting.

HR's efforts are coordinated. When diverse HR functions utilize the same technologies, they can more easily communicate and share information. This increased sharing increases intradepartmental coordination and cooperation.

HR has a global approach. Providing diverse business units that are spread around the world with up-to-date HR information can only be accomplished with the extensive use of information technology.

HR builds a brand. The extensive use of technology is by itself a powerful image builder.

THE NEXT STEP IN HR TECHNOLOGY

HR can move a long way towards becoming strategic by using existing technology. New technologies and approaches are just now being developed and implemented, however, that will greatly enhance HR's ability to have a significant business impact. In order to provide insights into the future development of HR technology I've highlighted areas where significant breakthroughs are occurring. In each area, the current practice is compared to the "future" HRIS system.

1. THE TYPE AND AMOUNT OF INFORMATION PROVIDED TO MANAGERS WILL BE "ADJUSTABLE"

Current—Managers have to know what information to ask for and what information is available in the HRIS database before they can determine whether the answers that are needed are available.

Future HRIS—Systems will anticipate managers' information needs based on HRIS's past experience with them. As a manager asks questions, the system will "learn" what type of information that the manager prefers, but more importantly the system will learn what information the manager actually utilizes.

The amount and type of information provided to the individual manager will be "modified" as experience informs it of what information is necessary, what is actually utilized, and what is "information overload" for that manager. Answers will be available in any language, 24 hours a day. Even better, the answers will be adjusted depending on the location, local laws, and the regional culture.

2. INFORMATION WILL BE "PUSHED" TO THE MANAGER "JUST-IN-TIME"

Current—A manager requests information *after* a problem occurs. This delay may cause the problem to worsen.

Future HRIS—Advanced systems will "push" information to managers just before or just as they need it. Most information that HR sends to managers and employees currently goes unused because it arrives when they have no sense of urgency to use it. Using JIT (just-in-time) "push" technology, HR can send out the tools and the appropriate information to the manager just before or just when the "smoke alarm" goes off, rather than *after* the manager's problem is out of control.

Information needs will be forecasted based on the experience that other managers face with similar situations. Analytics and heuristics will search HR and other business databases for precursors or leading indicators that "warn" us of potential problems. These statistical "smoke detectors" will help give managers enough lead time so that they can actually read the materials right before the problem begins to grow.

3. HR AND BUSINESS DATABASES ARE INTER-LINKED

Current—HR currently has a series of isolated functional "silo" databases. Quite often these HR functional databases do not even talk to each other, much less talk to other internal business databases.

Future HRIS—HR databases need to be linked to other HR databases as well as to other internal business databases (productivity, output, sales, PR, marketing, and finance). By providing HR with access to other business databases, HR can become more aware of business problems and changes in business unit performance. Linked databases can provide integrated information that can help "signal" both HR and managers to shift their focus in response to changes in the business.

Providing HR with links to external economic databases (including unemployment, inflation, economic growth, college graduation rates, etc.) informs HR about changes in the industry and the economic environment. Giving HR a heads-up about environmental changes provides HR managers with sufficient lead-time to adjust their approach.

4. HR DATABASES "LEARN" FROM MISTAKES

Current—HR databases are "dumb" in that they only include the data put in them. HR databases do not seek out information about failures and as a result, they don't "learn" from their mistakes. There are no "feedback loops."

Future HRIS—"Smart" databases learn from their experience. As HR systems recommend solutions to managers, data on their successes and failures will to be analyzed by HR analysts. Analysts can then feed their learning back into the database and to the relevant HR process owner. The result of this "analyst-assisted" feedback loop is that HR learns from its mistakes. Consequently, the quality of HR advice improves over time.

Smart databases or analysts may be able to calculate probabilities and risks (based on past experience and statistical trends) and improve the overall quality of the people decisions that both HR and managers make. Systems will include probability advice that actually educates managers about the probability of both problems occurring and of a particular solution working given the past success rate within the company.

5. TECHNOLOGY WILL HELP TO IDENTIFY THE "ROOT CAUSE" OF PROBLEMS

Current—Current HRIS reports list results or symptoms of the problem but make no attempt to report the causes and the whys of the problem.

Future HRIS—Advanced systems will tell not just what happened but why it happened. Using statistical models, HRIS will sift through the symptoms and identify the cause and effect. Managers who know why people programs work (or don't work) can more easily improve those programs' performance.

6. HR ACTUALLY IMPROVES PEOPLE-MANAGEMENT DECISIONS

Current—HRIS is an information provider but it does not assist managers in testing and evaluating their decision options. It also does not give them feedback on the quality of their people-management decisions.

Future HRIS—HR will provide managers with information to assist them in making decisions. However it will also provide managers with feedback on how their decisions turned out. Managers will also be provided with decision tools to allow them to test their decisions in advance. Managers will able to run on-line "what if" and "if-then" scenarios that will help them to see the potential impact of their different decision choices. This will help managers be more prepared for a broad range of future possibilities.

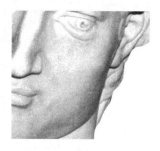

CHAPTER FIFTEEN

HOW CAN YOU TELL IF YOUR HR DEPARTMENT IS STRATEGIC?

OBJECTIVES

Now that each of the ten essential elements of strategic HR has been highlighted, what is next? Once a HR manager understands each of the elements, the question becomes how to assess how strategic the existing HR department is. This chapter will provide a variety of ways to make that assessment.

KEY POINTS

◊ There are a number of different approaches to assessing whether your HR function is strategic or not. This chapter provides numerous yardsticks or measures that allow HR managers to assess how well their department is doing.

◊ Unfortunately, when it comes to the actual practice of strategic HR, there is all too often little hard evidence to prove that most HR departments are strategic. Being strategic is a designation that it is often used without facts to back it up.

◊ Instead of relying on guesswork, it is important for senior HR managers to select a single set of criteria to use consistently when making a factual determination of whether the HR department is having a strategic impact.

THE DIFFERENCE BETWEEN STRATEGIC AND NON-STRATEGIC

The goal of this book is to provide HR leaders with directions and approaches for becoming more strategic. It's important to realize, however, that even strategic people must, on occasion, do tactical or operational things. In fact, in many cases it is a series of tactical actions that eventually builds to a strategic impact. Although it might seem superficially better to do only strategic things, that would be a mistake because the cumulative effect of several tactical actions often leads to a strategic impact.

> *The lesson to be learned here is that both tactical and strategic objectives are important; consequently, it would be a large "strategic" mistake to ignore tactical actions.*

Often tactical objectives get a bad name because they lack the glamour that is attached to strategic goals. And while it's true that not every HR tactical goal will have an obvious connection to business results, it's important that HR leaders continue to try to make that connection. For example, employee retention is a tactical HR goal for most organizations because it does not *directly* impact corporate profit. However, if you can demonstrate that losing key employees directly impacts traditional corporate strategic goals like product time-to-market, market share, and customer satisfaction, then you can prove that reaching a *tactical* HR goal has a *strategic* business impact.

Before you undertake an extensive assessment of whether your HR department is strategic, it might be wise to review some simple examples that highlight the difference between strategic and non-strategic actions. Although it may seem obvious, to some the difference between strategic and non-strategic is hard to discern. Some have difficulty in making the distinction, in part, because few HR employees are given a chance to see or do strategic things early in their careers. However, once HR professionals are confronted with a side-by-side comparison, the difference becomes apparent and they "see the light."

Below are a few examples that illustrate the difference between strategic HR actions and non-strategic ones. Immediately following these first few examples is a more detailed checklist providing even more side-by-side comparisons.

Recruiting

- **A strategic action**—Using metrics (measures) to identify the best sources in order to improve the on-the-job performance of hires.
- **A non-strategic action**—Reducing the cost of hiring by using cheaper but lower quality sources, with the net result being new hires that perform below average on the job.

Interviews

- **A strategic action**—Comparing candidate "scores" or ratings during an interview to their on-the-job performance and retention rate after they are hired. The goal is to see if the interviews predict on-the-job performance and, over time, to improve the performance of new hires.
- **A non-strategic action**—Attending interviews and asking good questions.

Training

- **A strategic action**—Adding new training programs where there is significant measurable difference in on-the-job performance after an employee takes a class.
- **A non-strategic action**—Offering the same training classes each year (regardless of their impact) because they are popular and well attended.

Retention

- **A strategic action**—Warning or alerting managers in advance about who is likely to quit and what tools are most effective in retaining them.
- **A non-strategic action**—Tracking and reporting a manager's turnover rates after the fact.

Compensation

- **A strategic action**—Educating managers and providing them with compensation tools that have a direct impact on employee productivity.
- **A non-strategic action**—Suggesting that a manager give across-the-board raises even though there is no evidence that they impact productivity or retention.

As you can see by these examples, strategic actions share certain common characteristics like using metrics, providing tools that impact employee productivity, and warning managers in advance. Taking this perspective, the contrast between the two actions becomes more obvious and it's easier to see that the strategic ones would provide more impact on productivity, revenue, or other corporate objectives.

ASSESSING WHETHER YOUR HR DEPARTMENT IS STRATEGIC

The way that "average" HR departments approach their role varies significantly from how world-class HR departments within a performance culture operate.

If it is your goal to become strategic or world class in HR, remember that the transition can't occur overnight.

This table provides side-by-side examples on how HR practices differ between traditional HR, strategic HR, and world-class HR. In this chart, a world-class HR department would mirror the practices that would occur in a true performance culture (remember, however, that fewer than one percent of HR departments would qualify as "world-class").

Table 15-A. *Progressing from traditional to strategic to world-class HR*

Traditional HR departments	Strategic HR departments	World-class performance culture
The essential elements of HR		
The HR department meets less than half of the 10 essential elements of strategic HR	The HR department meets all 10 of the essential elements of strategic HR	The HR department exceeds the norm in all 10 of the essential elements of strategic HR
Economic value		
HR adds value by cutting costs	HR increases corporate profit	HR increases stock price and market value
HR is an administrative and overhead function	HR is an employee productivity consulting center	HR is a profit center
HR maintains HR's capability	HR maintains business capability	HR increases the capabilities and the capacity of the business in the marketplace
Defining its customers and responsibilities		
HR's customer is the employee	The customer is senior management	HR's customer is the same as the customer of the business
HR is an employee advocate	HR is a line manager advocate	HR is a senior manager advocate
Employees' concerns drive HR	Managers' concerns drive HR	Business problems drive HR
HR "owns" people-management problems	Managers own people management problems	All employees and managers assume responsibility for people management
Equity is an HR goal; all customers are treated the same	HR prioritizes its customers	HR prioritizes its customers and services to mirror business objectives
HR focuses resources on poor performers	HR focuses on all employees	Focuses resources on top performers and key jobs
Planning and continuous improvement		
HR has only internal HR goals	HR has a written one-year HR plan	HR has a written multiyear plan with forecasts
Goal of HR is to be better than last year	Goal is to the best in the industry	Goal is to be the best HR department in the world
HR is satisfied with the status quo	Everyone in HR has a strong sense of urgency	HR is "paranoid" of top competitors and constantly strives to stay ahead
HR is satisfied with fixing HR problems with programs	Every HR program must continually improve	HR obsoletes most existing HR programs
HR is reactive to problems	HR is proactive in identifying problems	HR anticipates and predicts problems and opportunities
HR reacts to change	HR facilitates change	HR leads change

Table 15-A. Continued

Traditional HR departments	Strategic HR departments	World-class performance culture
HR improves at less than 5% a year	HR mirrors the rate of improvement of the firm	HR exceeds the competitor's rate of improvement
Measurements and metrics		
HR uses cost-based metrics	HR measures its success against workforce productivity metrics	HR measures its success with business impact metrics
HR uses anecdotal evidence to prove manager satisfaction with HR	HR periodically measures manager satisfaction	HR educates managers to expect more from HR prior to measuring satisfaction
HR makes decisions based on feelings and judgment	HR makes decisions based on current data	HR makes decisions based on current and forecasted data
HR benchmarks within U.S.	HR does global benchmarking	HR gathers competitive intelligence and benchmarking across industries
HR services		
HR provides face-to-face answers	HR provides face-to-face and call center answers	Intranet is the primary source of HR answers
Most employees receive 100% base pay	Key jobs have pay at risk	All employees have pay at risk
Other		
HR uses HR terms	HR uses general business terms	HR uses industry and firm specific terminology
No pay for performance within HR	Some HR employees have pay at risk	Every HR employee's pay is tied to HR departmental performance
HR assumes HR is effective	HR finds out which HR programs work and which don't	HR has HR "R&D" team to find out "why" HR programs work

As you can see, there is a noticeable progression from how traditional HR departments act to how world-class HR departments act.

*If what you do isn't mentioned in the annual report then you are **not** producing a strategic impact, because all things strategic are mentioned in the annual report. Complain if you must—but that's just the way it is.*

THE STRATEGIC IMPACT CHAIN

Connecting strategic goals with HR day-to-day actions

All efforts to become strategic must start at the top. Whether you are a manager in an overhead function like HR or in a business unit, you must always look to the top of the organization in order to identify what is strategic. Because senior management sets and communicates the corporation's strategic goals and objectives, senior executives *always* determine what is strategic and what is not. Once these goals and objectives have been set, the drive to impact them by people at all levels of the organization begins.

Lower level managers and workers have the hardest time in determining if the output they produce has a strategic impact. Many hours and numerous meetings in HR and other business units are spent trying to decide which of their outputs are strategic or not strategic. The connection between the output of the lowest department or individual and the strategic goals is known as the "strategic impact chain." The remainder of this section is devoted to demonstrating how individuals can find out if what they do is or is not part of that strategic impact chain.

Individuals who work at the top of organizations have little difficulty determining whether what they do has a strategic impact. Close to the top of an organization in hierarchy there is little ambiguity, as there are fewer levels between what you do and the strategic goals. If you are a janitor at the bottom of the organization and you are trying to make a strategic impact, for example, there might be ten levels of organizational structure between your job and the CEO.

EIGHT TESTS OF STRATEGIC IMPACT

There are eight tests that determine whether "what you do" is part of the strategic impact chain that links individual or departmental outputs with corporate goals and objectives. In summary, they are:

- There is word alignment or consistency between the output of your job and the corporate goal.
- Senior managers tell you that the output of your job directly impacts strategic costs.
- Senior managers are measured or rewarded for the same activities or outputs that your department or job produces.

- There is data to demonstrate a correlation between your work and a strategic impact.
- Your responsibilities naturally fit within high probability strategic areas.
- Your job has a high potential dollar impact.
- Your job includes strategic responsibilities or high impact duties.
- Your job is traditionally not classified as administrative or low impact.

Strategic impact link #1—"Word alignment"

As a result of the multiple levels between the top and bottom of an organization, it's hard to tell if what you do has a strategic impact when your day-to-day activities invariably use different "words" than the actual strategic goal. For example, if "cleaning the floors" is your job it's hard to see any obvious strategic impact on the goal other than the business goal of "increasing customer safety." Now if the strategic goal were "clean floors" there would be no ambiguity. But because of the many levels between a janitor and the CEO, it is very likely that the "words" that define a janitor's output will not be exactly the same or even closely related to the words in a strategic goal.

If the word usage is the same from the top to bottom (as it is in the area of sales), determining where you fit in the strategic impact link is relatively easy. If the word alignment is not clear, then you must use a different test to determine if you are part of the strategic impact chain.

Strategic test #1—Is there word alignment or consistency between the output of your job and the corporate goal?

Strategic impact link #2—Senior executives make the connection for you

Individuals in the lower levels of organizations often struggle to determine if their work is part of the strategic impact chain. But occasionally they get lucky because senior executives either deliberately (or accidentally) provide information that tells you that what you are doing is strategic. Take, for example, a CEO's speech, annual report or annual business plan that mentions the strategic goal of improved customer safety. Immediately following that reference the critical success factors (or strategic sub-elements) for attaining that goal are cited. In that case, anyone in the organization can assume correctly that those sub-elements are also strategic targets.

For example, if the CEO of a grocery store chain says that customer safety was important and then, in addition, he or she states that everyone must reduce customer slips and falls, reduce the number of falling objects, and increase security from crime, the janitor, as well as his or her manager, will know that what they do is part of the strategic impact chain.

> *Strategic test #2—Senior managers tell you directly that the output of your job directly impacts either the strategic goal, or one of the sub-elements of it.*

Strategic impact link #3—Senior executives' metrics and rewards tell you what to impact

Unfortunately, organizations seldom send a clear message about what is strategic. But one of the clearest messages they do send is to place significant metric systems and rewards on the performance area. It is a safe assumption that whatever senior managers are directly measured and rewarded for is an essential part of the strategic impact chain. Senior manager metrics and rewards have an added advantage in that, since they are designed for measurement, they are relatively clear and easy to understand.

When you use senior management measures and rewards to determine what is important, you generally get fairly specific and well-defined performance outputs that make the connection between your performance outputs and theirs much easier. Again, using the janitor example, if corporate senior managers have a monthly metric for " store cleanliness," you can be sure that the janitor's work has a strategic impact.

> *Strategic test #3—Senior managers are measured or rewarded for the same activities or outputs that your department or job produces.*

Strategic impact link #4—Research proves the connection

Occasionally, people with jobs at the bottom of the strategic impact chain are fortunate in that someone already has made the direct connection between their work output and the strategic goal. This would be true, for example, if the organization had collected and analyzed some data that showed a direct correlation between the corporate goal of "customer safety" and the output goal of the janitor's job goal of "clean floors." This connection or correlation could be demonstrated in a couple of ways:

Company data—The first level of proof would be a correlation, e.g., you can demonstrate (using a scale of cleanliness) that as the cleanliness of the floors increases, the number of customer accidents decreases, and vice versa. In this case, even though accidents resulting from dirty floors is only one element of customer safety (in addition to security from crime, falling objects, and fire danger), it is clear that there is a direct connection between clean floors and customer slip and fall accidents. Again, using this example, if existing company data demonstrates that customer safety/falling accidents increase as floors get dirty, you could say that there is a strategic link between the output of the janitor's job and strategic goals and objectives.

There are always some caveats to consider, however. If, for example the store dramatically changes the flooring so that slips as a result of uncleanliness are almost impossible, the strategic link would be broken. Incidentally, if the janitor also cleans floors that are not utilized by customers, then that work would have no strategic link.

As a result, if you are the manager, you would focus your time and resources on janitors who clean areas where customers have access. You would purposely put fewer resources into janitors or areas where customers had no chance of slipping. As cold as it may sound, you would also be less concerned about employees or vendors slipping because the corporation has already designated them to be of less strategic value than customers.

If existing information about the link between dirty floors and customers slipping cannot be found, the organization could generate new data to make the connection. Either a split sample or a pilot test could be used to prove the correlation. For example, a company could take half of its retail stores and improve their cleanliness dramatically while doing nothing to the other half of their stores. If accident rates for customers decreased proportionately, the strategic link would be clearly established. To be doubly sure, you could purposely reduce some of the cleaning levels at the successful stores just to see if the accident rate would go back up. You would also monitor the correlation over time to ensure that the connection remains strong.

Sometimes you can get naturally occurring samples within the corporation so that a pilot or split sample is not necessary. If for some reason several managers on their own deliberately had taken action to increase or decrease floor cleanliness, you could first track the numbers to see if any changes in accident rates occurred and second, to see if those store accident rates remained significantly lower than the other stores that chose to do nothing about floor cleanliness.

External data—A second level of proof also would be a correlation, but the data would come from external sources. Given the same situation, if external consultants, vendors or government organizations had already conducted research (in similar settings) that demonstrated the correlation, you could substitute their data. Obviously, internal data is superior because you have no way of knowing if the external situation was exactly the same as the one that your corporation is facing. External pre-existing data may be cheaper, however, so there is often a trade-off.

Strategic test #4—There is data to demonstrate a correlation between your work and a strategic impact.

Strategic impact link #5—Functional areas that are almost always strategic

Although every organization is different, there are some functions that are almost automatically classified as being part of the strategic impact chain. For example, most of what the CEO and the CFO do is assumed to be strategic. The same can often be said for entire job families, including those that demonstrate a high impact on:

- Product development;
- Direct sales;
- General managers of the business units;
- Mergers and acquisitions;
- R&D;
- Any job or function that impacts margins, market share, customer satisfaction and quality;
- Any function that must compete for its survival in a competitive marketplace;
- Any function where over 25 percent of the total corporate budget is spent;
- Internal functional units from which the current and the previous CEO came (individuals from non-strategic functions seldom become CEOs);

- Key jobs in any business unit that generate more than 10 percent of total corporate profits;
- Any function or job where adding headcount and overtime are frequently approved; and
- Anyone or anything that has an impact on more than one percent of company revenue.

If you look at 100 companies, in 95 percent of them each of the functions listed above would be an integral link in the strategic impact chain. Other functions to be included depend on the industry. For example, "IT" would automatically be a strategic function in any technology firm, while government relations would be an essential function in a drug research firm. For an industrial firm with a small number of large customers, customer service would almost always be part of the strategic impact chain. A firm that sells low-priced items to retail customers could not assure that customer service always would be considered strategic.

Strategic test #5—Your responsibilities naturally fit within "high probability" strategic areas.

Strategic impact link #6—High dollar impact

A high dollar loss potential is a good indication of something that's in the strategic impact chain. High loss avoidance areas are areas where the cost of a single mistake or error to the corporation is extremely high. Common high loss areas generally include death, a major lawsuit, or the threat of major governmental action. Jobs whose primary responsibility is to avoid or minimize those errors are high strategic impact jobs. For example, lifeguards at a pool, pilots for an airline, patent lawyers for high-tech firms, and government relations officers for drug or pharmaceutical firms are almost considered to be strategic. If an error does occur, the calculated costs are likely to be so high that they are guaranteed to have a strategic impact on the business.

Now let us return to the janitor's example and see how the high cost of error makes the janitor's job more strategic. If a customer slipped and fell on the dirty floor and the cost was $100,000 per error, the organization could justifiably classify avoiding slips from dirty floors as a strategic impact area.

This high-cost relationship works for almost any area of the business. You can assume that you are part of the strategic value chain:

- If you are paid a great deal of money (strategic individuals are heavily rewarded because they have a high impact);
- There is a great deal of insurance related to disasters or errors in your area;
- If you have the potential of generating a large amount of income for the firm;
- If you have a high replacement cost; and
- If the firm invests a great deal of money in your training.

Strategic test #6—Your job has a high potential dollar impact.

Strategic impact link #7—Some jobs are strategic because of the jobs they impact

Be careful never to assume that strategic jobs cannot occur in functions that generally are not themselves considered to be strategic. An example would be a janitor in a nuclear plant. While most janitors would be considered to have a low strategic impact, in the case of nuclear power plants, individuals responsible for cleaning up around the reactor could be classified as strategic individuals in a non-strategic department. These jobs are considered to have a strategic impact primarily because of the high dollar consequences that result if they make an error.

HR jobs. In the area of HR, the retention of an average employee is a low strategic value area because most individuals are easily replaced and, thus, there is little impact on productivity. Because of that low dollar impact, most retention jobs are not considered to be directly strategic. In sharp contrast, however, are certain retention jobs: if the head of R&D engineering went to a competitor, there would be an extremely high dollar cost of losing that particular employee. And as a result, the retention specialist in charge of retaining the R&D level jobs would be considered to be a strategic individual.

If you look at individuals who are included in the company's succession plan, it is probably safe to assume that those individuals are considered strategic. Consequently, the HR jobs that focus on retaining or recruiting these "succession-plan-level jobs" are also considered to be strategic. These retention examples illustrate an important point: two jobs in the same department may have a very different strategic impact, even though they carry the same title. The lesson to be learned is that it is the potential dollar impact that differentiates the high- from the low- impact retention jobs.

Recruiting is similar to retention in that most recruiting jobs are not automatically considered strategic. However, if the CEO orders an executive search firm to recruit for a key position, the CEO would be sending a clear message that he or she does consider the internal recruiters to be in strategic jobs. Similarly, if the HR department has an internal executive search function that is automatically assigned all executive searches, then those recruiters are considered part of the strategic impact chain.

Strategic test #7—Your job includes strategic responsibilities or high impact duties.

Strategic impact link #8—Things that generally are not strategic

Of course every organization is unique, but there are certain functions or job families that, in the absence of hard evidence, should not be assumed to be part of the strategic impact chain. Some of those "typically" non-strategic areas include:

- All administrative and overhead jobs and functions (including travel, purchasing, mailing, accounting, HR and maintenance). It is critical that you do not assume that the departmental goals of any overhead or administrative function are automatically strategic. This is because of the weak track record that most overhead functions have in directing resources towards programs that have a "real" strategic business impact.
- Jobs or functions that are frequently outsourced or considered for outsourcing.
- Any job or function where hiring and budgets are frequently frozen.

Strategic test #8—Your job is traditionally not classified as administrative or low impact.

Table 15-B. *Example of a strategic impact chain*
(For a retail corporation)

Example 1: Janitor	
Strategic goal	Customer safety (costs below $1 million)
Link #1	CEO said customer safety includes reducing customer accidents
Link #2	VP of administration is measured and rewarded on the dollar cost of customer safety events
Link #3	Data shows a correlation between floor cleanliness and customer accidents
Link #4	Cost per customer "slip" accident is $100,000
Operational action/ employee output	Clean floors

The four links clearly establish the connection or link between the janitor's "outputs" and the corporate strategic goal of customer safety.

Example 2: HR retention program manager	
Strategic goal	Customer satisfaction rate of 95 percent
Link #1	CFO said for every increased percentage point of customer satisfaction, revenues go up by $1 million
Link #2	CEO's bonus is based on customer satisfaction
Link #3	Data shows a .92 correlation between customer service rep tenure in the job and increased customer satisfaction
Link #4	For every 5 percent reduction in long term rep turnover, customer satisfaction increases by 1 percent
Link #5	Cost per long term customer rep termination and replacement is $40,000
Link #6	Retention program for long term reps reduces turnover by 50 percent
Operational action/ employee output	Operate customer rep retention program

The six links clearly establish the connection or link between the HR person's "outputs" and the corporate strategic goal of customer satisfaction.

A "SNAPSHOT" ASSESSMENT OF HR PERFORMANCE

Thinking strategically and measurement go hand in hand. It's not enough to say (or to think) that your HR department is producing the desired results; you need to actually measure them. The best way to measure the results of an HR department is with an HR index or with a "dashboard." However, both of those options require existing systems of metrics.

Another option is to get a quick "snapshot" assessment of the results you're producing. It's not as effective as a detailed HR audit (which is a worthwhile next step), but this snapshot assessment can add significant value even though it can be completed in a few days.

CRITERIA FOR SELECTING "SNAPSHOT" HR PERFORMANCE MEASURES

DEFINITION

A snapshot measure is a "quick and dirty" relative assessment of where you are today versus last year—and sometimes versus other firms.

In order to be quick but still accurate, the measures you select should meet most of the following criteria:

- They use existing numbers or easily obtained information;
- The measures are simple to understand;
- The measures are believable both within HR and within the CFO's office (run them by the CFO for validation);
- Information compilation and reporting is simple and cheap; and
- The most important measures are weighted according to their relevance.

FACTORS TO INCLUDE IN YOUR SNAPSHOT ASSESSMENT

There is no magic in selecting which factors to use in a "snapshot" audit. It is important to use a variety of them from different HR areas in order to get a broad assessment. It is of course acceptable to modify the ones provided in this book to fit your particular situation. Start with a small number and later add or subtract metrics in order to make the process easier or more accurate.

Financial performance measures

- **Revenue per employee**—This simple measure will give you a relatively easy assessment of your employee efficiency. By simply dividing the number of employees into the company's total revenue

  (company revenue/number of employees)

  you can get a general idea of your employee's productivity. The ratio should be continually improving (a poor rating would be lower than the industry average and also lower than your direct competitor).

- **Revenue per dollar of employee costs**—This more complex but more accurate measure will give you another measure of your employee efficiency. By simply dividing the dollars spent on your employees (include all salaries and benefits) into the company's total revenue

  (company revenue/employee cost)

  you can get a direct measure of your employee's productivity. Employee productivity is improving when you get more output for every dollar you spend all employees. This measure is superior to the revenue per employee measure because not all employees cost the same. The ratio should be continually improving (a poor rating would be an increasing number or one that was lower than the industry average and also lower than your direct competitor). Incidentally, another worthwhile measure is "people profit" (profit /employee cost), but because gathering the data can be a little complicated, it is often omitted as a quick measure.

- **HR cost per employee**—This simple measure will give you a relatively easy assessment of how expensive your HR department is. By simply dividing the number of employees into your total HR budget,

(total HR budget/number of employees)

you can get a general idea of whether your HR costs are increasing. The ratio should be continually improving (a poor rating would be lower than the industry average and also lower than your direct competitor). An amount above $1000 is generally high, but some have been as high as $3400 per employee. Remember the cost of HR is only relevant if it is compared to the quality and the volume of the services provided (for example, Tiffany's cost of selling an item is 5 times that of a discount store— but the value added is obvious). If you are high cost but can't prove you are high quality, then you are in trouble.

Retention and performance management measures

- **Turnover rate of top performers**—Does the company retain the top 10 percent of its workforce? Measure the turnover rate among those receiving the highest performance (appraisal) ratings. If performance ratings are not available, then use any ranking, recognition, reward or rating that the firm has used to identify "key employees." (A poor rating would be above 5 percent or higher than last year.)
- **Turnover rate of bottom performers**—Does the company actively move out the bottom 5 or 10 percent of its workforce? Measure the turnover rate among those receiving the lowest performance (appraisal) ratings. Again, if performance ratings are not available then use any ranking, recognition, reward or rating that the firm has used to identify "needs improvement" employees. (A poor rating would be below 2 percent or lower than last year.)
- **Turnover rate of poor performing managers**—Does the company actively remove its poor managers? Although it is possible to measure the performance of individual managers in a snapshot, it's generally not necessary. Instead just look at the percentage of managers that are removed for cause. (A poor rating would be less than 2 percent of your managers were selected and removed "for cause" during the last year.)

Compensation measures

- **Percentage of employees with pay at risk**—Does the compensation department succeed in ensuring that employees have their pay tied directly to performance? Identify what percentage of all employees have any portion of their salary or wages increased based on individual performance. Some organizations include employees who are eligible to participate in profit sharing and stock option plans, while others exclude them and look only at salary at risk. (A poor rating would include less than 5 percent of non-management employees with any of their pay at risk or a percentage that is not continually increasing.)
- **Managers' pay is based on excellent people management**—Because great people management has to be delivered by your managers, it is important that managers be measured directly and rewarded for great recruiting, retention and increasing productivity. (A poor rating would be 5 percent or less of your managers having some part of their pay based on successful people management practices.)

Recruiting measures

- **Executive search capability**—Is your HR function directly responsible for filling executive positions? Outsourcing a major part of this activity is an indication of a weak recruiting function. (A poor rating would mean that more than 75 percent of executive positions are filled by an external search firm.)
- **Percent of diverse employees**—What percentage of your exempt workforce is diverse? Although HR does not control hiring and retention, it should be able to influence it to the point where the firm attracts and retains a high percentage of diverse employees. (A poor rating would have a decreasing percentage over the last two years.)
- **Percentage of hires from referrals**—What percentage of all hires comes from employee referrals? Referrals are important because they indicate both employee satisfaction and willingness to recommend your company to others. Traditionally a high referral rate is a direct indication of great people management. (A poor rating would be less than 20 percent of the firm's positions are filled by referral.)

Training measures

- **Responsibility for sales and executive training**—Is the HR training department responsible for directly training the sales force and the executives? (A poor rating would be that the sales department is responsible for some training, and executive training is outsourced or is handled outside the training department.)

External recognition measures (employment "brand")

- **External recognition or awards**—Has the HR department received some external recognition, award or ranking? Is the firm listed on the *Fortune* 100 great places to work or has it received an Optima award or an industry or regional award? The key indicator is that there is some external recognition of the firm's "brand" as a great place to work as a result of a strong HR program. (A poor rating would be no external recognition during the last two years.)
- **Recognition of senior HR management**—Has the VP of HR (or other senior HR managers) either written articles or been mentioned specifically in articles published in your industry or HR journals?

Internal status and position indicators

These are some "soft" measures that the HR department can utilize to determine its internal status:

- **Mentioned in the annual report**—How many lines of text does the HR department receive in the firm's annual report? Compare this year to last, as well as to how many lines of print comparable overhead departments received. (A poor rating would include no specific mention of any individual HR program.)
- **Reporting relationship**—Does the VP of HR report directly to the CEO? (A poor rating would include reporting directly to the CFO.)
- **A member of the executive committee**—Does the senior VP of HR serve on the executive committee of the firm? (A poor rating means no representation.)
- **A scheduled meeting with the CEO**—Does the senior VP of HR have an automatic one-on-one meeting scheduled with the CEO? (A poor rating means no regularly scheduled meeting.)

OTHER THINGS GREAT HR DEPARTMENTS DO

The following is a list of actions and programs that are generally undertaken only by strategic HR departments. Although doing these things doesn't guarantee that your department is strategic, failing to do them almost always assures that you have a less-than-strategic HR department.

- **Distributed metrics**—Distributing to all managers a monthly scorecard ranking of all managers on their pay for performance.
- **Prioritizing customers**—Let's face it, with increasingly limited budgets HR can't do it all. As a result it is important for HR to prioritize its customers and its products while simultaneously dropping or spending fewer resources on those customers and services that have been determined to have a low impact.
- **Forecasting and "smoke detectors"**—HR has a bad habit of dwelling on the past. What managers want is an alert or heads-up about what will happen in the future. Great HR departments provide managers with forecasts and alerts about potential up-coming problems.
- **Utilization of technology**—In a global world, it is essential that managers have access to HR programs and answers 24/7. Great HR departments continually increase the percentage of answers their managers can get over company's intranet.
- **Rewards for cooperation**—Most HR departments contain functional silos that limit cooperation between HR units. Great HR departments have shared metrics and rewards that cross HR unit boundaries. As a result, individual units cannot receive their full bonus unless overall HR goals are met.

In a fast changing world, it is important to continually assess where you are going and how you are doing. I am a firm believer in sophisticated HR metrics and analytics but I also understand the need for quick assessments. The above assessment is a relatively simple measure of the "health" of your HR function. Because a limited number of measures are utilized, the results are relatively easy to track on a single page. If you want to go further, the next step is generally developing an HR "dashboard."

Once you develop your initial list of factors, run them by someone in the CFO's office. Their advice and counsel on how and what should be measured is priceless.

SURVEY MANAGERS TO ASSESS HR'S CONTRIBUTION TO BUSINESS UNIT PRODUCTIVITY

The most effective way of assessing HR's impact on business results is to measure it directly. However, in those cases where that is not possible, or when you need "a second opinion," another inexpensive option is to survey managers. Even though most surveys are subjective, when HR is trying to identify its relative impact on business unit productivity there is no one more likely to be aware of that impact than line managers.

One way to assess their view on HR's contribution to their success is an annual year-end "contribution-to-results" survey of all key managers. That survey asks them one simple question, "which administrative or overhead function contributed the most to your department's productivity and goal attainment?" All individual overhead functions and problems are included in the survey. The manager is given an opportunity to allocate 100 points among the different overhead programs. The scores of individual managers can be weighted based on the strategic priority (or the size) of the department the manager represents.

This survey is superior to most because it does not ask if the manager is "satisfied." Satisfaction tends to indicate whether you "like" the people providing the service. Instead, what you are trying to measure is the impact that these functions had on the department's accomplishments. These ratings then should be factored in when overhead department budgets are allocated to ensure that overhead function budgets are in line with business unit impact.

ASSESSING WHETHER GOALS ARE IN STRATEGIC ALIGNMENT

Alignment is a common buzzword, both in business and HR. It is used in connection with goal or objective setting. Alignment is important because it's highly desirable for the goals and objectives of the different business units and functions to be "aligned" with the overall corporate objectives. In this case "alignment" means similar to, parallel with, connected to, or consistent with. In any case, the key is that they are directly "in line" with the corporate goals and objectives.

The two sets of goals (corporate and HR goals) cannot be exactly the same because HR is a sub-function of the entire corporation and as a result, HR goals and objectives use "different words" than the corporate objectives. Because the "words" are not exactly the same, it takes some effort to ensure that the goals of HR are connected to and build directly to the corporate goals. In practice, the sum of every business unit's functional department goals and objectives should be *exactly the same* as the corporate goals and objectives.

For example, a corporate goal might be to increase customer satisfaction while the corresponding HR goal might be to increase employee retention. The two goals obviously use completely different words, but the test of alignment is not the words but whether the HR goal directly contributes to the corporate goal of increasing customer satisfaction.

Proof of the connection can be made, for example, because HR has conducted research and found that as employees gain experience on the job, their customer service ratings improve. So in this case extending the tenure of customer service reps by improving their retention rates will obviously increase the percentage of the workforce that has extended experience. And because HR already has demonstrated that more experience leads to higher customer satisfaction, it is accurate to say that extending employee tenure or increasing retention rates of customer service reps is "aligned" with the corporate goal of improving customer satisfaction.

WHEN HR ACTIONS DIFFER FROM GOALS

One not to be ignored caveat is that even if your *goals* are directly aligned, this does not in any way guarantee that your actual *actions* will support the words in your goals. It's possible to have all the lofty goals in the world and then essentially to ignore them and spend most of your time and resources on other things. This is often caused by the fact that HR has two separate committees or teams compiling the goals and the budget.

As a result of this not uncommon practice, it is essential to recognize that you still must measure whether your HR goals actually were executed, even though initially your actual goals were directly in alignment. That means that first, when the initial budget is drawn up, make certain that the budget allocations directly mesh with the departmental objectives. Second, once the budget year begins, track the actual amount of HR staff time and budget that you spend in each of the HR goal areas.

If you are not spending the same proportion of HR time and budget as the weight or importance of each objective then, first, you are misleading management and, second, you are diminishing your opportunity to have a major strategic impact.

It is important to make a note of this: A majority of corporations make no formal effort to connect the "actual" resource allocation with the goals and objectives set by and for HR.

ASSIGN WEIGHTS TO THE GOALS

All corporate goals and objectives are not the same. Some receive a higher priority or weight, and the same must be true of HR goals and objectives. Use the numerical weights or percentages, rather than just ordinal priorities, because the numerical weight has the added advantage of telling you what percentage of time and budget to spend on each of them.

For example, if you assigned "improving HR customer satisfaction" a weight of 50 percent and "reducing error rates" was weighted only five percent, it would be clear to all that they should spend 50 percent of their time on activities related to improving satisfaction, and only five percent of the budget and time fixing errors. It should go without saying that you need to ensure that the way that you assign HR goals and objectives is aligned with the weights for the importance of the corporate objectives that they impact.

ASSESSING ALIGNMENT

There are several ways that HR can assure that its goals are in alignment with the corporation's goals and objectives. Some of the indicators that HR goals are in alignment with corporate goals include:

- **They include the same words**—In the few cases where HR goals are the same as corporate goals, you are likely to be in alignment if you use the same words to ensure consistency.
- **Program-by-program assessment**—When HR research has demonstrated that there is a direct connection between the output of an individual HR program and a specific corporate objective.

- **A second outside opinion**—Having a company officer or an outside expert assess the goal alignment can be an indirect measure.
- **Outside funding**—When a senior manager directly funds an HR program, you can assume that it is aligned with corporate goals.
- **HR budget expenditures**—When the percentage of money spent in the different areas of HR is spent in the same proportion to the "weights" assigned to the HR goals.
- **HR time allocations**—When the percentage of time spent by HR staff members is in proportion to the "weights" assigned to the HR goals.
- **What you measure**—When the HR program measures the same or similar things as corporate or the next level up in the organization.
- **A survey of managers**—If a survey of senior managers ranks HR in the top 25 percent of all overhead functions for contribution to corporate goals.
- **What you reward**—If HR specifically rewards the same activities that occur under each corporate goal and objective.
- **Annual report**—In most organizations the annual report is prepared to coincide with the announcement of corporate objectives. As a result, if HR accomplishments are listed in annual report you can assume that you are aligned with corporate goals and objectives.

BEST PRACTICE

What are the most strategic HR departments?

I have been fortunate in my career to visit hundreds of companies and to talk to literally thousands of HR professionals. During that time I have constantly sought out a definition for what is "world class" in HR and then attempted to identify the firms that fit that definition.

During that search I have found that "world class" is in fact quite scarce in HR. I have also found that there are numerous world-class companies that are great for a variety reasons—almost in spite of what HR does. In other cases, the company performance is clearly driven in large part by a great HR department.

As a result of this contradiction, my list of "world-class HR departments" excludes many "great" companies. Using the 10 essential elements of a strategic HR department, below is my list of the most strategic HR departments. (Please note I have purposely excluded some likely great HR departments of which I do not have first-hand knowledge.)

- Intel

- Cisco

- Microsoft

- GE

- HP

The next chapter will highlight several approaches that an individual HR professional can utilize to determine if he or she is taking strategic actions.

CHAPTER SIXTEEN

HOW TO TELL IF YOU ARE A STRATEGIC INDIVIDUAL

OBJECTIVES

The last chapter highlighted how to assess whether an HR department was strategic. This chapter will take a similar approach but will focus in on the different ways that *individuals* can assess their strategic level. Any individual starting a quest to become strategic must realize that strategic individuals are not born, they are made. You become strategic over time by *practicing*.

KEY POINTS

◊ This chapter will provide tools for individual HR professionals to assess whether their own actions can be characterized as strategic. Individuals should periodically assess their own actions, even if they are currently in lower-level HR jobs.

◊ Becoming strategic is a long-term evolutionary process. By periodically sitting down and assessing the strategic impact of your own actions, you get in the habit of using metrics and making fact-based decisions.

◊ If you utilize the information from the self-assessment to develop a continuous learning and improvement program, then you are well on your way toward becoming strategic.

Few individuals are strategic early in their careers. This is true simply because most of our early working lives are spent doing operational things. It's rare for someone early in their career, whether in school or in a job, to even get the opportunity to act strategically.

Of course the argument can be made that individuals quite often *think* strategically even if they do not get a chance to *act* that way, but thinking is hard to measure. The best way to assess a strategic individual is the way he or she acts in—and beyond—the job.

Unfortunately, it is possible for individuals within HR department to act strategically without producing any strategic results. This is because it's difficult, at best, for any one individual to overcome the tactical focus of an entire HR department.

ASSESSING WHETHER YOU ARE A "STRATEGIC INDIVIDUAL"

This checklist is designed to help individuals in HR assess whether they are acting strategically. It can be used by individuals for self-assessment or by HR senior managers to help assess their staff. The checklist is divided into the 10 essential element categories in order to facilitate comparison between individual strategic actions and departmental actions.

If you are going to be a strategic contributor in HR, these are some of the things you need to do. Although no one individual has all of these characteristics, generally truly strategic individuals meet more than half of them.

1. INCREASE EMPLOYEE PRODUCTIVITY AND CORPORATE PROFIT

- **Goals**—As individuals, they set strategic goals for both themselves and any program they manage.
- **Formula**—They know the formula and how to calculate employee productivity.
- **Measurement**—They measure their own productivity at least once a month. They also measure the productivity of any program they manage.

- **Tools**—They know the tools that work within their organization to increase employee productivity. In addition, they also know "why" each works and why it fails.

2. PROVIDE SOLUTIONS WITH EXTERNAL FOCUS ON IMPACTING THE BUSINESS

- **Business objectives**—They keep a written list of the corporate goals and objectives and for each goal they identify the various ways they potentially can impact it.
- **Calculate impact**—At least twice a year they attempt to estimate the dollar amount of their business impact.
- **Critical success factors**—They know the company's core competencies and the critical success factors of their industry.
- **Business environment**—They identify and track economic and business factors that may impact their own as well as the company's success. They track the company's margins, profits, market share, and stock price on a regular basis.
- **Rotation**—They make an effort to work outside of HR in "line" businesses through rotations, transfers or cross-functional teams.
- **Plan**—Even if they are individual contributors, they have a business plan for their job responsibilities. If they run a program, every major element of their plan must directly connect to the firm's overall business plan.

3. USE PERFORMANCE CULTURE TOOLS TO IMPROVE PERFORMANCE

- **Mindset**—They believe in the effectiveness of the primary tools for a performance culture: competition, a sense of urgency, measurement, and rewards. They believe that competitive market forces and pay for performance drive excellence.
- **Prioritize**—They prioritize their customers and services to maximize their impact on employee productivity. They consciously spend most of their time and resources on top performers.
- **Risk taking**—In a performance culture, risk-taking is the norm and failure is part of the improvement and learning process. A strategic HR person calculates each risk and learns quickly from each failure.

- **Sense of urgency**—They have a high sense of urgency and energy level. They are constantly concerned about competitors catching up, and they spread that paranoia and sense of urgency to their coworkers. They volunteer for strategic projects related to improving performance.
- **Drop programs**—They consciously identify and drop programs and program elements that are ineffective. They continually drop low-performing activities and reinvest the resources in areas of higher return.
- **No excuses**—When they are given an assignment, if they encounter difficulties they always find a way to accomplish the task. They are constantly overcoming and finding new ways to do the impossible.
- **Speed**—Because best practices are quickly copied in today's world, strategic individuals streamline processes, decrease response times, and, in general, make speed their competitive advantage.
- **Pay for service**—Strategic individuals produce work of high-enough quality that managers would be willing to pay for it on a fee for service basis. Strategic HR people get managers to directly fund some of their work.
- **Identify patterns**—They use data to identify patterns to predict similar events. They identify tools that allow them to look around "corners."

4. PROVIDE A COMPETITIVE ADVANTAGE

- **Benchmark**—They actively benchmark results and best practices both within and outside the industry. They can name the best people-management practices within the firm and at the top firms in the industry and the world.
- **Competitive analysis**—They complete a competitive analysis of their own area of the HR function. They complete side-by-side comparisons of program results and direct competitors. They identify areas where improvement is needed.
- **Competitive intelligence**—They proactively get information about what the competitor is doing and planning, so that they can block competitive efforts and aim ahead of where competitors will be heading.
- **Continuous improvement**—In a fast-changing world, standing still isn't sufficient (because the competition isn't), so they build

continuous improvement elements in every program in an effort to maintain their lead.

5. MAKE FACT-BASED DECISIONS USING METRICS

- **Mindset**—They believe in the importance of making fact-based decisions. They seek out data and information prior to making a major decision.
- **Prioritize efforts**—They do periodic critical assessments of their programs based on ROI and business impact. They continually relocate resources to areas of higher return.
- **User satisfaction**—They periodically measure user and manager satisfaction with their work or their programs.
- **Information source**—They are driven to have answers to every manager's question. They are passionate learners and, as a result, they are a data and information "warehouse" because they stay on the "bleeding edge" of business and HR knowledge.

6. PROACTIVE AND FUTURE-FOCUSED

- **Forecast**—They forecast the company's and industry's emerging trends and use them as part of their program-planning efforts. In addition, they identify potential problems and opportunities within their own job's sphere.
- **Competencies**—They develop a list of the future competencies that the firm (and this individual) will need in the next few years. They then develop a plan to acquire the relevant ones.
- **Alerts**—They proactively identify potential problems and opportunities, and, when appropriate, they alert or warn the appropriate managers as well as offer solutions.
- **Continuous improvement**—They recommend to their boss possible ways to improve other HR processes.
- **Learning plan**—They have a written, individual learning and development plan that identifies future knowledge and skill areas that must be developed. They have a step-by-step plan for developing those skills.
- **HR problems**—Even when it is not their responsibility, they proactively identify and forecast the upcoming problems and opportunities that the HR department will face.
- **A range of options**—Rather than being directive, they act as an "advisor," much like a financial advisor does. As a result, they

provide a variety of options to managers including the risks, the probabilities, and the upside potential of each.

7. THEIR EFFORTS ARE COORDINATED

- **Coordination**—If they run a program, they closely integrate it with other related programs. If they are an individual contributor, they identify and then still seek out related individuals to make an attempt to learn from each other.
- **Connect the dots**—They have a written flowchart or process map that identifies programs or processes that are interdependent with their own. They look both for "friction points" and new areas of potential cooperation.
- **Sharing**—They proactively share learning and "what works" with colleagues, both within and outside the department.
- **Consult with management**—Strategic HR professionals view themselves as consultants and advisors to management. Instead of using the "HR cop" routine to threaten (*i.e.*, "you'll get sued"), they stop saying no and become more of an advisor. They give advice and add to it probable consequences, probabilities and liabilities. They also have formal mechanisms for continually seeking out their managers' opinions. They educate managers to expect much more from HR, and they change their agenda and resource allocations based on the problems that management identifies.

8. A GLOBAL APPROACH

- **Global knowledge**—They are aware of the best practices in their HR functions around the world. They regularly read about global business and HR on the Web.
- **24/7**—If they work for a global company or one that has offices in multiple locations, they understand the needs of people in different time zones. As a result, they find ways to offer basic services and information even when "they" are out of the office.

9. BUILDING A BRAND

- **Exposure**—They proactively seek out opportunities to get their programs publicized. They periodically speak at regional and national professional meetings where they highlight their firm's best practices.

- **Internal image**—They develop a plan to ensure that they are visible within the organization. When they design programs, they ensure that they include features that are likely to be exciting enough to be talked about.
- **A business case**—They develop business arguments to support what they do currently. They seek out financial professionals to validate their business case. They also help train others in making successful business arguments.
- **Expertise**—Strategic HR professionals pick one specific HR area in which to be a recognized expert. They use their position as the best in the company or industry as a PR tool to build their credibility and exposure. Being a recognized expert improves their ability to influence managers and other HR professionals.

10. TECHNOLOGY PERMEATES EVERYTHING

- **Knowledge**—They read about new technological innovations in their field and view installations at area firms.
- **Integration**—They integrate technology into every new program and initiative. They ensure that any technology solution that they utilize is compatible with existing HR and business systems. In addition, they ensure that HR databases are linked to other business databases.

OTHER TRAITS OF STRATEGIC INDIVIDUALS

- They know the definition of strategic.
- They routinely read leading business publications like *Business Week*, *The Economist* and *Fortune*, as well as leading industry publications and at least two publications or online services within HR.
- They have read the annual report and the 10k of both their company and its chief competitors.
- They seek out and accept leadership roles in teams in order to build their leadership and strategic capabilities.
- They are known for rapid learning.
- They have a (non-HR) line manager as a mentor to broaden their learning.

Although the items in the list above have not been "weighted," it's wise not to consider all of the items as having equal importance. Organizations and their needs vary dramatically based on their size and situation. After completing the assessment, identify areas where you need improvement. It is also a wise move to get a second opinion and assessment by someone who is impeccably honest and straightforward.

TRANSITIONING FROM BUSINESS PARTNER TO HR LEADER

Becoming a business partner has been a goal of most HR professionals for years. Although becoming a business partner and perhaps even achieving professional certification by the Society for Human Resource Management (SHRM) are desirable short-term goals, I recommend that you aim for the next level, becoming a HR leader.

DEFINITION

While both business partners and HR leaders strive to be strategic, the significant differences between the two are that an HR leader is more aggressive, is future-focused, and makes "fact based decisions." A business partner differs from a HR leader much the same way that an accountant differs from a finance person. It is a progression, but once you develop the "finance" or leader mindset, your approach forever changes to a more "take-charge" expert approach.

The goal of a business partner is to partner with or become equal to management. Becoming a partner is certainly a desirable goal, but an HR leader strives to a higher level. An HR leader does not strive to become an "equal partner." His or her goal is to become a "leader" who proactively seeks out people-management problems and pushes to get management's attention. In essence, HR leaders want to be the "managing partner" on people-related issues because of their detailed knowledge and their ability to make fact-based decisions.

Business leaders differ from business partners in that:

- They want to be an "unequal" partner in people-management issues;
- They proactively seek out problems and opportunities when they are in their infancy;
- They are experts and, as a result, they aggressively take control and guide managers;

- They accept accountability for getting things done even though they do not have control; and
- They are future-focused so they forecast and anticipate future events.

There are several other contrasts between business partners and HR leaders. A "business partner" generally reacts to requests and events, while an HR leader anticipates business opportunities and problems and suggests action prior to being asked by management. An HR leader relies on data and expert knowledge, while a business partner relies more heavily on relationships.

Also, HR leaders differ in the area of focus. While they generally strive to provide equal treatment, an HR leader must differentiate because he or she is laser-focused on performance. Because of that focus, HR leaders constantly insist on the use of financial measures and data for decision-making.

HR leaders, because of their expert knowledge and their ability to make fact-based decisions, strive to move beyond business partner status to become the equivalent of the "managing partner" on people-related issues.

The next chapter highlights how to build a strong business case for HR. It includes tips on how to convince the CEO and the CFO that HR provides a high economic value-add.

CHAPTER SEVENTEEN

MAKING THE BUSINESS CASE FOR HR

OBJECTIVES

The goal of this chapter is to provide the tools and strategies that can be used to influence senior managers because, to them, almost every decision requires a "business case."

KEY POINTS

◊ Because senior managers have learned to think in analytical terms and to quantify everything, HR must also do the same.

◊ The prime reason that so many HR departments are being subjected to budget cuts is not because HR does not provide a strategic value, but instead because HR does not provide the proof of its strategic value in a manner and language that CFOs and CEOs have come to expect.

Human resource functions always have undergone intense scrutiny by executives and financial officers. Although CEOs are notorious for saying that "people are our most important asset," they often become relative "misers" when it comes to funding people programs. And, incidentally, it is extremely rare for the manager of the most important asset (the VP of HR) to be promoted into the most important job in the corporation, the CEO's job.

In tough economic times, HR programs come under siege by the cost-cutters who have taken control of businesses during tough times. If human resource professionals are to survive and prosper, it is essential that they refocus their efforts on *building the business case* for investing in human capital programs. HR professionals need to shift from their all too common "I think" and "I believe" approach to a more businesslike approach where decisions are made based on data and facts. ROI and payback need to become more prominent in the jargon of human resource professionals.

Unfortunately, to say that HR professionals have been weak in building the business case for HR programs is more than just a mild understatement. I have spent over 25 years teaching HR teams how to build their business cases. Even so, from HP and Cisco all the away down to the small-business owner, there is little variation in what makes an effective business case. It's not as difficult as you might think because it turns out that most financial professionals and executives are very logical people. What they expect is surprisingly consistent in all different-sized businesses.

DEFINITION

Building a business case is a separate issue from "doing metrics" in HR. Metrics is mostly a statistical exercise that focuses on internal HR effectiveness, while building a business case is really just selling with numbers. Making a business case differs from metrics because it includes:

- Using business logic to sell an idea;

- Proving business results using common business financial ratios;

- Identifying the decision criteria that key executives use;

- Effective wordsmithing; and

- Making a short but powerful presentation (including a detailed decision-support document, a few effective PowerPoint slides, and a "wow" verbal presentation)

THE ELEMENTS OF AN EFFECTIVE HR BUSINESS CASE

Each of the steps you must take in order to build an effective business case is highlighted below. While going through these steps it is important to step back occasionally and to view the "big picture." A business case is selling an idea, just as a salesperson sells his or her product.

In order to be successful you must *focus on the decision-making criteria that your target audience uses.* Be aware that the decision criteria listed below are, by their very nature, generic. If you want to maximize your effectiveness, do your own internal research in order to identify the specific decision criteria and the "passing scores" that are utilized within your own organization.

I. IDENTIFY WHO YOU ARE TRYING TO INFLUENCE

Although we live in a world of computers, in most "buy" or "don't buy" situations, real people make decisions. Even though they might serve as a team or work together as a unit, each individual has his or her own set of decision criteria to determine if a project is fundable. You can't treat all of the decision-makers the same, and you probably don't have time to influence them all. Instead, you must prioritize them and focus on those individual decision-makers who have the most "influence" on program decisions.

> *"Knowing" key decision-makers and how they make decisions is the first and most important step in building a business case.*

1. Identify and prioritize your target audience—Identify which people are the most influential ones. Also identify any strong individuals who frequently serve as gatekeepers or who frequently exercise "veto" power over proposed programs. Next, prioritize the target audience and focus your efforts on the most influential ones. When possible, try to get one of the most influential individuals to sponsor the program. If, for example, you can convince an executive known as a "HR program-hater" to sponsor it, the game is already halfway over.

2. Identify their decision criteria—After reviewing a variety of past program decisions (get your non-HR colleagues to help you to track them), you need to identify the critical success factors in influencing each individual to vote "yes." For each influential individual, identify the primary decision "mindset." Individuals make decisions in a variety of ways, but they generally fall under these "mindset" categories: financial, logical, scientific, emotional, image, personal relationships, selfishness, or immediacy of impact. Also identify the minimum acceptable number or "passing score" you need to reach for each of the criteria (for example: 11 percent is the minimum acceptable ROI percentage).

3. Determine who is likely to resist or support it, and why—Identify which individuals routinely support or vote against HR or other overhead programs. Then try to identify a commonality or a pattern in the decision-making in order to identify why they approve some but reject others.

II. DEMONSTRATE THE CREDIBILITY
OF PROGRAM SPONSORS

It's unfortunate but true that mediocre programs supported and presented by great people get funded more often than great programs presented by mediocre people. In order to prove that you and your team are credible, you must make a strong case that you are "experts" in your industry, your business and in this topic area.

4. Prove that you are an expert in the industry and the organization—Prove that you are an expert at forecasting the future problems and opportunities in your industry and at your firm. Increase your credibility by citing examples of the business impact that your past programs have had. Show that you have done detailed research in your program area and that you can answer any question on the subject without hesitation.

5. Forecast trends and patterns—Show that you know where the business and industry are going by highlighting key trends and patterns. Include forecasts for the changing business and environmental factors.

6. Demonstrate your success rate and your track record—Demonstrate that the previous programs and projects you have presented have reached their goals and had positive, measurable business impacts. Quantify the success rate of your past projects in percentages.

7. Show that the HR "owner" of the project is well known, trusted and respected—Make sure that the person running the program is known and respected by the decision-makers. Improve your case by providing information to show that he or she has the experience, track record and expertise necessary to run a successful program. Determine whether the program sponsor has any major enemies or major program failures in his or her background. Remember that if the program sponsor is new to the firm, it can be assumed that the NIH ("not invented here") syndrome will surface. Provide information to show that the program sponsor "thinks like us."

III. DEMONSTRATE THAT THE PROGRAM MEETS ORGANIZATIONAL GOALS AND CULTURE

All overhead programs come under scrutiny because it's not always easy to show how they directly impact business results. Executives will need to be shown the direct relationship between the proposed HR programs and the stated corporate goals and objectives for the year.

No matter how effective a program might appear on the surface, decision-makers often use a cultural filter to screen out programs that don't seem to fit the corporate culture or values. If you are unsure, get a "grizzled veteran" to do a quick cultural fit assessment. Convincing executives that there is a cultural fit often means using key buzzwords judiciously, citing historical precedents, and mentioning corporate heroes. Having a corporate "veteran" sponsor the program can also alleviate fears that it doesn't fit the corporate culture.

8. Show that the program helps meet corporate business goals and objectives—Be sure and repeat the key objectives in your documentation and show how the proposed solution directly aligns with the major corporate objectives. Quantify the estimated impacts.

9. Clarify whether the program fixes an existing problem or presents a new opportunity—Most executives choose fixing existing problems over seeking out "new" profit opportunities. If you select a problem to fix, first identify the problem, show its causes, and quantify the problem's impacts. Next show how your solution solves the problem. Where possible, give examples of how this type of solution has solved the problem in other similar organizations. If it is an opportunity, demonstrate how the results will be superior to competing opportunities, and demonstrate that there is a sense of urgency that requires immediate action.

10. Demonstrate how it fits the corporate culture and processes—Show how each major program element fits, supports or enhances the organization's culture and values. If the program has broad impacts, show how the solution aligns—or at least does not conflict—with ongoing processes and systems.

11. Show the program's impact on diversity—Where possible, quantify the impact the program will have on increasing the diversity of the workforce.

IV. DEMONSTRATE HOW THE PROGRAM IMPROVES COMPETITIVE POSITION

Executives and decision-makers are almost always competitive people. They love programs that give a sustainable competitive advantage over rival firms and their products. An HR program is most effective when it is the first and only one in the marketplace. Once everyone has one, it becomes essentially a commodity, which means it's necessary to have one, but having one provides no significant edge.

12. Show how the program provides a competitive advantage—Demonstrate (and then quantify) how this program is superior to those of your competitors. Provide a side-by-side comparison of the program's features, including what your program offers and what competitors offer.

13. Demonstrate how it allows competitive differentiation—Show that the program is unique so that it will stand out among the rest. Show how that uniqueness will get the organization "talked about" in the industry. Describe the unique programming elements and demonstrate how they are difficult to copy.

14. Show how it models benchmark organizations—Senior managers almost always have a "model" organization that they want to be like. Demonstrate how this program will make your organization more like that model or other benchmark organizations. Show what "they" do and how this program will emulate "them."

15. Demonstrate benchmarking research—Show that you've done your research and benchmarking by outlining the best practices at each of the leading firms.

16. Forecast where competitors "will be headed"—If you assume that any program implementation will take some time, show that you have calculated how far the competitor will have advanced by the time your program is implemented and what you have done to counter that progress.

17. Forecast what response competitors will make to your program—Include in your program plan the steps you will take in order to combat competitors' inevitable counter-moves or copying of your program.

V. DEMONSTRATE A HIGH PROBABILITY OF SUCCESS

All programs involve risks, and "people programs" have some of the highest failure rates. It's essential that you demonstrate—both in probabilities and in dollars—the likelihood of success of your program. Be prepared to show how you arrived at the forecasted success rate.

18. Prove how often these types of solutions work—Demonstrate that you've done your research and quantify how often these types of programs work and how often they fail.

19. List the critical success and failure factors—If you can't show why programs succeed, you are clearly not an expert. Show that you've done your research by listing and prioritizing the critical success factors for this type of program. Also make a list of the common problems that can occur in implementing this type of program, and show that you have a solution for each.

20. List the environmental and economic factors that impact the likelihood of success—Programs and solutions are impacted by changes in both the internal and external environment. List the key environmental factors that impact program success. Show how you will monitor and track each of these factors.

21. Demonstrate that you have the talent, technology or other competencies necessary for success—Great ideas fail without the right resources. Demonstrate that the organization has the necessary talent to manage and operate the program. Show that you have the necessary competencies and experience as well as the infrastructure or technology necessary for success.

VI. DEMONSTRATE THE POSSIBLE ECONOMIC IMPACT

Speaking the language of business means using dollars and numbers. HR professionals need to "talk" the language of business and finance if they expect to be heard. Although every company has its own unique measures of business success, the following list is a good representation of most business success measures.

Don't get hung up on "perfect" numbers. Finance estimates such things as sales, profits, and goodwill all the time. However, be sure that you run your proposed project success measures and metrics by someone in the CFO's office before you formally present your program plan. Where possible, involve financial professionals in setting up the acceptable success measures.

Beware of traditional internal HR success measures because they are too tactical. Senior executives focus on *overall* business impact. Incidentally, great hiring, retention and people-productivity programs generally have among the highest ROI of any business programs, so don't be shy with the numbers.

22. Improve revenue, income, profit, margins, customer value and shareholder value—Estimate the potential impact of the program on profits. Next focus on shareholder value or stock price. Finally, show whether you can demonstrate, through better hiring, training, pay practices, or technology, that the firm will improve its productivity and profits.

23. Calculate the payback period—Executives hate to wait a long time for the program's break-even point. Demonstrate how many months it will be before the program begins generating results and when the initial investment will be paid back.

24. Minimize the amount of up-front money needed—The "best" overhead programs operate out of existing resources. Hiring new people and buying equipment are "red flag" items. Executives want to minimize the amount of up-front money that is needed to get programs started. If possible, show that results will be demonstrated before any additional cash is needed.

25. List the program success measures (metrics)—List the five key success measures for the program or project. Be sure to include the minimal "passing score" for each measure.

26. Calculate the program's ROI—New programs or projects are frequently measured by their return on investment (ROI). Demonstrate that for every $1.00 invested, at least $1.15 will be returned (a 15-percent ROI). Be aware that a ROI of above 50 percent is not credible.

27. Calculate the program's impact on your products and services—Anything that improves your organization's product almost always impresses executives. Demonstrate where you can do that with improved hiring, training, etc., to dramatically improve each of the following business impacts measures:

- Increased margins;
- Increased market share;
- Time to market for product development;
- Added product features or product quality;
- Improved response time or customer service;
- Decreased errors or rejects;
- Decreased cycle or process time;
- Increased customer satisfaction;
- Increased image, PR or brand recognition; and
- Increased product sales (which might differ from increased profit).

28. Show the program facilitates the company's rapid growth—Modern executives love "top-line" (revenue) growth. Programs that facilitate or allow rapid growth almost always receive a high priority.

29. Likelihood of external financial support—Programs that are partially funded by outside sources (strategic partners, the government, customers, or vendors) have an increased likelihood of support. You have already demonstrated that others see value in what you're proposing, and these external partners are willing to "vote with their wallets."

VII. DEMONSTRATE THAT THE PROJECT PLAN IS CREDIBLE

Great programs often are not approved because their implementation plans are weak. Generally project plans are not judged as credible when they fail to answer key questions or to anticipate potential problems. Have your plan reviewed by a successful internal project manager and, over time, develop a checklist for assessing program implementation plans.

30. Show that the project leader is credible—If you have to "sell" the individual to the management team, you are *already* in trouble. Pick someone they know and trust.

31. Demonstrate that your team is competent—Provide a brief profile of each team member highlighting their skills and demonstrating their accomplishments in recent projects or programs. Delete any team members that may have a "negative" image.

32. Show that the organization can attract any talent it may need—If it is a new program, you must demonstrate that you will be able to learn quickly or attract experienced talent either internally or from the outside.

33. List the program steps—Don't skimp here. Provide an appendix document that lists—in some detail—each of the steps you will take to implement the program. This is to demonstrate that you have thought of all eventualities and that you have a logical step-by-step process.

34. Show that you have undertaken a pilot—Executives *say* that they are risk-takers, but in fact they are really *calculated* risk-takers. By proposing or actually operating a pilot project or beta test, you can demonstrate that you are willing to try out and refine your idea before any big dollars are required. If you have already conducted a successful pilot using your own resources, you're halfway there.

35. Highlight the program monitoring system—Great implementation plans include milestones or assessment points where the program is re-evaluated. Sometimes weak programs are approved when they demonstrate that they have an effective feedback loop that allows them to continually improve and learn.

36. Provide best- and worst-case scenarios—Executives live in a reality where things often go wrong. Effective project plans anticipate things going wrong; consequently, they highlight every possible eventuality. Demonstrate that you have considered both best- and worst-case scenarios, that you have calculated their probabilities, and that you have a backup plan for each.

37. Show a plan for identifying any unintended consequences— Even great programs can have side effects. Demonstrate that you have a formal program that is designed to identify any potential negative or positive unintended consequences that may occur as an indirect result of your program.

38. Identify any potential legal issues—Executives often hate lawyers, but they hate surprises even more. Show that you have calculated any legal risks and taken them into account.

VIII. IDENTIFY DIRECT PERSONAL BENEFITS FOR KEY DECISION-MAKERS

Executives can be prone to selfishness; getting to the top generally *requires* some degree of selfishness. Don't ignore that fact. Treat them as individuals with egos, insecurities and feelings. Make sure you demonstrate to each of the influential decision-makers how the program will benefit them personally. In reverse, you also need to look at how the program might threaten them or their business unit. *Ignore this element of the business case at your peril!*

39. Establish a personal relationship with the decision-maker—On more than one occasion, great programs have been rejected because the program manager failed to build a personal relationship with the influential decision-makers. Remember, it's easier to reject strangers than it is friends. Make sure decision-makers are aware of any common interests or experiences you might share.

40. Demonstrate that the program improves the chance of promotion or increased income—Where possible, demonstrate to each individual decision-maker how the program might help their career or boost their income level.

41. Demonstrate that the program might build decision-makers' images—Executives can have enormous egos, so be sure to demonstrate how the project might improve their visibility and image, both inside and outside the corporation.

IX. CONSIDER OTHER FACTORS

42. Anticipate being offered a reduced budget—Be prepared for the eventuality that decision-makers will approve your project *but* at a reduced budget level. Anticipate this eventuality and have a backup plan that allows you to operate at partial funding. Be prepared, however, to say "no" if partial funding will doom the program to failure.

43. Include a continuous improvement process in your plan—Include in your plan a process for continually upgrading and improving every key element of your program. This program element will excite even the most mundane decision-maker.

44. Take into account executives' past experiences with your department—Many executives have had negative experiences with the HR department. Don't be naïve; study the history and be prepared to show how you are different or have changed.

X. IF ALL ELSE FAILS ...

Be aware that executives are almost always a macho group. Whether they are men or women, they are universally impressed with people who stick their necks out, because they themselves must stick their necks out every day. They are also painfully aware that most "overhead" people (and HR is no different) are risk-averse. If you really want the project to be approved, you need to "put a stake in the ground" and put your job on the line. This means:

- Guarantee the date the program will be operational;
- Set that date to be within 90 days;
- Guarantee numerical results (specify them) within six months of operation;
- Guarantee further numerical results at the end of the year;

And finally ... offer to resign if the above four don't occur ....
Any questions?

MAKING A BUSINESS CASE IN HR

A business case is a logical step-by-step approach for selling a program or project to senior management. HR people unfortunately have a long but weak history in making business cases. The following is an example illustrating how to create a business case for adding a new recruiter to the HR staff to focus on marketing and IT. It follows the format outlined above and, while it is only an outline, it will provide some idea of the basic approach.

I. Identify who are you trying to influence

1. Who is the target audience?

The CFO's office processes and approves budget requests for additional staff during a hiring freeze.

2. What are their decision criteria?

After reviewing the minutes of the budget committee meetings, we found that the CFO's office approves only 45 percent of the proposals that come before her. After reviewing the trend analysis of the last 100 decisions over the previous year, we identified the differences in the projects that were approved and projects that were rejected. Successful programs are approved based on the following criteria:

- 50 percent of the decision is based on the calculated financial impact of the proposed project (where the minimum passing score is a 15 percent ROI and at least a revenue impact of $1 million);
- 25 percent of the decision is based on a promise of immediate return or payback period (where the minimum passing score is that at least 25 percent of the promised results are achieved within six months); and
- 25 percent of the decision is based on the risk of failure associated with the project (where the minimum passing score is that the project has less than a 25 percent chance of failure during its first two years).

3. Who is likely to resist or support it (and why)?

- The CEO consistently vetoes high-risk proposals where the chance of failure is over 25 percent.
- The CIO and the VP of marketing consistently support (95 percent of the time) new revenue-increasing programs that increase revenue by at least $1 million; and
- The CFO rejects 90 percent of all HR proposals. The CFO constantly complains that HR's proposals are heavy on emotion but weak on data. The CFO has rejected 50 percent of all of the requests for new staff during the hiring freeze because they lacked a significant financial impact.

II. Demonstrate the credibility of program sponsors

It's unfortunate but true that programs supported and presented by people without a track record or knowledge of your industry get funded at a rate of less than 10 percent. If this project is to be funded, you must make a strong case that you are an expert in the industry, in the business, and in the area of recruiting.

4. Prove expertise in the industry, firm, problem or solution

The project director is a recognized national expert in the field of HR. She has been at XYZ Corporation for eleven years and she completes 95 percent of her projects under deadline and under budget.

5. Forecast trends and patterns

The project director recently has demonstrated a correlation of 0.92 between a decrease in the unemployment rate and the need for increased

HR staffing personnel. With the lower unemployment rate, there is a corresponding lower quality of candidates and a longer time to recruit, both of which dramatically decrease departmental productivity (especially in high-growth areas like marketing and IT). As a result of the projected drop in the unemployment rate of 1 percent, there is a need to increase HR recruiting personnel by hiring an additional recruiter.

HR has successfully demonstrated in the past that the return to the firm (in the form of increased employee productivity) for every new hire in the HR staffing office results in a minimum of a $1,000,000 increase in employee productivity during the first year. Every month of delay without hiring the recruiter will cost us nearly $100,000 in lost productivity, two points on our profit margin, and one percent of our market share.

6. Demonstrate your success rate and track record

The last five increases in HR program staff have generated more than $10 million in increased productivity without a single failure. The average return on investment on HR projects is 62 percent, where the firm average for all programs is only 41 percent. The last three HR projects approved had an average ROI of 97 percent. Each of the last five increases in staff produced results on time and under budget.

7. Show that the HR "owner" of the project is well known, trusted and respected, and show that a senior non-HR manager is "sponsoring" the project

The CIO and the VP of Marketing are the sponsors of this project. They have already identified the need for additional hiring to aid their departmental growth. The HR project director (the director of staffing) has presented six different projects to the CFO's staff and all six were approved. He came from the CFO's staff and maintains to this day a high level of credibility and believability with that department.

III. Demonstrate that the program meets organizational goals and culture

8. Show that the program helps us meet our goals and objectives

Maintaining productivity levels in the marketing department is the number two goal on the CEO's priority list; maintaining productivity levels in IT is the number three goal. Increasing HR's talent capabilities is the fifth goal on the list, and increasing hiring speed and quality is number twelve.

9. Clarify whether the program fixes an existing problem or presents a new opportunity

Hiring an additional recruiter solves an existing problem in the marketing and IT departments because they're understaffed by 10 percent (slow hiring speed), and their productivity is down by 15 percent (poor quality of current hires). The program provides us with a positive opportunity to expand our talent capabilities while at the same time it helps address low staffing levels in marketing and IT.

10. Demonstrate how it fits our culture and our processes

Our push to maintain our position as the low-cost provider in our industry requires us to assess new programs based on their ROI. Increasing the staff in the HR staffing department does run counter to our attempts to keep overhead costs to a minimum, but the need to act quickly as a result of the imminent decrease in the unemployment rate, the decrease in productivity in IT and marketing, and the high ROI for this project, makes cost reduction a secondary concern.

11. Impact on diversity

The HR staffing department has a 47 percent diversity rate compared to the firm's overall 29 percent rate. The project manager has agreed to advertise for the position in all major minority publications, and the hiring of additional recruiters with the ability to source diversity candidates will help us meet and even exceed this year's diversity goals.

IV. Demonstrate how the program improves competitive position

12. Show how it gives us a competitive advantage

We are currently the industry leader in attracting talent. This additional recruiter will allow us to maintain that competitive advantage. Additional HR staff will allow us to successfully poach top talent from other area firms, thus obtaining a disproportionate share of the quality marketing and IT talent in our industry. We need to act quickly because talent will soon be harder to acquire as a result of the decrease in the unemployment rate.

13. Demonstrate how it allows us to differentiate ourselves
Additional speed and response time to applicants (as a result of the new HR hire) will help us build our external brand image as a great place to work. Adding of a recruiter will result in increased staffing levels in marketing and IT, which will directly increase our ability to develop innovative products and increase our product development speed.

14. Show it makes "us" just like them
Cisco is our target firm to emulate. It currently has an HR staffing ratio of 15 recruiters per 1,000 employees. This addition to our staff will bring us up to that ratio.

15. Demonstrate competitive benchmarking
Five other peer firms have recently added HR recruiting staff in response to this decrease in the unemployment rate phenomenon. Cisco is the leading firm when it comes to recruiting talent. Their speed and quality of hire are 15 percent better than ours. The other emerging firm to watch our industry in regards to talent is Juniper Systems.

16. Forecast where our competitors "will be"
Our competitive intelligence tells us that our competitors can add no additional staff beyond their currently planned additions due to recruiting software limitations that will take 18 months to resolve.

17. Forecast the competitive response to our program
We expect no response because of their recruiting software limitations, but if they do copy our approach we propose to give each of our recruiters basic sales training in order to increase their effectiveness without the need to increase our overall staff headcount.

V. Demonstrate a high probability of success
18. Prove how often these types of solutions work
Eighty-five percent of the time in our industry, and 95 percent of the time in our firm, hiring a recruiter (during times of decreasing unemployment rates) results in an increase in hiring quality and a decrease in hiring speed.

19. List the critical success and failure factors

The critical success factors (CSFs) for hiring a new recruiter were developed after studying 22 cases of recruiter hiring success and failure during the last three years. The CSFs include:

- Hiring within 30 days after a position is approved;
- Hiring experienced recruiters away from other firms; and
- Paying them 10 percent above market.

Common problems related to adding new recruiters include:

- A lack of computers and recruiter training can hamper HR recruiting efforts;
- Outdated candidate lists can reduce HR recruiting effectiveness by 5 percent; and
- Failing to source on the Internet slows hiring speed by 50 percent.

20. External factors that impact the likelihood of success

If the unemployment rate should stop decreasing and instead start increasing by more than 10 percent, this will mitigate the low unemployment rate effect, which in turn would cause a 20 percent decrease in the expected revenue gain (as the result of the increased recruiting success in IT and marketing). The probability of such a shift in the unemployment rate happening is estimated at less than 10 percent, and even if it did occur, the ROI for the program would still exceed the firm's average by 10 percent.

21. Demonstrate that we have the talent, technology or other competencies necessary for success

Our current HR recruiting staff is the most effective in the region. We have demonstrated our ability to hire the best recruiters in the industry in three out of the last five years. There is ample mentoring, computing capacity, and training available, as well as office space for any new hire within HR.

VI. Demonstrate the possible economic impact

22. Revenue

Revenue is expected to increase $1 million in the first year as a result of the faster and higher quality of the hires in marketing and IT. We expect it to increase our overall margin by one percent. We anticipate no change in the stock price as a result of this program.

23. Payback period

We anticipate it will take only six months until the initial investment is returned.

24. Amount of up-front money needed

$75,000

25. Program success measures (metrics)

Things to measure in order to assess the program's effectiveness include

- Increased revenue attributed to the new hires in IT and marketing as a result of the additional recruiter;
- Decrease in the time to hire attributed to the new recruiter;
- Increased quality of hire (performance of new hires vs. current employees);
- Manager satisfaction rate (of those managers in IT and marketing that had new hires with the new recruiter);
- Our external image (percent of positive recognition as a great place to work) as measured by industry surveys; and
- The project's overall ROI.

26. Calculate the program's ROI

The project ROI is 62 percent.

27. Calculate its impact on our products and services

We estimate that product development time will decrease by 7 percent, and our overall product quality will improve by 5 percent as a result of the new hires in marketing and IT.

28. Show that the program facilitates the company's rapid growth

The backlog of hiring requisitions will be eliminated in thirty days and the candidate call-back waiting time will be decreased by 6 hours as a result of this new recruiter. Hires will start 60 days earlier, so product development time will decrease by 7 percent. The increased hiring (as a result of the new recruiter) will decrease product error rates in IT by 2 percent. There is no projected error rate impact in marketing. Projects in marketing and IT that are now held back due to lack of staff have an estimated value of $500 million.

29. Likelihood of external financial support

There is no likelihood for obtaining external financial support.

VII. Demonstrate that the project plan is credible

30. Show that the project leader is credible

The project leader has a 95 percent success rate (*e.g.*, he met 100 percent of the goals) on projects, and he has in the past decreased product development time (7 percent) and decreased hiring time (50 percent).

31. Demonstrate that your team is competent

N/A

32. Show that you can attract any talent you might need

We have ten top recruiter resumes currently in our applicant pool, so we anticipate no difficulty in hiring. Seventy-eight percent of the previous recruiters selected for hiring accepted our offer.

33. List the program steps

1. Update the job description;
2. Place an ad;
3. Search Internet chat rooms and list servers frequented by recruiters;
4. Ask our own best talent which recruiters are best at trying to recruit them away;
5. Ask other recruiters and managers for referrals;
6. Interview;
7. Make an offer;
8. Provide two days of initial training; and
9. Measure the results and provide additional training or incentives as necessary.

34. Show that you have undertaken a pilot or beta test

Although it was not possible to undertake a pilot, our current staff is already seeing an increased difficulty in recruiting as a result of the decrease in the unemployment rate. Similar recruiter hiring has produced positive results during the last two periods when the unemployment rate dropped.

35. Highlight the program monitoring system

All HR recruiting is coded so that we can identify which staff member generates which new hires. Marketing and IT productivity and product development will be measured on a monthly basis. Manager and candidate satisfaction will be measured quarterly. The CFO has approved the project metrics and monitoring system.

36. Provide best- and worst-case scenarios

Best case is increased revenue of $2 million per year and ten hires within a year; the worst case is $200,000 in revenue during the first year and two hires in the first year.

37. Show a plan for identifying any "unintended consequences"

Additional recruiter hiring for marketing and IT may increase conflict between IT and marketing for attention from the recruiter. Other operating units may become jealous because they have received no additional recruiting help.

38. Identify any potential legal issues

There is a .02 percent chance of a lawsuit as a result of the increased volume and speed of hiring.

VIII. Identify direct personal benefits for key decision-makers

39. Establish a personal relationship with the decision-maker

The VP of HR and the CFO have a strong working relationship. They will serve on the executive committee and they are golfing partners.

40. Demonstrate that the program improves chances of promotion or increased income

We estimate that the increased growth and revenue as a result of increased hiring will increase all executive bonuses by five percent this year.

41. Demonstrate that the program might build executives' images

There is no estimated impact on the CFO's image.

IX. Consider other factors

42. Anticipate being offered a reduced budget

Even if only a part-time position is offered, we estimate it will generate a positive ROI of 12 percent.

43. Include a continuous improvement process in the plan

Revenues will be monitored to see if the additional staff, new hiring incentives, or recruiter training lead to an increased yield. If so, additional resources will be requested to take advantage of these possible program enhancements.

44. Consider executives' past experience with your department

The negative "business partner" image from the 1990s has been worn away by our attempts to become business leaders. We anticipate no negative political or "reputation" issues.

Pretest your arguments

A great business argument starts with providing decision-makers with the essential information for making a decision as reflected by the preceding factors. But making a convincing business argument is only 75 percent logical; the remaining 25 percent of any decision-making process is emotional.

> *In order to ensure you have made a great emotional argument, you must "pre-test" your argument using real people.*

There are several ways to assure that your argument is convincing, including (from least to most powerful approaches):

- Videotape your presentation and review it yourself "frame-by-frame." Identify weak arguments and presenters.
- In order to identify its readability and scanability, have ten people scan your support document for five minutes. Then ask them (from memory) to recite the key arguments.
- Have them read the support document and have them highlight the five weakest and the five strongest arguments.
- Provide an anonymous (no names) document to a panel of experts and have them vote on funding. Use the results as a guide to determine how convincing the support document is.

- Do a mock presentation in front of a panel of experts (some from outside your department or firm). Have them highlight the five weakest and the five strongest arguments, and then vote on funding.
- Give a "draft" document to a friendly member of the decision team. Ask that person to rate your chances and identify your weaknesses. If you have the courage, do the same with someone who is skeptical of you and your program.
- Practice your actual presentation in front of critical people multiple times until you can answer every one of their "bone-chilling" questions quickly and to their satisfaction.

After you complete the pre-testing process, revise and improve both the support document and the actual presentation script and plan. But don't stop there. Identify why mistakes were made and then improve your program development process to avoid similar future errors. Share these learnings so that others also can improve.

X. If all else fails ...

53. Program promises

- The date the program will be operational (the recruiter will be on board and functioning) will be January 30th (60 days from today);
- Within six months of operation the hiring backlog in marketing and IT will be zero;
- By the end of the first 12 months of operation, revenues in marketing and IT will be up two million dollars; and
- If the above don't occur I will offer my resignation.

WHY NEW HR PROGRAMS ARE REJECTED

Many senior HR people seem totally surprised when their new "pet project" is heavily criticized by a team of MBA financial analysts with a battery of what I call "questions from hell." In case you are planning on proposing a new HR program, use this checklist of questions to prepare for the inevitable bombardment from the "non-believers and nay-sayers."

When new programs are proposed in HR, there are invariably a series of "it won't work" criticisms that you will get from cynical managers and executives. You must be able to anticipate and respond to each of these potential criticisms and questions if you expect to get any new HR program approved. These common concerns are presented in the following checklist of criticisms, complaints and issues you will likely hear when proposing new HR programs.

CHECKLIST OF REJECTION QUESTIONS

It impacts our business results

- It doesn't fit our business plan or model.
- You have not demonstrated its impact on employee productivity.
- It increases overhead costs, which negatively impacts our product margins.
- It has no positive dollar impact on shareholder or customer value.
- It raises headcount or requires new hiring (during slow growth periods).

Proof it works

- There is no hard data that proves it actually produces results.
- No one has done a side-by-side comparison to show this program is clearly superior to the other alternative programs.
- We tried it already last year (in another business unit) and it didn't work.
- You have not demonstrated the program's normal success and failure rate.
- It never works on the first try or on initial implementation.
- Its effectiveness will only last for ___ months (it will become obsolete rapidly).
- Yeah, the benchmark firm uses it, but that doesn't mean it actually works.

Benchmarking and "learning" from others

- No one else has tried it (or had success with it).
- No one in our industry has tried it (or had success with it).
- Many firms have dropped it.
- It won't work in our size firm.
- It won't work in our industry.
- It won't work in our region (location).

Competitive advantage it provides

- This project or its components are based on information that is available to all, so there is no competitive advantage for us.
- Your program can be easily copied. So how many months will it take for a competitor to copy or produce a similar program?
- This program is "vanilla" and no different than what other firms use or have.
- The vendor will also sell it (the service or program) to the competitor, so where is the competitive advantage?

Managers' concerns

- Top executives hate the idea; there is no executive buy-in.
- Managers hate it (they haven't asked for it).
- Managers don't have the time to participate in it or use it.
- Managers don't have the necessary people skills to make it work.
- Managers (and others) aren't measured on whether or how well they do it.
- Managers (and others) aren't rewarded for doing it, so why should they do it?

Money and costs

- No one ever calculated the proposed project's ROI.
- Its ROI is too low compared to our firm's normal expectations.
- The proposed program won't work on half the budget allocation (and that's all we have available).
- The payback period is too long (the wait to get our initial investment back).
- It's not in this year's budget, so it will have to wait.
- It requires too much up-front money to get running.
- The cost per unit of service is too high.
- No one calculated the risks (probability of occurring and potential dollar impact) related to this new project.

Time and delays

- We need it now (it takes too long to implement).
- It takes too long to design.
- It takes too long to get up to a minimum performance level.
- It takes too many hours a week to operate and maintain.

- The service isn't available 24/7.
- The response time is too slow.

Quality and errors

- The error rate is too high.
- The user or employee satisfaction rate is too low.
- It's too easy to cheat or bypass the system or rules.
- It doesn't meet Six Sigma or ISO standards.

Volume and scalability

- The program can't rapidly vary the volume it handles or its output (scalability) as our needs suddenly change.
- If we need to double the volume (after a merger, new plant or international expansion), can the process handle it?
- It won't work as our firm's size (and thus our needs) shrinks and we need a lower volume.

Metrics and performance measures

- The data or information you need to operate your project is not available to us.
- There is no one who can do the data collection.
- The data needed is collected inconsistently, is inaccurate or is too expensive to collect.
- We don't know what an "acceptable" score (or performance level) is.
- The program has no measurement plan or the metrics that are used are too "soft" to be of any real use.

HRIS and technology

- The system (hardware or software) you are considering using isn't compatible with our current systems.
- We don't have the hardware to support it.
- We don't have the software to support it.
- We can't afford to update the system as the vendor upgrades it.
- We can't afford to maintain the system.
- We can't offer it outside our firewall (on laptops).
- The system or data isn't Web-based.
- Our employees don't have access to a computer.

- Our employees don't have the necessary computer skills.
- The IT department will never allow it.
- We can't use technology or we will lose the "human touch."

Project or program management

- There is no continuous improvement element designed into the process.
- We don't have the time to manage another program.
- We don't have the management skills to manage another program.
- No one (person) is available to manage it.
- The vendor isn't reliable, so we need to be able to shift rapidly to a back-up plan.
- You actually believed the "story" the vendor told you?
- It's a "corporate HQ"-designed program, so it won't work outside of "corporate HQ." In addition, it doesn't fit "our" unique needs.
- The program designer (or project team) has no successful track record or credibility in this area.
- There is no formal performance monitoring process or system that is designed into your proposal.
- The program doesn't have a component for forecasting (or predicting) our firm's future needs or problems.

Global scope

- It's a "U.S.-designed" program that won't work in different geographic regions because of legal issues.
- It won't work in different cultures around the world.
- It isn't designed to work in different languages, or different language versions aren't available.

Legal issues

- There is a high probability that the program will discriminate or have an adverse impact on protected classes.
- It doesn't protect employee privacy.
- The union agreement doesn't allow it.
- It might lead to unionization.
- We might get sued if we do it.

Environmental factors

- It won't work if the unemployment rate changes.
- It won't work if the economy goes in the tank.
- It won't work if the interest rates change.
- It won't work if the laws change.
- It won't work if the currency valuation rate changes.
- It won't work if the competitors can copy it quickly.
- It won't work if the stock market (our price) crashes.

Training

- The training is too expensive.
- The training is too time-consuming.
- Managers won't go to it; they have no time for the training.
- The training doesn't work (there's no proof).
- The training isn't available on-line.

Miscellaneous "soft" factors

- It won't work in or it conflicts with our company culture.
- It doesn't fit our values or ethics.
- You don't understand, we are different and we need a customized (local) approach.
- It doesn't directly contribute to us developing a more diverse workforce.
- We have always done it this (a different) way and there is no need to change it.
- It violates or runs against our past practices or policies.
- There is no consensus for doing it.
- We need to study it further (let's form a committee!).
- Equity demands we treat everyone the same.
- It produces waste and harms the environment.
- It's just another HR "flavor of the month" program, and it too will fade away in time.

If you only propose a new HR program once every three years, you are likely to forget the type and ferocity of the concerns that others are likely to raise against your proposal.

Being "rusty" might doom your project to failure if you don't have a checklist to guide you in preparing for and directly addressing each concern your team will encounter.

CALCULATING THE HIGHER BUSINESS IMPACT OF TOP PERFORMERS

Managers often have the mistaken impression that they should treat all workers equally. In fact the opposite is true. Great managers treat top and average workers "differently." This doesn't mean that you should abuse or ignore average employees; it just means that you should not treat all employees equally.

Whether you look at corporate or academic research, nearly all of the studies in this area demonstrate a significant difference in performance between average employees and top performers. In some cases, the differential between "superstar" employees and average employees was as high as 12 times.

Identifying the dollar value of the output produced by top performers over the output produced by average workers isn't as difficult as you think. Start by identifying several jobs with measurable results. Sales positions and other individual contributor roles make for an easy starting point. Other easily measured roles you might consider include software engineering, quality assurance, or customer service roles. The goal is to compare the differences in output or results between those with average performance and those ranked as the best in each job category.

METRICS

Calculating top performer output step-by-step

1. Calculating output—Start with the output of the average performer. This is called the *average output per employee*. Then look at the output of the very top performer (or the average of the top 1 percent). This is called the *top performer output*.

2. Top performer increase factor—Start with the top performer output per employee as the base. Then divide the output of the average performer into that number. That is the *top performer increase factor*.

3. Revenue per employee—Calculate the *average revenue for an employee* for these jobs (total divisional revenue for a year divided by the number of divisional employees. If that is not available, take the total revenue of the firm for a year and divide it by the total number of employees).

4. Revenue increase for top performers—Take the average revenue per employee and multiply it by the top performer increase factor. That number is the revenue generated by the top performer.

5. Value difference between top and average performer—Subtract the average revenue per employee from the revenue of the top performer. The difference is the value added each year by hiring or retaining a top performer.

6. Add additional jobs—Next, do it for other measurable output jobs. If the ratio (the percent difference) is close for most jobs (and it usually is), use that ratio for all jobs in the firm. If there is some variance, average the ratios together to come up with a firm average.

Example

(1) Sales for an average salesperson are $150,000, while top employee sales are $400,000.

(2) $400,000 divided by $150,000 = 2.6, where 2.6 is the *top performer increase factor*.

(3) Total employees (400) is divided into total revenue ($100,000,000), resulting in $250,000 *average revenue per employee*.

(4) $250,000 times 2.6 (the *top performer increase factor*) equals $650,000 (revenue generated by top performers).

(5) $650,000 (revenue of top performers) minus $150,000 (average revenue per employee) equals $500,000. This means that top performers generate over $500,000 per year in revenue more than the average employee. If you hire or retain 10 of these top performers you likely increase the revenue of the firm by $5M each year.

METRICS

Advanced variations

People profit increase by top performers —Take the total dollars of profit and divide it by the dollars paid to all employees (including all salary, benefits and training). This gives you *profit per dollar of employee costs*. Then multiply it by the top performer increase factor. The difference between the top and the average is the profit per dollar of employee cost differential for top employees.

Pay (cost) vs. performance—Since top performers are typically paid no more than 30—50 percent more than average performers, you can easily calculate the differential in dollars spent (in salary) to dollars generated.

A BUSINESS CASE FOR REPLACING BOTTOM PERFORMERS WITH TOP PERFORMERS

Top performers are cheap. Because we typically pay top performers only between 30 and 50 percent more than average performers, it turns out that top performers are, in effect, "a bargain."

Just as a company can calculate the top performer increase factor, it also can calculate the poor performer decrease factor using the same method discussed above. Combining these two calculations, a company can determine the potential impact of hiring more or retaining existing top performers and cutting poor performers.

Example:

Using the same formulas presented above, we calculated revenue per employee for an organization of 9,790 people with revenues of $1,736,500,000 to be $170,283.

Revenue generated by top performers:

Assuming a top performer increase factor of 3.16, we determine that top performers, on average, contribute $538,523 to total revenues.

Revenue generated by poor performers:

The poor performer decrease factor is assumed to be -0.58, indicating that performance is not only lower than average performers, as expected, but that their very presence in the company has a negative impact of revenues. Running the same calculation as above, we identify that poor performers generate a loss of $71,485 in revenue.

Combined dollar impact:

By combining the two figures calculated above, it's possible to determine the potential dollar impact of replacing each poor performer with a top performer. To perform this calculation, subtract the revenue generated by poor performers from that generated by top performers. ($538,523 - ($71,485) = $610,008). What this means to a manager is that every time a poor performer is replaced (through termination or transfer) with a top performer (through hiring or transfer), it will generate over $610,000 more per year. If management made five such substitutions in this theoretical firm, the additional revenue generated would be over $3 million per year.

PROVING TO SKEPTICAL MANAGERS THAT HR PROGRAMS WORK

How can you prove the impact of new or improved HR programs, even to the satisfaction of skeptical CFOs?

Begin the process of convincing senior managers that your HR programs "work" by realizing that most senior managers didn't get to where they are without being cynical. They have learned over time not to make decisions based on feelings and hunches. Instead, realize that they became successful by being numbers people. For example, the Wall Street Journal once described typical meetings between senior executives and subordinates at Microsoft as "big math camp" where executives don't feel comfortable talking about things that aren't quantified. In fact, most senior executives have come to expect hard data to prove that any program works, regardless of discipline.

HR is no different than other business functions; if HR enters a meeting and provides senior management with merely its "ideas," HR is destined to fail. What senior managers want is *proof* that ideas will produce measurable results. Although senior executives often say that they are risk-takers, generally they are not. Instead, they focus on minimizing their risks by taking only calculated risks. That means they expect and demand that you provide "dead-bang proof" that your program works and that it produces an increase in employee productivity.

Take testing of drug effectiveness as an example. Merely showing that people get better or are satisfied after taking a new drug is not really proof that the drug works because of the "placebo effect" (meaning that some individuals improve just because they are given *something*). To prove that a program or practice actually causes a phenomena, you need to think—and act—like a scientist.

The best way to prove that a new HR program works is to compare the difference in results that occurs before and after a program is implemented. Unfortunately, the reality is that most new HR programs are implemented without results metrics of any kind. A few programs do attempt to measure their results but only indirectly through user satisfaction surveys.

It's important to remember that senior executives are cynical. Even if you measure the before and after results of a new HR program, there is no guarantee that you will impress executives, because most executives understand that performance increases can be influenced by numerous other factors. Without accounting for all of these factors, the increase in performance cannot convincingly be tied to the introduction of the HR program.

LEARN FROM OTHERS HOW TO PROVE THE RESULTS OF "SOFT" PROGRAMS

People management is definitely a *soft* discipline, but that doesn't mean that you can't prove that it works with *hard* numbers. Business is full of functional areas that are considered "soft" that successfully have found ways to quantify their activities. The functions of PR, branding, and even most advertising have been much more successful than HR in quantifying their results. Psychologists and drug manufacturers have also successfully overcome similar challenges in trying to quantify their results and prove that their products and services work.

The lesson to be learned from each of these functions is that soft things can be quantified and soft programs can demonstrate their economic value. The key learning is to think and act like a scientist. Every step must be taken to provide convincing "dead-bang proof" that the program works. That means eliminating other possible causes of program success through the use of basic scientific and statistical methods and approaches.

The four basic methods of proving effectiveness

There are four basic ways to provide some degree of hard-to-dispute, senior-executive-level proof that a program works (*i.e.*, it improves employee productivity). Each is similar to the way that other business functions demonstrate the effectiveness of their programs (*i.e.*, how a new drug gets tested or how new ads or new products are assessed). The most effective ones are listed first.

1. **Split sample contrast**—This is the approach used by most scientists and drug companies where absolute proof often is required. Instead of applying the program across the entire organization, instead use a split sample with a control group to show the performance differential between the groups that utilize the program and those that don't. By applying a new HR program to only one-half of the team or business unit (and not to the other half) and controlling for other variables, you can easily convince your executives that any performance improvement is a result of the program and not external variables.

    Primary weakness—The costs of a control group are high in that, if the program actually works, a significant portion of the population (the control group) will not get the HR service or treatment until after the study is completed.

2. **Demonstrate a correlation**—This method uses statistics or a "trend line" to demonstrate a direct correlation (relationship) between the increased usage of a tool or program and a corresponding increase in productivity or profit. A correlation can also prove that when program usage goes down, so does productivity.

    Primary weakness—Correlation shows a relationship between the use of a program or service and an increase in productivity. However, because many relationships are complex, it is not possible to prove "cause and effect" using correlations. Calculating statistical correlations can also be over the head of many HR professionals.

3. **Before and after contrast**—Another effective approach relies on performance measurements collected at two different times. If you have a new HR program, be sure to measure employee per-

formance prior to the program's implementation. Next measure employee performance in the same manner after the program has been implemented. If the program has an immediate impact, there should be a "hockey stick" effect, where, if the results are plotted, a noticeable rise occurs in employee performance. Similar to the split sample approach, the performance differential between the "before" and "after" proves the program's impact.

Primary weakness—Even though performance increases after the program is implemented, the performance increase could be due to other changes that occurred within the business or the external environment. For this method to be effective, most other changes in the management process must be held constant.

4. **Results after implementation**—This method is similar to the before and after approach except, in this case, there is no measurement of performance before the program is implemented (note that often when a new team or business unit is put together, there is no "before" performance that *can* be measured). Start by measuring performance on the day the program starts, and then measure employee performance again after the program is in full operation.

Primary weakness—In this case, the lack of "before" performance data collection means that other internal or external factors could cause the performance increase. In addition, because business trends occur in cycles, it's possible that the increased performance might be something that periodically happens on its own, but without historical data, you have no way of knowing that.

If you are unsure on how to use any of the above approaches, work with your own advertising, PR, branding and product development departments to better understand how they use these tools to prove the value of what they do.

"Lesser proof" that HR programs work

The four most effective ways of demonstrating that an HR program produces results were listed above. Unfortunately, not all HR professionals have the time, inclination or resources to utilize one of those four techniques. As a result, it's important to list other types of "weaker" proof that an HR program produces results.

A good start. This final list contains some relatively good approaches for demonstrating that an HR program works. If you can't provide "dead-bang proof" that your program works, one of these other approaches might suffice.

It's probably an effective program if ...

- Managers are willing to pay for it, even during tough economic times;
- A small pilot program or beta test is successful;
- Managers request or demand it;
- If the program or service is paid for on a "fee-for-use" basis, top performers consistently select it from a list of available choices (especially if some of the choices are markedly cheaper); or
- The program can demonstrate a higher return on investment than your other top-performing programs.

Not quite as convincing. If none of the approaches above is an option, you may have to look to these indicators ...

- Program attendance, return rates or usage rates are among the highest in the organization (assuming it's voluntary);
- A large percentage of former participants in the program refer others to it;
- Internal experts who have been accurate in similar recent program assessments say that the program works;
- Data-based academic research studies prove that the program works;
- Supervisors or top management estimate that it produced a positive impact on workforce productivity; or
- The program produces positive results only part-way through the program's implementation phase.

Be careful of these approaches when attempting to prove that a program works. HR professionals frequently use weak arguments in their attempts to prove that their programs work. Be aware that the items listed in this section are *not recommended*, even though they are frequently used. Please don't fall into the trap of thinking that the arguments listed below are convincing proof that a HR program produces results; *don't use these arguments*.

- **Everyone uses it**—Common usage (or "everyone uses it") is never proof. Everyone acted like the world was flat before Columbus *proved* them all wrong. Use alone is *never* proof because so many executives in HR follow trends or fads.

- **But it works at XYZ**—Proof it works at one firm is not a guarantee that it will work at all firms because cultures, management processes, and resources differ significantly between organizations.
- **Words alone**—Any argument that relies exclusively on "words" alone to prove its effectiveness is a weak argument. Be especially careful of words like "I feel" and "I think." Without data, it's just an opinion.
- **An article says it works**—Be especially cynical of magazine articles that say that a particular program works. Unless the article provides hard data, assume that the people in the article are just bragging to make themselves look good.
- **Experts say it works**—Be careful; many experts have a hidden agenda or even a poor track record of predicting success. Be especially wary of consultants and vendors that tell you their program works but they have no data to back up their assertions.
- **Relative proof**—Even if a program has data that proves that it produces "results," the data might be suspect without comparison numbers. Unless you know the quantified results that the very best program produces, you must take even a steady increase in the numbers with a grain of salt. A firm with a 10 percent improvement rate might actually be "weak" if the average rate of improvement in the industry is 50 percent. Also be careful of programs that compare their results to an "average." In large industries, the average number may be misleading at best. Compare your results to the results obtained by the top firms if you really want to prove how good you are.
- **Sales as proof**—Be careful of programs that claim they are successful because revenues or sales have increased. Remember that revenues might have increased in fact, but costs may have also increased beyond the revenue gain. ROI or profit is the only true measure of relative program success.
- **Surveys can be misleading**—Surveys of people that use a particular program or tool (and say it works) are generally of marginal value because few will acknowledge that what they do for a living is ineffective. Surveys are just opinions, and people with a vested interest don't always respond honestly in surveys.
- **Impact delayed**—There are many factors that can confuse the issue of what causes program results. For example, doing great R&D may result in great products, but the delay or lag between the R&D

work and the first product sale makes proving the relationship between R&D and sales more difficult.

- **U.S.-only data**—Having data that proves that the program works in the United States can be misleading. Be aware that quite frequently things that work in one country do not work in other countries around the world.

- **Anecdotal evidence**—Be especially suspicious of testimonials (a story or single incident). The fact that someone says in an article or quote that something works may be simply a recollection of a single incident.

- **Stock price increases**—Just because the firm's stock price went up at the same time as it implemented a new HR program does not mean that this "program" must be working. Because stock price often varies as result of so many things, it's best to assume up-front that unrelated factors might have caused the stock price to change. In addition, everyone else's stock price may have gone up significantly more (relative to yours) during this period, making your firm's improvement relatively insignificant.

Note: Even if a program does produce results, make sure it does not have unintended consequences (negative side effects that were not expected). For example, gaining weight after stopping smoking might outweigh the benefits from the original smoking cessation program.

UNDERSTANDING LINE MANAGERS' EXPECTATIONS OF HR

One of the prime areas for measuring the effectiveness of an HR department is whether it satisfies line managers. Let's face it: line managers are the ones that make a corporation "work" on a day-to-day basis. Some HR departments even define the line manager as their primary "customer." As a result, it's important to understand what line managers expect so that you can tailor your programs to meet those expectations.

Unfortunately, most HR people have never served as line managers so they sometimes have difficulty in understanding the line manager's perspective. It's important to gain insight into specifically what line managers expect. They are typically a demanding group and all too often are not particularly proactive in sharing their wants and needs with HR.

Although it's obviously important for HR to have strategic goals and objectives, it is also important to be recognized as an organization that serves its internal customers well. In order to do this, HR needs to develop a comprehensive list of tactical or operational objectives. There are many tactical goals and objectives for HR that, while not always strategic, are important to the efficient operation of the organization.

The following section is a checklist based on line or operating managers' needs and expectations. It's important that HR sets its tactical goals and objectives with the needs of the managers and business units it serves in mind.

HR people see their job as a "high touch" job where their role is to listen, be available and "build relationships." Managers, on the other hand, want tools that increase people productivity today.

Table 17-A. *Checklist: Manager expectations of HR*

Recruiting and retention	
The ability to attract and hire top candidates around the globe	Increasing the diversity of the workforce
Employee retention	Backfill or replacement capacity for unexpected needs
Preventing departing employees from going to competitors	Transferring work to low labor cost areas
Motivation and satisfaction-related	
Employee motivation	Reducing employee fatigue and stress
Employee satisfaction and morale	Competitive pay
Reducing employee frustration	Increasing the connection between pay and performance
Leadership and management	
Leadership development	Reducing the amount of management time required to supervise employees
Fully trained replacements	Team cohesiveness and intra-team cooperation
Improving the quality and speed of people-related decisions	
Employee performance and performance management	
Identifying, fixing or eliminating bottom performers	Time to reach minimum output (for new hires and transfers)

Willingness of employees to work overtime, when needed	Reducing bad job fit—Untrained or "rusty" people doing unfamiliar jobs
Employees' ability to do higher level tasks	Absenteeism, sick usage and tardiness
Employees' understanding of their job and responsibilities	Error rates
Time required to complete the tasks	Performance measurement and reporting
On-the-job-failure rate (and the need for retraining or termination)	
Learning and sharing	
Best practice and "what works" sharing	Increase individual learning, challenge and growth
Failure-sharing across the organization for problem avoidance	Technical skill development
Benchmarking and competitive intelligence	Training in planning and providing focus and direction
Operations	
Plant and equipment utilization rates	Reducing material waste
Scheduling efficiency	On-time project completion
Budget and resource issues	
Eliminating the need for new positions	Reducing the costs of accidents and insurance
Reducing the need for expensive overtime	Training and technology allows the use of less skilled or less educated workers
Reducing the need for temporary employees and consultants	
Other	
Ethical behavior	Reducing and preventing legal issues
Maintaining and enhancing the corporate culture	Reduced union activity
Reducing employee and management time spent on administration (away from the job)	Global, 24/7 availability of basic HR information
Reducing time in meetings	Reinforcement of culture and values

Once you understand the typical concerns that line managers have, the next step is to identify the specific concerns that managers have within *your* organization. Some HR managers take the approach of asking line managers directly about their expectations of HR. There are two basic problems with this approach. The first problem is that many times line managers are not great people managers, and as a result, they do not really know what to expect from HR. The second issue is that managers accustomed to dealing with the "administrative" HR function often have very low expectations of

HR. If you expect to be strategic, you cannot be satisfied with these low expectations. In fact, what HR must do is to educate line managers about the more sophisticated approaches and tools that HR has to offer.

WHOSE JOB IS IT TO DO HR?

All too often, managers blame HR for their problems. Why? Because they often feel, sometimes legitimately, that HR has tied their hands and been overly restrictive by telling them all the things they cannot do. In short, they often view HR in the role of "cop." When HR restricts a manager's actions, it allows managers to avoid taking full responsibility for their own people issues.

A similar problem resulted in the 1980s when organizations hired quality control people to identify and address quality problems. This approach failed because you can't allow any central department (in this case quality assurance) to remove accountability from the managers and the employees who ultimately should be responsible for producing the product. The lesson learned then was that quality is everyone's business.

The same is true of HR work. Managers will never accept responsibility until they have sufficient ownership and control. HR has been calling for managers to take more responsibility for people issues for years; now is the time to enforce that mind-shift. HR needs to take the shackles off managers and let them do their jobs. HR can provide them with tools and information, but then it should step aside and assume its true strategic role as advisors and expert consultants.

INFLUENCING YOUR CEO

Impressing the CEO is certainly on everyone's strategic HR agenda because, almost by definition, nearly everything the CEO does is strategic. However, impressing CEOs is not easy, especially if you come from an overhead function. The first step in influencing them, however, is understanding them. Think of yourself as a biographer and study CEOs like you were going to write their story.

Executives and CEOs are unique individuals. They didn't get to the top without developing their own agenda and their own way of thinking. If you are truly going to help them, you must first understand what gets their attention. Although possible, this is especially difficult if you are in a low-profile department like HR so often is.

As a result of my many interactions with CEOs, I have identified specific areas that seem to get their immediate attention. I put my recollections into a checklist to help trigger your thinking about what steps you might take. Of course, every item will not work for every CEO or senior manager, but the checklist below should get you started on developing a plan to influence your own CEO.

CHECKLIST: KNOW YOUR CEO

- Know the top five problems the CEO is currently facing. (Read the CEO's speeches on the company intranet, read the CEO's meeting agendas, ask his or her direct reports or the administrative assistant, or just ask the CEO).
- Know the performance criteria that the Board of Directors uses to determine the CEO's bonus. (You may be able to get this information as well from the CEO's direct reports, administrative assistant, or from the CEO directly. The head of Finance and/or Compensation would also know CEO reward criteria. It might even be in the annual report.)
- Know the CEO's key information needs. CEOs are big on competitive intelligence. If you know how your organization's direct competitor does "it," you will be an instant hero. (Talk to former employees that now work as competitors, and to consultants and shared suppliers. Learn how to "trade" information with others.)
- Know the top three future problems the CEO soon will be facing. (Track environmental or economic factors, read articles by the top performers in your industry and reports written by industry analysts. Listen to your CEO's speeches, or ask direct reports or the CEO directly for his or her predictions.)
- Know your CEO's expectations of you. Make sure you know specifically what is wanted from you. You must prioritize what the CEO wants into a "more of/less of" list. (Start with just asking your CEO the "more of/less of" question. Ask your CEO to prioritize his expectations. Ask her to quantify your expected outputs. Update this information quarterly. If you have difficulty meeting your CEO's expectations, send a note listing what you believe the expectations to be, and ask the CEO to comment on it.)
- Profile what it takes (based on what others have done) to become one of your CEO's key advisors so that the CEO will turn to you when some honest advice is needed. Begin the process by learning

what it takes to gain the CEO's respect and confidence. (Identify people that your CEO currently "seeks out" for advice. Ask them what they did to gain the CEO's confidence. Also ask their administrative assistants.)

BE THE CENTER FOR EXCELLENCE

The goal here is to have your department known as the "place to go" to find new ideas, best practices and developing talent. Even if you are an obscure department, you can impress your CEO.

1. Be the "talent launching pad" for the company. Be the place where the best employees start and develop. Think of business as being similar to professional sports. Everyone is impressed with the coach who can recruit and develop top talent. Some ways to impress your organization with your talent-building ability include:

- **Hire the best and brightest**—Be the place where the best rookies start and develop. Be a great recruiter and you will get everyone's attention, and, in addition, the top rookies will make it possible for you to do better quality work.
- **Be "the" talent provider**—Keep your talent as long as you can and then give them to other departments.
- **Be the development "farm team"**—Take raw talent and develop it faster and to a higher level than others. Have the best skill development systems and make sure every individual has a learning plan.

The goal is to make everyone believe that you *must* pass through your department on the way to the top.

2. Become the "idea place." Become your organization's "Skunk Works" for new ideas and innovations. Become the test pad for refining new management processes and answers. Be the place others come to benchmark against for management processes and systems. The goal is to make the CEO believe that whenever any outstanding idea or innovation is implemented, the original source of the innovation was your department.

- **Anticipate**—Develop forecasts and prepare "if-then" scenarios in order to anticipate future management problems; then develop management systems in advance of the need. Whenever a new problem arises that is a surprise to most, step forward with a pre-prepared plan before others have time to react.

- **Know the customer** —CEOs as a rule are "in love with" their customers because they realize that without customers there would be no profit. As a result, it's important to become close to the customer and be the "voice of the customer" inside the organization. Use your in-depth knowledge of customer needs to generate ideas for sales, customer service and product development.

- **Be the "information source"**—Be the benchmark master. Know what information the CEO wants but can't get (or doesn't have time to get). Focus on how key competitors do things; summarize what you've learned for all, so that in the future everyone naturally will come to you with their "how do the best do it" questions. Be proactive and send the CEO and senior managers relevant information and answers before they ask for them. Identify how the very best managers learn, and use that information to become the "answer guy."

- **Give the CEO "heads-up" warnings**—CEOs are very busy and they hate to be blindsided. By covering their blind side and giving them early warnings or alerts, you will earn their respect and will be considered a "smoke detector." Identify others in the organization that seem to be the first to know and find out how they do it. Put together an early warning network and use it to build your reputation as a "future thinker."

- **Know technology**—Quite often CEOs are "technologically challenged." Become an expert in the latest technologies and provide your CEO with informal tutoring so that he or she can appear to be "up" on the latest technology trends.

3. Become the "go-to guy." Be the person the CEO seeks out in time of crisis. Identify future issues and be ready with answers when the issue inevitably heats up. Identify what the CEO looks for in a "go-to guy." Study the situations when help is needed and the characteristics of the CEO's current "go-to guy." Become the first alternative in time of crisis. Anticipate problems and develop answers before the questions are asked. Also learn to be a risk taker; CEOs are, and they admire other risk-takers, so be bold.

4. Build respect and avoid errors. Build a reputation for quality in everything your department does. Have double quality checks to avoid mistakes. CEOs hate mistakes, sometimes more than they like success.

- **Manage your "internal image."** Occasionally CEOs don't respect you because they (and others) think your job is easy. Manage their perceptions so that they see that such mundane areas as "harvest businesses," staff functions, and "cash cows" require great skill to manage. Make them aware that being close to the customer requires agility and responsiveness. Demonstrate how managing and motivating workers in non-glamour roles is difficult and demanding. Show how your department (because of its profit generation) makes what they do possible. Become a "hero."

- **Build your "external brand."** Whenever possible, get written about in company advertising, the press, and technical journals apply for functional and industry awards. Where possible, give speeches and write articles highlighting what a "great place to work" and how well-managed your company is (always mention the CEO's name as a driving force). It's important to be recognized externally because CEOs do not always know what a good HR professional really is, so they substitute an "external" assessment of your ability for their own.

5. Exceed their expectations. My personal experiences in being a former CEO have shown me there are several things that almost always impress CEOs. These include:

- Making them a lot of money.
- Making them a lot of money (in case you missed it the first time).
- Making them look good, especially in front of the board of directors and in the press.
- Knowing the business at least as well as they do, and showing them you share their passion for it.
- Being agile and flexible. Giving them options and having multiple answers for their questions.
- Being interesting, impressive and exciting as an individual.

6. Talk like them. Use dollars and numbers and data in *all* your conversations. Always quantify your accomplishments with output, competitive advantage, ROI and a focus on the future, not on process and the past. Be optimistic and don't whine. Forget the words "no" and "I can't." Learn to find a way to get things done. No matter what, don't aim just to satisfy your CEO; instead, exceed all expectations and WOW them!

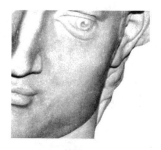

CHAPTER EIGHTEEN

"SCREENING FILTERS" IMPROVE STRATEGIC DECISION-MAKING

OBJECTIVES

Because HR managers are continually confronted with decisions on new programs or initiatives, it's important to have a program or decision "screening filter."

KEY POINTS

◊ HR is frequently known for making decisions based on emotion and feeling. It also has a reputation for letting "everyone have their say." The development of formal departmental decision filters will go a long way in helping to shift HR's image toward the more "businesslike" approach to decision-making.

◊ Unlike some of the recommendations in this book, decision-screening filters are seldom used in HR departments. Yet these decision filters are quite common in finance, technology and product development.

◊ Screening filters allow "nonconforming" ideas to be jettisoned early in the decision process and long before large amounts of time and money have been expended.

One of the primary responsibilities of an HR manager is to make high quality decisions. Because some HR departments are known for pursuing ideas or programs that are clearly not strategic or are "off task," it's important to implement a tool that keeps everyone laser-focused on the organization's strategic objectives. The most effective tool is a type of "funnel" or routing process that forces all concerned to "filter" or "screen" new ideas or programs through a series of screening criteria. These criteria, in fact, act to minimize wasted discussions and eliminate program ideas that are not directly related to business or HR strategic objectives.

Once learned and practiced by all, the process shortens meetings and discussions dramatically. It acts to limit program development ideas to those with a high potential for strategic impact and that closely adhere to departmental strategic goals.

DEFINITION

A screening filter allows you to determine first, whether you have enough information to make a good decision and second, whether the supporting information meets the minimum criteria necessary for it to qualify as a program or idea that is likely to have a high strategic impact. For example, if someone proposes a solution that is likely to generate a cost savings of $1000, even though all savings are important, $1000 of cost savings cannot have a strategic impact in a billion-dollar company.

This chapter contains a relatively long list of commonly used filters. Every corporation and situation is different; consequently, it is not important that you use every criteria listed here. It is a good idea, however, to have general agreement among senior HR managers about what filters or "screens" should be used to evaluate HR program ideas.

Screening filters have an added benefit in that they tell HR professionals up-front what must be present for an idea to receive serious consideration by senior HR management. This can save your HR department hours of time and perhaps millions of dollars in "weak" program decisions.

STRATEGIC HR "SCREENING FILTERS"

The following list of filters or screens can be used to determine if an HR program or idea meets the minimum standard for discussion or consideration. If an idea or program fails to meet each of the filter criteria, the sponsor of the idea should be told to revise it and return when it meets the department's "screening filters."Good decisions meet the following criteria:

Increases employee productivity

- One of its primary goals is to increase employee productivity.
- It also has a measurement component for measuring the change in employee productivity.

Impacts the business and monitors the environment

- One of its primary goals is to increase profit and it has a measurement component to assess the impact.
- It proposes a solution that directly impacts one of the designated corporate business problems.
- It identifies external economic and business factors that, if these factors change, impact program results. The operational plan has a component for continually monitoring these factors.

Emphasizes performance and competitive advantage

- The program includes performance culture tools like market forces, quantifiable measures of performance, and pay for results.
- Individuals are accountable, and there are defined consequences for failure.
- The program includes analysis that compares this program directly to the programs run by competitors. The analysis includes evidence that the program provides us with a superior advantage.

Fact-based decision-making and metrics

- The proposal includes sufficient data to allow for "fact-based decision-making." It also provides evidence that each program premise is backed by quantifiable data.
- It has extensive performance metrics (including response time, output and cost per unit of service).

- It includes a component that specifically measures "quality" (including error rate).
- It has a manager and user satisfaction measurement component.

Proactive and future-focused

- It contains components that proactively seek out problems and opportunities.
- It is directed towards a problem that will occur in the future.
- It contains a forecast.
- There is evidence that several "what-if" scenarios have been completed that cover most things that could go wrong.

Program integration

- It contains components that demonstrate that it is integrated with other HR and business processes.
- It provides evidence that the managers of any related HR programs support it.

Global impact

- It has a global component and it is capable of being rolled out around the world.

Image and brand

- It has a PR or image-building component.

Technology

- It utilizes technology that allows for 24/7 and paperless operations.
- It has a component that provides managers with "desktop" information.

Other strategic indicators

- The program has clear and measurable goals that are weighted or prioritized.
- It has an off-cycle component that allows it to take advantage of opportunities where other companies are "slacking off."

- The possible "unintended consequences" all have been considered and quantified.
- A continuous improvement component is built into the program.
- There is a feedback loop that ensures that the program "learns" from its errors.
- The probability of program success has been calculated based on benchmark data.
- Potential risk factors have been identified and quantified.
- "Fresh eyes" or an external person has reviewed the plan critically.
- There is evidence that it "fits" the corporate culture and values.

Indications of value

- An ROI or a cost-benefit analysis was performed, and the numbers exceed the 75th percentile of departmental ratios.
- The potential dollar impact exceeds one percent of revenues.
- The payback period is within expectations.
- It is requested or demanded by senior managers in the business units.
- It has a "fee-for-service" component or there is some evidence that managers are willing to pay for it.
- It includes a service-level agreement that guarantees a quantifiable level of service.
- It targets or primarily serves a high priority customer, business unit or key job.

Program benefits and features

- It reduces headcount.
- It contains a degree of flexibility and variation to allow it to meet local needs.
- It has an "early bailout" component which allows us to abandon unsuccessful programs early in their lifecycles.
- It's easy to use and understand.

Leadership and management

- The person making the decision has a track record of good decision-making and project management in this area.
- There is a single individual responsible for success or failure.
- The program manager has put together a quality team to manage the effort.

CHAPTER NINETEEN

THE "ACID TEST"— IF YOU ONLY READ ONE CHAPTER, THIS IS THE ONE

OBJECTIVE

The goal of this chapter is to provide insights into how people who make "fact-based decisions" think. From my perspective, it is by far the most telling chapter in this book. It is the "acid test" as to whether an individual is strategic. If you can answer all of the questions in your functional area with data, you are *already* a strategic individual; about that there can be no question.

KEY POINTS

◊ This chapter includes a series of "common sense" questions that almost everyone outside of HR finds to be logical and reasonable. These questions cut to the heart of what strategic effectiveness in HR is all about.

◊ Unfortunately, in my long career as a practitioner, consultant and educator, I have found only a handful of HR professionals who were capable of answering these "questions from hell."

◊ If these questions excite you, I challenge you to direct that passion into becoming the type of HR person who thrives on finding the answers to these questions.

"I want to increase the productivity of my team by 20 percent, while cutting labor costs by 15 percent, with a 10% increase in quality and no negative impact on customer service. What is the name of the HR program that will do that?"

COMPELLING STRATEGIC HR QUESTIONS

Can you answer the "CEO questions from hell?"

It takes facts to prove that you are an expert.

In the general business world, the use of numbers and metrics is part of life. CEOs, CFOs, and shareholders all measure results using numbers and dollars. Within major firms, all projects, products, and business units are evaluated on the basis of numerical results.

Earlier chapters in the book highlighted how many former "overhead functions" like quality control, manufacturing, and even customer service have moved to the forefront of management's attention because they shared a single common component. That common element is the use of metrics to become recognized as "true experts" in producing business results. If HR leaders are to become the next "corporate champions," they must prove to senior managers, *using dollars and numbers*, that they are experts in increasing employee productivity and effectiveness.

ARE YOU AN HR EXPERT?

Individuals in HR often complain that they have a difficult time getting managers to follow their advice. I have found that the traditional approach most HR professionals rely heavily on—"building relationships"—is no longer sufficient. The corporate world's shift towards technology has made managers dependent on data in order to make almost all of their decisions.

What this means to HR is that if you want managers to follow your advice, you now need to be perceived as a subject matter expert. These days, that means rather than answering their questions with opinions, you instead substitute dollars and numbers. Instead of taking a different approach, HR now must learn to answer questions similarly to the way that experts in quality control, finance and marketing do.

The section is designed to challenge your thinking and to test your expert knowledge of HR. Just for a few minutes, forget all of the HR certifications, degrees and "titles" you may have obtained and see, when put on the spot, just how much you can actually "prove" about HR.

I call this series of questions the "CEO questions from hell." As you read each of these questions ask yourself three things:

1. Is this a *reasonable question* that a strategic HR professional should be able to answer?
2. Could I answer this question *today* with numbers and facts (as opposed to guessing and stating opinions)?
3. What must I do *tomorrow* to get these answers in order to improve HR effectiveness and employee productivity?

For some individuals, reading the questions alone makes them uncomfortable. That's what they are designed to do! If you are one of the few who believes that these questions are "unrealistic or unobtainable," let me assure you that each and every question can be answered.

Questions about your firm's HR strategy

1. **Know the strategy**—What is the name of your HR strategy? If you asked your ten most senior managers to name the HR strategy, what percentage would know the name of it?
2. **Flex with the economy**—Does your HR strategy shift so that HR acts differently as the economy changes?
3. **Competitive advantage**—How does your HR department give the company a competitive advantage? Have you done a side-by-side competitive analysis to show which of your HR functions is clearly superior in performance to the comparable functions at your direct competitors?
4. **Employment brand**—What evidence do you have that your employees and potential applicants see the organization as superior to its competitors and as a great place to work?
5. **Rewarding people management**—If people management is so important, how come a significant portion of each manager's bonus is not based on employee retention, recruiting, employee development and productivity?

6. **Forecasting**—Does the HR function forecast accurately? Do you adequately warn or alert managers about upcoming people problems? And, if so, what is the name of that forecasting report that is sent to managers?

Is it worth it to have great people?

1. **Performance differential**—Does having great people really matter? What is the difference in the value of the output of a top performer compared to the output of an average employee? A bottom performer? Is the output differential higher than the pay differential?
2. **Critical jobs**—Which job, if you staff it with top performers, has the most impact on the business? Which jobs have the lowest impact?
3. **Focus on top performers**—Why does HR spend most of its time on the bottom performers? Does spending resources on top performers have a higher return?

General questions about HR's impact

1. **Profit impact**—Do the most profitable firms have a great HR department? Do the bottom-performing firms have weak HR? As the percent of HR expenditures increases, do profits grow proportionately?
2. **Budget impact**—If you doubled the HR budget, would employee productivity, profits or stock value double? If so, how long would it take for the impact to show? If you cut the HR budget in half, would the same result occur in reverse?
3. **Employee productivity**—What is your people productivity? And are your people more productive than your competitors' (i.e., do they produce more output per dollar spent)?
4. **Compared to other functions**—Does a great HR function have a greater economic impact on a business than a great finance, marketing, IT or manufacturing department? And if so, what is the ROI of HR?
5. **Critical success factors**—Which firms have the best HR departments in the world? What are the critical success factors that make up a great HR department?
6. **Overall metric**—What is the one single overall metric or measure that best assesses the effectiveness of an HR department? What is a good score on it?

7. **Stock price impact**—What elements of HR do financial analysts look at when assessing a firm's investment potential? How much stock valuation does great HR add?

8. **Price impact**—Does our organization produce products and services that allow it to charge higher prices (and generate higher margins) because we have higher quality talent?

Questions about HR departmental performance

1. **Highest ROI function**—Which HR functions (compensation, recruiting, retention, benefits, etc.) have the highest and lowest impact on your profitability (ROI)?

2. **Allocating resources**—What percentage of your HR budget and time is spent on high-performing business units and individuals? Does your spending and time allocation directly coincide with your corporate business goals?

3. **HR costs**—How many dollars are spent on each employee in HR costs (the HR budget divided by the number of employees)? How does this figure compare to your competitors?

4. **Focus on top performers**—Do you routinely assess your people programs to ensure that they improve the productivity of your best employees? How much does great HR increase top performer productivity?

5. **Continuous improvement**—What was the percentage improvement rate in the performance of the HR department last year? How does that percentage improvement compare to other business functions?

6. **Satisfaction with HR**—What percentage of your line managers and employees are satisfied with the performance of your HR department?

7. **Responsiveness**—How responsive is the HR department? How long does it take for managers to get a correct answer to a question they may have? How has that improved since last year?

8. **Manager ranking**—If you did a forced ranking survey asking your managers which overhead function contributed the most to their productivity and profitability, where would HR be ranked compared to other overhead functions?

Questions about the employment function

1. **Profit impact**—Do the most profitable companies in your industry have the best employment function? Do they spend the most money on recruiting?
2. **Productivity of hires**—Have the people that you hired this year been more productive (e.g., they produced a higher average output or received higher ratings) than the people you hired last year?
3. **Overstaffing**—Do we have the "right number" of people? How does a manager know if they are over- or understaffed?
4. **Impact of bad hires**—What is the cost of a bad hire? What percentage of the people that you hire are mistakes? What happens to them?
5. **The best sources**—Which recruiting source produces top performers? Which source produces the top diversity hires? Which source produces the worst quality hires? Which recruiting source produces candidates that stay a long time (a high retention rate)?
6. **Hiring speed**—Does slow hiring impact the speed of your product development or time to market? If so, what is the dollar cost of a vacancy in a key position per day? Does speeding up the time to hire increase or decrease the quality of the hire?
7. **Applicant satisfaction**—Are the applicants who apply to your firm satisfied that you've treated them like your customers? How do you measure applicant (customer) satisfaction?
8. **Best schools**—What schools do your top performers come from? Do you spend the most time and money recruiting at those schools? How long before a college hire reaches the performance level of an experienced hire?
9. **Recruiting impact**—Which has a higher ROI, recruiting great talent from the outside or retraining and developing your current "average" employees?

Questions about retention

1. **Impact on profit**—Do the most profitable companies have the lowest turnover rates?
2. **ROI of retention programs**—Which is more cost-effective, spending money on programs for current employees or spending money on recruiting?

3. **Accountability for retention**—If retention is such an important issue, why is there no department (a "retention department") that is solely responsible for it?

4. **Cost of turnover**—What is the cost of losing a key employee? If the amount varies by job, which job has the highest turnover cost?

5. **Going to a competitor**—Where do top performers go when they leave the firm? What percentage goes to direct competitors? How much does going to a direct competitor increase the cost of turnover?

6. **Reasons for leaving**—Why do top performers leave the firm? How do you know for sure? Do top performers leave for different reasons than average performers?

7. **Identifying potential turnover**—Does HR accurately forecast and inform managers about which employees are "at risk" of leaving?

8. **Effective tools**—What are the most effective and the least effective retention tools? Does offering employees more money get them to stay over the long-term?

9. **Ideal turnover**—What is the turnover rate of your key or top performers compared to your competitors? What is the turnover rate of bottom performers? What should it be?

10. **Low turnover**—Can your turnover rate be too low? Could your turnover rate be low because your employees are not desirable?

Questions about the compensation and benefits function

1. **Profit impact**—Are the firms that compensate their employees in the highest pay percentile the most profitable firms?

2. **Revenue per compensation dollar**—How much revenue does each employee generate per dollar spent on his or her compensation and benefits? How does that ratio compare to last year, and to your direct competitors?

3. **Pay impact on performance**—Which pay "type" influences performance the fastest? How long does it take, and how long does the performance impact of the pay change last? Do traditional salary increases cause a corresponding increase in performance?

4. **Impact on retention**—Is it the money that causes people to leave or to accept a new job? When top performers leave your company and go to a competitor, how much more salary (percentage increase) do they actually get at the competitor? How do you know?

5. **Pay at risk**—What percentage of each employee's pay is "at-risk," based on his or her own individual performance and the company's performance? How does this overall percentage compare to last year and your direct competitors?

6. **Non-monetary rewards**—Which has a bigger impact on employee motivation and productivity, monetary or non-monetary rewards? What percentage of the compensation department's budget, time and programs focuses on non-monetary motivation? Is that the right proportion?

7. **Impact of benefits**—Does having great benefits impact attraction, productivity and retention? Can you prove their impact? If so, which particular benefit has the most or least impact per dollar spent?

8. **Reward for recruiting and retention**—If a manager hired a "superstar" candidate, what would be the manager's average monetary reward for making a great hire? If a top performer left, what would be the average monetary penalty?

Questions about the employee relations function

1. **Impact on performance**—Do you currently improve the performance of the people in the organization? What percentage of bottom performers ever become top-level performers? If that improvement occurs, how long does it take and how much does it cost? What percentage of the bottom performers is terminated each year? How does that compare to the organization's top competitors?

2. **Performance appraisal**—How come the average of the individual performance appraisal scores for a department never equals the total department's overall performance (as measured by the percentage of its yearly departmental goals that were met)?

3. **Impact of bad managers**—What is the dollar impact of keeping a bad manager? Do you have a bad manager identification program? What percentage of bad managers actually improve, and how long does it take? What percentage of your turnover does having bad managers cause?

4. **Employee/ manager agreement**—If you asked a random sample of your employees the question, "how would your manager rank your performance level?" what percentage would accurately know (and agree with) how their manager ranked them?

5. **Identifying motivators**—If knowing what motivates an employee is so important, why do you never ask individual employees what excites and motivates them? Do we know what frustrates them?

Questions about the training function

1. **Profit impact**—Are the companies that provide their employees the most training time in your industry the most profitable ones?
2. **Training impact**—Which training programs have the highest and the lowest impact on productivity?
3. **Productivity impact**—If you increase training hours in a department, does productivity increase proportionately? If you put a poor-performing employee through training, does the training impact his or her productivity? How?
4. **OJT**—If most learning occurs "on the job," what percentage of your training time and budget is spent on "on-the-job" training and learning?
5. **Some "learning"**—If you hire great people, why do you need to train them?

Miscellaneous "questions from hell"

1. **Diversity**—What is the dollar impact of having a diverse workforce? As the percentage of diverse people on a team increases, does the productivity and output increase proportionately?
2. **Impact of technology**—Does increasing the level of technology in the HR department increase its effectiveness or overall employee productivity?
3. **Lawsuit probability**—HR always says the organization might get sued, but have you calculated the actual probabilities of that happening? Have you calculated your likelihood of losing? Have you calculated the actual financial risks? Are you even a lawyer, or are you just crying wolf?

Fact-based decision-makers
can answer these questions

Consider using these questions and their answers as a guide for starting your HR department toward excellence. By starting the process that eventually results in answering each of these important questions, HR professionals will be able to begin the transformation from "emotional decision-making" to "fact-based decision-making."

If individual HR departments are to prosper in a world run by "number crunchers," they must learn to anticipate each of the CEO-type questions listed here. In this new world of HR, opinions are no longer sufficient. HR professionals are expected to demonstrate quantifiably that they are experts in all areas of people management. These CEO-type questions can be used as a roadmap to guide the transition of HR from an overhead function into becoming an HR champion.

Although this last chapter was relatively short, it is no less quite powerful. The questions included cut to the heart of what strategic effectiveness in HR is all about. They are not intended to be subtle questions; frequently people become angry after reading them. I believe that the anger comes from the simplicity of the question coupled with the stark realization that they do not even know how to begin to find the answer.

For those who are energized by the questions, I believe you will find that the approach to finding the answers can be found throughout this book. For those who suspect that the answers cannot be calculated, let me assure you that they have been.

CHAPTER TWENTY

A STRATEGIC ACTION TOOLKIT

OBJECTIVE

I often meet HR managers who do not have the authority to develop a comprehensive HR strategy. They often actually make this comment—something to the effect of, "I just want to do *something* strategic." If you are in that category, this chapter contains a list of actions that have proved to be strategic in other organizations. (Note that additional strategic actions are found in Chapter 8 on competitive advantage.) These actions tend to be a little "bold," but that's okay; you've probably already tried all of the basic HR actions that can result in a strategic HR impact.

KEY POINTS

◊ This chapter is designed to provide some thought-provoking ideas for your next strategic action.
◊ A secondary purpose is to demonstrate the extent to which strategic actions vary from what most consider "normal." These approaches are truly different and radical—and that is precisely their strength. In order to be innovative and strategic, an idea must literally shock 75 percent of the audience.

EXAMPLES OF STRATEGIC ACTIONS AND APPROACHES

GENERAL MANAGEMENT

Integrate your managers through metrics—Managers often work independently and fail to share best practices among each other. By offering each individual manager on the management team an incentive, based on the overall performance of the management team, you can encourage managers to cooperate. By tying managerial performance together with a common bond, you can encourage top managers to help improve the performance of the below-average managers.

By asking employees to rate the quality of their own management and then rewarding managers with high scores, you can also encourage managers to play closer attention to their people-management practices.

Bad management identification program—One of the primary reasons that employees quit their jobs is the bad management practices of their direct supervisor. Develop a program that can identify "bad managers," and then develop strategies for fixing these managers, transferring them back to more technical jobs, or releasing them.

Measure and reward managers for good people management—Managers who practice good people management have the most productive employees. Unfortunately, most firms have no measurement system for assessing individual managers on how they manage their people. HR should send a clear message to individual managers that managing people is important by developing a system for rewarding managers for great people management.

Off-cycle actions—Going "against the grain" might seem unwise on the surface, but in some cases, it can lead to being the first or the only competitor in the field. For example, if the economy is down and no one is recruiting on college campuses, you might find that if you actively recruit, you might get some "superstar hires" that you would have had little or no chance of getting when everyone else was going full speed in college recruiting. Yes, this means creating open positions when the company is not doing well, but it might also mean that you will be able to "explode" out of the box better than your competitors can when the economy improves.

There are other off-cycle actions, for example, intensifying retention programs even though your turnover rate is currently very low. Most employees expect special treatment when they know there is a high demand for their talent. This off-cycle approach is so effective because, when you pay attention and recognize employees when it's not needed, employees tend to appreciate it more. In addition, when the job market improves, they might just remember how well you treated them when you did not have to.

HR ADMINISTRATION

Reward results in HR—HR managers must be recognized and rewarded for their results in maintaining a competitive advantage over the organization's competitors. HR lags woefully behind in the use of incentives for its people and programs, however. Combining metrics with significant bonuses for performance can have a dramatic impact on HR productivity.

In particular, rewards should be offered to all if HR meets its overall goals. Incentives are also effective for recruiters, generalists (if their business unit achieved its goals), and those in leadership development. It does not take much; as little as a five percent bonus will improve performance by significantly more than five percent. A note of caution, though; bonuses must be tied to numerical results, not subjective terms like "merit" or leadership.

Reward cooperation—HR is known for having functional silos; this runs counter to the goal of developing a competitive advantage. In order to ensure that HR functions work together, HR needs to develop a common metric and reward that crosses all critical HR functions. This way HR professionals are incented to work together.

Prioritize programs—It's not important to be great in every area, just in critical ones. That means that HR must identify which programs and processes are critical to the firm's success and focus on maintaining a competitive advantage in those areas.

Shifting resources—In addition to prioritizing programs, HR leadership must ensure that HR budget and time allocations continually shift from low-priority HR programs to high-priority ones.

Employment brand—One the areas that is critical if you are to build a competitive advantage is the organization's "brand" as a good place to work. Because most HR departments spend little time and effort on building a brand, this is an area where it is relatively easy to provide a competitive advantage.

Managers are your "delivery system"—It's important to remember that supervisors or line managers "deliver" a great deal of a firm's people-management services like policy interpretations, performance assessment, and motivation. Although HR does deliver some information directly to employees, most of that is filtered or redefined by line managers. As a result, it is important for HR to realize that the primary delivery system for people-management services is the manager.

HR must accordingly design its programs based on the strengths and the weaknesses of the delivery system—the manager. It is not enough to develop an HR program; it must be pre-tested utilizing managers in order to see if what you intended actually will filter through to the employees.

HR advisory group—Like most other functions, HR tends to be isolated from outside criticism. To counter that insularity, HR should put together an advisory group to provide critical input and ideas, and to act as "beta testers." The group should include line managers, individuals who hate bureaucracy, individuals from finance, and some other diverse thinkers. Ask this group to be critical of everything you propose and offer suggestions in order to make your programs easier to implement and more strategic.

Competitive intelligence—A significant side benefit of doing a competitive analysis between firms is that you frequently gain competitive intelligence information about the operation of their people-management programs. This information can be used to improve existing programs so that you can leapfrog over your competitors. Cooperate with the competitive intelligence staff within your own business units and piggyback on their processes and sources.

Experimentation—Constantly try new things in every area of HR on the assumption that you can't beat them if you don't act differently. Rapidly drop the ones that don't work. Run pilot and test programs to see if great "ideas" really become great "programs."

On demand—HR has a bad habit of offering "flavor of the month" programs to managers. Flooding managers with programs that they don't want can be a tactical error that can result in a lot of wasted resources on "unwanted" programs. A wiser approach is to first identify manager needs and provide information to managers on programs and services that you could provide. But only offer new HR programs after managers request or "demand" them. Proof that managers really want an HR program is typically if they are willing to fund it.

RECRUITING

Develop a "most wanted" list—A "most wanted" list is an element of a recruiting strategy that espouses asking your key managers which individuals working at competitors that are "to die for." By identifying the specific individuals you want to hire, by name, at the beginning of the hiring process, you take a good deal of the "chance" out of the recruiting process.

Pre-identifying targets allows you to focus a significant portion of your recruiting time and resources on convincing a relatively small number of "highly desirable" individuals to come to work with your firm. And the net result is that you can, first, really "wow" your managers and, second, you can increase the effectiveness of your firm dramatically by bringing in these "high-impact" individuals.

Hire to hurt—Identify key individuals at your competitors who, if they were hired away, would significantly hurt your competitor. Look at competitors as you would a sports team with no backups in crucial positions. Be sure and exclude people who are easily replaceable in the marketplace or who have a strong "second" who can step in easily. Ask your current employees who formerly worked for your competitors to help you identify these key individuals.

Benchmark to recruit—Call the top firms (or piggyback on others at your firm who are actively benchmarking) to benchmark their best practices. Use that benchmarking process to identify and build relationships with potential recruiting targets.

First day of hire, ask "who else is good?"—When you hire someone from a competing firm, it is essential that you use that opportunity to gather the names of employees from their former firm who you might want to recruit. Ask the new hire who else at the firm is really good or will soon be good, as well as who is undesirable. Ask new hires (and reward them) if they will help you in recruiting top talent from their former employers.

Pre-need hiring—Hire people in key positions *before* there is an urgent need. If you wait until someone leaves a key job, that means that there inevitably will be a delay before the new hire is up to speed. This can dramatically slow your time to market. Hire people before they are needed so they can ramp up their skills and be ready when you need them. Calculate the learning curve and the time-to-fill periods, and use that to determine when to "pre-need" hire.

On-site professional seminars—People who continually learn and improve are the type of talent you want to recruit. These are the same kind of people who regularly attend seminars. By holding professional seminars on your site, you can physically draw them to your premises while simultaneously improving your organization's "brand."

When they arrive you can excite them with your facility, get them to meet your people, and show them your cool projects and tools—all under the guise of helping them learn to perform their current job better. Bring in outside experts as speakers in order to draw them in. Invite potential hires to speak along with your own top employees. Demonstrate to attendees that your firm and its employees are on the leading edge of knowledge.

Invited open house—An "invite a friend to work" program has a simple premise. Any organization needs to get candidates "in the door" in order to have a real chance of closing the sale. Car dealers and realtors have used this strategy for decades. A "bring a friend to work program" gets potential candidates to come to your facility and talk to your team. It targets employed but "passive" job seekers who wouldn't apply for a job but might come to an event to see what it's like where "my friend" works.

"Bring a friend to work" is a high-touch variation of the traditional employee referral program. It differs from traditional "open house" programs (that are open to the public) in that individual employees invite people they know on a professional basis and who have the competencies the organization needs. If the "friend" is hired, the employee gets the standard referral bonus.

Retention and employee relations

Who is at risk of leaving?—Instead of guessing who is going to leave the organization, it is better to take a proactive approach in identifying who is at risk of leaving. Possible strategies include searching the Web for your own employees' resumes; placing a blind ad to see if your own employees apply; or asking other workers to identify who is "looking." Also consider hiring an executive search professional to tell you who is a prime candidate for other firms, who is looking, and who is safe. By getting real data and outside opinions, you increase the odds of identifying the correct individuals who truly are at risk.

Challenge plans or learning plans—One of the top reasons employees leave a job is that they are not challenged in their current job. By giving each employee an individual challenge plan, employees can continue to grow and learn. A challenge plan would include new projects, tasks and presentations in front of management. Managers and employees both could choose from a list of "tried and true" challenges if they are unsure of what might challenge them.

Pre-exit interviews—Instead of waiting until someone quits, it pays to be proactive and ask key employees why they stay. By identifying what keeps them in the job and at your organization, you can reinforce the positives and eliminate what frustrates them the most. Interviews should be held every six months for employees who are at risk.

Re-recruit—Superstar employees often leave because they are courted and praised by outside recruiters. Managers must remember to do the same periodically in order to reduce turnover. Why wait until recruiters call and "sweet talk" your top talent? Every six months treat your employees as potential recruits and "re-do the deal" to re-energize and excite them.

Blocking tools—In this aggressive world, managers must anticipate large-scale raiding by competitors. Managers must develop "blocking tools" in order to protect the organization's talent resources. These tools include anticipating competitors' actions through competitive intelligence, developing a blocking team, re-recruiting top talent, offering "stay-on" bonuses, and doing a competitive analysis of the raider. Other blocking strategies might include tools to make it difficult for competitors to identify your top talent, to know your pay ranges, and to find your weaknesses.

Attention plans—Many employees desire recognition and attention. One-way to systematically ensure that key employees get exposure is to develop an individual "attention plan" for each of them. Ask the employee what kinds of exposure he or she wants, and plot out a plan to insure it happens. Attention areas might include committee assignments, presentations, write-ups, chances to be a team leader, meetings with the CEO, and meetings with members of the Board of Directors.

Post-exit interviews—Many people fail to give the real reason for leaving a job because they fear potential retaliation by their manager in the form of a bad reference. If, however, you postpone the interview until three to six months after the termination, the chances of getting a candid reason for leaving increase dramatically. Use an independent market research firm to identify why employees have left, what the salary differential is at their present job, and even if they're interested in returning.

Change the players—Even when sports teams win championships, the next year they frequently change more than 10 percent of their team. Teams change their players in order to stay fresh or to adapt to the changing competition or environment. Unfortunately, such high turnover rates are quite unusual in business. If you are trying to be strategic, a low turnover rate could be a big mistake, especially if you have poor hiring practices, weak training, or ineffective incentive and motivation programs. My advice to managers is that "if you continually lose the game, change the players."

Drop the "deadwood"—Improve people productivity by dropping the deadwood. Instead of giving everyone a second and third chance, run the metrics to see if investing in poor performers has a higher return than getting rid of the poor performers as soon as it becomes obvious they aren't performing. Instead of crying "we might get sued," quantify the real risks of lawsuits. Develop "no-fault divorce" approaches to termination in order to encourage managers to drop bottom performers quickly.

WORKFORCE PLANNING

Bench strength (back-fill) plan—In a time of high turnover, it's increasingly essential to have a strategy for identifying and developing individuals who can take over if an employee leaves. A "bench strength" plan differs from traditional succession planning in that it only covers replacing key jobs within a single department. It is not a company-wide succession plan. Individual managers are held responsible (and are rewarded) for developing at least one individual to fill every key job.

Redeployment—Quite often businesses reduce their productivity not because they have the wrong people but because they have good people in the wrong job. This is especially true in businesses that are undergoing continuous rapid change. Initially placing an "innovator" in a business unit, for example, might have been a wise move when the business was in its early growth stages. Once the business has transitioned into a commodity business, however, it makes more sense to move the "innovator" out and into another business where "innovative ideas" can be put to better use—this can have more of an impact as well.

Rather than waiting for the employee alone to figure out where his or her own best internal job placement should be, a better approach is for HR and managers together to proactively identify and move talent from areas of relatively low return to jobs with a higher return. This process is known as proactive intra-placement or redeployment.

Targeted succession plans—Targeted succession plans are narrowly focused strategies for ensuring that individuals are available to fill vacant key positions. They also tell key employees in advance that they have a future at the organization. Targeted areas often include major software implementation efforts and product development teams. Most succession plans fail because they are too broad and cover too long a period of time. Targeted plans allow the focus and forecasting to be more narrowly applied with the goal of increasing the accuracy of the planning.

Corporate headcount "fat" assessment plan—Rather than learning at the last minute that the organization needs to do a layoff, establish a set of assessment tools that will let you know *in advance* where headcount may be excessive. Monitor ratios, such as output per employee, employees to managers, overall department headcount to productivity, and overall labor costs per unit of output, to identify possible "fat" areas.

COMPENSATION AND INCENTIVES

What should I pay?—Salary surveys can be out of date by the time they are published. If they are, you run the risk of "under-offering" top candidates. In order to improve the accuracy of your offers, it is critical to capture the "other" offers that each of your new hires and applicants have in order to confirm what the competitive offers really were. You should also ask your current recruiters and outside executive search professionals what the real market rate is.

Pay for performance—Increase productivity by changing the way you pay people. Shift from the "money distribution department" to a function that incents productivity and the behaviors that increase it. Place a significant emphasis on, and allocate resources to, non-monetary rewards and recognition. Identify and educate managers on which kinds of pay, recognition, and incentives have the most impact on productivity per dollar spent.

Measure and reward increasing productivity. Increase the percentage of every worker's pay that is "at risk" based on his or her output, because there is evidence for most jobs that, as you increase the percentage of an employee's pay that is at risk, performance increases.

MOTIVATION AND COMMUNICATION

"More of/less of" motivation list—A simple way of identifying what employees want more of in their jobs (and what they want less of) is to ask each employee what job and environmental factors they wish to have increased and decreased. Done quarterly, this process gives managers a chance to understand what employees want. Surveying employees and new hires about what motivates them helps managers better understand how to keep them excited. Topics should include what frustrates you? What challenges you? What are your learning goals?

You do not have the right to remain silent—This is a tool that explains the shared responsibility that an employee has in his or her own management and motivation. You must educate each employee (begin on the *first day*) that employees have a shared responsibility to help their managers and the organization understand what motivates and frustrates them. Employees are also asked about their aspirations and the key aspects of their "dream" job. Two-way communication needs to be established at the very start so that employees understand they have an important role in educating their manager about what excites and challenges them.

Develop an employee "balance" sheet—In addition to assessing the economic impact of programs, some managers find it helpful also to provide employees with an assessment of their individual economic impact. One way to do that is to give each of your key employees an employee balance sheet at the end of each year. This sheet compares the economic value of the employee's output with the cost of salary, benefits and training. This format encourages workers to be more aware of their economic impact to the company.

DEVELOPMENT

Employee learning plan—One of the main reasons that people either accept or quit a job is their rate of learning. Top professionals demand the opportunity to learn continuously. By asking each top performer about their learning goals and how they learn best, managers can develop individualized learning plans to ensure that the employee learns at a speed necessary to excite and stimulate them.

Parallel benchmarking—Benchmark the best practices in related or parallel industries that traditionally implement advanced programs faster than your industry does. Learn from the advanced programs and processes of other disciplines, industries or geographic regions. For example, I once developed an incredibly fast "speed of hire" process for a *Fortune* 100 company based solely on information gathered from "fast lube" and fast food chains. I studied the existing processes throughout HR, but they were all slow, so there was really little to learn.

Part of any strategic approach is being aware of the best practices that exist outside your discipline. In particular, disciplines of finance, marketing, PR, and decision sciences are frequently ahead of HR in metrics and program development.

Where top performers learn—In a fast-changing world it is essential that everyone is continually learning. Unfortunately, in a fast-paced world there's often little time for traditional learning. One way to speed up the learning process is to provide employees with "presorted sources." By asking top performers directly which resources they use to learn quickly (*e.g.*, what sources have top performers utilized and found effective), HR can relatively easily identify which sources are effective and which sources have little value. Then provide this "best practice" learning list to managers and employees so that they can begin learning the same way that the company's top performers do.

Virtual learning networks—A learning network is a group of individuals that exchanges information and ideas in real time. By sharing reading and learning, members can learn faster and from each other. Normally, a learning network consists of 4–10 individuals with a passion for learning. Information can be exchanged through e-mail, fax, telephone, in person, or by a combination of approaches. Information that might be exchanged includes best practices, problems, articles and other learnings.

There are three basic types of learning networks: e-mail, fax, and telephone. In the first two types, a problem, article or proposal is sent to the group for comment. Ideas and criticisms are given and the results are summarized and sent to all (or to all who participated). Telephone groups use conference calls and hold roundtable discussions.

COMMON "STRATEGIC ERRORS" OF HR DEPARTMENTS

Now that you've seen a list of provocative and innovative strategic HR ideas, it's time to consider the opposite. After conducting an audit of HR department operations, it is common to find the following errors or omissions:

- Not measuring or rewarding managers for great people management.
- Not tracking management satisfaction with HR.
- Not allocating HR resources in line with strategic goals.
- Treating all employees and business units the same in recruiting and other HR functions.
- Not having a feedback loop to learn and revise the HR processes when things don't work (*i.e.,* bad hires, bad promotions and losing key individuals).
- Failing to do zero-based budgeting to critically assess existing HR programs, and then dropping the weak ones.
- Promoting managers based on technical skills rather than their people skills.
- Having no formal non-monetary motivation team compensation.
- Not including on-the-job training and job rotations as an essential element of the development function.
- Using the same target pay percentile for all jobs and business units when clearly all jobs do not have the same business impact.
- Having no formal retention department or program.
- Only using cost-based and no qualitative HR metrics.
- Having few transfers to and from line management.
- Having no periodic measurement of individual HR and business knowledge.
- Having no periodic HR audit.
- Not developing and continually running "what-if?" scenarios to ensure there is a plan "B" for the entire range of possible problems.

- Failing to develop HR programs that cannot be easily copied by competitors.
- Hiring HR staff without business or line experience.
- Not coordinating HR plans with other business functions to ensure a coordinated effort.
- Failing to ask new hires why they considered and accepted the job in order to determine which organization efforts had any direct impact on their decision (pay, training, benefits, career web site, etc.).
- Not having new HR programs assessed by someone with "fresh eyes" and by managers that hate HR.
- Failing to measure HR response time and on-time service delivery.
- Failing to assess the value of the HR department's "brand name" and market share.

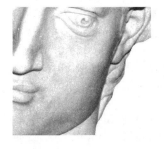

CHAPTER TWENTY-ONE

THE STRATEGIC PARADOX

It's time for HR to go to the next level. The "business partner" model has taken us about as far as it can go. HR professionals can no longer be satisfied just being a business partner; they must instead push to become HR leaders and drivers of change. This shift requires dropping the old traditional ways that we have approached HR. This new approach requires a new attitude and maybe even some new "DNA." Dramatic change is always difficult, but there is no better time than today for HR to view this economic downturn not as a negative event, but rather an opportunity to step back and to transform what is probably a small HR function.

SPEED DOESN'T KILL, SLOW DOES

CEOs are known for saying that people are their most important asset. Because HR has built only a weak business case for people management, however, the HR department is all too frequently one of the first departments cut during tough business times. The fact that CEOs are willing to lay off their most important asset demonstrates that HR still has a long ways to go in proving that people are a *strategic* asset. If HR is to avoid this boom-and-bust cycle of prosperity regarding budget cuts, it needs to do many things differently.

In recent years, the prime driver of organizational change has been the speed of change in the world. Since this rapid change is likely to continue unabated for years, addressing this issue should be a prime goal for HR.

> *Everything in HR needs to get faster. Speed needs to become the foundation for everything we do.*

HR must increase its delivery speed and its responsiveness. HR programs need to evolve faster and to develop just-in-time capabilities. Instead of reacting to problems and then attempting to catch up, the leaders of the new HR need to adapt to a constant state of rapid change.

In the new world of business, best practices are copied at breathtaking speed. As a consequence, instead of aiming directly at a target, HR must instead learn to aim "ahead" (at least six months ahead) because HR targets are no longer stationary. They are constantly changing. Aiming ahead requires us to begin to anticipate and forecast not where the target is, but where it will be.

Instead of looking at new HR program development in isolation, we also need to plan for the inevitable responses to new HR programs that are likely to be taken by our direct competitors. Like most business functions, HR is stuck in a game of "leapfrog," where whatever we do will be copied quickly by our competitors.

What is the net result of these rapid changes? HR has no choice but to shift from its "keeping up with the Joneses" approach towards trying to develop a *sustainable competitive advantage* over our rivals in people practices. In a world that rapidly copies *everything*, a sustainable advantage requires a degree of rapid innovation that previously has been seen only in other functional areas like product development. The days of slow, deliberate decision-making and consensus-building need to be replaced by an agile, just-in-time, innovative HR organization.

BE PREPARED TO BE UNCOMFORTABLE

If speed alone doesn't make you uncomfortable, then the complex challenge of becoming strategic should.

One of the most startling revelations by individuals who are for the first time striving to be strategic is that they are almost always "shocked" when they first see "real" strategic ideas. They somehow expect strategic ideas to be easy to understand and instantly credible. They also assume that the clear logic and workability of strategic solutions will just "jump out at you." In reality, nothing can be further from the truth.

In fact, when you present innovative strategic ideas to the average HR person, their reaction invariably includes one or more of the following. It is:

- Unworkable
- Unrealistic
- Too radical
- Too risky

The lesson to be learned is that innovation in general, and strategic innovation in particular, look like "swampland" at first glance. Innovative strategic ideas in HR in fact make most people nervous. They appear on the surface to be high-risk undertakings, and most individuals discard them at first glance as being "unworkable."

What this means to a strategic HR professional is that if you ever expect to move beyond just talk of becoming more strategic, you need to learn to seek out the very ideas that most would consider to be crazy.

In fact, that is the test. When you present any innovative strategic idea and everyone says "wow," "great," or "let's do it," the odds are that your idea is neither innovative nor strategic.

THE STRATEGIC PARADOX

Numerous professionals in HR have spent the last few years attempting to become strategic. One of their primary focuses was to minimize most transactions and information-providing services in order to "free up" time to be more strategic. While the use of technology, self-service and outsourcing HR has in fact freed-up a good deal of time from administration, the strategic paradox is that in many cases HR is still in the same situation it always has been. Budgets have been cut or headcount has been reduced at least as much as they have been in the past when times were tough. And that's the paradox; even with *more* time, too many human resource functions have failed to demonstrate any additional strategic impact.

Now, of course there are exceptions, but all too often the reason that HR has failed to increase its strategic impact is because HR has refused to give up its old philosophies and tendencies.

- Being strategic means being aggressive, and most of the people in HR are still not aggressive.
- Being strategic means adopting metrics and the ways of finance, and many in HR remain reluctant to shift to the use of metrics and fact-based decision-making.
- HR has traditionally been the champion of the underdog, and being strategic means focusing on top performers.
- Being strategic means focusing on corporate goals rather than HR processes and efficiency.

My conclusion is that if the old guard can't change, they must be replaced with new players. These new players need to be highly competitive, aggressive and innovative. The time has come to shift from the old HR cop role to the competitive model where the process of winning is less important than the result.

New technology, new models, or all the consultants in the world won't change the fact that in order to be strategic, "liking people" is less important than making people more productive, and that is the answer to the paradox. The new HR must be a productivity consulting center where experts in people management and business practices provide expert, data-driven advice that produces immediate results.

In addition, these results must be clearly superior to both last year's results and the results your competitors produce. Becoming strategic doesn't stop with producing results, either. HR must go the next step and market itself internally, build its image, and quantify its results, so that all can see the key driver behind organizational success is excellence in people management.

INDIVIDUALS MUST CHANGE ALSO

Shifting from a tactical approach to a strategic approach requires the most difficult thing of all; it requires "you" to change. Changing means you can no longer be comfortable with just having opinions. Instead, you must develop a high level of technical knowledge about the tools that actually increase worker productivity. You must become an expert—not in "trying things" or in initiating new HR programs—but instead in actually changing employee and management behavior.

Producing strategic results means that you can no longer be satisfied with just providing advice to managers and then shrugging your shoulders when they *inevitably* fail to listen or change. This is because being strategic means taking responsibility and being accountable for cajoling, influencing, or doing whatever is necessary to *make* managers change.

If, after reading this book, you are still unsure about whether you are an expert in people management and whether you're capable of making data-based decisions, go back to Chapter 19's "questions from hell." Revisit it and use it as the "acid test" of where you are compared to where you need to be.

AN INCREDIBLE ECONOMIC OPPORTUNITY

Because employee productivity is the area where HR can have the most business impact, HR needs to focus its efforts on employee productivity. The first chapter of this book says that its primary goal is to demonstrate how, with aggressive HR actions, you can improve the productivity of your workforce. A later chapter demonstrates that "people" costs are a huge segment of all organization costs (up to 50 percent of total variable expenditures). Still later the book demonstrates that top performers are "cheap," in that they can produce up to 12 times more than an average worker while only costing as little as 30 percent more in pay.

If we were not talking about people, most business people would see these related facts and conclude that, "This is an unbelievable financial opportunity. If I can develop systems to increase the percentage of top performers in the workforce, I could get as much as a 1000 percent return on my investment. And if I applied that approach to 50 percent of all corporate expenditures, the net economic gain to a corporation of only moderate size would easily exceed $1 billion."

But here lies another paradox. HR professionals talk constantly about the desire to have a strategic business impact, but when they are confronted with the HR decisions and changes they have to make in their *own* behavior, they quickly retreat to the old behaviors and approaches that experience has demonstrated cannot ever produce a strategic impact. The unfortunate part of this is that, because we are talking about "people," for some reason the current cadre of HR professionals are resistant to adopting an approach to HR that is focused exclusively on increasing "people" productivity.

This reluctance and even resistance to confronting workforce productivity seems to come from an almost "1984" fear that, somehow, increasing human productivity reduces the human spirit and turns us into nothing more than machines. I could accept that resistance if there were not so many other areas of human endeavor, like sports and the military, where both athletes and soldiers work together with management striving as a team to squeeze out every ounce of increased human productivity.

Other non-human management systems have been developed to squeeze every ounce of productivity out of the supply chain, production, product quality, and customer service, for example. But in those cases, there were no concerns of sweatshops, high stress, and reduced work-life balance. Instead, everyone accepted the common goal of continually increasing productivity. Why professionals in HR are unwilling to approach what they do as a productivity problem remains a puzzlement to me.

THE FINAL INGREDIENT

The difficulty of getting individuals even to look at, much less try, innovative strategic ideas reminds me of a question that I received from a Wall Street Journal reporter after leaving a stint as the Chief Talent Officer for Agilent Technologies (a Fortune 200 firm with 40,000 employees). The question was simple but to the point. "What does is to take to make rapid, innovative but impactful strategic change in large global corporations?"

I know that the reporter anticipated that I would say something traditional like "brains," "resources," or "access to technology" but my answer was quite different. I said then and still believe today that it takes but one talent to be strategic in HR, and that is courage.

INDEX